Design
with
Nature
Now

Design
with
Nature
Now

EDITED BY

FREDERICK STEINER

RICHARD WELLER

KAREN M'CLOSKEY

BILLY FLEMING

LINCOLN INSTITUTE
OF LAND POLICY

Published in association with the
University of Pennsylvania Stuart Weitzman
School of Design and The McHarg Center

Library of Congress Cataloging-in-Publication Data

Names: Steiner, Frederick R., editor. | McHarg, Ian L., 1920-2001. Design with nature.

Title: Design with nature now / edited by Frederick Steiner, Richard Weller, Karen
   M'Closkey, and Billy Fleming.

Description: Cambridge, Mass. : Lincoln Institute of Land Policy in association with
   the University of Pennsylvania Stuart Weitzman School of Design and The McHarg
   Center, [2019] | Includes bibliographical references and index.

Identifiers: LCCN 2019015302 (print) | LCCN 2019019208 (ebook) |
   ISBN 9781558443969 (epub) | ISBN 9781558443938 (hardcover)

Subjects: LCSH: Landscape architecture. | Sustainable architecture. |
   Land use, Urban.

Classification: LCC SB470.5 (ebook) | LCC SB470.5 .D47 2019 (print) | DDC 712—dc23

LC record available at https://lccn.loc.gov/2019015302

Designed by Studio Rainwater

Composed in Graphik by Westchester Publishing Services in Danbury, Connecticut.
Printed and bound by Friesens in Canada. The paper is Rolland Opaque, a recycled
PCW sheet.

PRINTED IN CANADA

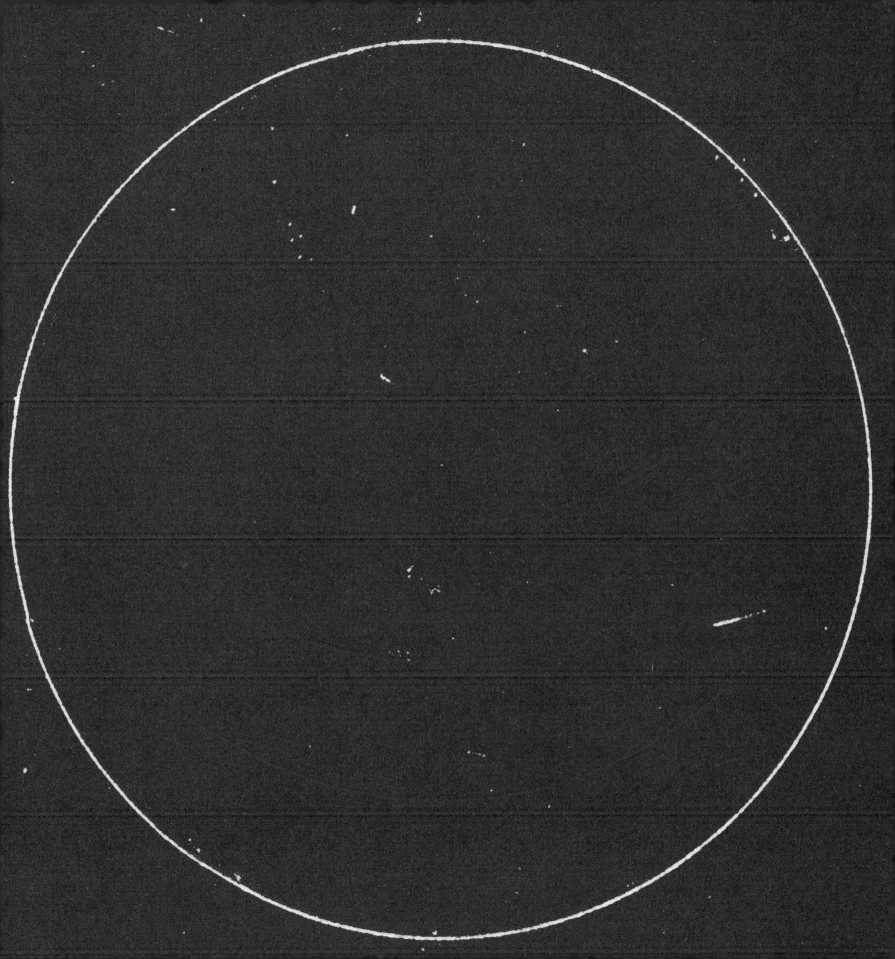

Contents

Design with Nature: Reflections, Tributes, and Inspirations

Human Ecology and Design

Projects: Five Themes

244 Projects: Commentaries

Design as a Quest, Not a Task

Andrew Revkin

In early March 2001, amid the intensifying flow of news at the heart of my beat covering the environment for the *New York Times*, word arrived that Ian L. McHarg had died. When I was asked to step away from the news grindstone to write his obituary, I considered it an honor. It was also a bit of a relief to tackle a more uplifting topic for a day or two. I'd just had a front-page story on the "message in eroding ice," as Mount Kilimanjaro's fabled white cap shrank under the effects of climate change.[1] I was tracking conflicting signals out of Washington as lobbyists and environmentalists fought to reverse or defend George W. Bush's campaign pledge to regulate heat-trapping emissions from power plants. (Industry won the tussle later that month.)[2]

What better tonic for those dark days than to explore such a pioneering and productive life? Until then, I had no more than a superficial awareness of McHarg from courses in college. As I dug into our clip file and data bases and began phoning his peers and pupils, it quickly became evident that while *Design with Nature* was revolutionary in its call for conforming to, rather than competing with, ecology, this landmark book was just one of McHarg's legacies.

The resulting obituary focused on McHarg's achievements and innovations, such as his famous "layer cake" of transparent site maps, designed to help clients or communities weigh the value of any human development against the functions of underlying soils, water flows, and other environmental conditions. But I am glad at least one line conveyed what felt like McHarg's other enduring gift: "His greatest legacy was not his method, or even his seminal book; it was his passion for respecting the living land and his volcanic determination to brand successive generations of planners and landscape architects with the same ethic."[3]

In *Design with Nature Now*, an array of McHarg's contemporaries—along with practitioners, scientists, and scholars in fields from planning to ecology to comparative literature—explain why there has never been a greater need for McHarg's way. That might seem a tough case to argue given the pace of change in both the Earth system and human systems as the third millennium speeds along. What is the role of design in a world where sea level, climate, invasive species, surging cities, and technologies are all changing simultaneously? How does one define *nature* in the Anthropocene—a moment on Earth in which humans are jolting ecosystems and climate as powerfully as an asteroid strike has done in the past? And of course we are simultaneously poised to redefine nature at the genetic level as tools like gene drive technology offer the prospect—for better and for worse—of not just shaping some crops' genetic traits but pruning the tree of life of inconvenient species like a disease-toting mosquito.[4]

Actually, it is precisely that fast-forward state of the planet, and of *Homo sapiens*, that makes McHarg's methods and motivation more vital than ever—and gives them influence far beyond the fields of landscape architecture and planning. Consider his eagerness to incorporate any discipline necessary to clarify an answer. Following the success of *Design with Nature*, McHarg strove to expand his design models from geology and ecology to include the human element, with the plasticity of culture introducing so many new variables. "How could we extend this model to include people?" McHarg wrote. Along that path, McHarg added anthropologists and ethnographers to his circle. There is still much to learn from this aspect of his work, given how, all these decades later, many academic, governmental, and corporate structures and norms—and journalistic norms, for that matter—still impede interdisciplinary collaboration.

There are also lessons to glean by examining how McHarg shaped his presentations. He tended to use them less to make his case for an environmentally sound design than to enable stakeholders to find their own logic in sensible choices. To absorb this, it is best to see him in action—something not possible in this book. But fortunately he is on dynamic display in the remarkable 1969 public television documentary *Multiply and Subdue the Earth*, which includes McHarg's 1968 presentation to the Metropolitan Council of Minneapolis–St. Paul and surrounding counties, in which he makes the case for resilient, ecologically attuned planning.

"I have spent years of my life offering my palpitating heart to various people who couldn't care less," he says, pacing in front of the panel of planners and other local figures. "So palpitating heartism doesn't really get you anywhere at all. It seems to me that one really needs to have two things. You not only need to be able to say, 'Don't.' You also want to be able to say, 'Do.'"[5] He calls this two-pronged approach a "positive inducement process."

An accumulating body of behavioral and social science has validated this approach for dealing with a divisive issue like global warming and the local and planet-scale design debates it has sparked. As Dan Kahan of Yale Law School has demonstrated in empirical studies, more information, with or without great graphics, can deepen, rather than dispel, divisions.[6] He calls the phenomenon "cultural cognition." But that same body of work shows how a conversation, like a landscape, can be designed—in this case with *human* nature in mind. The result can be consensus on resilient and sustainable paths even amid divergence.

In several essays, contributors to this book note another factor that is critical to the success of a McHargian strategy for this century. That factor is not better data visualizations or better dialogue among experts and officials. It is representation: who gets heard at the table where decisions are made about roads and reservoirs, parks and pavement, or environmental laws and agreements. The success of a climate agreement, or a city, will depend on inclusion.

But the most resonant facet of McHarg's method in the context of this century's challenges is his focus on designing for the *properties* of a landscape or system. With biology, particularly evolution, as his constant touchstone, he aimed for "dynamic equilibrium" more than a static, durable end point.

That approach is invaluable given the complexity and enduring uncertainty in confronting human-driven climate change and related challenges. It would be easier to design a safe coastal city in a world with either a stable sea level or a known rate at which seas will rise. Neither is the case now, and will not be for decades, if not centuries, to come, according to a host of recent studies.

The same design philosophy is emerging in very different realms. Through the first quarter-century of international treaty negotiations aimed at avoiding dangerous global warming, the goal of most countries was a binding, robust, contract-style treaty that would govern the actions of signatories. In the 2015 Paris Agreement, negotiators finally forged an outcome that is itself a process—with norms for reporting nationally determined steps toward a safer human relationship with climate. At its core, that agreement is an iterative tool for "positive inducement" that McHarg would have appreciated.

We need an expansion of McHarg's methods, as suggested in the pages that follow, creatively reimagined to accommodate more complexity and diversity and to design—as much as that is possible— a planetary future with both nature, and human nature, in mind.

Design in the Anthropocene

IN 1969, IAN L. McHARG, professor of planning and landscape architecture at the University of Pennsylvania (Penn), published a manifesto titled *Design with Nature*. Translated into Chinese, French, Italian, Japanese, and Spanish, and still in print to this day, it is arguably the most important book to come out of the design professions in the 20th century. *Design with Nature* not only captured the zeitgeist of the late 1960s by decrying modern civilization's—or at least North America's—sprawling urbanism and environmental degradation; it went further than most by proposing a practical method for doing something about it.

Using rudimentary digital tools and painstaking analog drawings, with his students and colleagues at Penn, McHarg developed a method of overlaying maps of the biophysical characteristics of a given place to make decisions about future land use. Part science and part common sense, the method provided an empirical, rational, and ostensibly objective basis for deciding which land was most suitable for which purpose—for example, farms on the good soil here, forest upland from water supply there, and of course, housing outside of flood zones and behind coastal dunes.

Throughout history, cultures have either withered or flourished as a result of how they live with land and water, or per McHarg, how they designed with nature. For cultures attuned through experience to the specific conditions of their landscapes, designing with nature becomes a form of lore. In this sense McHarg's design philosophy is nothing new. But his advocacy of ecology as the basis for design and its application to the modern city was. McHarg's great achievement, then, was to create a simple, universal method for assessing and then incorporating environmental science into the decision-making processes of modern development. When applied well, his method offered a way to both guide and substantiate design decisions, especially those that limited the scope and scale of otherwise sprawling development.

However, *Design with Nature* is more than a land use manual (figure I.1). It soars from geology to cosmology, it cuts from Christianity to Buddhism, and it interleafs speculations on entropy and evolution to arrive at a unifying theory of design. For

FIGURE I.1 Cover of *Design with Nature*, 1969. Doubleday/Natural History Press, American Museum of Natural History.

McHarg, to design with nature meant for humanity to intentionally and benignly fit itself to the environment. Drawing on the most advanced ecological science of his time, this idea of fitness flowed from a belief that cultural and natural systems could coexist harmoniously, in balance, if each part were in its proper place. For him, this was not just biological determinism at work; it was the highest of arts.

McHarg's vision, like that of his mentor the great polymath Lewis Mumford and Patrick Geddes before him, was that by living *with* rather than against the more powerful forces and flows of the natural world, humanity would gain a biocentric sense of place; and this, in the deepest sense, would replace the Abrahamic theologies and capitalist culture of consumption he held responsible for the environmental crises of the 1960s. For McHarg, Western culture's greatest promise was a synthesis of the sciences and the arts that had yet to be applied to how we dwell on the land, and it was the profession of landscape architecture that could steward society through this evolutionary process. To this day, at least in theory if not in practice, this remains the field's primary raison d'etre.

On the occasion of the 50th anniversary of the publication of *Design with Nature*, with this new book and its associated exhibition and conference, we ask what might be meant by design(ing) with nature *now*? As faculty at PennDesign, the school to which McHarg devoted his life, we feel a particular responsibility to explore these questions at this time and from this place. While McHarg's prescience warrants celebration, our intention in marking the 50th anniversary of his magnum opus is not hagiographic. Rather, we view our responsibility, and the purpose of this volume, as one of constructive and critical discourse—to ask how the ethos of designing with nature has evolved over the past half-century, and to speculate on its prospects over the next fifty years.

By making recourse to nature as a higher authority on the one hand and reducing it to interpretation through data-driven positivism on the other, McHarg was always going to get into philosophical trouble and attract criticism. Indeed, much of what has happened in landscape architecture over the past fifty years can be read as either an endorsement or a critique of his philosophy and method. Had McHarg titled his book *Design with Landscape* instead of *Design with Nature*, and had he offered caveats about the limits of his method to inform human creativity and ingenuity, then accusations of hubris and artlessness that were periodically leveled at him could have been largely avoided. But in his rush to change the field—and indeed to change the world—McHarg overlooked some of those critical details.

That McHarg inspired debate is, however, no small part of his enduring significance. Whereas these debates once may have threatened to split the profession between "the designers" and "the planners," we can now see a profession that has intellectually matured around these tensions. We see a profession that is diversified in its practices but united in its sense of ecological and artistic purpose. We see a profession equipped with a range of design techniques that build on, rather than obviate, their foundation in the McHargian method of landscape suitability analysis described earlier in this chapter. And yes, we also *still* see the rift between McHarg's grandiloquence and daily practice—a rift that to some extent must always exist between the ideal and the real. Without gaps between the theory and practice of designing with nature, there would be nowhere for landscape architecture to grow or evolve.

The projects around which this book is constructed were selected because each in some way narrows this gap and opens up a wider horizon for the future of landscape architecture. Arriving at this set of projects at this moment in time involved a long, collaborative process. We began by asking colleagues from around the world to nominate projects that they thought best exemplified and extended McHarg's design philosophy and method.[1] The nomination process resulted in a list of over eighty projects, and after much discussion, we, the editors of this book and curators of the exhibition, agreed on the final twenty-five. The projects are organized into five themes: Big Wilds, Rising Tides, Fresh Waters, Toxic Lands, and Urban Futures. Although these themes cover a lot of territory, it will be obvious to readers that the collection does not represent all the types of work the professions of planning and landscape architecture do. We have included projects that engage large complex sites and pressing socioecological issues, and that variously translate into reality what could be referred to as a McHargian ethos of stewardship. It must be said, however, that some projects show the limitations of the discipline's ability to effect change at the scale that is needed—the projects improve the social and ecological function locally, but may also be part and parcel of development patterns and infrastructural projects that are environmentally degrading at other scales. We wish this collection comprised a greater diversity of projects from a greater diversity of places. Much as this collection identifies gaps in the thematic areas engaged by contemporary practice, so too there are glaring gaps in the geography of contemporary practice. In short, the project selection is imperfect, but we have found, and hope the reader will also find, that the collection is a good place to begin.

As well as forming the centerpiece of this book, the selected projects formed the basis of an eponymous international exhibition and conference, both held at Penn in Philadelphia in 2019. Highlights of this exhibition are reproduced in chapters 12–16. The exhibition also included a survey of McHarg's life and work by William Whitaker, curator of PennDesign's Architectural Archives, a summary of which is included in chapter 26.

A third component of the *Design with Nature Now* exhibition was a specially commissioned series of artworks by the landscape architect and artist Laurel McSherry. Derived from her deep immersion in the landscapes of McHarg's childhood in Scotland, juxtaposed with those of his adulthood in the Northeastern United States, McSherry's artwork approaches McHarg's legacy in an entirely novel way—a way he would surely have appreciated. This work is included in chapter 9.

Apart from this editorial introduction, all of the writing in this book stems from the Design with Nature Now conference. Except for the two keynotes by geographer Erle Ellis and literary scholar Ursula Heise (reproduced here in full), the speakers (Alan Berger and Jonah Susskind, Tom Campanella, Rob Holmes, Kate John-Alder, Nina-Marie Lister, David Orr, Catherine Seavitt Nordenson, Allan Shearer, and Jillian Walliss) were all asked to address McHarg's legacy through the lenses of the selected projects. Taken as a whole, their essays offer a spectrum of opinion regarding the ways in which landscape architects and environmental planners are now shaping the world and how their work is indebted to McHarg.

The opening chapter is a biographic essay by McHarg's long-time friend, mentor, and advocate Frederick Steiner. Respect for McHarg's oeuvre is further articulated in a series of short tributes by eminent scholars and practitioners who were taught by and worked closely with McHarg—Ignacio Bunster-Ossa (AECOM), James Corner (James Corner Field Operations), Anuradha Mathur (Penn), Laurie Olin (OLIN), Anne Whiston Spirn (MIT), and Dana Tomlin (Penn). As central figures in landscape architecture—in the way McHarg once was and remains—they offer insight into how his ideas shaped their own, and how their own ideas are shaping a new generation of scholars and practitioners. Similarly, Brian Evans of The Glasgow School of Art discusses the enduring influence of McHarg on his native Scotland in chapter 8. Indeed, as anyone who knew him or even attended just one of his lectures will attest, McHarg was an unforgettable character, a man of passion and erudition in equal measure.

Ian McHarg died in 2001, his life's work completed well before the expressions "climate change" and "the Anthropocene" became central societal concerns. The environmental reality these terms now signify, the debates and anxieties they engender, and the increasing calls for climate action make McHarg's prophetic injunction to *design with nature* more pertinent that ever. Paul Crutzen, the atmospheric scientist usually credited with first declaring this to be the epoch of the Anthropocene, has described its advent as beginning with the Industrial Revolution and then radically accelerating after 1945. In 2011, along with his colleagues Will Steffen and John McNeill, Crutzen argued that we should begin moving into a new period in which we "steward the earth."[2] This of course was the essential message of *Design with Nature* some fifty years earlier, and in this regard the profession of landscape architecture has been at the vanguard of a broader cultural revolution that now comes into its own in the context of the Anthropocene. This is not to say, however, that the profession has fulfilled its McHargian mandate of leading global environmental stewardship. Such a claim would be absurd. More to the point, it could hardly be argued that the world is environmentally better off now than it was when *Design with Nature* was first published. On the contrary, the dawn of the Anthropocene signals the opposite. We are plunging, headlong, into an epoch of global environmental change at an unprecedented scale and pace. How we learn to live with that change is the central challenge for the next half-century of design. In the work we have collected here, there are real clues as to how, through design, we can better tune our cities and their infrastructure to the forces and flows of the Earth system. The fact that such projects are the exception and not the rule only underscores their importance as landmarks of a more widespread historical change yet to come.

The 21st century is marked by the fact that humanity has directly or indirectly modified every habitat on the planet, and much of it deleteriously so. With the unintended consequences of global warming, species extinction, and resource depletion, it is now possible that our extraordinary success as a species could also become our demise. Our recognition of this "tragedy of the commons" is what distinguishes us from other species that have also flourished in the course of evolutionary history. To not only know this, but to act on that knowledge in a precautionary way, is to intentionally design environments so that they are more life-giving and more life-sustaining, for all forms of life. This is not a punitive or messianic project; it is a political and above all a creative project, one that transcends geographies, economies, and the forces of globalization that have overwhelmed and divided the planet—between developed and developing, rich and poor. That is the enduring and inspiring meaning of *Design with Nature*, and it is to that end that this book is dedicated.

Design with Nature: Reflections, Tributes, and Inspirations

CHAPTER 1

Green the Earth, Restore the Earth, Heal the Earth

Frederick Steiner

IAN LENNOX McHARG (1920–2001) entered World War II as a lanky teenage volunteer private. He left military service after the war as a confident major in command of one of Britain's elite combat units. Before the war, he was a child in a Calvinist household during the Great Depression in the industrial Clyde River Valley near Glasgow, Scotland. After the war, "the major," as he was called then, marinated in modernism at Harvard.

He left Harvard with the intent to help rebuild his war-ravaged homeland. McHarg worked as a planner in the United Kingdom and experienced a near-deadly bout with tuberculosis before Dean G. Holmes Perkins enticed him to build a new graduate program in landscape architecture at the University of Pennsylvania. At Penn, McHarg fused his desire to practice with a newfound love for teaching.

His most important contributions derived from this academic practice. At first, this practice was grounded in the modernist principles McHarg had learned at Harvard. Influenced by his mentor Lewis Mumford, McHarg began to move away from the aesthetic dogma of the international style. He grew highly skeptical of the one-size-fits-all stylistic palette of modernism, instead remaining committed to the *ideals* of modernism. Specifically, he believed knowledge should guide action—and furthermore that this action would result in better housing, more open space, more efficient transportation systems, and, in the end, healthier and safer communities.

He explored these ideals through the design studios at Penn and through his growing consulting practice (figure 1.1). For many years the boundaries between the Department of Landscape Architecture (then the Department of Landscape Architecture and Regional Planning) and his consulting practice—Wallace-McHarg Associates (later

Wallace McHarg Roberts & Todd)—blurred. Both the academic department and the firm engaged in action research, advancing several disciplines and professions. This work represented a meaningful dialogue between the academy and professional practice. A synthesis of this dialogue is provided in *Design with Nature*. While this clarion call-to-arms presents insightful case studies, it also advances a new theory for planning and design and a new mandate for public policy. What are the origins of his ecologically based theory?

Again, it came both from within the academy and from experience. From the early 1960s on, Ian McHarg was a public personality. He hosted his own high-profile CBS talk show and later narrated a popular PBS documentary. McHarg served on several important commissions and panels, including the influential 1966 White House Commission on Conservation and Natural Beauty. In the process, he befriended Lady Bird Johnson, Stewart Udall, and Laurance Rockefeller, among others.

His early 1960s CBS television show, *The House We Live In*, emerged from, and then informed, his teaching, and in turn put forth the theory in *Design with Nature*.[1] For a series

FIGURE 1.1 Ian McHarg with students and faculty, circa 1958. Karl Linn, Frederick Towers, Robert Carson, William Roberts, McHarg, and John Whalley (left to right). *With permission, The Architectural Archives, University of Pennsylvania.*

of twenty-six Sundays in 1960 and 1961, Ian McHarg invited the leading theologians and scientists of the day to discuss our place in the world on network TV (including Margaret Mead, Julian Huxley, Paul Tillich, and Luna Leopold) (figure 1.2). He had initiated this format in his "Man and Environment" course at Penn in 1959. Leading scholars (including pioneering biologists such as René Dubos, Paul Sears, Robert MacArthur, Paul Ehrlich, and Eugene and Howard T. Odum) were invited to discuss values and ethics, as well as entropy, the universe, evolution, and plate tectonics in the classroom and on television. McHarg's razor wit, intelligence, and relevance attracted students and TV viewers alike.

Through the 1960s and into the 1970s, "Man and Environment" was the most popular course on the Penn campus, and it alone changed many lives. I had a colleague who was a Wharton School undergraduate when he took "Man and Environment." He promptly transferred from finance to hydrology, eventually earning a PhD and becoming a significant environmental planner and educator. Ian McHarg's growing academic following and environmental activism coalesced during Earth Week in April 1970. McHarg and his students led the events of that week in Philadelphia. Across the nation, other faculty and students organized similar events.

For example, I was the cochair of the student-led Earth Day events at the University of Cincinnati. Our activities included a book fair. In comparison with the present, there were relatively few environmental books then—notably those by Rachel Carson and Aldo Leopold. The one with the word "Design" on the front cover and the whole Earth from space on the back stood out to those of us undergraduates studying landscape

FIGURE 1.2 Ian McHarg (right) interviewing psychologist Erich Fromm, on the set of *The House We Live In*, December 18, 1960. *With permission, The Architectural Archives, University of Pennsylvania.*

architecture, architecture, planning, and design. Over the next couple of decades, many of us flocked to Penn. Many more read *Design with Nature* and were inspired by its hopeful message.

Nothing is as practical as a good theory. The dictum "design with nature" not only changed design and planning, but influenced fields as diverse as geography and engineering, forestry and environmental ethics, soils science, and ecology. The evidence is ubiquitous: almost every geographic information system (GIS) presentation begins with a depiction of a layer cake of maps about environmental and social phenomena, although rarely crediting McHarg and often without his eloquence or insight into how the data should be collected and analyzed. Environmental impact assessment, new community development, coastal zone management, brownfields restoration, zoo design, river corridor planning, and ideas about sustainability and regenerative design all reflect the influence of *Design with Nature*.

However, Ian McHarg's theoretical and practical contributions extend beyond this important book. Two other topics occupied much of his considerable energy in the decades after the initial Earth Day. First, he sought to advance the understanding of the ecology of our own species. Second, he advocated the extension of his theoretical framework to the national and global scales. McHarg's ecological approach helped designers and planners illustrate how organisms relate to one another as well as to our physical and biological environments. Like other organisms, our species is part of the web of life. The challenge is to see ourselves as part of that web. According to Alexander Caragonne: "Like the fish that swim in the seas, we are apparently oblivious to and incapable of describing either the nature or extent of the medium we inhabit."[2]

Ian McHarg recognized the need for us to understand the medium we inhabit as well as how we shape it and it us. He sought support from the National Institute of Mental Health to address this topic, writing, "My colleagues and I had concluded that geomorphology synthesized physical processes and that ecology synthesized both physical and biological processes. How could we extend this model to include people?"[3]

He turned to the science of anthropology for the answer. Just as he had recruited geologists and ecologists to his department beginning in the 1960s, he added anthropologists and ethnographers in the 1970s. These colleagues taught us that culture is our most important instrument of adaptation. Furthermore, our ability to evolve our culture distinguishes us from other species. Design and planning can then be viewed as adaptive mechanisms—that is, tools for resilience. Adaptation and resilience are related to our health, which has been defined by the World Health Organization as the ability to recover from disease, injury, or insult.

For years, McHarg coordinated the introductory graduate landscape architecture and regional planning studio. Ecologists, geologists, soil scientists, and ethnographers worked alongside landscape architecture and planning faculty to help students learn how to read landscapes. Specific sites from the Pennsylvania Piedmont to the New Jersey Coastal Plain were studied to reveal opportunities and constraints. Maps (initially hand-made and colored with markers and eventually computer generated), transects, block diagrams, sketches, photographs, and prose were employed to explain geologic and human processes and patterns. Always, faculty and students visited sites to understand in the field what they had mapped, drawn, diagrammed, and analyzed in the studio (figure 1.3).

Ian McHarg generated big ideas. As he witnessed the growing application of those ideas through GIS and visualization technologies, he realized that they could be used at the national and even the global scale. In the early 1990s, McHarg and several colleagues produced a prototype data base for a national ecological inventory. Then U.S. Environmental Protection Agency (EPA) administrator (and McHarg admirer) William Reilly commissioned the study, and the prototype was submitted to the EPA in 1993.

FIGURE 1.3 501 Studio field trip to Hawk Mountain, Pennsylvania, September 30, 1983. Ian McHarg sitting on left; geologist Robert Giegengack sitting and pointing in center; and ecologist James Thorne (with beard) standing on right. *Photo, Frederick Steiner. With permission, The Architectural Archives, University of Pennsylvania.*

McHarg and his team proposed an extensive inventory at three scales—national, regional, and local—including information about physical oceanography (where applicable), geology, geomorphology, physiography, hydrology, soils, vegetation, limnology, marine biology, wildlife, and land use. They urged that chronology be employed as "the unifying rubric." In his autobiography, *A Quest for Life*, McHarg states, "We observed that the greatest problem lies not with data, but with integration."[4] Decades later, the greatest problem remains integration and the wisdom to apply data in decision making.

In the final years of his life, McHarg advocated this national ecological inventory for the United States and other nations, and also believed the approach could and should be expanded to the entire planet. This global view was deeply rooted in McHarg's philosophy. For example, as early as 1968 he wrote: "We must see nature as a process within which man exists, splendidly equipped to become the manager of the biosphere."[5] He called this global responsibility our "greatest role." If we agree, then how do we indeed fulfill our "greatest role"?

As he changed from Presbyterian to Friend, from soldier to scholar, from the Old World to the New, from Harvard to Penn, from site-level concerns to regional and global visions, several of McHarg's characteristics held firm: the irreverence and the generosity, the humor and the leadership, the broad knowledge of science and art, the love of jazz, the ability to spin a yarn and to captivate an audience.

Ian McHarg established new territories for his twin disciplines of landscape architecture and city and regional planning. He altered their flow—how the fields are perceived by others, how practitioners view themselves. His influence transcends landscape architecture and planning. Architects and ecologists, geologists and foresters, soil conservationists and artists heard his summons and altered their thinking as a result. McHarg was a public figure who chatted with talk show hosts and debated the origins of the universe and meaning of life with rabbis and Jesuits on national television broadcasts. He walked with presidents and Hopi elders, with Loren Eiseley and Andy Warhol, with physicists and hippies.

We are linked to something larger, but we are also what we make ourselves to be. We become the shadows of our aspirations. We become who we present ourselves to be. Ian McHarg chose a big role to present. We should all possess such courage to address the environmental and social challenges and opportunities of our time: to design with nature *now*.

CHAPTER 2

McHarg: The Long View, Shortened

Ignacio F. Bunster-Ossa

DURING STUDIO CRITIQUES at the University of Pennsylvania, Ian McHarg would lean back in his chair, lace his fingers behind his head, and stretch his neck as if to take the longest possible view of the work pinned in front of him. In the celebrated PBS documentary *Multiply and Subdue the Earth*, he expounded on ecology while standing knee-deep in a sun-bathed amber meadow, marrying the urgency of his message to the boundless grassland in front of him and deep blue skies above him.[1] McHarg doubled down on that message in *Design with Nature* by evoking on its cover the image of a polluted planet viewed from outer space.

The long and urgent view of things was his gift to designers, planners, and everyone else with a grain of concern about the environment. I received this gift the day McHarg invited me into his office at Penn as a prospective student. Upon recognizing how ill prepared I was in the earth sciences, he asked that I take introductory courses in biology and climate at a community college as a prerequisite for admission. The coursework discussed the Everglades (I was living nearby in Miami at the time), and few places on Earth better capture McHarg's grand view of the landscape from extent and ecological standpoints. And so, if there is one thing that McHarg seared into my soul, it is the imperative to take the longest, widest view possible of humanity's impact on our small, fragile planet.

To be sure, the long view was, to McHarg, more than the big picture. As conveyed in the chapter of *Design with Nature* on form and function,[2] he believed in the inherent wonder and appropriateness of each and every part of every landscape, regardless of locale, extent, or level of detail. At Penn he beseeched students to relate their projects to the whole—that is, to how a path, a plant, a wall, or a building yielded, in however modest a measure, a greater understanding of its place on the land.

The urgency of McHarg's long view roused attention in 1966 when he and a handful of esteemed colleagues penned the Declaration of Concern, the mission statement of the newly established Landscape Architecture Foundation (LAF). It read in part, "Lake Erie is becoming septic, New York City is short of water, the Delaware River is infused with salt, the Potomac River with sewage and silt. Air is polluted in major cities and their citizens breathe and see with difficulty. . . . All too soon life in such polluted environments will be the national human experience."[3] *Design with Nature* was published three years later. Alas, neither the declaration nor his landmark book portended the environmental calamity we face today. Back then, of course, little was understood about humanity's capacity to alter the planet's climate. Fifty years later a correction was made. Following a summit of world landscape architecture leaders, the LAF published the New Landscape Declaration. The document places emphasis squarely on climate change, calling for the creation of bioregional landscapes that can "adapt to climate change and mitigate its root causes."[4] The new declaration has been translated into nineteen languages, a fitting tribute to, and advancement of, McHarg's environmental legacy.

But can the profession truly move the needle on climate change? The Earth's atmosphere has already surpassed 410 parts per million of carbon dioxide. The upward trend continues. Some scientists are doubtful that global emissions can stop before global warming exceeds two degrees Celsius, the maximum level set in the 2015 Paris Agreement on climate change. Landscape architects could guide the planting of millions of carbon-sequestering trees around the globe and push for the preservation of millions of acres of extant forests and wetlands, yet these nature-based measures would hardly make a dent in the problem. Climate change is a massive planetary issue, and only massive governmental and corporate action directed at stopping the burning of fossil fuels, investing in clean energy technologies, and implementing geoengineering measures, such as an aerosol atmospheric veil, can avert catastrophe.

Landscape architects may not have the capacity to mitigate the root causes of climate change, but for the profession the adaptation side of the equation remains critically in play. Through the design of flood control features, green stormwater management, living systems of coastal protection, heat-abating urban places, community-scaled productive landscapes, and (soon to come!) the rewilding of lands that affected communities are forced to abandon, the profession today is poised to raise its societal relevance, perhaps more so than at any time since the Declaration of Concern. However, McHarg's legacy of environmental concern goes beyond scale of relevance or manner of application.

Design with Nature was published in 1969, a time of accelerating suburban development, but also a time of environmental ferment that saw the enactment of the National Environmental Policy Act (NEPA) in 1970, the Clean Water Act (CWA) in 1972, and the Endangered Species Act (ESA) in 1973—a stunning run by today's standards of legislation. NEPA and ESA explicitly include the word "ecology" in their statement of purpose. CWA does so implicitly. McHarg's greatest contribution as an educator and activist was, arguably, to help bring the term into wide practical prominence. And it came with a method—namely the layering of ecological data (geology, soils, hydrology, physiography, etc.), as a way to determine development suitability. The so-called layer cake was instrumental in the innovative conception of suburban communities such as the Plan for the Valleys in Baltimore County and The Woodlands community north of Houston. The Plan for the Valleys was not fully realized, but The Woodlands matured to become a shining example of the ecological design method.

In an irrevocably urbanizing world, the layer cake might seem inadequate as a planning and design tool. Yet the method continues to resurface. GreenPlan Philadelphia, a 2005 seminal study led by Mami Hara, a former principal in the firm Wallace Roberts & Todd[5] and current Seattle Public Utilities General Manager/CEO, included the technique as a way to prioritize the citywide deployment of green infrastructure. Armed with a geographic information systems data base, the plan layers open-space accessibility and flooding, as an example, to determine potential locations for bioretention areas that can also double as urban parks.

But more than translating McHarg's signature method from one domain to another, his legacy demands the application of ecology as an overarching ethic. An ecological ethic predicates the actionable understanding of the interrelated physical, environmental, political, economic, and cultural conditions that make up any portion of our urban "house" or, as McHarg used to put it, "Why are people there, what are they doing, where are they going?" For McHarg, "people" meant the inhabitants of a particular locale. Today it means the totality of humanity. Half a century ago it may have been notable to integrate a new community into a patch of mixed woods north of Houston. Today we must act to save urban and wild lands across all nations. If yesterday ecology was a method, today it must be a mind-set—one that enfolds environmental stressors and threats, inclusive of aspects of culture, equality, and social justice, *regardless of locale, extent, or level of detail*.

It is standard in our industry today to equate such a holistic mind-set with resilience. Sadly, resilience owes its rise to the abject failure of sustainability as a model for growth. Clearly, future generations will not have access to the same planet that we have today. As the land submerges, shorelines recede, the permafrost heaves, plants migrate and animals follow, and regions are abandoned in part or in whole, the landscape we see out our window will, in a hundred years, not look and function as it does today. McHarg in his grave would not be turning, but weeping. If this sounds like a doomsday prediction, so be it. McHarg taught us to see the ignorance and irresponsibility of human action. May we all work diligently to extend his long view, shortened as it is by the imperative to act, with equal unapologetic fervor.

Thinking Big:
Design with ~~Nature~~ Culture

James Corner

FIFTY YEARS AFTER the publication of *Design with Nature*, the book seems more prescient, urgent, and relevant than ever before.[1] Caring for the bounty of the natural world while ensuring the advancement of human economy was not just of academic interest to the inimitable Ian McHarg; it was an absolute passion, a lifespring so deep and meaningful that it was his life's work, his devotion, and his love.

One can only wonder what he would think of our world today. On the one hand, he would surely admire the many successes related to the rise of environmental movements, new technologies, and access to data, as well as the abundance of exemplary planning and design projects around the world informed and inspired by his work. On the other hand, he would surely be dismayed by the inadequacy of our politics and regulatory structures to adequately address the effects of climate change and environmental decline, as well as the continuing failure to effectively confront and reverse habitat destruction, hunger, poverty, and extinction of species. One wonders just how far we have actually come since 1969.

In retrospect, I think that McHarg's work continues to teach us four important and valuable lessons. At the same time, I believe there are three confounding challenges to the environmental planning and design mission espoused in *Design with Nature*. I will get to these challenges in a moment, but first let me review the four lessons, the first of which is "think big." McHarg never shied away from the issues of the day—the Vietnam War; the proliferation of nuclear arms; the negligent dependence on polluting fossil fuels and nonrenewable energy; the loss of life caused by mostly preventable natural disasters; the deterioration of living standards in cities; soaring human population growth; rapidly diminishing nonrenewable natural resources; the pollution and contamination of air, water, and soils; and the loss of habitat and species diversity around the planet. Humanity has inherited a bounty in the gifts of the Earth, and yet people seem determined to plunder, impoverish, and sully their own environment. This massive challenge is as much philosophical, political, moral, and imaginative as it is technical and logistical. Hence the "bigness" of McHarg's thinking, which embraced multiple disciplines, ideas, and practices to at least begin addressing these enormously complex issues.

Design with Nature chapter titles such as "City and Countryside," "Nature in the Metropolis," and "The City: Health and Pathology" continue to speak to the big issues of our own day, especially how cities, towns, villages, and other forms of settlement can better absorb a growing global population while maintaining a healthy and diverse natural environment, fundamental for the provision of clean water, air, food, natural resources, biodiversity, and open space. The rhetorical positioning as well as the professional planning and design methods described in *Design with Nature* encourage us all to think bigger, to act more holistically, and to be both brave and capable enough to take on the big issues.

Related to thinking big is a second lesson: multidisciplinary collaboration is valuable. Knowledge for McHarg was neither useful nor constructive when isolated in disciplinary silos; knowledge is more insightful and more "real" as a holistic construct. Consequently, in the 1960s and 1970s McHarg built his academic program at the University of Pennsylvania around a diverse multidisciplinary faculty, comprising not only landscape architects and urban planners but also natural and social scientists, computational and data analysts, public health and governance experts, and others. Multiple sources of input could then be "layered" upon one another to construct a more comprehensive understanding. Again, this kind of broad-based curiosity, combined with rigorous techniques for mining the insights of real collaboration, is as relevant today as it ever has been.

The third lesson is that science, data, and metrics can be effective in shaping a vision and moving it forward. McHarg was well aware that passion and rhetorical poetics only go so far in the world of politics and large-scale decision making; hard data and evidence helps to construct a more unassailable argument. There can be a cold, positivistic side to scientific data that I have been critical of before, with its lack of cultural nuance and situational pliability, but the point still remains that rational argument based on data undergirds how a convincing case can be made for enacting new decisions, regulations, and controls in an open and diverse democracy. McHarg's method presented cases for how land might be best developed, preserved, managed, and planned for in responsibly rational terms, utilizing data and metrics to construct logical and compelling arguments.

Related to this is the fourth lesson: messaging and media are powerful. McHarg was profiled on national television, interviewed by leading newspapers and magazines around the world, published and cited in a huge number of books and articles, and invited to speak at many important events around the world. He was a powerful spokesman, skilled in rhetorical argumentation, gifted with poetic introspection, and charged up with a passionate energy that people found magnetic. He avoided science-speak, engaging people with a more accessible and inspiring discourse. He made it clear that our work with environmental planning and design does not happen in a vacuum but must inevitably reach out, connect, and lead the larger conversation. McHarg was inspiring in this regard and relentless in getting the message out.

At the same time, however, three challenges continue to confound McHarg's work and the environmentalist movement generally.

The first of these is the role of governance and coordinated action. The big social and environmental issues of our time cannot be resolved at the local level alone; they require much larger-scale efforts and cross-jurisdictional coordination. Land and infrastructure planning are state-dependent activities that demand an activist government capable of enacting clear decisions, regulations, and controls. In a democracy, and especially in a republic such as the United States, it is practically impossible for coherent, long-term, and effective land planning to be done with any consistent clarity. Lobbyists, special interest groups, conflicted stakeholders, and even the not-in-my-backyard (NIMBY) activists confuse, complicate, and ultimately stall otherwise good and productive initiatives. The various Rockefeller Foundation–funded initiatives to look at urgent climate-change resiliency design and planning ideas for both New York and San Francisco inevitably flounder because of the sheer scale and massive order-of-magnitude coordination and funding required. The 2015 Paris Agreement on global climate change among multiple nations was a miraculous achievement, although the United States under a nationalist President Donald Trump has proven just how fragile that alliance is. Clearly, the challenge at all scales of environmental design and planning requires broader coordination, longer-term strategies, and clarity of policy, leadership, and action. Design and planning need to operate more effectively within the political sphere, while at the same time encouraging more progressivist and longer-term initiatives that are fundamental to effective environmental action at the appropriate scale.

Related to this is the challenge of people: the challenge of disparate cultural points of view, which are especially prevalent in an open democracy. Some actions and policies that are good for one group will inevitably not be good for another group. There will always be multiple opinions and values accorded to any particular initiative. McHarg's maps and metrics made an unassailable argument that seemed both obvious and urgent; and yet people could interpret the proposals, actions, trade-offs, and ideas in divergent ways, mostly according to who would gain and who would lose. Similarly, in the context of climate change and global environmental decline, one would think the case is so crystal clear that we could all more easily unite to address these challenges collectively, and yet, in recent years especially, we have seen a complete cultural divide around whether the issues are even real and valid. Ironically, the science and data in which McHarg placed so much faith has become weaponized—diminished through the rise of disinformation campaigns and a generational skepticism that data are never neutral or objective but subject to manipulation and bias.

There is a struggle between people who believe in different realities, live in different worlds, and have different aspirations. It appears that no amount of scientific evidence, rational argument, or innovative technology can resolve, persuade, or conflate cultural differences; the environmental equations for trading one thing off for another will inevitably produce winners and losers, supporters and adversaries. We are perhaps at the point where instead of continuing to think about operating on the world "outside," we need also to start better engaging our own internal social world, the world of ideas, language, culture, and human nature. How do we engage and work with one another productively? How do we develop and articulate shared values and visions for our collective future? How do we come to terms with the fact that rational planning, scientific expertise, technological innovation, and other forms of optimization do not always resonate, make sense, or hold any value for the majority of people?

This brings me to the third challenge: the challenge of design, creativity, and imagination. Art helps to lighten the load and permit new ways of seeing, new ways of doing, new ways of being. The design of landscapes and cities, the design of our Earth, is not simply cosmetic; more fundamentally, it shapes how people see, value, and interact. If we are to try and more fully address the issue of diverse cultural values coalescing around some kind of shared vision, then design will have a powerfully important function. Although many thought it easy to pigeonhole McHarg as a quantitative environmental planner, he was not at all immune to design: he authored a number of significant design projects while at Wallace McHarg Roberts & Todd, was a fan of "big and bold" landscape architects such as Roberto Burle Marx and Lawrence Halprin, and was proud of the innovation of "ecological design" as spearheaded primarily by his proteges Carol and Colin Franklin and Leslie and Rolf Sauer of Andropogon. He also wrote poetry and loved the diversity of culture generally. He saw creativity as fundamental to the evolution of life, both biological and cultural. Life continues to "body itself forth," with form, consequence, and potential. Nonetheless, the effective conjunction of imaginative design with rational planning remains elusive; seemingly the metrics and pragmatics of planning too easily govern the more subjective, imaginative aspects of design, and the profession has unfortunately splintered into two camps.

If one views *Design with Nature* as simply a methodological set of practices, inspired by an ecological ethos, then the larger conceptual, artistic, and cultural potentials of ecological ideas will be too easily overlooked and underdeveloped. There is still an enormous reservoir of untapped creativity related to the interface between ecology and culture, and most of this belongs to the world of design. Humanity continues to propagate new forms, new ideas, and new ways of being; it is just a question of sparking the imagination and inspiring collective aspiration.

Fifty years after the publication of *Design with Nature,* we are beginning to realize that the ecological is not something "out there" to be remedied, fixed, and transformed— "nature"; it is instead something to be nurtured deep within human and social consciousness—"culture." Cultural values need continual engagement if we are to find a truly sustainable and equitable future on Earth. Thinking big, crossing boundaries, utilizing knowledge, creatively addressing challenges of governance and social difference, and using design innovation to project alternative futures lie at the heart of the greater McHargian project: not just restoring the Earth per se, but uplifting our very humanity.

Traverse Before Transect

Anuradha Mathur

IAN McHARG INTRODUCED me to the ecological transect. It situated me uniquely in the land to which I had recently arrived as a student from India, 7,500 miles (12,000 kilometers) away. I was not just in Philadelphia; I was on a line drawn from the Appalachian Mountains across the Piedmont Plateau down to the Coastal Plain and the Atlantic Ocean. Having learned about Patrick Geddes's Valley Section from his work in India in the 1910s, the transect resonated with me. In Geddes's words, it was "that general slope from mountain to sea which we find everywhere in the world."[1]

The transect, however, not only situated me; it also gave the students of my class, who hailed from five different continents, a common ground. It cultivated an eye for seeing landscape that we could carry wherever we went. For many of us that meant back home.

Each week we set out to a point on the transect—the coal mines near Scranton, the boulder field in the Poconos area, the forests of the Wissahickon, the meadows near Valley Forge, the falls at Manayunk, the bogs and waterways of the Pine Barrens, and the dunes along the Jersey Shore. We dug soil pits, identified vegetation, searched for clues to what lay above and below the Earth's surface, and in our field notes pieced together the sectional history of the land. In studio, we worked in groups, familiarizing ourselves with particular sites on the transect. Each site was an area of 25 square miles (65 square kilometers), represented by a topographical map on which we called out diverse soils, vegetation, land uses, slopes, and geology. We highlighted the lines of streams, floodplains, wetlands, and aquifers, constructing clear distinctions between features that belonged to land and those that belonged to water. Although the base maps were the same each year, using a scale of 1 inch to 500 feet (1 centimeter to 60 meters), we took particular pride in choosing our palette of colors, which extended into subtle gradients of green, blue, and brown, perhaps in an attempt to dissolve boundaries constituted by the map that did not correspond with our experience on the ground. It was inevitable, however, that the transect on the ground would recede into distant memory as the map took over as the primary site of analysis and design. After all, it allowed the layering of information from multiple disciplines onto the same geographic surface. The map is what we as students of design and planning were tasked to respond to. This was our experience in the 501 studio at PennDesign in 1989, the foundational landscape studio initiated by Ian McHarg and Narendra Juneja in one of its last years.

A decade later it was my turn to teach the foundational landscape studio.[2] I took students not to the transect of my student days but to a place from which they could construct their own transect. They carried measuring tapes, string, improvised spirit levels, pencils, newsprint, index cards, and charcoal. They did not carry maps to orient themselves, only the blank pages of their sketchbooks as they began to negotiate an unfamiliar terrain. I urged them to walk not so much to find their way, but to *make* their way. Some made their way from creek to ridge, others from forest to industrial remnants, yet others from wetlands to infrastructural corridors. Like route surveyors at the head of armies charged with mapping unknown terrains, they triangulated between points, connecting these points with lines of sight and measurement. They learned to be attentive to their selection of points. Some were fixed; others were ephemeral. They also learned to appreciate the lines that connected them, paying particular attention to the line between land and water. This line was fraught with controversy. It was known to shift daily and seasonally, but in a land of settlers, it was also shifted at will. They learned to appreciate wetness everywhere—in the ground, air, plants, rocks, creatures—rather than accept the presence of water as it was indicated on maps. The terrain was not exhausted in a single walk. It was walked differently each time. Once they triangulated, students sketched, sectioned, and photographed with an eye and ear tuned to meter and movement, material and horizon, continuity and rupture. Distinctions and boundaries that they had been cultured to see dissolved, and they began to articulate new relationships and limits.

Students were learning what it took to make a map. They were also learning what it took to construct a transect. It took traversing, traversing being the act of journeying across a terrain with the objective of recording findings as much as imposing a new imagination on place. In this sense, they were already designing while constructing a transect. Design was in the eyes with which they were seeing, the legs with which they were striding, the choices that they were making, the instruments with which they were measuring. They were learning what Geddes and McHarg knew all too well, that landscape and design emerge simultaneously in the act of traversing to construct a transect.

The work on the walls and on student desks drew a smile and characteristic sharp inhale from McHarg every time he walked into my 501 studio, expressing an appreciation for the graphite sections and triangulations being drafted, photographic montages being made, and plaster castings being worked. It was an appreciation that could only come from someone who knew what the transect owed to the traverse.

Today I take students in more advanced studios to places of conflict, poverty, and unfolding tragedy such as Mumbai, Bangalore, the Western Ghats of India, the deserts of Rajasthan, Jerusalem, and Tijuana. These are places on slopes from mountain to sea of their own, slopes that Geddes and McHarg believed to be "everywhere in the world."[1] But I am acutely conscious, as they would be, that these "transects" are products of traverses by "designers" before us—surveyors, explorers, colonizers, conquerors. Their extraordinary transgressions articulated the landscapes that have become the ordinary in these places, including what is taken for granted as natural and cultural, land and water, urban and rural. In short, they created today's ground of conflict. Surely the least we can do in the spirit of McHarg and Geddes is to traverse these places again, to venture a new imagination aimed not necessarily at solving problems, but at keeping the transect alive as an agent of change.

A Few Choruses Low Down, but Not So Blue for Ian

Laurie Olin

THE PUBLICATION OF *Design with Nature* forever changed the field of landscape architecture. The book, its ecological point of view, its rational method, and its author also had a significant and positive effect on my own life and career. I first heard of Ian McHarg when architecture classmates from Seattle stayed at my apartment in New York City in 1966. They were traveling to and from the Delmarva Peninsula for a landscape architecture studio at Harvard, where Ian was teaching while on sabbatical from the University of Pennsylvania. I was somewhat taken aback that they were making a plan for an entire peninsula that encompassed large portions of two states.

I first heard McHarg speak in Seattle and met him in March 1971 while teaching with Grant Jones at the University of Washington. He had come to give the John Danz lectures, which consisted largely of excerpts from *Design with Nature*.[1] The three lectures were titled: "Man, Planetary Disease"; "An Ecological Metaphysic"; and "Design with Nature." He was spellbinding. His presentation of the problems arising from our ideology, politics, and habits of practice was persuasive. Like many others, I got it. Ian was at loose ends during the day between his evening lectures and social events, so he came over to the school and hung out in our studio. Up close he was charming, warm, and kind to the students, who were preparing a landscape master plan for Bainbridge Island. He was an astute critic and generous to Grant and me. A year later, I went off to Europe to work on a landscape history of southern England and to study the sociology of the public realm of Rome.

By happy coincidence, I joined the Penn faculty in 1974, at a time when the Department of Landscape Architecture and Regional Planning had a bumper crop of natural and social scientists in addition to landscape architects, architects, and planners on its faculty. The curriculum was ambitious, wide ranging, and exhausting, but exciting and remarkably productive in its research, teaching, and production of future educators and practitioners who departed to all parts of the globe, spreading the message of *Design with Nature*. Since then, ecological analysis—the integration of data by overlay techniques, and an interactive matrix-based method for planning and design at a range of scales as advocated by Ian and in our curriculum—has seeped into the working methods of design practices, teaching curricula in academic institutions, and public agencies around the country and the world.

Ian was twenty in 1940, and World War II had begun. His youth was put on hold while he blew up bridges as a commando behind enemy lines. Afterward, he was part of a generation that wanted to fix things, to not make the mistakes of previous generations. Marxist and Freudian thought, which had been influential in intellectual endeavors for several decades before the war, were displaced by a new perspective: structuralism, which provided meaning and methods in disciplines ranging from linguistics and literature to philosophy and ecology, even economics and design, through the 1950s and 1960s. The intellectual, academic, and professional world of the postwar years was imbued with instrumental systems thinking and a belief that reason and rational methods must be applied regardless of topic and field. McHarg used his graduate study at Harvard to give himself a crash course in science, sociology, and urban planning theory. He was determined to develop a landscape planning method and practice that was objective, not subjective; that was as rational and replicable as the hard sciences, not intuitive and willful—"not like the design of ladies' hats," as he would bellow. Step by step he developed the curriculum at Penn with the aid of research money that allowed him and his colleagues to consider the problem of human habitation and the most fundamental issues of community planning and design at a scale from neighborhood to physiographic region.

In concert with a number of natural scientists who had become public figures, McHarg used national television to advocate for environmental planning. There is no question that his rhetoric, performance, and publications had considerable influence on the creation and early years of the Environmental Protection Agency and the Clean Water and Clean Air Acts of the Lyndon Johnson and Richard Nixon administrations in the United States. The problems he raised and attempted to address—issues related to health, safety, settlement, resources, ecology, and resilience—are still the most important problems we face, and seem even clearer and more desperate today than when he was at his most strident.

Occasionally people ask me what the department was like, or suggest to me that they think McHarg was unsympathetic to design. It is simply not true. Others have speculated that Bob Hanna, Carol Franklin, other design practitioners, and I were something of a design antidote to the so-called method. In fact, with Ian's support and conviction we were trying to demonstrate that science and ecology were not antithetical to design, but underpinned it when well done—that we were actually part of the follow-through. He sought to clarify this in a book extending his ideas to human ecology, but the planned "Design for Man" volume never happened, in part because of the intractable difficulties inherent in social science. In the final analysis, landscape architecture is not a science. Like architecture, it is a useful art, one that employs the findings and knowledge of science along with knowledge of art, craft, design, and construction to address human needs in social environments. We knew that, and we discussed ad nauseam how our students at a certain point had to strap all of their analysis to their backs like a parachute and jump, hoping for a soft landing, not a crash. It informed their choices as ethical professionals regarding costs, safety, health, and environmental outcomes. McHarg's ideas were for guidance and to be used as a checklist for responsibility, not a set of rules to limit imagination, and as a constraint on foolishness and ignorance, not on creation.

Interestingly, I found that the overlay method of examination, comparison, and interaction between various factors and topics—natural, social, historical, theoretical—could be as stimulating and useful in building up and creating a scheme through additive considerations as it was in digging through history and natural factors to produce suitability matrices. In over two dozen projects with Peter Eisenman, I explored using overlays of information in a forward-projecting manner in an effort to find alternative design structures, formal and artistic solutions to complex planning and design problems. Examples of my built and unbuilt work range from the Wexner Center at The Ohio State University and Rebstock Park in Frankfurt, Germany, to the City of Culture at Santiago de Compostela in Spain. After many somewhat experimental projects, I also came to find natural processes and ecology to be powerful metaphors that have been enormously helpful and inspirational in my work. Several of my most recent projects have derived from careful considerations and analysis of ecological history to produce both an understanding of a place and situation and complex and responsive physical designs. The recently completed University of Washington north campus residential community in Seattle, Apple Park in Cupertino, California, and OLIN's current and ongoing Los Angeles River Master Plan and its pilot projects exemplify this approach.

In the past two decades a number of critiques have been leveled at McHarg and *Design with Nature* that are misplaced and often as ill informed as the denigration of Frederick Law Olmsted and his parks by a recent generation of professionals. Most of the criticism of McHarg, however, has focused on the means, methods, and data in the work, arguing that they are outdated and simplistic. There is some truth in this, for structural systems of thought are inherently political and moralistic; they inevitably raise ethical issues, whether in science, the humanities, or the professions. Debates within the department and in his own office over planning and design often centered on social rather than biological issues, particularly fears of determinism derived from particular methods of responding to data; the data themselves; the costs and benefits resulting from the relative weight assigned to various factors; and the role of imagination, politics, and choice in human decisions. Unquestionably, the technologies used for remote sensing, mapping, and digital processes and computation have become more sophisticated. In the social sciences, likewise, quantitative methods have evolved, as have concerns for complex and vexed human relationships, economics, and all manner of groups not considered fifty years ago. Nevertheless, Ian's fundamental insight and approach, despite his method—imperfect as all forms of research inevitably are—frames landscape and regional planning today. For all the developments in geographic information systems, no one has shown that he was working on the wrong problems, or that those problems are not still vitally important. As well, his critics have underestimated Ian's responsibility for creating the professional context in which landscape architects and planners now operate; today's practitioners are focused on similar concerns and are using the technology that he promoted and encouraged.

Ian was a force who changed our perspective forever, but also a deeply human and contradictory person. Difficult as he could be at times, he was extremely loyal and devoted to friends and family and fiercely proud and protective of his faculty, quarreling and making up with them socially and privately, in reviews and in faculty meetings—all in an endless effort to improve our work, our lives, and the planet. One of my fondest memories is of him standing atop a log, backlit in the blazing sun, wearing pajama bottoms and holding a cigarette in one hand and a hose in the other, watering the giant kitchen garden on his farm in Marshallton, Chester County, Pennsylvania. Sheep, pigs, and Highland cattle wandered about in the background as he drenched the rank and jumbled masses of plants and hummed a favorite Coleman Hawkins tune. Ian always understood that humans were part of nature, and that only through ecological understanding and constructive action could we save ourselves and have a good life.

A Landscape of Ideas and Action: Place, Process, Form, and Language

Anne Whiston Spirn

I KNEW NOTHING ABOUT landscape architecture until I read Ian McHarg's description of the field in the brochure of the Graduate School of Fine Arts at the University of Pennsylvania in 1969. McHarg's text was a call to action. It spoke directly to me, offering the opportunity to join a profession that would give scope to all my disparate interests: landscape, environment, history, art, photography, social action. I decided to switch from Penn's doctoral program in art history to landscape architecture.

At Penn in the early 1970s, all our work began with the identity of place, its history, its present, and the socioenvironmental dynamics that would influence its future. In 1967, McHarg's article "An Ecological Method for Landscape Architecture" had laid out the ideas that were the foundation of our curriculum:

> Written on the place and upon its inhabitants lies mute all physical, biological and cultural history awaiting to be understood by those who can read it. This is the prerequisite for intelligent intervention and adaptation. So let us begin at the beginning. The place, any place, can only be understood through its physical evolution. Both climate and geology can be invoked to interpret physiography, the current configuration of the place. If one now knows historical geology, climate, and physiography,

Portions of this chapter are drawn from the essay "Ian McHarg, Landscape Architecture, and Environmentalism: Ideas and Methods in Context," in *Environmentalism and Landscape Architecture*, ed. Michel Conan (Washington, DC: Dumbarton Oaks, 2000).

then the water regimen becomes comprehensible—the pattern of rivers and aqui-fers, their physical properties and relative abundance, oscillation between flood and drought. Knowing the foregoing and the prior history of plant evolution, we can now comprehend the nature and pattern of soils. . . . by identifying physiographic, climatic zones and soils, we can perceive order and predictability in the distribution of con-stituent plant communities. Animals are fundamentally plant related so that . . . with the addition of the stage of succession of the plant communities and their age, it is possible both to understand and to predict the species, abundance or scarcity of wild animal populations.[1]

Our grasp of this method was honed in mapping the "layer cake" of air, earth, water, and life, and in fieldwork, where we learned to read landscape processes with the aid of a core faculty of environmental scientists. But, apart from ecology, we learned little about the theoretical context of ecological design and planning. McHarg emphasized invention over precedent. Throughout the 1970s our curriculum was ahistorical, offer-ing no introduction to, or comparison of, alternative approaches to landscape design and planning.[2] In the 1980s, as a faculty member at Harvard, when I encountered the work of Patrick Geddes and Jaqueline Tyrwhitt, it was a revelation. This glimpse of im-portant precedents prompted me to trace the roots of ecological planning and design and to construct a pantheon, from Hippocrates through Vitruvius and Alberti, Freder-ick Law Olmsted, and Frank Lloyd Wright to Patrick Geddes, Lewis Mumford, McHarg, and Kevin Lynch.[3]

McHarg used his position at the University of Pennsylvania to develop ideas about ecological design and planning. In the 1960s and 1970s the university studio was a place for theoretical and methodological experimentation, the professional office a place to test ideas in actual places, with real clients and programs. I observed this interaction first-hand, as a student at Penn from 1970 to 1974 and at Wallace McHarg Roberts & Todd (WMRT) from 1973 to 1977, where I worked on several landmark projects, including The Woodlands (Texas), the Sanibel Comprehensive Plan (Florida), Pardisan (Tehran, Iran), and the Toronto Central Waterfront (Canada). At the office, McHarg only took jobs that could advance the field, and he often spent "overhead" funds on research. In one case, I sketched out my ideas for a manual for the planners and designers who were begin-ning to work at The Woodlands and whom I feared would not take the time to assimi-late all the material WMRT had produced. My proposal was to condense and summarize our ecological inventory and present our design strategies.[4] When I showed McHarg my sketches, he told me to take a month and develop the idea. We had no contract for that work. Ultimately, he sold the idea to the client, and it became a funded project, but he took a risk. That was typical of McHarg's approach. Ideas trumped budget. And

Nature trumped the client's program. Our site boundaries, always dictated by natural processes, often extended beyond the client's property. In the case of The Woodlands, our "site" encompassed the larger watershed, and our program expanded to address the recharge of an aquifer that underlay the city of Houston. McHarg persuaded the client, Texas oilman George Mitchell, to take on this enlarged mandate, which turned out to be in the client's interest.[5]

Many of us students challenged McHarg about the curriculum's focus on suburban and rural sites and its neglect of the city. His defense was that little was known about the urban natural environment, but a WMRT project for the Toronto Central Waterfront revealed a wealth of information.[6] A few years later I decided to produce a book about how to design with nature in the city, and I wrote *The Granite Garden: Urban Nature and Human Design* for a general audience in order to create a demand for the kind of work I wanted to do, as McHarg himself had done with *Design with Nature*.[7] At WMRT, I had witnessed firsthand how many clients sought out the firm because his book had persuaded them to take an ecological approach. Even in the midst of the recession of 1973–1975, when so many architects and landscape architects were unemployed, McHarg still had work. And *Design with Nature* persuaded people like myself to become landscape architects. All this taught me to appreciate the power of a book.

After *The Granite Garden*'s publication in 1984, prospective clients reached out, and I had to decide whether to open an office. I was teaching at Harvard and remembered the cases in *Design with Nature* that had been studio projects at Penn. McHarg explained that "a professional landscape architect or city planner is limited in the projects he undertakes to problems presented by his clients. A professor, in contrast, suffers no such constraints and is enabled to undertake projects he deems worthy of study."[8] I decided to create a research practice in which teaching, grants, and a university salary would enable me to set my own agenda and support demonstration projects for some clients, like community gardeners and children, who cannot afford a designer, and others who do not know they need one, like community development corporations, city agencies, and public schools. What began, in 1984, as a study of how vacant urban land could be exploited as a resource to restore the city's natural environment and rebuild inner-city neighborhoods, grew, in 1987, into the West Philadelphia Landscape Project (WPLP), an ongoing action-research project of more than thirty years' duration.[9] WPLP proposals have inspired many other programs, such as Philadelphia's landmark Green City, Clean Waters program, proposed in 2009, which will reduce combined sewer overflows through green infrastructure. WPLP employs landscape literacy as a cornerstone of community development.[10] The project was a laboratory for my book *The Language of Landscape*, which argues that landscape is a form of language and that, in shaping landscape, people express purpose, values, and ideas.[11]

Central to all my work is Ian McHarg's insight that every place "is in the process of becoming. This we must be able to read, and ecology provides the language."[12] To me, however, it is landscape, as a mutual shaping of people and place, that provides the language; and it is ecology, a science, that helps us understand the interplay of processes that shape landscape. Landscape is, inevitably, a fusion of nature and culture. The language of landscape integrates natural processes and human purpose, where "form and process are indivisible aspects of a single phenomenon," allowing one "to understand form as an explicit point in evolutionary process."[13] The language of landscape "permits us to perceive pasts we cannot otherwise experience, to anticipate the possible, to envision, choose, and shape the future."[14]

The Power of Nature and/or the Nature of Power

Dana Tomlin

IAN McHARG DESIGNED my home. In fact, it was one of his first major projects. Neither of us knew it at the time, however, since he had yet to finish his schooling, and I had yet to be born. McHarg was one of thirteen students working on the project in a seminar conducted by Harvard professors John Black and Ayers Brinser, who published their work as *Planning One Town: Petersham—A Hill Town in Massachusetts*.[1] This small volume documents the process by which that group formulated "possibilities" for a landscape in rural New England.

As I write these words, I find myself both in and of that landscape. Having lived in Petersham for several decades, it is easy to reflect in hindsight on both the insight and the foresight of that work from almost seventy years ago. More meaningful to me now, however, is not the work itself so much as the way I came across it. Soon after moving to Petersham, I stopped in to the town library to take out a copy of *Planning One Town*. The librarian was a woman named Delight, for whom that name was appropriate. On this particular occasion, however, her response to my inquiry was anything but delightful. Instead, she spoke with disdain about what she would only call "that book." Her explanation was both unexpected and easy to appreciate. In short, the terms that were used by those academics to characterize her town (and now mine) were not always easy to reconcile with self-image.

When I recounted this to Ian years later, his response was typical and telling. Rather than dwell on Delight's concern, he immediately and enthusiastically started asking me about my new home. Had I seen this? Did I know about that? Was so-and-so still around? I think what struck me most was his curiosity about my neighbors. He was still able to refer to several by name almost four decades after his infamous work on "that book."

I ultimately came to know Ian McHarg as a mythical figure, a welcome mentor, a close colleague, and a friend. It is for this reason that I now face both the opportunity and the obligation to edit my remarks: to organize and express my impressions in ways that may either reveal or conceal, confirm or confound, teach or preach, explore or exploit, eulogize or criticize . . . You get the idea. This is not merely a descriptive task but also a prescriptive exercise that will inevitably reflect on its author as well as its subject. After all, what I am about to project onto Ian is an image of my own choosing.

I say this not only because that role is so familiar, but also because I believe that role is fundamental to understanding the power of Ian McHarg. To be sure, this character enjoyed a remarkable ability to embrace the world around him, to understand it intellectually, to celebrate it spiritually, and to convey all that to others with both clarity and charisma. That much is apparent. Less apparent yet equally important, I believe, is the degree to which his presence and his prominence have served to promote the ideas and ideals of others. Throughout his career and even today, proponents and opponents have projected onto him images of their own choosing. In landscape architecture, where the particular manner in which one draws from both the arts and the sciences is often what distinguishes one practitioner from another, the images projected onto McHarg have reflected that distinction. Even today, as we continue to reinterpret Ian's legacy, my mind returns to Delight's critique of his early work on "that book." Now as then, it is still true for some that he is not always easy to reconcile with self-image.

So was he an artist? Or was he a scientist? And why did such questions never seem to matter as much to him as they did (and do) to those around him? My own contention is that they did. For McHarg, however, these were questions that related more to production than to promotion. Though he certainly knew the importance of appearance, he also knew that the best way to maintain appearance was through performance.

As I consider his considerable impact on my own ways of seeing and being over the years, what comes to mind first and remains there last is not the head, the heart, the hands, or even the mouth that generated such an irrepressible voice. The image that I would choose to project relates instead to the ears. Whether we were contemplating the magic of Petersham, musing about information technology, or airing differences of opinion on a student project, Ian was one of those people who actually listened. He did so actively, he did so passionately, and he did so with genuine interest. More often than not, he also did so with an impish twinkle in the eye that at once conveyed both challenge and support.

And it still does. Among the others who worked with him, that influence remains apparent. More significantly, it also remains apparent among those who never encountered the man himself but who resonate with his message.

So is it fair to claim that Ian McHarg designed my home? Or is that statement just another instance of self-serving projection? In order to view it as anything else, one would have to broaden the definition of "home" enough to encompass an entire town. One would also have to broaden the definition of "my" enough to include the world in which one happens to reside. And one would have to broaden the definition of "design" enough to make room for the kind of interpretations and recommendations that are offered in "that book."

I, for one, think Ian McHarg would be comfortable with all three.

Ian Lennox McHarg, Scotland, and the Emergence of Green Consciousness

Brian M. Evans

THE ROYAL MILE extends from Edinburgh Castle to the Palace of Holyrood. It is Scotland's Panathenaic Way and was redolent of imperialism—from military to monarchy—until the insinuation of the new Scottish Parliament in 1999 introduced a distinctive and democratic "discontinuity."[1] The principal entrance to Scotland's Parliament sits juxtaposed with the regal entry to Holyrood. On the elevation to the Royal Mile, in the approach to the entrance for Members of the Scottish Parliament, the words of a famous few Scots are cut into the stone to remind them whom they serve as they go about the business of government.

The words are those of authors, entrepreneurs, philosophers, and poets.[2] Sir Walter Scott observed that politicians kept close at hand are easier to hold to account. But his most famous quote, which captures the way that many, then and now, feel about Scotland, is missing: "Breathes there the man with soul so dead / Who never to himself hath said / This is mine own, my native land! . . . / Oh Caledonia, stern and wild / milk nurse for a poetic child."[3]

This essay explores the relationship between Ian Lennox McHarg and the environmental consciousness of Scotland, the country where he was born, schooled, and lived before European conflict took him away to soldier for king and country—a challenge to which he responded with some distinction—until his first sojourn in Harvard University in the United States, which changed the course of his life.[4]

Five thinker-scholar-practitioners each published a seminal work in the 1960s and changed forever the way we think about and practice urbanism. The *primus inter pares* of the group is Jane Jacobs and her masterwork *The Death and Life of Great American Cities*. The others are Kevin Lynch's *The Image of the City*, Gordon Cullen's *Townscape*, Edmund Bacon's *Design of Cities*, and, for those who begin with the land, Ian McHarg's *Design with Nature*.[5]

This list reflects my personal view. There are notable omissions—Lewis Mumford, for example—but, as an aspirant thinker-scholar-practitioner working in the intertwined fields of urbanism and landscape design, I view these "famous five" as the progenitors of late-20th-century urbanism, which enabled a step change in the empirical, rational, and pragmatic thought applied to city and landscape planning and design.[6]

They gave us the basic tools for understanding the socioeconomic realities of the city (Jacobs), its experiential qualities (Lynch), the observational skills needed (Cullen), the orthography of the city (Bacon), and in *Design with Nature*, the natural and ecological qualities. They knew one another, shared, and collaborated. An iconic photograph from 1958 shows McHarg with Jacobs and Lynch and many other notable contemporaries, including Lewis Mumford, J. B. Jackson, Catherine Bauer, and Louis Kahn.[7] Cullen and Bacon are missing from the photograph, but Bacon taught for many years at the University of Pennsylvania, and Cullen was also on the faculty after McHarg invited him to teach there.[8]

Urban and landscape thought, research, and practice have evolved since the publication of these books. However, the contention may be made that the foundation of more recent, leading contributions can be tracked back to these five principal texts, whether that be the legacy of Kevin Lynch for Jan Gehl or Ian McHarg for Michael Hough. I do not mean to suggest, however, that Gehl and Hough are derivative of Lynch and McHarg, any more than McHarg is derivative of Patrick Geddes, but rather that a clear intellectual connection exists.[9] Here, then, is a personal view of the key thinkers who established the intent of late-20th-century urban thought and practice, placing McHarg and *Design with Nature* at its core.

Like the First Nations of many countries, the Celts of Scotland (and Ireland) had a predominantly oral culture, with law and traditions entrusted to the *seanchaidh* (English: shanachie)—part storyteller, part historian, and part shaman.[10] Today a substantive literature exists on the antecedents and legacy of Celtic and Gaelic culture in Scotland, notably in associations with land and environment.[11]

An enduring theme in the narrative about landscape and environment is the distinction between *land* and *the land*. In his musings on the subject in *Second Nature*, Michael Pollan distinguishes between the developer's love of *land*, as distinct from *the* land, for "*the* land is abstract and in some final sense unpossessable by any individual," whereas "*land* is a reliable if somewhat mystical source of private wealth . . . to hold and multiply in value" [italics added].[12]

This distinction goes to the heart of Celtic and Scottish sensibilities about environment and land. It is a recurrent theme in Celtic poetry and folklore, and it is further evoked and developed in the canon of Scottish literature, as exemplified by the likes of Lewis Grassic Gibbon in the quotation, "Nothing endures . . . but the land."[13] Norman MacCaig, renowned poet and chronicler of the Gaelic traditions of Scotland, wrote: "Who possesses this landscape? / The man who bought it or I who am possessed by it? / False questions, for this landscape is masterless / and intractable in any terms that are human."[14]

There is a difference in the time frames of these different approaches to land; one is driven by short-term financial motivation and the other by protracted climatic and cultural horizons. But it is the "commodification" of land, rather than an inherited appreciation of natural and social good, that is the most immediate difference between these approaches.

In the United Kingdom and in British history, the distinction between *land* and *the land* is a fault line that differentiates Celtic and Anglo Saxon attitudes toward the social, economic, and cultural appreciation of territory. This difference was at its most pronounced during the Highland Clearances in Scotland (and similar indignities in Ireland)—Britain's own program of ethnic cleansing.[15] The Clearances were not the first, or the last, systemic displacement of First Nations in the name of progress and exploitation of land rather than living with them in a harmonious balance, but for any scholar of Scottish history and landscape they are the most real, the tangible evidence that brother can prey on brother, lured by the pursuit of economic advantage. This same disparity is apparent in the political ideologies of social democracy and neoliberal capitalism.

In his lecture to the British Academy in 1990, Thomas Christopher (T. C.) Smout explored the (Scottish) Highlands and the roots of green consciousness.[16] Smout, like John Muir, Patrick Geddes, and Ian McHarg before him, has written about green consciousness as reflected in human relationships with the land, its use and management, and how this enters art, culture, and poetry. In his writings, Smout set out the attitudes toward landscape and the environment (predominantly in the Highlands of Scotland) as (1) "traditional"—a resource for living (farming and forestry), a resource for sport (huntin', shootin', and fishin'), and a resource for industry (mining, smelting, and power); and (2) "post-romantic"—a resource for outdoor recreation, spiritual contemplation, and taking refuge in nature. Smout was one of the first in the United Kingdom, on the cusp of the 21st century, to observe the transition in green thinking from the romantic views of nature in the 18th and 19th centuries to the scientific analysis and taxonomy of the 19th and 20th centuries to its emergence into the political mainstream in the late 20th and early 21st centuries. That journey is increasingly seen as essential to addressing the threats of global population growth and climate change foreseen by Muir, Geddes, and McHarg, three native Scots who have had a global impact on environmental consciousness.

Muir was born in Dunbar, Scotland, in 1838, and eleven years later his family moved to Wisconsin, bringing with it Scottish love for the land and dedication to hard work, values shared by many pioneer immigrants and frequently referred to by McHarg himself.[17] Muir and McHarg were inspired by the landscape of the United States and seized the opportunities presented there, but I would suggest, particularly in McHarg's case, that the cultural context and environmental awareness they grew up with had a lasting effect on the attitudes they carried with them and their subsequent exploration of opportunities presented to them.[18]

Unlike Muir and McHarg who emigrated to America by default and by choice, respectively, Patrick Geddes (born 1854), originally from the village of Ballater in the northeast of Scotland, remained in the U.K., studied in London, and achieved great prominence nationally and internationally as one of the founders of town planning.[19] Geddes advocated the unity of city and region as the basis for town and country planning; he explored these ideas at the *Cities and Town-Planning Exhibition* of 1911 and later in the book *Cities in Evolution* in 1915.[20]

Geddes's proposition of a journey from *eotechnic* (preindustrial life in balance with nature) to *paleotechnic* (the life-threatening industrial age of exploitation and city growth) to *neotechnic* (life renewed and transitioning to a healthy environment through the use of newer, cleaner technologies) was initially seen as utopian but has since come to be appreciated as expressing the antecedents of sustainability—a proposition explored in "Dear Green Place: A Question of Equilibrium," the theme of the U.K. exhibit at the 18th Triennale of Milan in 1992.[21]

The review and reappraisal of Geddes's ideas has been more or less continual since the late 20th century, as urban and landscape thought has evolved, and as research and practice have sought a means to integrate the ideas first espoused by Jacobs, Lynch, Cullen, Bacon, and McHarg into a more holistic approach to urbanism. In a special issue of *Landscape and Urban Planning* in 2017, contributors discuss the strengths and weaknesses of Geddes's ideas.[22] For example, Michael Batty and Stephen Marshall highlight Geddes's introduction of the theory of evolution to city planning, which he applied to social evolution, with its inherent contradictions and tensions between bottom-up and top-down action. Nonetheless, they conclude that the enduring appeal of Geddes is that he left, albeit incomplete, the expression of a "big picture in a way that later generations could easily grasp and build upon" while revealing the "key paradox of modern planning which seeks to intervene in systems that have enormous complexity, growing and evolving rather than being designed in any top-down fashion." But, as Volker Welter suggests, "The study of cities was, for Geddes, ultimately a means to study and advance life."[23]

Geddes's contribution to green consciousness is clear, as Frederick Steiner and Laurel McSherry assert:

The hill and valley landscapes of Scotland influenced how Patrick Geddes viewed cities and regions. His theories were grounded in interdisciplinarity and visual thinking and produced enduring tools still used by planners and designers, such as transects, diagnostic surveys, and conservative surgery. . . . His ideas in turn influenced other important planning theorists such as Lewis Mumford, Jaqueline Tyrwhitt, and Ian McHarg and remain timely and useful for contemporary regional planning, urban design, and landscape architecture. . . . The theories of Patrick Geddes continue to be relevant for cities in evolution.[24]

Lewis Mumford was influenced by Geddes's work and did a great deal to promote it in the United States. Geddes's work predates McHarg's, but as Anne Whiston Spirn argues, "[does not] diminish McHarg's contribution."[25] Spirn posits several reasons for "the failure to appreciate the importance of Geddes's work as a precedent," including "the desire [of landscape architects] to be seen as original," and she has established that Geddes's papers were lodged at The Glasgow School of Art when McHarg returned to Scotland to teach there in 1952.[26] The exact nature of any influence, however, is not the central issue here. It is rather to establish a patrimonial link between three of the world's leading environmentalists—John Muir, Patrick Geddes, and Ian McHarg—Scots who developed ideas that resonate with, and emerge from, Scottish attitudes toward the land, the environment, and the landscape in what Smout has described as an emerging green consciousness (figure 8.1).

All three came from a cultural landscape tradition in which the appreciation of place is rooted in its relationship with the land—a deep respect for it and the traditions derived from it. Scots Gaelic uses the word *dualchas* to connote that part of the patrimony that somehow conveys physical character, heritage, culture, and tradition; it is akin to the polyvalence currently devoted to "place" as a concept. The closest contemporary term is the German *Heimat*, which carries the same allusion to place and to home. *Dualchas* is heard today in the phrase *"dualchas àraid agus luachmhòr ann"* (a unique and valued heritage).[27]

It is unknown whether Muir or McHarg had any knowledge of the Gaelic language, although we know that Geddes did have some. All three did, however, share a love and understanding of and affinity with the land that is commonplace in many aboriginal societies, Celtic and Gaelic communities, and still apparent in contemporary Scots culture. Writers have paid tribute to *the land* in Gaelic and Scots literature for centuries.[28] Scotland is the only part of the U.K. to have an "everyman's right," a freedom to roam.[29]

FIGURE 8.1 John Muir, Patrick Geddes, and Ian McHarg (left to right). John Muir. *National Park Service, John Muir National Historic Site*; Patrick Geddes. *Chronicle/Alamy stock photo*; and Ian McHarg. *Photo, Becky Young, 1979. With permission, Ian McHarg Collection, The Architectural Archives, University of Pennsylvania.*

As McHarg observed: "Scotland has no law of trespass, so the countryside [is] fissured by rights-of-way."[30]

The Highland Clearances displaced many thousands of Highland people in a widespread diaspora to North America, but also to the burgeoning industrial city of Glasgow, which became and remains, with Manchester and Birmingham, one of a very few metropolitan cities in the U.K. other than London.[31] All of these cities are or have been destinations for successive waves of immigration, what Doug Saunders has described as "arrival cities."[32] Among these British metropolitan cities, Glasgow is unique in the sizable proportion of its population that is of "Highland" Scot (significantly, west as well as north) and Irish extraction—a tradition that McHarg himself hails from.[33] In this respect, and sparing Dublin's blushes, Glasgow is the greatest Celtic city in the world.

It was to Glasgow that the Highland and Irish dispossessed arrived in numbers almost as great as to the New World. In turn they provided the muscle and canny intelligence to support the creation of an industrial behemoth that had had its beginnings in the visionary settlement of New Lanark in the upper reaches of the River Clyde. It became the "workshop of the world" and the "second city of empire"—shibboleths both and now reviled in Glasgow for many reasons, mainly to do with the exploitation of indigenous Scots and colonial peoples.[34]

The first industrial expansion of Glasgow was populated by these displaced Highland and Irish peoples, and their culture, values, and humor pervaded the burgeoning Glasgow working class. Gaelic was widely spoken, and even today Glasgow's links with the highlands and islands of Scotland and with Ireland north and south are pronounced.[35] Attitudes toward the land and the environment were embodied in this new urban culture; they are transcendental and remain evident today, and they are evident in McHarg's own recollections in *A Quest for Life*: "A beautiful and powerful landscape contrasted with a mean ugly city. . . . Nature was freedom. . . . I was born and bred on a fulcrum . . . [between] city and countryside."[36] After reading the literature and speaking with those who knew him, it is perhaps glib but nonetheless accurate to assert the old aphorism that "you can take the boy out of Glasgow, but you can't take Glasgow out of the boy."[37]

There is a cultural and intellectual link between this Celtic/Gaelic legacy (perhaps an attitude of mind) and bioregionalism in Scotland. The tradition of regional planning in the west of Scotland is strong and has been continual since the publication of the Clyde Valley Regional Plan in 1946 led by Sir Patrick Abercrombie (influenced by Geddes) and assisted by the young Robert Grieve, who went on to become Scotland's chief planner and professor of town and regional planning at the University of Glasgow (figure 8.2). Grieve was knighted as the founding chair of the Highlands and Islands Development Board.[38]

As a teenager, McHarg was returning to Glasgow after walking in the Scottish countryside when he met Grieve by chance at a bothy (mountain hut), where older men often met to socialize and tell stories.[39] Later, after graduating from Harvard, McHarg worked for Grieve in the government in Scotland and viewed him at a distance and with some considerable respect.[40] So McHarg knew the Clyde Valley Regional Plan, knew Grieve personally, and recognized the influence of Geddes's work as reflecting "the brilliant mind of . . . biologist-turned-planner . . . fascinating but difficult to read."[41] During his early years in Scotland, McHarg was asked to look at aspects of implementing the Clyde Valley Regional Plan, including the siting of Cumbernauld New Town.[42] McHarg's contribution inspired William Gillespie, who was the new town's chief landscape architect and went on to found Gillespies, subsequently one of the U.K.'s most prominent landscape practices.[43]

The Clyde Valley Regional Plan of 1946 was revisited in the West Central Scotland Plan of 1974 and became the talisman for the Strathclyde Structure Plan of 1976 (in several editions), and then the Glasgow and Clyde Valley Strategic Plan from 1996 until its most recent iteration in 2017 (figure 8.2). Along the way, informal strategies, including the Strathclyde River Valleys Strategy, Greening the Conurbation, and the Central Scotlands

Woodland Project were the antecedents of today's Central Scotland Green Network, one of fourteen national priority projects in Scotland's National Planning Framework.[44]

Clearly, the condition of his native city and its surrounding landscape spurred McHarg's thinking and ideas. He was not alone, and many with influence, such as Sir Robert Grieve and William Gillespie, shared his concern. Eventually they and their ilk gained an upper hand in the environmental, landscape, and heritage regeneration of Glasgow in successive waves in the 1970s, 1980s, and 1990s, inspired by Geddes and by McHarg, by *Design with Nature*, and by the techniques it espouses to help turn a city that McHarg had described as "one of the meanest of industrial cities" into one "nomi-

FIGURE 8.2 Clyde Valley Regional Plan, 1946, led by Patrick Abercrombie. *With permission, Clydeplan. Glasgow and the Clyde Valley Strategic Development Planning Authority.*

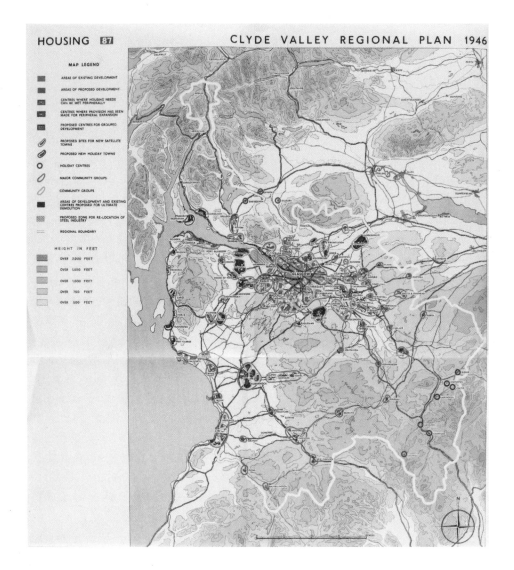

nated in 1992 [sic] as the European city of culture—quite a transformation from the days of my boyhood."[45]

The degraded landscape of central Scotland has seen remarkable remediation (of land and the cleansing of pollutants), renewal (of the land surface through landscape enhancement), regeneration (of the built heritage and fabric), and renaissance (of communities and their social fabric) through a series of initiatives originating with the land reclamation program of the Scottish Development Agency in the 1970s and 1980s.[46]

The Central Scotland Woodlands Project that began in 1975 became the Central Scotland Forest and finally, in 2011, the Central Scotland Green Network, a £2.5 billion project for greening the central valley of Scotland from Ayrshire to Fife and the Lothians (figure 8.3).[47] The first chair of this initiative was Robert (Bob) Steedman, one of McHarg's first alumni, who worked for Wallace-McHarg Associates in the early 1960s.[48]

Much of this work may not have been delivered as early as McHarg wished. He lamented the failure of the government's Department of Health to immediately take up his ideas (well before *Design with Nature*), but, in the fullness of time the Central Scotland Green Network has become one of the most strategic and consistent applications of the ideas of *Design with Nature* anywhere.[49]

Ian McHarg trained many of the U.K.'s finest landscape architects of the 20th century, and his legacy continues to inspire the next generation today.[50] Scotland was also a beneficiary of McHarg's pedagogic diaspora, some of whom made a significant contribution to establishing the ideas of *Design with Nature* in Scotland. McHarg makes several references to James Morris and Robert Steedman, two of his first students at the University of Pennsylvania, in *A Quest for Life*.[51] Penn has a list of this group of alumni, many of whom formed influential alliances and practices in the U.K. Like both Morris and Steedman, Wilson Mark Turnbull (graduated 1970) first studied and later worked with McHarg on assembling *Design with Nature*.[52]

There are numerous examples in this volume of the influence of McHarg's alumni globally. Steedman and Turnbull have had a profound and lasting impact on the theory and practice of landscape architecture, planning, and design in contemporary Scotland. Both Steedman and Turnbull were appointed to the Royal Fine Art Commission for Scotland (RFACS) and the Countryside Commission for Scotland (CCS), the only two architects/landscape architects to hold the distinction of being commissioners of both organizations.[53] As Fine Art and Countryside commissioners, Steedman and Turnbull exerted considerable sway on the built and natural environments of Scotland in the thirty years from the 1970s until the 1990s. They were both influential in the debate around some of the most pressing matters of the time, including the establishment of guidelines to incorporate industrial infrastructure into Scotland's landscape after the discovery of North Sea oil in the 1970s, the development of a park system for

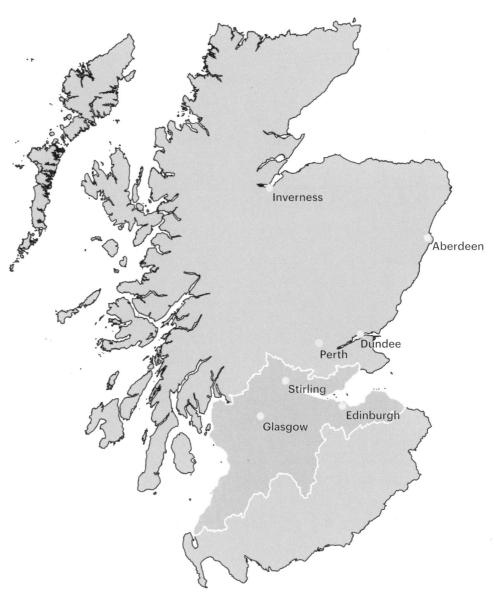

FIGURE 8.3 Central Scotland Green Network. The Central Scotland Green Network has an operational area that extends to some 10,000 square kilometers (3,861 square miles) across nineteen local authority areas with a population of 3.5 million. © *Central Scotland Green Network Trust. Crown Copyright and database rights 2019. All rights reserved. Ordnance Survey 100002151.*

Scotland (in the 1970s), and the intense debate leading to the establishment of Scotland's first national parks in 2002.[54]

Through my collaboration with Steedman, and later with Turnbull, I developed, with my practice (Gillespies), a theoretical and practical understanding of the techniques of *Design with Nature*. Later, when I was working in developing countries, this experience provided the basis for landscape planning using McHarg's method in new settlements employing ecological, landscape, and environmental principles of design, notably in Russia and China. The culmination of this effort came in 2012, when the Anglo-American team led by Urban Design Associates and Gillespies was joint winner of the international competition for the expansion of Moscow (figure 8.4), held by the federal government of Russia and the city's mayor. The international jury commended the team for their understanding of, and a designed response to, the environment, ecology, and landscape of the Moscow region as a key to the team's success.[55]

Did McHarg ever look at Scotland and think wistfully in Sir Walter Scott's words, "This is mine own, my native land." In his own words and in the view of those who knew him and worked with him, the answer is an emphatic yes.[56] *A Quest for Life* is riddled with proclamations to that effect. But, after his early years, McHarg never practiced again in Scotland and he saw himself as—and was—a Scots American.[57] The narrative in this essay gives rise to some immodest claims. But none seek to reclaim Ian McHarg for Scotland. Nonetheless, there is an argument presented here that Scottish (and in particular, Celtic/Gaelic) culture has given America and the world three hugely influential sons who have, together with their cultural antecedents, provided more impetus than many nations—large and small—to the emergence of green consciousness.

Ian McHarg is part of the pantheon of thinkers and practitioners who changed urban thought in the late 20th century. More than John Muir's, less perhaps than Patrick Geddes's, McHarg's awareness of the Scottish land and culture pervaded his thought, and together with Muir and Geddes represents a remarkable global contribution to environmental awareness and green consciousness born of traditions and culture founded in aboriginal, Celtic, Gaelic, and Scottish precepts concerning the land.

Scotland can be slow to recognize its children who make a contribution on the world stage. It came to appreciate Patrick Geddes and Charles Rennie Mackintosh only after they had received world acclaim. Thankfully, today we have the John Muir Trail, which leads from Muir's birthplace to Loch Lomond and the Trossachs, Scotland's first national park. It is hoped that in 2019 with the celebration of the 50th anniversary of *Design with Nature*, it will be possible to stimulate a similar public awareness of Ian Lennox McHarg to match his professional recognition and legacy.

McHarg emerged from a city, region, and nation that was in trauma from the Great Depression and World War II. His appreciation of the environment from the region to the

FIGURE 8.4 Landscape plan for the expansion of Moscow. In 2012, the Capital Cities Planning Group led by Urban Design Associates of Pittsburgh and Gillespies of Glasgow were joint winners of the international competition for the expansion of Moscow, capital city of the Russian Federation. The two diagrams on the left show an integrated landscape and ecological strategy for the existing city (top) and the expansion area (bottom). The plan in the center shows the integrated landscape and ecological strategy for the combined area. The plan on the right shows the final development plan for the existing and expanded areas of the city extending to 2,500 square kilometers (965 square miles) with an existing population of 11.5 million and a future anticipated population of 14 million. *With permission, The Capital Cities Planning Group: Urban Design Associates & Gillespies LLP with Beazley Associates, JTP Masterplanners LLP, Nelson/Nygaard Consulting Associates, Group Ark, Buro Happold LLP & Stuart Gulliver.*

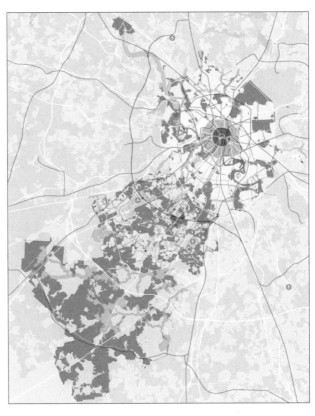

garden echoes Geddes and has in the past thirty years been paralleled at home, where his native Glasgow has been transformed from industrial to postindustrial city. It is now becoming a proto-knowledge city worthy of its Gaelic name, *Gleschu* (dear green place).

There is a multistranded helix of historical and contemporary experience in this narrative: the traditions of Scotland that influenced Muir, Geddes, and McHarg; the bio-regionalism of the west of Scotland; McHarg's influence on his native land through his Scottish alumni; the largest greening project in Europe; and, in the developing world, the transformation of Moscow.

McHarg's graduates have reinvigorated his beliefs and his work at home, and have inspired the next generation of individuals and projects. One such, the Central Scotland Green Network, is one of fourteen national priorities. Today, and at last, Scotland *is* designing with nature. Perhaps at some point in the future, McHarg's words, like those of Muir and Mackintosh, will be cut into the stones of Edinburgh. As President George H. W. Bush said in his tribute to McHarg, "Let us hope that in the next [21st] century the finest accomplishment of art will be the restoration of *the land*" [italics added].[58]

A Book of Days

Laurel McSherry

PRESENTED HERE ARE THREE EXAMPLES drawn from a larger body of work that I produced in the winter and spring of 2018 during a six-month Fulbright residency at The Glasgow School of Art. This occasion to experience the city and countryside vividly described by Ian McHarg stimulated my desire to see with equal purpose and intensity. Some days were fleeting. Others were slow. My challenge became twofold: to effect markings on paper, metal, film, and cloth; and in parallel, to make my abstract meditations legible, and perhaps even palpable, to others.

Glasgow Daylight Series Nos. 3 & 4 uses traditional intaglio and relief printing to record the length of daylight changes from January through June. In printmaking, intaglio refers to images produced from ink held in the indentations in a metal plate. These indentations are made either directly by cutting with a tool, or indirectly through the use of acid applied to the plate's exposed, unprotected surface. In this series, steel plates were engraved and immersed in six sequential acid baths of different duration, which incrementally represented the daylight gained per month in Scotland and cumulatively over the six months. Since each successive immersion sacrifices earlier markings, I pulled prints at each of the six stages to register the moments and record the changes.

Dual Transect is a contemporary adaptation of a time-honored descriptive and analytical tool. Derived from the collection and encoding of archival material and field photography, the drawing records the presence, absence, and disappearance of discrete landscape phenomena along the reach and fall of two rivers foundational to the work of McHarg: the Clyde (in Glasgow) and the Delaware (in Philadelphia). Fords, naturally occurring shallows used formerly as river crossings, which consequently vanished as a result of human activity, natural processes, or both, provided an entry point to the work. My subsequent marks registered artifacts and occurrences drawn from living memory and beyond. Overlaying them provides an immediate sense of the density of human and ecological associations bound up in these river landscapes. The result produces a distinct relationship between traditional cartography, digital technologies, and autographic processes.

 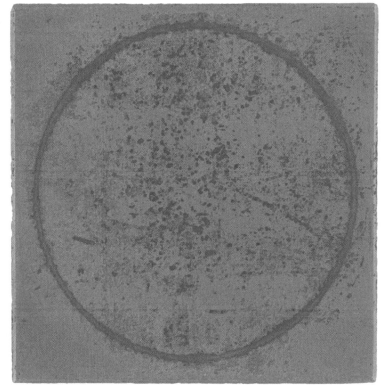

FIGURE 9.1 *Glasgow Daylight Series
Nos. 3 & 4.* Etched plates, steel, 4" × 4",
2018. © *Laurel McSherry.*

FIGURE 9.2 *Glasgow Daylight Series*
No. 3. Durational intaglio prints, stages
1, 3, and 6, ink, paper, 4″ × 4″, 2018.
© *Laurel McSherry.*

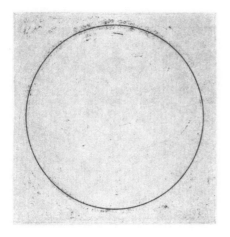 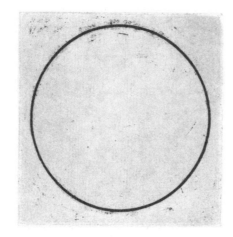 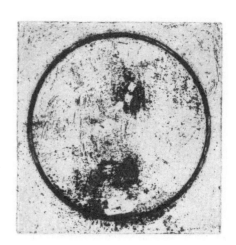

FIGURE 9.3 *Glasgow Daylight Series No. 4.* Durational relief prints, stages 1, 3 and 6, ink, paper, 4″ × 4″, 2018. © *Laurel McSherry.*

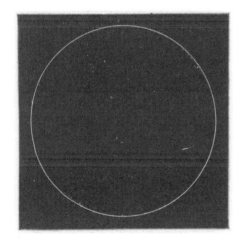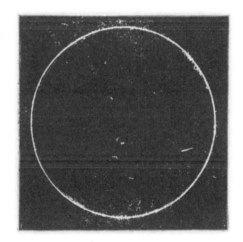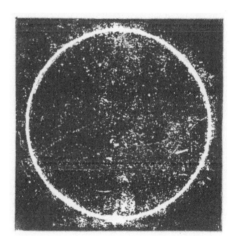

FIGURE 9.4 *Dual Transect*. Digital print, ink, cloth, 16″×220″, 2018. © *Laurel McSherry*. (This two-page spread and the following spread.)

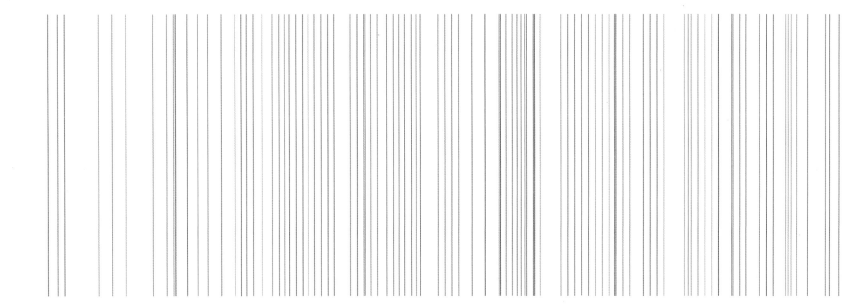

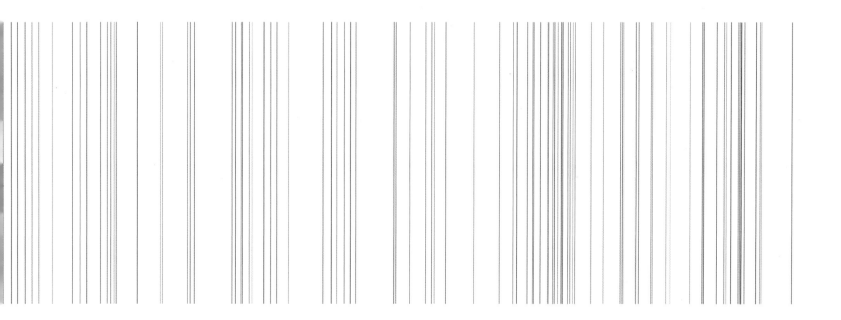

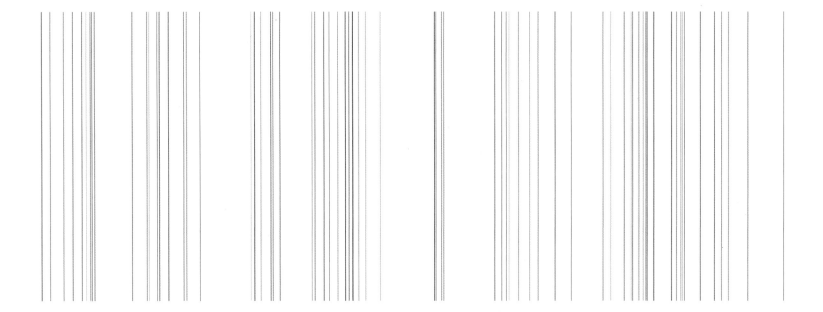

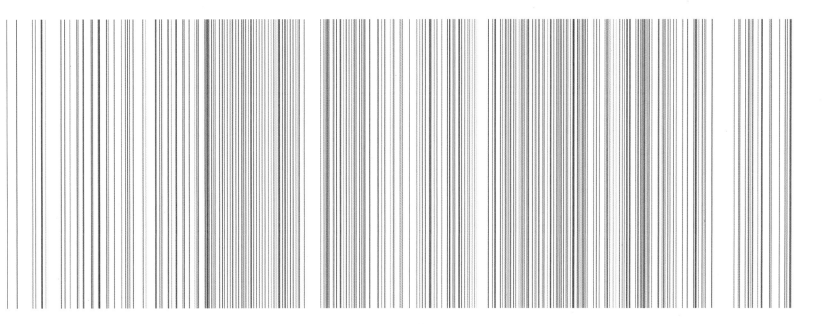

Human Ecology
and Design

Nature as Designer: Emancipating Nonhuman Ecologies in an Increasingly Human World

Erle C. Ellis

FOR MILLENNIA, WE HUMANS have had our designs on Earth. By reshaping this planet to sustain ourselves, we have left no more than a quarter of Earth's ice-free land beyond the direct influences of our settlements, agriculture, and other infrastructures.[1] Combined with rapid changes in climate and the species we are moving around the planet through trade and transport, the increasing reach of our globalizing societies is felt virtually everywhere.[2] Wild spaces beyond the intentions of human design still linger at the margins of our working landscapes, cityscapes, and seascapes, yet are nevertheless influenced by the unintended emanations of human societies.[3]

On this planet of nearly eight billion people, and billions more to come, humans already form a mass ten times greater than that of all of Earth's remaining wild mammals combined.[4] In this vast expansion of the human world, too many populations of wild creatures and wild ecologies of the prehuman past are shrinking toward extinction. Now, Earth's climates, soils, species, and ecosystems change with us, not without us. As Earth moves deeper and deeper into its human age, the Anthropocene, its landscapes have become anthroecological palimpsests, written and rewritten over and over by generation after generation of societies, locally, regionally, and globally.[5]

By constructing our niche across this planet, the sociocultural forces of our societies have become inextricably entangled with the workings of Earth's entire biosphere.[6] Even where wildlands still persist, from the forests of Amazonia and Białowieża to the Siberian Tundra, biological communities and ecological processes already bear our fingerprints.[7] Now, with contemporary societies increasingly cherishing and working to conserve what is left of the wild nonhuman world, our massive global influences continue to reshape Earth's form, functioning, autonomy, and wildness, even without intending to. Every day, there is less and less space to be nonhuman on this increasingly human planet.

Is there any hope of sustaining the evolutionary treasures of the prehuman world across the long arc of the Anthropocene? Can new forms of design break the Anthropocene narrative of an ever-expanding humanity presiding over an ever-declining nature? Can the human world be redesigned to regenerate, expand, and sustain wild places free of ongoing human influences, even while sustaining humanity at increasing scales?

Losing the Wild, Gaining the Anthropogenic

Remarkably, times have never been better for many creatures, especially those of our own design, our domesticates—from cattle to kittens—which together now far outnumber and outweigh us.[8] The same holds for those adapted to, commensal with, or parasitic on the human world. The anthropogenic biosphere is a world of opportunity for life adapted to the niches we have constructed—our crops, livestock, pets, ornamentals, weeds, pests, parasites, hitchhikers, and hangers-on. From the human microbiome to the indoor biome to the used and novel ecosystems embedded within the anthromes that cover more than three-quarters of Earth's land, the species we favor and that favor us are flourishing, evolving, and adapting to an ever more dynamic human world.[9]

Not so the rest. Wild species, especially wild animals, are being lost at alarming rates. The cause is mostly habitat conversion and loss, combined with unregulated hunting and resource use, pollution, competition with species transported and introduced by us from other parts of the world—both intentionally and unintentionally—and, increasingly, global changes in climate.[10] While hunter-gatherer societies of the late Pleistocene initiated this mass defaunation of the biosphere, contemporary extinction rates, especially on islands, raise serious concerns about the potential for a sixth mass extinction event in Earth history.[11] Although it is far too early to tell whether a mass extinction will come to pass, the consequences of Anthropocene defaunation include not only losses of Earth's evolutionary heritage but also the wholesale transformation of ecological form and function across the biosphere.[12] For example, Earth's temperate forests and grasslands have already been largely converted to croplands and rangelands, and an entire biome has been lost: the Mammoth Steppe.[13]

Yet even as wild species and wild spaces give way to novel anthropogenic ecologies, it is important to acknowledge that there is nothing unnatural about this or about them. The human world of a human epoch is producing novel ecologies and even new species.[14] They differ, often profoundly, from those that evolved before us. But Pleistocene ecologies differ greatly from those of the Pliocene that came before them, and the Miocene before that. Anthropocene ecologies are merely Earth's latest natures, with novel evolutionary pressures acting on the species of the past, leaving some as they are, bringing new ones into being, and mixing them together in the novel communities and ecosystems that will represent the Anthropocene's contribution to the geological epoch that comes next, perhaps as long as millions of years hence.

Natures Emerging

Measurements show that some of the densest urban settlements on Earth contain biological communities as species-rich as some of the most remote tropical rainforests, from zoos and arboretums to urban ornamental landscapes.[15] While these communities are usually rich in the same cosmopolitan species found around the world, large numbers of wild native species can also thrive, or at least survive, in urban settings.[16] Yet just to live within such novel anthropogenic ecologies is to be reshaped by them, as, for example, urban environments reshape the foraging habits and even the bodies of wild species dwelling within them, driving them toward nocturnal lifestyles (like *Homo sapiens*?) and boosting the size of moths, butterflies, and crickets, for example, while shrinking beetles and weevils.[17]

Evolution continues, and life will go on. The socially shaped ecologies and species of the Anthropocene are new and novel natures, but they are natures just the same. But the single most important fact about the emergence of these unprecedented new ecologies is that these in no way require that those of the past be lost. Most of the species that came before us, albeit with far too many notable exceptions, are still here with us. Even some species of very distant epochs, tens to hundreds of millions of years before today, from horseshoe crabs to crocodiles to *Ginkgo biloba*, have persisted across profound changes in Earth's functioning as a system to thrive into the present day. There is no ecological requirement that the anthropogenic ecologies and species of a human epoch must exclude those that came before.

For all their rich diversity, the novel biological communities, ecosystems, and environments of urban, agricultural, and other anthropogenic landscapes are no substitute for the wild nonhuman ecologies of the prehuman world. Just as "frozen zoos" (and arboretums) might guarantee species' survival into the future, no one would consider these an adequate substitute for lives lived in the wild. The ecologies of the human world are not enough. It is time to go beyond the sociocultural designs that are rapidly reshaping this planet, to embrace the designs of the nonhuman and prehuman world. To accomplish this, we must recognize that the greatest challenge of ecological design in the Anthropocene is not how to design with nature, or even how to design for nature. In this human epoch, the most challenging design of all is to empower nature as designer.

Design *with* Nature

McHarg's call to design with nature deserves to be celebrated as a profound theoretical, technical, and ethical advance over conventional designs disconnected from environmental realities.[18] By fitting designs to ecologies, McHarg's approach has produced both better outcomes and new norms of design practice, including preferences for native plantings and ecoregional planning. Building on this approach, nature-based solutions have many well-known advantages over conventional gray infrastructure designs, including greater resilience.[19] Green spaces have also been proven to enhance human well-being.[20] Design with nature is clearly good for us—and certainly better than designs without nature.

Yet McHarg's "ecological view" and its integration into design remains a product of the environmental thinking of its time, emerging in the wake of the publication of Paul R. Ehrlich's *Population Bomb* and right before Donella Meadows et al.'s *Limits to Growth*. In *Design with Nature,* McHarg calls "the quest for survival, success, and fulfillment" of humanity into doubt based on serious environmental concerns. While calling for a purge of "dominion and subjugation" as the model for "man's relation to nature," McHarg still echoes Stewart Brand's "We are as gods and might as well get good at it."[21] The faith is placed in "Man" as gardener of the planet. Good for people, perhaps, but good enough for the rest of nature?

For McHarg, "The farmer is the prototype," and the goal is twofold. First, to ensure that "his creations will be appropriate to the place," and second, to lead "the way for the man who would be the enzyme of the biosphere—its steward, enhancing the creative fit of man-environment, realizing man's design with nature."[22] No doubt McHarg's aim is also better outcomes beyond the human world. But the focus is firmly on setting the human world right with nature, not on making space for the rest of nature to thrive without us. The natural world is incorporated into design projects as functional and aesthetic elements, and designs are tuned into environmental constraints and opportunities. Human habitats are improved, while also creating and sustaining ecologies that benefit our nonhuman fellow travelers, including the broad host of species capable of utilizing hybrid human-natural habitats and living in varying states of cohabitation with the human enterprise.

For all these good intentions, though, even design with nature, let alone design without it, has often proceeded without adequate effort to preserve, sustain, and enrich nonhuman lives. As a result, these continue to become ever rarer and ever poorer.

Design *for* Nature

Long before design *with* nature, there were efforts to design *for* nature. Contemporary industrial societies are not the first to make space for wild lives. Polynesian tapu areas and species,[23] India's sacred groves,[24] and the royal hunting grounds of Europe and elsewhere[25] are but a few of the many traditional sociocultural designs that restrict or redirect human influences away from the nonhuman world. Contemporary conservation designs, including the designation and management of public lands for conservation, are both innovations and variations on the evolving cultural priorities of societies around the world that have helped to sustain biodiversity for generations in many regions.

New reserves, parks, wildlife habitats, and other spaces designed to sustain nonhuman species and wild ecologies continue to evolve and adapt to cultural trends within and among societies. In the emerging industrial world, design criteria for conserving wild places and wildlife have long been divided between a focus on "nature for nature's sake" and "nature in service of humanity," as epitomized by the century-old debate between the preservationism of John Muir and the conservationism of Gifford Pinchot.[26] Even Aldo Leopold's efforts to achieve "harmony between land and men" failed to settle these arguments.[27] Debate has most recently erupted over valuing ecosystems based on the services they provide to societies[28] rather than through a broader appeal to diverse cultural valuations through the framework of "nature's contributions to people" recently adopted by the Intergovernmental Science-Policy Platform on Biodiversity and Ecosystem Services (IPBES).[29] Further afield from mainstream conservation, but increasingly popular among environmentalists and scholars, are constructs of conservation for the sake of "biodiversity,"[30] and emerging posthumanist narratives that decenter the human from a position of control[31]—cultures of nature that seemingly circle back toward those of indigenous hunter-gatherer societies. Yet even the most ancient, traditional, and ecocentric nature valuations of human societies must be seen as evolving sociocultural constructs—cultures of nature that are just as subject to change as are human languages and material cultures.[32]

In this time when human transformation of the biosphere has never been greater, nature conservation has developed into a vast and expanding human enterprise already engaged in governing more than 15 percent of Earth's land.[33] Guided by evolving conceptions of "naturalness," conservation designs vary dramatically, shaped both by a wide diversity of cultures of nature and the social aims and effectiveness of the many different governance systems in operation,[34] from well-funded national park systems to public rangelands to traditionally managed indigenous lands[35] to "paper parks" offering little to no protection to the nonhuman world. Despite recent calls for designs for nature's governance to encompass more consistent and scientifically tractable principles, including "historical fidelity, autonomy of nature, ecological integrity, and resilience, as well as managing with humility,"[36] the evolving sociocultural processes that govern all human enterprises apply equally or perhaps even more to practices of nature conservation and restoration.

As societies develop and evolve, so do their conceptions and experiences of nature and naturalness, yielding shifting baselines for conservation design and management.[37] Moreover, efforts to maintain historical conditions and sustain dwindling populations of rare species often require increasingly intensive management interventions to counteract the effects of shrinking populations and gene pools, deforestation, agriculture, extractive industries, urbanization, species introductions, fire, pollution, and other human influences, not to mention long-term shifts in the ranges of species and habitats induced by climate change. The interventions needed to reverse these effects are themselves causing further alterations of ecological patterns and processes.[38]

Even when the goal is naturalness, a nature managed is inevitably a human nature. Even designs for nature evolve with the human social worlds that create and sustain them. Perhaps that is all that is possible in an increasingly human world. But let us consider the prospect of designs that empower nature as designer.

Nature Beyond Design

Is there any human being who truly wishes to live on a planet without spaces where wild creatures live free of human interference in habitats as wild as they are? While some might ignore or dismiss the possibility of such a world, I, like E. O. Wilson and many others, believe that the answer is no. We humans, as creatures of the biological world, are biophilic; all human beings love the wild world, albeit in their own individual, acculturated, and socialized ways.[39] For some, wild nature is best kept far away—better seen on TV. Others seek fulfillment from weeks alone in a remote protected wilderness. Still others find it in the ultimate hunting trip, a walk in the woods, the fringes of farmscapes, or the vacant lot next door.

No doubt there are as many ways to love nature as there are to be human. And, for almost every nature humans have desired, there has been, is, or will be a design. Indeed, societal capacities to design and engineer ecosystems have already reached levels capable of transforming the entire biosphere and the Earth system.[40] Designing the natures that sustain us, designing with nature, designing for nature, and even designing just for people: all are nature designs, and all are empowered by the global force that is human social change. In this time when humans have emerged as a force of nature, not to design at all is to reshape nature just as surely as any design does.[41] Indeed, such nondesigns, emerging through the unintended consequences of human actions in globalized societies, may now be the most potent global shapers of the natural world, far beyond the urban or agricultural landscapes designed specifically to sustain human societies. From global changes in climate to biotic homogenization, the global impacts of failing to design our interactions with the rest of nature—by polluting air, land, and sea; fragmenting habitats; transporting species; overharvesting; overfertilizing; draining, flooding, and channeling—likely exceed the total harm to the nonhuman world produced intentionally and directly by replacing natural habitats through the construction of agricultural, urban, and other human-sustaining landscapes.

In the wake of such widespread human transformations of this planet, both intended and unintended, novel anthropogenic ecologies now emerge rapidly wherever lands are left unmanaged, including even the remotest areas on Earth that have been set aside to conserve wild nature. As these transformative influences continue increasing in scale, extent, and intensity, human needs and desires are reshaping the biosphere, even where we do not intend them to.

Under such seemingly inescapable forces of anthropogenic transformation, is there any prospect for designing natures uninfluenced by the human world? Ironically, as human societal capacities for design and engineering continue to advance, the answer should be yes.

Yet the conception of a nature designed without a designer is clearly paradoxical. In designs of, with, and for nature, a human or humans, together with their social worlds, are always the designer, making the rules and enforcing them. In all such designs, even in conservation areas carefully managed to counter the influences of the human world, these influences nevertheless intrude, often overwhelmingly, as they do for the rest of life on Earth. Any design that would sustain wild spaces for wild species beyond the influences of the human world needs to be a design of unprecedented ambition capable of operating at the scales and intensities necessary to reverse, or at least hold back, Earth's newest force of nature. Although many possible such designs remain to be imagined, the following two have recently emerged and demand further thought and development.

Designs on the Biosphere

The Half-Earth Project, which aims to set aside half of Earth's surface as an interconnected conservation reserve, is likely the most radically ambitious aspirational vision of conservation ever.[42] Best known through E. O. Wilson's book of that name,[43] though originally proposed by Harvey Locke, as *Nature Needs Half* in 2013, the goal is to produce enough space to conserve more than 85 percent of Earth's species into the deep future. The precise way forward is not made clear in the book, or even in subsequent studies,[44] but the design vision is radically simple, crisp, and clear: sharing Earth half-and-half sure seems like a fair shake, and a better Earth for the rest of nature will also be a better Earth for us. Most important, even though the political, economic, and other social implications of such a project are staggering and potentially unattainable,[45] the Half-Earth vision is positive and easy to embrace—miles ahead of the typical doom-and-gloom environmental messaging that has discouraged so many.[46] And done right, such a plan has an unprecedented capacity to facilitate the conservation of Earth's ecological heritage into the future.[47] Half-Earth, or a related design of similar scale, may be the only design capable of ensuring the continuation of the species and ecologies that came before us.

Reshaping half of Earth's land into a global conservation reserve would undoubtedly be the most challenging landscape design and planning process in history. Sharing the planet unequally with one another is hard enough. Sharing land equitably across ecoregions—including Earth's most productive and densely populated regions—would demand global trade-offs in land use that are hard even to imagine, though computations of its potential impacts on agriculture demonstrate it would almost inevitably affect food systems at some level.[48] Whose half will be conserved or restored? Where will lost agricultural production be made up? Who wins and who loses in the great global land trade-off? Who would compensate whom?

Design of a truly equitable, effective, and sustainable global conservation system would need to be more than a global property portfolio in the hands of a few powerful institutions. Multilevel, not top-down, modes of governance, defined by strong local and regional institutions, as well as novel forms of social collaboration among private and public stakeholders, would be required at all levels. Elinor Ostrom's visions on the governance of common-pool resources offer insights into the institutional practices that might facilitate such collective management of a shared reserve covering half the Earth.[49] The dichotomy between used lands and protected areas would also need to transition into a continuum of strategies for integration, from interconnected regional national parks and indigenous reserves to urban green spaces, prairie strips, hedgerows, wildlife bridges, dam removal projects, and experiments with conservation management. Diverse emergent codesigns will be essential to navigating the compromises that will make a shared planet valuable to people and viable for wildlife.

What would a globally interconnected reserve covering half of Earth's land look like? A global patchwork of organic farms, green cities, rural villages, and indigenous reserves interspersed and interconnected with less disturbed habitats? Separate seas of dense cities and intensive farms, with protected wilderness areas in between? Would shared spaces, where people and wildlife coexist, increase? Or would they disappear? Would nature feel closer or farther away? These are just some of the hard questions. Even more important, will it ever even be possible to conserve or restore habitats extensive enough, and interconnected enough, to enable life on Earth to roam across the continents and evolve its own solutions to the changing climates and environments of the Anthropocene?

With 15 percent of Earth's land already protected and another 2 percent on the way, interconnecting 50 percent of Earth's land to create a global conservation reserve is at least in the realm of possibility. And one thing is sure. Though the challenges are as extraordinary as the opportunities, in these times of unprecedented global connectivity and interdependence among human societies, the time has never been riper for a global social enterprise to open up the vast spaces needed for wild species to evolve beyond the confines of the human world.

Nature as Designer

Redesigning human use of the biosphere through design for nature is necessary to sustain the biodiversity and wild spaces we treasure. Even the most old-school nature conservation strategies, including traditional hunter-gatherer management regimes, must play a fundamental role in conserving Earth's remaining biodiversity. Together with the development and evolution of more and more effective conservation designs and practices, these classic strategies will continue to be critical for sustaining nonhuman natures in the face of human pressures. Indeed, the radical expansion of these approaches is essential to ensure the future of the nonhuman world across the age of humans. But making space for nature, and even designing for nature, are just first steps on the road toward emancipating the ecologies of the nonhuman world from their transformative entanglement with the human world.

With or without people, nature will always change. There has never been a balance of nature, only flux.[50] Conservation in even the most remote wilderness areas struggles with the need to manage a state of constant change driven by a combination of natural and anthropogenic causes, from human hunting to climate change and species invasions. But in the most undisturbed areas, at least, long periods without anthropogenic change offer historical precedents to help guide management and design for nature.

In the novel hybrid communities and ecosystems emerging across the remnant and recovering habitats embedded within the human world, there are no clear precedents to guide conservation. Across more than 35 percent of Earth's ice-free land, where landscapes remain unused or unmanaged, dynamic mixtures prevail, in which species that came before intermingle inextricably with species newly arrived on human coat-tails. These hybrid communities and ecosystems are without precedent or any realistic hope of returning to some known or even imagined prehuman historical condition.[51]

Yet leaving nature alone is not an option in the Anthropocene.[52] In the face of Earth's newest force of nature, not managing transforms ecology just as surely as managing does. Even in some of Earth's best protected wilderness areas, ever more frequent and intensive management interventions, from herbicides to systematic weeding and culling, have become standard practice to keep invading species and other pressures of the human world at bay. One may argue for or against any of these specific measures, as human pressures mount, but the practice of conserving nature is edging ever closer to gardening and zookeeping. As a result, conservation values and the nature design and management practices they inspire now shape wild populations and ecosystems just as surely as agricultural values and practices can reshape a wild forest into a farm. Calls for rewilding, Pleistocene or otherwise, are just new and different nature values and practices. Ultimately, Pleistocene park is no different from Central Park.

With all of nature now entangled with the transformative forces of globalized human societies, is it still possible to sustain the wild fluxes of nature in forms uninfluenced by the evolving cultures of the human world? Or must wildness only diminish over time?

Listening to the Animals, and Plants, and . . .

What are the prospects for painting the human world out of the picture? Can nature be empowered as the designer and manager of spaces within the human world into which no human influence can intrude? Clearly, the challenge to design such wild spaces is like no other. But it is a challenge worth taking up.

Conceptual approaches to such designs are already being investigated, under the rubric of "Designing Autonomy."[53] Central to this rubric is the creation of a "distanced authorship" through the empowerment of a designer with capacities distinct from and beyond those of any human—an artificial intelligence equipped with tools for sensing and interacting with organisms and environments to enact values and practices learned directly from the nonhuman world.[54] Such designs will likely remain preliminary and speculative in the near future. Yet they are no mere fantasy. Rather, they are within the realm of technologies under development, including capacities for deep learning and interactive management uninformed by human culture and equipped with skills beyond those of any human being.[55] They include the ability to listen to and sense the activities of animals, plants, and entire biological communities and ecosystems,[56] to interact helpfully with organisms and environments—facilitating movements, reproduction, and basic needs—and to interfere with, reduce, and eliminate the intrusions of the human world, from noise cancellation to trash removal.[57]

Although technological approaches to empowering nature as designer may raise more problems than solutions, it is ever harder to imagine ways to decouple the human and nonhuman worlds without the intervention of a third party with capacities beyond those of either. At the very least, the philosophical and ethical implications of creating autonomous wild spaces demand consideration in a time when autonomy from the human world is increasingly challenging to enact or even to envision.

Ensuring that nonhuman natures can continue to evolve independently of the human world feels like the right thing to do. The very idea connects with the deepest and broadest human love of nature. In emancipating the nonhuman world from human transformation—by creating wildness—we may find even more than preservation of the world.

CHAPTER 11

Mapping Urban Nature and Multispecies Storyworlds

Ursula K. Heise

A LOT HAS CHANGED in the fifty years since the publication of Ian McHarg's seminal *Design with Nature*. New theories and new storyworlds have radically shifted how we map, narrate, and understand changing urban natures.

Mapping Urban Nature

"There are maps and there are maps and there are maps," one of the main characters in Karen Tei Yamashita's novel *Tropic of Orange* thinks as he surveys the city of Los Angeles.[1] An elderly Japanese American man who was formerly a surgeon but is now homeless, Manzanar Murakami often looks at the city from freeway overpasses, perceiving layers of its nature, history, and infrastructure that would not normally be visible to the naked eye. The "mapping layers" he detects reach from artesian rivers and earthquake faults to utility lines, sewage tunnels, streams of toxic runoff, electric lines, and computer networks:

> On the surface, the complexity of layers should drown an ordinary person, but ordinary persons never bother to notice [. . .] the prehistoric grid of plant and fauna and human behavior, nor the historic grid of land usage and property, the great overlays of transport—sidewalks, bicycle paths, roads, freeways, systems of transit both ground and air, a thousand natural and man-made divisions, variations both dynamic and stagnant, patterns and connections by every conceivable definition from

the distribution of wealth to race, from patterns of climate to the curious blueprint of the skies.[2]

Murakami's cognitive mapping of Los Angeles is the most comprehensive in the novel because he moves seamlessly from maps of natural elements to maps of the built environment and back, but he is by no means the only character who is fascinated with urban cartography. Buzzworm, an African American neighborhood advisor, timekeeper, and self-designated "angel of mercy," looks at a map of 1970s gang territories in Los Angeles that an acquaintance of his has torn out of a book, "*Quartz City* or some such title," an obvious allusion to Mike Davis's classic *City of Quartz*.[3] The question of what territory belongs to whom, and on what authority, makes him think of his conversations about real estate

> with people saying they used to live here or there. Now here or there is a shopping mall, locate the old house somewhere between Mrs. Field's and the Footlocker. Or here or there is now the Dorothy Chandler Pavilion, or Union Station, or the Bank of America, Arco Towers, New Otani, or the freeway. People saying if they coulda owned the property, if the property had been worth anything at the time, if they'd a known then every square foot of that land was worth millions. If they'd a known the view'd be so expensive. If they'd a known. And then Buzzworm thinking about before that. About the Mexican rancheros and before that, about the Chumash and the Yangua. If they'd a known.
>
> Somebody else must have the big map. Or maybe just the next map.[4]

If maps open up urban geology and infrastructure for Murakami, they provide an entryway into history for Buzzworm.

At the same time, Buzzworm is deeply invested in the numerous palm trees of Los Angeles, which he perceives as historical timekeepers, neighborhood guardians, and also as signals of neighborhood boundaries. As he walks from Los Angeles's Koreatown to African American and Latino neighborhoods, he notices palm trees in various states of neglect and instructs residents on how to take care of the different species. He also sees them as guideposts that provide a botanical map of urban life.

> One day, Buzzworm got [. . .] to pass over the Harbor Freeway, speed over the hood like the freeway was a giant bridge. He realized you could just skip out over his house, his streets, his part of town. You never had to see it ever. Only thing you could see that anybody might take notice of were the palm trees. That was what the palm trees were for. To make out the place where he lived. To make sure that people noticed. And

the palm trees were like the eyes of his neighborhood, watching the rest of the city, watching it sleep and eat and play and die. [. . .] Everything going on down under those palm trees might be poor and crazy, ugly or beautiful, honest or shameful—all sorts of life that could only be imagined from far away.[5]

The attempt of different characters to understand urban maps and the realities they model is not just a minor motif in Yamashita's novel. In typically modernist fashion, her portrait of Los Angeles is presented from the split perspectives of seven major characters—Mexican, Chicano, Asian American, and African American, of different genders and generations. As the novel follows their activities over the course of seven days, each day is broken down into seven chapters, one devoted to each character. These chapters are listed at the beginning of the novel sequentially in a normal table of contents, but the list is followed by a page titled "HyperContexts" that presents the days, characters, and ways in which they break down urban space and time in the form of a spreadsheet.[6] Even before the novel proper starts, then, readers are invited to reflect on different ways of mapping the spatial and temporal structure of both text and city.[7]

The plot itself is in a sense a reflection on the remapping of urban space through migration. It starts in Mazatlán, Mexico, where one of the Chicano characters, Gabriel Balboa, has built a house that he hopes will put him back in touch with the place his ancestors came from. As the novel opens, his housekeeper, Rafaela, is looking after the house, into which an odd assortment of dead and live animals enters every night, no matter how well she shuts windows and doors: "moths and spiders, lizards and beetles. [. . .] An iguana, a crab, and a mouse. And there was the scorpion, always dead [. . .] And the snake that slithered away at the urging of her broom."[8] This scene sets the tone for a storyworld in which nature and the built environment bleed into each other and keep entering into new fusions, no matter how hard the human characters seek to set up barriers between them.

On Balboa's Mazatlán property, situated right on the Tropic of Cancer, an orange tree grows; Rafaela's son, Sol, picks its single ripe orange and carries it with him as he and his mother travel back to Los Angeles. They are joined on their northward journey by an old man who seems to possess supernatural strength, and who remembers and recounts the history of Mexico, and indeed the entire Latin American continent, to his fellow travelers. As the orange moves farther and farther northward, it becomes clear that it is physically attached to the Tropic of Cancer and starts to pull the degree of latitude northward as the travelers approach Los Angeles, producing strange distortions of time and space. Buzzworm notices the shifts as he tries to locate "a constellation of palm trees in the distance. Used to be he could fix his sights by those palms, but weren't the same no more."[9] Trees, in Yamashita's storyworld, function as spatial markers but also indicate the distortion of topographies and maps.

Obviously, Sol's orange is meant to allegorize the sociocultural changes that Latin American migration brings to the urban space of Los Angeles, which Yamashita narrates as partly funny and partly tragic. The distortions of urban time and space lead to accidents and upsets, including an epic traffic jam on a freeway that causes drivers to abandon their cars and homeless people to set up a temporary encampment among the abandoned vehicles, only to be brutally dispersed by police after a few days. The plot culminates in a wrestling match between two characters named SUPERNAFTA and El Gran Mojado (The Great Wetback, who is in fact none other than the old man with supernatural strength) and in Rafaela's reunion with her Chinese-American husband, Bobby: complementary endings that signal conflict and reconciliation occurring simultaneously.[10] *Tropic of Orange* hybridizes North American and Latin American cultures not only through its plot but also in its narrative form: the old man is directly borrowed from a short story by the Colombian writer Gabriel García Márquez called "Un hombre muy viejo con unas alas enormes" ("A Very Old Man with Enormous Wings"), and the plot takes up elements of magical realism, which Yamashita came to be familiar with during a ten-year stay in Brazil from the mid-1970s to the mid-1980s. Combining elements of Latin American magical realism, North American ethnic fiction, and Japanese techno-postmodernism, *Tropic of Orange* presents the contemporary city as a hybrid of cultures as well as different kinds of nature.

What might "design with nature," as Ian McHarg conceived of it in the late 1960s, mean for such a perspective on the contemporary urban landscape that refuses clear distinctions between natural and sociocultural ecologies? McHarg belonged to a group of pioneering thinkers at the moment the modern environmental movement emerged in the United States, and was one of the first to link ecological analysis with urban and regional planning. His seminal book sought to map the topological and hydrological profiles of particular urban and peri-urban areas, as well as their sociocultural profiles, in terms of such variables as "land values," "historic values," "scenic values," "recreation values," and "residential values," among others.[11] Superimposing the individual, meticulously detailed maps, McHarg argued, would allow planners to determine the most naturally suited areas for particular uses, yielding a "gross hierarchy of urban suitability"[12]—where best to place transit routes and green recreation areas, for example. "Growth," he complained, "is totally unresponsive to natural processes and their values."

Optimally, one would wish for two systems with the metropolitan region—one the pattern of natural processes preserved in open space, the other the pattern of urban development. If these were interfused, one could satisfy the provision of open space for the population [. . .] [R]ather than propose a blanket standard of open space, we wish to find discrete aspects of natural processes that carry their own values and prohibitions: it is from these that open space should be selected, it is these that should provide the pattern, not only of metropolitan open space, but also the positive pattern of development.[13]

Planning and building in this way, McHarg argued, would allow the "genius of the site as composed of discrete elements, some derived from the natural identity, others from artifacts" to be discerned and preserved, and lend a unique identity to each city.

[P]rinciples should be constructed into policies that will ensure that the resources of the city, site and artifacts, are recognized as values and determinants of form, both in planning and the execution of works. Rio differs from Kansas City, New York from Amsterdam, and Washington from all of them, for good and sufficient reasons. They lie, at base, in the geological history, climate, physiography, soils, plants and animals that constitute the history of the place and the basis of its intrinsic identity.[14]

This kind of design, McHarg believed, would allow urban development to move beyond the "countless city slums and scabrous towns, pathetic subdivisions, derelict industries, raped land, befouled rivers and filthy air."[15]

This approach has undoubtedly proven useful for environmentally oriented planning over the past few decades. But "the map is not the territory. It may not even represent the territory that well. But what it invariably does quite well is represent ideas about the territory," as the environmental historian Jon Christensen highlights.[16] Yamashita seeks to capture such shifting ideas and changing urban maps in her narrative by pulling the Tropic of Cancer northward with Mexican migrants who carry an orange, itself an example of a nonnative fruit that became as iconic of the city of Los Angeles in the early 20th century as its palm trees did later.[17] Depending on which of her characters looks at and cognitively maps the city, different kinds of nature move into the foreground. In Yamashita's approach, Los Angeles *is* designed with nature— but what that nature is varies from observer to observer, and what the observers see in turn shapes and reshapes urban space, from its freeways to its trees. And sometimes urban nature itself speaks back to humans: "Palm trees looked like they were all bending, all stretching their necks in the same direction. Pointing. Trying to say something," Buzzworm thinks at one point.[18] In Yamashita's narrative, written almost three decades after McHarg's seminal book, nature is not something that humans can unequivocally map and use to model cities, but a socioecological construct, some of whose features change with changes in observers and in culture, and which might at times even have an agency of its own.

Multispecies Cities

Tropic of Orange was written at a moment when ideas about the relationship between nature and cities were undergoing fundamental transformation in ecology, geography, urban planning, design, architecture, and landscape architecture. Whereas McHarg was mostly on his own in seeking out connections between ecology and the city, interest in urban ecology has grown exponentially since the 1990s, and new paradigms have arisen in planning, architecture, and environmental activism: actor-network-theory, ecological urbanism, landscape urbanism, urban political ecology, urban environmental justice, urban metabolism, biophilic design, and climate urbanism have all transformed theory and, at least to some extent, practice in these fields. From nature in and around the city of the kind McHarg focused on, interest has shifted to the study of nature for the city—the deliberate creation or restoration of green and blue spaces and their benefits for humans as well as for ecosystems—and of the city as nature, a novel type of ecosystem with its own distinctive properties.[19]

Many of these paradigms have remained anthropocentric in their focus, envisioning cities as spaces created by humans and for humans, and analyzing their natural dimensions mostly as a function of human uses, benefits, and harms, or of changing human perceptions of nature. But since the mid-1990s, some scholars and activists have also called for a reconsideration of cities as habitat for nonhuman species whose agency, exposure to human impacts, and claims on humans' ethical and legal consideration need to form part of urban theory. In this vein, environmental historians have traced the rise of the "sanitary city" in 19th- and early-20th-century Europe and North America that led to the gradual displacement of livestock as well as other types of animals from cities, even as the presence of farm animals continues to shape urban spaces in the developing world.[20] Anthropologists, historians, and sociologists have explored the way in which particular animals and plants give both economic and cultural shape to cities, as do practices of gardening and pet-keeping and their impacts on urban ecologies.[21] Urban parks and their different uses have generated studies that reach from Jane Jacobs's classic *Death and Life of Great American Cities* to recent attempts to make green spaces hospitable to the increasingly diverse urban communities that surround them.[22] More generally, works grounded in feminism, critical race theory, and postcolonial theory have highlighted the ways in which urban nature is perceived, experienced, and used differently by different sociocultural groups both within particular cities and across the globe.[23] Although these explorations of urban nature have ranged widely over the past three decades, they have remained largely anthropocentric, focused on the human inhabitants of cities and on urban space as human habitat.

This fundamental anthropocentism has not remained unquestioned, however. The geographer Jennifer Wolch has most forcefully argued that contemporary urban theory and the planning practices it informs should integrate the impacts of urban growth on nonurban wildlife, and on the ecologies of animal life in the city itself. Beyond concrete issues such as the creation of wildlife corridors to connect fragmented habitat, she argues, transspecies urban theory or "zoöpolis," as she calls it, also offers the possibility of new alliances between different branches of environmental activism: "Zoöpolis invites a critique of contemporary urbanization from the standpoint of animals but also from the perspective of people, who together with animals suffer from urban pollution and habitat degradation and who are denied the experience of animal kinship and otherness so vital to their well-being."[24] Reconsidering cities as inhabited by more than just one species ultimately leads to questions of ethics and justice in this perspective, which is inflected by actor-network-theory as well as theories of animal rights and human-animal relations.

We have just begun to think about the moral choices we make in building and living in cities, and what they mean for animals. [. . .] If animals are granted subjectivity, agency, and even maybe even culture, how do we determine their survival in the city? [. . .] If urban and environmental justice is eventually broadened to include animal justice as well, questions also arise about how radical an urban democracy we can visualize, or handle in practice.[25]

More recently, these questions have also been taken up by multispecies ethnographers, anthropologists who approach what we usually conceive of as human societies and cultures as in reality multispecies assemblages that involve humans along with the fauna and flora that keep them alive, the animals and plants that form part of culture and religion, and the bacteria and viruses that variously ensure or harm humans' organic functions. "Human nature is a multispecies relationship," Anna Tsing has argued.[26] Some of the research in this line has focused on urban animals, such as Deborah Bird Rose and Thom van Dooren's study of penguins and flying foxes in Sydney.[27] Animals have been at the center of Wolch's as well as the multispecies ethnographers' work, but given the recent interest in critical plant studies, it is likely that plants, too, will come to form part of this theoretical reimagination of urban nature.

Based on Wolch's concept of transspecies urban theory and the work of multi-species ethnographers, I have proposed the idea of multispecies justice as a way of thinking about concerns of environmental justice, such as unequal exposure to environmental risks and unequal environmental benefits, together with concern for nonhumans' claims on our moral consideration.[28] Many conservation debates and decisions in urban and regional planning involve fundamental questions about what it means to do right by other people and other species, and what groups or institutions should resolve such questions. Debates over whether to allocate urban space to parks or housing, how to distribute water so as to ensure supplies for urban communities as well as vegetation, how to adjudicate between human cultural preferences for certain kinds of garden-scapes and nonhumans' needs for plant habitat, when and how to use pesticides, and how to weigh the rights of cats against those of songbirds, to name just a few examples, are not just pragmatic questions but also involve underlying issues of justice. Thinking of them in terms of multispecies justice is not meant to deliver readymade solutions to these problems, but rather to encourage consultation and debate that involves both human and nonhuman stakeholders. Given that definitions and foundations of thinking about justice themselves differ between communities, which communities are represented, how, and by whom become important issues in this context.

Multispecies Futures and Urban Storytelling

Multispecies justice demands thinking in legal and political frameworks, but also in cultural ones, and especially in terms of narrative. What stories particular communities tell about their own origins and futures, and about their relationship to other communities and species, is often a crucial means of establishing and perpetuating scenarios of justice and injustice. Fictional storyworlds, in addition, offer the possibility of playing out the implications of different kinds of design and planning in the context of a polyphony of voices and divergent plot lines. This has, of course, always been one of the functions of the novel, and especially of novels in the genre of science (or speculative) fiction, which uses the device of futuristic or alternative worlds to explore the consequences of individual and collective decision making. These storyworlds offer another window into how our thinking about "design with nature" has changed since McHarg first published his book. Two relatively recent speculative novels have addressed questions of the city and nature, Kim Stanley Robinson's *New York 2140* (2017) and China Miévielle's *Perdido Street Station* (2000). Though both books belong to the broad genre of speculative fiction and were written by novelists with a deep affinity for leftist and specifically Marxist politics, they present radically different urban scenarios. Robinson sets his plot in Manhattan toward the middle of the 22nd century, when climate change and two pulses of massive sea-level rise have put entire neighborhoods of the city under water —an extreme but not impossible scenario according to current climate science, and one that allows him to trace the development of urban capitalism in a broadly realist idiom. Miévielle's *Perdido Street Station* is set in the fictional city of New Crobuzon, which is part Dickensian London with a dash of steampunk and part alien planet with a profusion of intelligent species. Varied human and nonhuman perspectives and projects clash and converge in the struggle for survival against a deadly invasive species—itself no doubt Miévielle's allegory of capitalism—in a bleakly dystopian and yet exuberantly vital metropolis. By turns fantastic, horrific, and baroque, Miéville's urban portrait could not be more distant from Robinson's realist, scientifically informed, and often humorous prose; and yet both texts engage at a deeper level with similar problems of multispecies justice in a capitalist metropolis.

Two pulses and fifty feet of sea-level rise in the late 21st century, due to warming temperatures and melting polar ice, have transformed Manhattan, as Robinson portrays it, in *New York 2140*. The northern tip of the island, which lies 150 feet above sea level, is not directly affected, but lower Manhattan is under water, and midtown has turned into an "intertidal" zone where water comes and goes, and where some buildings remain standing and others collapse. But even though one of the characters does refer to this change as "apocalyptic, Armageddonesque," the narrative does not take the form of a familiar disaster plot. New York, in fact, has in some sense benefited from the flooding, becoming an "aquatropolis," a "SuperVenice, fashionably hip, artistic, sexy, a new urban legend. Some people were happy to live on the water if it was conceptualized as Venetian, enduring the mold and hassle to live in a work of art."[29] The drowning of major cities around the globe, for which New York serves as one paradigmatic example, has also given rise to new forms of collaborative economy and culture:

> Hegemony had drowned, so in the years after the flooding there was a proliferation of cooperatives, neighborhood associations, communes, squats, barter, alternative currencies, gift economies, solar usufruct, fishing village cultures, mondragons, unions, Davy's locker freemasonries, anarchist blather, and submarine technoculture, including aeration and aquafarming. Also sky living in skyvillages that used the drowned cities as mooring towers and festival exchange points; container-clippers and townships as floating islands; art-not-work, the city regarded as a giant collaborative artwork; blue greens, amphibiguity, heterogeneticity, horizontalization, deoligarchification; also free open universities, free trade schools, and free art schools.[30]

These communitarian and socialist initiatives exist side by side with continued real estate speculation and a stock market that has adapted to turn a profit from the uncertainties of the intertidal zone, Robinson's major spatial metaphor for the world and the city under conditions of global warming. One of the novel's protagonists, Franklin Garr, is a stockbroker who has devised a new index, the IPPI or Intertidal Property Pricing Index, "because if the intertidal has any value at all, even if it's only a million or two, then someone wants to own that. And other people want to leverage that value right out to the usual fifty times whatever it might be."[31] So capitalist speculation on property values, and more generally the global capitalist market, has adapted to climate change. But the novel is bookended by two attempts to subvert the capitalist order. The first one, a digital revision of the global banking code carried out by two computer hackers, fails; the second one succeeds, a market crash precipitated by common people's refusal to pay their loans and mortgages, and a government bailout of the affected banks and companies that is contingent upon their effective nationalization.

Robinson's final utopia—or "optopia," as he prefers to call it, not an ideal society but the best possible given the circumstances—therefore emerges from the engagement with urban space, its zones, its property values, and their transformation through ecological risk. Modeling the structure of his novel on the one developed by John Dos Passos in *Manhattan Transfer* (1925) and his *USA* trilogy (1930s), Robinson tells the story of future Manhattan through the viewpoints of multiple characters: a historian, stockbrokers, computer programmers, a community organizer, an African American cop, a pair of teenage boys hunting for underwater treasure, an East European building superintendent. Like Yamashita, he makes the architecture of his novel all by itself tell a story of multiple viewpoints and divergent interests, but he focuses far more on the urban inequality caused by class differences than on those of nationality, race, and ethnicity that Yamashita foregrounds. This emphasis is also obvious in segments of historical documentation and running political commentary by a voice only named "the citizen." The city, its neighborhoods, its buildings, and its nature mean very different things to these varied characters, and parts of the city that have lost old structures, buildings, uses, and meanings take on new ones constantly over time.

New York City's urban history has not overwritten its ecological foundations, however, and as it turns out, climate change, along with destruction, has helped new ecological dimensions emerge. "Forest? Okay, now it's a forest of skyscrapers. A city, and such a city that it used to take some looking to see it as an estuary. Since the floods that's become easier, because although it was a drowned coastline before, it is now more drowneder than ever," the citizen wryly comments.[32] Amelia, an activist and Internet celebrity who travels around the globe in an airship for an online broadcast about biodiversity conservation, especially the assisted migration of endangered species to new habitats, describes her arrival above New York in her signature colloquial idiom:

See how Hoboken's been built up? That's quite a wall of superscrapers! They look like a spur of the Palisades that never got ground down in the Ice Age. Too bad about the Meadowlands, it was a great salt marsh, although now it makes a nice extension of the bay, doesn't it? The Hudson is really a glacial trench filled with seawater. It's not just an ordinary riverbed. The mighty Hudson, yikes! This is one of the greatest wild-life sanctuaries on Earth, people. It's another case of overlapping communities [. . .] Brooklyn and Queens make a very strange-looking bay. To me it looks like some kind of rectangular coral reef exposed at low tide.[33]

Even as literal and metaphorical uses of ecological terminology get hopelessly confused in the "airhead" language Amelia cultivates, this confusion has a purpose on Robinson's part, if not Amelia's. Her ecological travel journals persistently highlight the hybridization of human and nonhuman systems, the extinction of species and ecosystems, and the emergence of new habitats that are often shared by humans and nonhumans.

That the passages dedicated to Amelia in *New York 2140* are among the most humorous in the book indicates that Robinson's vision of urban and ecological futures is not one of unmitigated disaster, but a mixture of tragedy and comedy. In one of her most daring ventures, Amelia transports half a dozen polar bears from the Arctic to the Antarctic in a last-ditch effort to help the species survive. After comical mishaps in transit—the bears break out of their cages and corner Amelia on her airship—she delivers them successfully to their new habitat, only to see them killed shortly afterward by the human inhabitants of Antarctica, who see the new arrivals as an invasive nonnative species with no history or place in their region, one that will disturb "the last wilderness. . . . [t]he last pure place."[34] A new environmental vision of multispecies communities collides in this tragicomic plot line with an older vision that militantly defends local places and local species, even and especially when faced with global ecological change. The carefully planned strategy to redesign species habitats globally through assisted migration fails, at least in this instance.

But in New York City, reshaped by sea level rise, ecology redesigns itself.

Life is more than algorithmic, it's a snarl of green fuses, an efflorescence of vitalisms. Nothing we devise is anything like as complex as the [New York] bay's ecosystem. On the floors of the canals, the old sewer holes spew life from below. Up and down life floats, in and out with the tides. Salamanders and frogs and turtles proliferate among the fishes and eels, burrow in the mulm. Above them birds flock and nest in the concrete cliffs of the city. [. . .] Right whales swim into the upper bay to birth their babies. Minke whales, finbacks, humpbacks. Wolves and foxes skulk in the forests of the outer boroughs. Coyotes walk across the uptown plazas at 3 a.m., lords of the cosmos. [. . .] The Canada lynx? I call it the Manhattan lynx. [. . .] At the center of the estuarine network swims the mayor of the municipality, the beaver, busily building wetlands. Beavers are the real real estate developers. River otters, mink, fishers, weasels, raccoons: all these citizens inhabit the world the beavers made from their version of lumber. Around them swim harbor seals, harbor porpoises. A sperm whale sails through the Narrows like an ocean liner. Squirrels and bats. The American black bear. They have all come back like the tide, like poetry.[35]

As in Amelia's earlier portrait of Manhattan, the citizen here describes a New York City that has become a newly lively ecosystem, along with the diverse and vibrant human neighborhoods that have established themselves after the flood. Climate change drives polar bears close to extinction, but it also opens up new habitats for species that had long disappeared from New York City—just as sea-level rise floods and topples buildings but also opens up new opportunities for financial speculation and for communal living. And where conservationist planning efforts fail, as in the assisted migration of polar bears, the contingencies and unforeseen transformations of sea-level rise themselves open up new migration routes and habitats.

This does not imply that Robinson seeks to suggest a laissez-faire attitude in the face of either ecological or economic change. On the contrary, it is multitudes of citizens refusing to make their loan payments who topple the capitalist world market at the end of the novel, and Amelia, for all her apparent superficiality, actually becomes one of the voices who encourage people to participate through her widely viewed show. But cultural as well as ecological change often takes unexpected turns in Robinson's history of the future and does not seem susceptible to the kind of planning that McHarg envisioned for urban spaces. Often, the city in *New York 2140* must engage with contingencies, accidents, and consequences that none of the characters had foreseen, and that frequently cause risks or catastrophes along with new opportunities. Amelia admits as much in her *Assisted Migration* show when she tells her audience, "Mainly it's just a disaster, a fucking disaster. So we have to nurse the world back to health. We're no good at it, but we have to do it. [. . .] it's the only way forward."[36] Caring for the planet, in her perspective, does not mean restoring a lost purity but accepting hybrid ecologies, or what she calls a "mongrel planet."[37]

It's a mongrel world. We've been mixing things up for thousands of years now, poisoning some creatures and feeding others, and moving everything around. Ever since humans left Africa we've been doing that. [. . .] It's a mongrel world, and whatever moment they want to hold on to, that was just one moment.[38]

Intertidal New York City, with its mix of terrestrial, waterborne, and airborne infrastructure, its collapsing buildings and newly constructed superscrapers, its native, introduced, and returned flora and fauna, functions as the main symbol of this global mongrelization or hybridization in Robinson's novel.

The idea that cities are hybrids composed of natural and human-made elements and rely on material as well as semiotic networks is not, of course, new or unique to Robinson's novel. Theorists of urban political ecology have similarly used the vocabulary of the hybrid or cyborg city, often drawing on Donna Haraway's description of the cybernetic organism in her well-known "Cyborg Manifesto" (1984) as "a hybrid of machine and organism, a creature of social reality as well as a creature of fiction,"[39] and on Bruno Latour's actor-network-theory. Erik Swyngedouw and Maria Kaïka, for example, approach cities as "cyborg cities," "constituted through dense networks of interwoven socio-ecological processes that are simultaneously human, physical, discursive, cultural, material, and organic. Circulatory conduits of water, foodstuffs, cars, fumes, money, labour, etc., move in and out of the city, transform the city, and produce the urban as a continuously changing socio-ecological landscape."[40] They elaborate:

This hybrid socionatural "thing" called city is full of contradictions, tensions, and conflicts. [. . .] The metabolized flows that weave together the urban fabric [. . .] narrate many interrelated tales of the city: the story of its people and the powerful socioecological processes that produce the urban and its spaces of privilege and exclusion, of participation and marginality. These would-be stories of rats and bankers, of diseases and speculation in frozen pork bellies, or Nikkei-index futures and options, of chemical, physical, and biological reactions and transformations, of global warming and acid rain, of the capital, machinations, and strategies of city builders, of urban land developers, of the knowledges of the engineers, the scientists, and the economists. In sum, excavating the flows that constitute the urban would produce a political ecology of the urbanization of nature.[41]

In his portrait of intertidal New York City and more broadly a planet transformed by climate change, Robinson narrativizes precisely this urbanization of nature—but also the rewilding or renaturalization of urban nature that occurs in part because of collective initiatives and in part by way of unintended consequences.

In his far more fantastic novel *Perdido Street Station*, Miéville also characterizes New Crobuzon as a "*mongrel city*,"[42] and this phrase accretes a number of different meanings over the course of the plot. It refers, on one level, to *the immigrants, the refugees, the outsiders who remake New Crobuzon every day. This place with a bastard culture.*"[43] But the character who thinks these thoughts, Yagharek, is himself not human, but a garuda, a member of a six-foot-tall species of intelligent birds. He is only one of a multiplicity of sentient species that populate New Crobuzon: humans; khepri, a matriarchal species whose females have humanlike bodies and heads in the shape of a scarab, while the males are simply unintelligent beetles; vodyanoi, a large froglike species; hotchi, vaguely hedgehoglike creatures; and cactacae, essentially walking, talking, and thinking cacti, among many others whose material needs and cultural communities shape the particular character of individual neighborhoods as well as the multispecies character of the overall city. In addition, some of these species combine human and nonhuman physical characteristics—at least when they are seen from a human perspective—and the novel often describes the facial expressions, gestures, or movements of individual characters as "shockingly human" or "shockingly inhuman" to highlight the surprising hybridizations in the bodies and minds of the city dwellers.

As if this natural species variety were not enough, the hybridization and cyborgization of individual bodies with parts from other species and indeed mechanical parts is a highly advanced technology in New Crobuzon. It is used as a systematic device of punishment by the legal system, producing so-called Remades in a grotesque and proliferating variety, but this "biothaumaturgy" is also used by some individuals of their own accord. An example is one of the most impressive and most frightening characters in the novel, the drug kingpin aptly named Mr. Motley, whose anatomy exceeds any possible species identification:

> Scraps of skin and fur and feathers swung as he moved; tiny limbs clutched; eyes rolled from obscure niches; antlers and protrusions of bone jutted precariously; feelers twitched and mouths glistened. Many-coloured skeins of skin collided. A cloven hoof thumped gently against the wood floor. Tides of flesh washed against each other in violent currents. Muscles tethered by alien tendons to alien bones worked together in uneasy truce, in slow, tense motion. Scales gleamed. Fins quivered. Wings fluttered brokenly. Insect claws folded and unfolded.[44]

Mr. Motley rejects the question to which species he might have originally belonged with outrage, insisting that hybridity is "'what makes the world . . . the fundamental dynamic. Transition. The point where one thing becomes another. It is what makes you, the city, the world, what they are. . . . The zone where the disparate become part of the whole. The hybrid zone.'"[45]

New Crobuzon, in his perspective, is just one more example of this transitional hybridity:

And what of the city itself? Perched where two rivers strive to become the sea, where mountains become a plateau, where the clumps of trees coagulate to the south and—quantity becomes quality—are suddenly a forest. New Crobuzon's architecture moves from the industrial to the residential to the opulent to the slum to the underground to the airborne to the modern to the ancient to the colourful to the drab to the fecund to the barren . . . You take my point.[46]

Yagharek, the birdman, perceives a more dystopian version of this varied and hybridized cityscape when he first arrives in New Crobuzon by boat:

The river twists and turns to face the city. It looms suddenly, massive, stamped on the landscape. Its light wells up around the surrounds, the rock hills, like bruise-blood. Its dirty towers glow. [. . .] It is a vast pollutant, a stench, a klaxon sounding. Fat chimneys retch dirt into the sky. [. . .] Faint shouts, here and there the calls of beasts, the obscene clash and pounding from the factories as huge machines rut. Railways trace urban anatomy like protruding veins. Red brick and dark walls, squat churches like troglodytic things, ragged awnings flickering, cobbled mazes in the old town, culs-de-sac, sewers riddling the earth like secular sepulchres, a new landscape of wasteground, crushed stone, libraries fat with forgotten volumes, old hospitals, towerblocks, ships and metal claws that lift cargoes from the water. [. . .] What trick of topography is this, that lets the sprawling monster hide behind corners to leap out at the traveller?[47]

In descriptions such as these, Miéville insistently maps the hybrid individual organism onto the monstrous design of the city (here metaphorized as its "anatomy"), and the variety of its biological bodies and species onto the variety of its architectures and neighborhoods: a hybridity and multiplicity that can only be captured by means of enumeration, the cataloging of parts and zones.[48] And by mapping: *Perdido Street Station* opens with a compact but complex map of the fictional city whose overall outline vaguely resembles that of a human brain, with innumerable neighborhoods, roads, and rivers that appear to be this urban brain's ganglia.

Knowledge is similarly hybrid in New Crobuzon. The scientist on whom two of the major plot lines converge, Isaac Dan der Grimnebulin, defines his expertise as a combination of disciplines that he explains in terms of urban infrastructure: "'I'm not a chymist, or a biologist, or a thaumaturge . . . I'm a dilettante, [. . .] a dabbler. [. . .] I think of myself as the main station for all the schools of thought. Like Perdido Street Station. [. . .] All the trainlines meet there [. . .] everything has to pass through it. That's like me. That's my job. That's the kind of scientist I am."[49] His main research interest is how the energy that crisis mobilizes in individual bodies as well as in collectives might be materialized and used, and over the course of the novel, he is called upon to deploy his knowledge about crisis energy to solve two different problems.

One of these involves Yagharek, whose wings have been amputated as punishment for a rape he has committed, and who travels from his faraway home community in the desert to seek out Grimnebulin's help in restoring him to flight: a project of biological restoration, in a sense. The other one is a problem of biological invasion. As Grimnebulin researches flight mechanisms in a variety of species, he accidentally releases a member of an intelligent species from another continent, a so-called slake moth that is able to hypnotize other sentient beings into submission and nourishes itself by consuming their minds, leaving them alive but deprived of sentience and unable to care for themselves. This moth frees four other members of its species from a research lab, and with no natural predators or effective defense weapons that might defeat them, the moth group turns into a deadly urban danger that Grimnebulin has to help combat.

Miéville, in all of his writings, is primarily interested in the social and political life of cities rather than in urban nature, and this overriding interest justifies reading the species variety as well as the themes of biological restoration and ecological invasion in *Perdido Street Station* as political allegories. The corruption of Mayor Rudgutter's government, which turns out to be in cahoots with Mr. Motley's organized crime, the brutal putdown of a strike that the vodyanoi dock workers initiate, the burning of the headquarters of an underground political newspaper, and the death by torture of its editor are overt allusions to political oppression, as is the plot that gradually but inexorably draws Grimnebulin's scientific research into politics. In this context, the variety of species might merely illustrate varieties of exploitation and social division, and the ever-growing number of casualties from the mind- and life-sucking moths can easily be read as an allegory for the depredations of capitalism.[50]

But the extravagant detail with which Miéville describes the biological and material realities of organic as well as urban structures in his novel far exceeds the needs of such political allegory and warrants a somewhat different analysis of the multispecies community in New Crobuzon, as ecological in addition to political allegory. From this perspective, the profusion of imaginary species in Miéville's metropolis is not just a general allegory for sociocultural and economic diversity, but a portrait of the more real but often unimagined biodiversity of actually existing cities. By the same token, the meticulously described neighborhoods that are dominated by one particular species—the khepri communities of Creekside and Kinken, the cactacae neighborhood under the ancient and dilapidated Glasshouse—can be read as acknowledgments that urban space is not shaped by one species, humans, alone. The fact that Miéville relies on the genres of science fiction, horror, and fantasy to portray nonhuman individuals and communities with sentience, social structure, culture, politics, crafts, and their own aesthetic values highlights in and of itself how far removed from our usual sense of urban reality such a perception of other city species is, yet how much it might change our knowledge and understanding of real urban spaces.

This changed understanding may at first glance be most obviously reflected in the cross-species relationships of love, friendship, and collaboration that the novel portrays. Grimnebulin has a love affair of several years' standing with the khepri artist Lin; he forms bonds of respect and friendship with the garuda Yagharek; and he puts together teams and alliances to fight the slake moths that involve multiple factions, from humans to Remade and vodyanoi. In the culminating confrontation with the moths, he has put together a technological device to mobilize crisis energy whose construction and operation involve two even more unusual figures: the Construct Council, an Artificial Intelligence that has self-organized from robotic remains and other debris in the New Crobuzon garbage dump; and the Weaver, a spiderlike creature that can cross over into other dimensions and perceives the world's weave from a purely aesthetic viewpoint, commenting on it continually in a lyrical singsong that might well qualify as a "stream of unconsciousness." In Miéville's scenario, then, the maintenance of the hybrid socioecological urban system requires all the forces that biological life and technological ingenuity can muster.

But why are the slake moths ultimately excluded from this encompassing, enormously diverse system of relationships? The urgent need to exterminate a nonnative, predatory species that does not have any natural enemies to keep it in check in its new ecosystem is a familiar motif from invasion ecology, and it does explain a turn of the plot that is not well explained in terms of political allegory. As Christopher Palmer has pointed out, the culminating battles in *Perdido Street Station* eliminate the immediate danger to the city, and they demonstrate the collaborative mechanisms that are necessary for a successful political revolution. But their outcome is to leave the city in the same state in which it started out—functional but riven by inequality, corruption, and oppression.[51] The moment of revolution, in other words, perpetuates the status quo rather than introducing a new order. This makes little sense as political allegory, but it does make sense ecologically: the extermination of invasive species is, in this scenario, most often meant to return the ecosystem to its pre-invasive status.

But it remains that the violent killing of the slake moths does not sync well with Miéville's exuberant descriptions of the multispecies city, and the narrative vocabulary of gothic horror that is associated with the gigantic black moths who turn other beings into zombies only exacerbates the problem. Portrayals of some sentient beings as inherently evil and destructive are not easy to reconcile with either political or ecological thinking that relativizes such moral judgments in relation to divergent cultural standards and ecological networks that include predator-prey relationships as much as cross-species symbioses and collaborations. One can blame this contradiction in the narrative logic on a shortfall of Miévielle's imagination, or on the more general problem of narrativizing sociopolitical problems by means of biological metaphors.[52] But a look at the other important plot line in *Perdido Street Station,* the story of Yagharek's crime and sentence, sheds light on this problem.

Yagharek's miserable condition initially appeals to Grimnebulin's empathy and to his passion for scientific research. Yagharek clearly suffers from the loss of his ability to fly: being earthbound amounts to a fundamental change—as he initially perceives it, a demotion—in his social and ontological status. In his despair, he seeks help from Grimnebulin, who is both moved by his client's plight and intrigued by the technical problems of helping a larger-than-human bird who has lost his wings regain flight. But he changes his mind after a visit from Kar'uchai, the female garuda whom Yagharek has raped. In her and other garudas' perspectives, rape seriously violates the communitarian respect for others' choices that the garudas conceive of as the foundation of their society, a socialist utopia of sorts in which the well-being of others and of the community as a whole is the "concrete" value that supersedes the "abstractness" of individualism. Kar'uchai pleads with Grimnebulin not to reverse the garuda justice system and its judgment on Yagharek, and Grimnebulin accepts this entreaty by abandoning the quest to restore Yagharek's ability to fly. Yagharek, in turn, accepts the terminal loss of his avian capabilities by removing all of his feathers and reentering New Crobuzon as a more humanlike, unfeathered if still beaked, creature about to begin an entirely new life.

This plotline approximates—in allegorical terms, of course—the ethics that might go along with the transspecies urban theory that Wolch and others have called for. Grimnebulin is portrayed as both sympathetic to the plight of a nonhuman creature whom he comes to accept as a friend and a comrade in arms; at the same time, he is, in the end, respectful of the cultural and ethical norms that govern a nonhuman society he only understands incompletely. Yagharek emerges as a subject who has to abandon his original identity and adopt a new, unprecedented one—a nonflighted, unfeathered garuda in a human-dominated metropolis, but one whose active acceptance of his new identity comes with the hope that remains associated with transition and hybridity throughout the novel.

Miéville, then, structures the architecture of his urban novel so as to oppose two divergent plotlines of multispecies justice: one—Yagharek's sentence, search for redemption, and acceptance of his judgment—in which different ideas of what constitutes justice are accepted and accommodated by the different species involved; and a second one—the slake moths' introduction into the city, their persecution and extermination—in which a "foreign" species is portrayed as the source of a lethal danger that has to be and is eliminated in the end. *Perdido Street Station*—and this is part of why it appears as a dystopia—does not minimize or sentimentalize the costs of either decision. Yagharek, with his feathers ripped away from most of his body, scarred and unflighted, appears at the end of the novel as the mirror inversion of a Remade human whom the protagonists encountered earlier as an exhibit in a freak show, a man into whose face feathers were rammed and to whose face a beak was surgically attached as part of a legal punishment. Grimnebulin and his closest friends leave New Crobuzon after the defeat of the moths, with Lin, Grimnebulin's khepri lover, reduced to a state of permanent infantilism after a slake moth has robbed her of part of her mind. Multispecies justice does not, in Miéville's portrayal, offer easy solutions—or even difficult ones that come without a significant cost in well-being. Respect for as well as elimination of other species exacts a heavy toll, and through this toll Miéville suggests that multispecies justice in his storyworld has to remain provisional, subject to being revisited as city and ecology change.

Designing Multispecies Nature

McHarg was inspired by a vision of urban and regional planning that works in synchrony with the geological, meteorological, and ecological characteristics of the natural landscape. Many of his basic principles and procedures remain valuable fifty years after the publication of *Design with Nature* and resemble some of those used by landscape ecologists today, as Wolch, West, and Gaines have remarked.[53] McHarg's maps, in particular, bespeak his confidence that the characteristics of the natural world and the cultural and human uses and values they might lend themselves to can be identified with precision. The fictional urban narratives I have discussed here also seek to draw maps of urban nature and its cultural meanings. But they emphasize the shifting uses and perceptions of nature for different cultural communities, as Yamashita does through her views of Mazatlán and Los Angeles through the eyes of nationally, racially, ethnically, and generationally differing characters; at different historical moments, as Robinson does with his palimpsest of New York history; and even for different species, as Miéville suggests through his imaginary multispecies city of New Crobuzon. What nature is and how different kinds of humans and nonhumans cocreate it is subject to a great deal more variation in these narratives than McHarg's approach allows.

Mapping itself becomes a far more self-conscious, self-reflexive activity in these urban stories. The brain-shaped map of New Crobuzon that appears at the start of Miéville's novel suggests that the city is complex but graspable, whereas the accumulation of detail in the descriptions of the city's multiple neighborhoods overwhelms any such sense in the narrative itself. Robinson makes the unstable "intertidal" topography of Manhattan under conditions of climate change the central metaphor of his novel. And Yamashita's work destabilizes maps and schedules of Angeleno space and time as the Tropic of Cancer is pulled northward in her deployment of Latin American magical realism. These instabilities and transformations do not make maps useless or superfluous; on the contrary, Yamashita's and Miéville's explicit and Robinson's implicit interest in cartography highlights the continued importance of maps as models of urban space. But all three authors juxtapose the map with narrative as a different cognitive tool for exploring shifts in urban nature itself, as well as shifts in humans' (and other species') perceptions and uses of it.

Conflicts of justice—between humans, and between humans and nonhumans—lie in different ways at the core of these narratives. McHarg, of course, was not insensible to the deprivations of poverty, slum dwelling, and war, as his account of growing up outside of Glasgow between the two World Wars clearly shows. Yet his most vocal criticism in *Design with Nature* is directed at the sheer ugliness of modern cities, their lack of vitality, and their despoliation of nature. Glasgow was "a memorial to an inordinate capacity to create ugliness, a sandstone excretion cemented with smoke and grime. Each night its pall on the eastern horizon was lit by the flames of blast furnaces" in his description, and he claims that "you can confirm an urban destination from the increased shrillness of the neon shills, the diminished horizon, the loss of nature's companions until you are alone, with men, in the heart of the city, God's Junkyard. [. . .] It is the expression of the inalienable right to create ugliness and disorder for private greed, the maximum expression of man's inhumanity to man."[54] What critique of capitalism might be implied in his reference to "private greed" is quickly overwritten by a more general indictment of "man's inhumanity to man."

Recent urban narratives of the kind I have discussed here link the characteristics of urban nature more directly to social, economic, and legal injustice of different kinds. Whether the emphasis is Yamashita's on nation and race, Robinson's on class, or Miéville's on class and species, the kind of nature that the characters have access to, their perception of it, and their imagination of its futures is intimately related to their legal, sociocultural, and economic status. But precisely by refracting urban nature through a wide variety of lenses, city narratives also reach for a new vision of totality that is built out of the immersion into juxtaposed perspectives and superimposed layers. Yamashita's portrayal of Manzanar Murakami aims most directly at this new totality: "*There are maps and there are maps and there are maps*. The uncanny thing was that he could see all of them at once, filter some, pick them out like transparent windows and place them even delicately and consecutively in a complex grid of pattern, spatial discernment, body politic."[55] Any struggle for multispecies justice—justice for the humans and nonhumans that inhabit cities together—emerges from the juxtaposition of these divergent maps and their combination with compelling narratives about multispecies pasts, presents, and futures.

Projects: Five Themes

Big Wilds
Rising Tides
Fresh Waters
Toxic Lands
Urban Futures

Big Wilds

CHINA

National Ecological Security Pattern Plan

NEW ZEALAND

Landscape Regeneration of
Western Waiheke Island

Great Green Wall

Africa

Formally known as the Great Green Wall of the Sahara and Sahel Initiative (GGWSSI), the Great Green Wall spans approximately 8,000 kilometers (5,000 miles) from Senegal to Djibouti and is 15 kilometers (9 miles) deep. Its purpose is to combat desertification by restoring degraded lands on the front lines of the encroaching desert. The idea of a wall of trees at the edge of the Sahara and the semiarid belt of the Sahel is not a new one; it was originally proposed in the 1950s, revisited in the 1980s, and considered again in 2002 by President Olusegun Obasanjo of Nigeria. However, it was not until 2007 that the governments of the twenty nations that encompass the wall endorsed the idea and began to undertake the project. When it is complete in 2030, it will be the largest designed living structure in the world.

Some of those who live along the wall's proposed path are considered the world's most multidimensionally poor, meaning that their poverty is not just financial but that they also lack access to sufficient education, work, food, and health care. The countries that contribute to the wall's progress have faced or are currently facing extreme challenges, including food shortages, drought, exodus, conflict, and in some cases, civil war.

Since 2007 the Great Green Wall's mission has evolved. A monolithic greenbelt of trees is no longer part of the vision. Instead, restoring the degraded land with native trees, bushes, and grasses, and embracing agricultural technologies such as farmer-managed natural regeneration, agroforestry, and zai pits (small holes dug to retain runoff and manure) have helped to attune the project to the specificities of local ecologies and cultures.

Incorporating farming, animal grazing, and food production into the project has created new jobs and opportunities for communities. Scientific monitoring of the project has aided the project's growth and helps determine which techniques are most successful.

As of this writing in 2018, 15 percent of the wall had been completed. The politically stable countries of Senegal and Ethiopia have led the restoration and provided strong governmental support. Niger, Nigeria, and Burkina Faso have also made headway. Like many other large landscape conservation and planning projects, the Great Green Wall is a work in progress.

FIGURE 12.1.1 Chad, Mao, Kanem region. Oasis in the Lake Chad Basin, October 13, 2012. Women from the local village help to reforest the oasis by planting indigenous plants with the Great Green Wall program. © *Andrea Borgarello for TerrAfrica /World Bank.*

FIGURE 12.1.2 Light green zones show areas in need of landscape restoration. The large central swath is the Sahel region where the Great Green Wall is taking shape. *Drawing, Anni Lei based on mapping by the Food and Agriculture Organization of the United Nations, esri, and Google Earth imagery. With permission.*

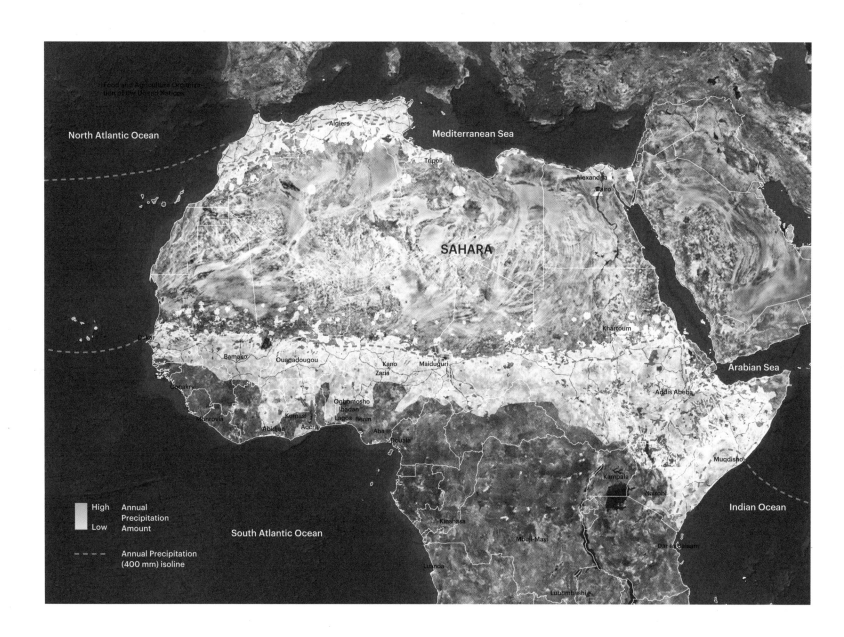

FIGURE 12.1.3 Growing the Great Green Wall, Senegal, November 2015. *With permission, Ignacio Ferrando*.

Yellowstone to Yukon Conservation Initiative

USA and Canada

In 1993, lawyer and conservationist Harvey Locke first proposed a continuous corridor of protected habitat from Yellowstone National Park in the United States to the Yukon in Canada. Four years later, the Yellowstone to Yukon Conservation Initiative (Y2Y) was founded, and its plan is now being implemented. Inspiration for Y2Y is traced to a female wolf named Pluie, who was tracked with a GPS collar migrating from Canada's Banff National Park to America's Glacier National Park to near Spokane, Washington, over an eighteen-month period. This journey was testament to the wolf's stealth and cunning and also suggested the need for continuous corridors of wildlands to allow other species to migrate throughout the territory in relative safety.

The Y2Y corridor spans nearly 2,000 miles (3,200 kilometers) and encompasses over 500,000 square miles (1.3 million square kilometers) of land. In its effort to connect habitat across a vast region of different land uses, Y2Y works with and supports over 300 organizations, First Nations, private landowners, and government entities. Its role is to unite these diverse groups in an effort to promote the science behind the corridor, maintain and restore degraded land within the corridor, and advise and address development that is good for the economy without harming wildlife.

Wildland corridors both facilitate seasonal migration and open up pathways that will allow species to adapt to climate change over the long term. For these species to survive indefinitely, parks such as Yellowstone need to be linked to other protected areas, thereby connecting individual animals to a larger and more diverse gene pool. For example, Banff National Park has built six animal overpasses and thirty-eight underpasses so animals can cross the major highway that bisects the park. Since the project started the land area designated as protected under the Y2Y initiative has risen from 11 to 21 percent. Another 30 percent of the designated land has benefited from improved conservation practices implemented through local land use management plans.

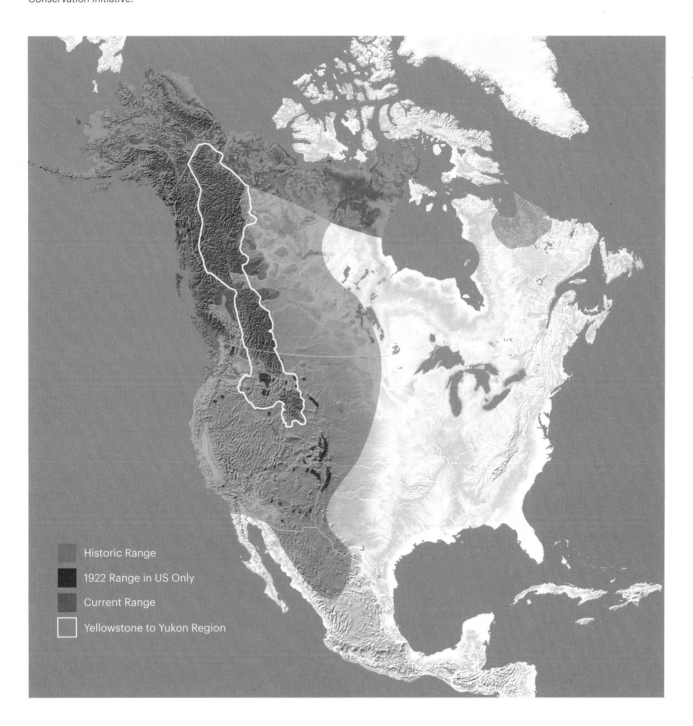

FIGURE 12.2.1 Map shows the change in grizzly bear habitat over time. The Yellowstone to Yukon region is outlined in white and overlaid on color zones. *Redrawn by Yang Zhao based on map by C. H. Merriam, Dr. B. McLellan, and IUCN. With permission, Yellowstone to Yukon Conservation Initiative.*

Historic Range

1922 Range in US Only

Current Range

Yellowstone to Yukon Region

FIGURE 12.2.2 AND FIGURE 12.2.3 Maps of Protected Land in 1993 (this page) and 2013 (opposite). Green shows protected lands and yellow indicates other conservation designations, including recreation areas, high conservation value forests, and restricted use wilderness areas. *With permission, Yellowstone to Yukon Conservation Initiative.*

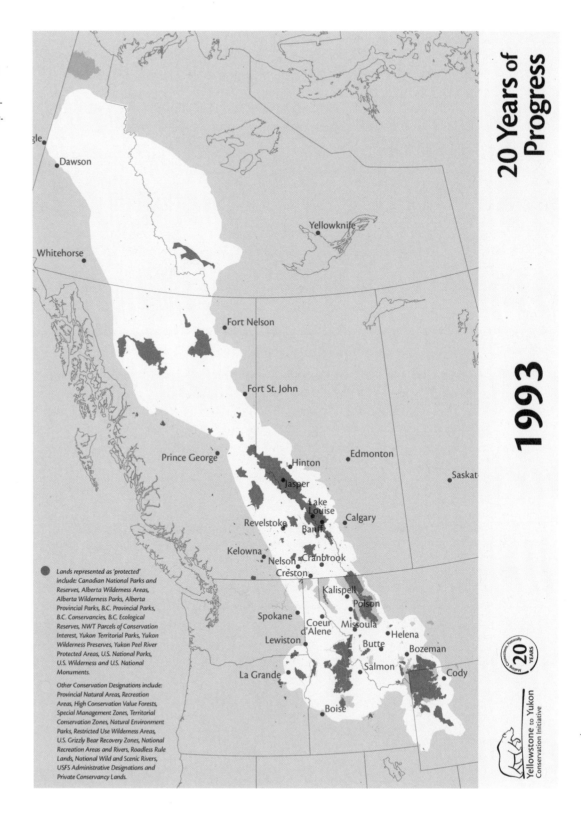

20 Years of Progress

1993

Lands represented as 'protected' include: Canadian National Parks and Reserves, Alberta Wilderness Areas, Alberta Wilderness Parks, Alberta Provincial Parks, B.C. Provincial Parks, B.C. Conservancies, B.C. Ecological Reserves, NWT Parcels of Conservation Interest, Yukon Territorial Parks, Yukon Wilderness Preserves, Yukon Peel River Protected Areas, U.S. National Parks, U.S. Wilderness and U.S. National Monuments.

Other Conservation Designations include: Provincial Natural Areas, Recreation Areas, High Conservation Value Forests, Special Management Zones, Territorial Conservation Zones, Natural Environment Parks, Restricted Use Wilderness Areas, U.S. Grizzly Bear Recovery Zones, National Recreation Areas and Rivers, Roadless Rule Lands, National Wild and Scenic Rivers, USFS Administrative Designations and Private Conservancy Lands.

Yellowstone to Yukon Conservation Initiative

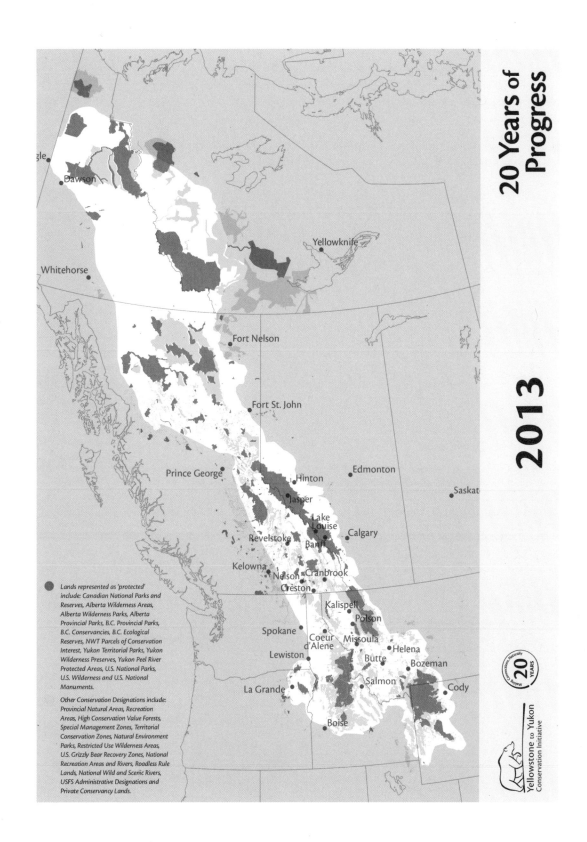

gle

Dawson

Whitehorse

Yellowknife

Fort Nelson

Fort St. John

Prince George

Hinton

Edmonton

Jasper

Saskat

Lake
Louise

Revelstoke

Banff

Calgary

Kelowna

Nelson Cranbrook

Creston

Kalispell

Polson

Spokane

Coeur
d'Alene

Missoula

Helena

Lewiston

Butte

Bozeman

La Grande

Salmon

Cody

Boise

Lands represented as 'protected'
include: Canadian National Parks and
Reserves, Alberta Wilderness Areas,
Alberta Wilderness Parks, Alberta
Provincial Parks, B.C. Provincial Parks,
B.C. Conservancies, B.C. Ecological
Reserves, NWT Parcels of Conservation
Interest, Yukon Territorial Parks, Yukon
Wilderness Preserves, Yukon Peel River
Protected Areas, U.S. National Parks,
U.S. Wilderness and U.S. National
Monuments.

Other Conservation Designations include:
Provincial Natural Areas, Recreation
Areas, High Conservation Value Forests,
Special Management Zones, Territorial
Conservation Zones, Natural Environment
Parks, Restricted Use Wilderness Areas,
U.S. Grizzly Bear Recovery Zones, National
Recreation Areas and Rivers, Roadless Rule
Lands, National Wild and Scenic Rivers,
USFS Administrative Designations and
Private Conservancy Lands.

Yellowstone to Yukon
Conservation Initiative

Making Connections Naturally
20 YEARS

FIGURE 12.2.4 Bighorn in traffic, Highway 93 South, Jasper, Alberta. © *Northern Focus Creative.*

FIGURE 12.2.5 Various animals using the underpass to cross 93S. *With permission, Parks Canada.*

FIGURE 12.2.6 Animal crossing overpass,
Banff National Park, Alberta. © *Paul Zizka*.

National Ecological Security Pattern Plan

China

Between 2006 and 2008, Kongjian Yu, founding principal of the design firm Turenscape, led a research planning exercise on behalf of the Chinese Ministry of Environmental Protection and the Chinese Ministry of Cultural Protection. The project—translated into English as National Ecological Security Pattern Plan (NESP)—was to develop geospatial plans on a national scale that indicated where the "ecological security" of land should be prioritized. The plans were to address issues such as water catchment protection, flood control, desertification, soil erosion, and biodiversity conservation. This research represents an increasing recognition at the highest levels of government that ecological concerns are in the Chinese economic interest and should be reflected in Chinese land use planning guidelines.

The project emerged from Yu's doctoral thesis, "Security Patterns in Landscape Planning," in which, under the tutelage of Carl Steinitz, Richard Forman, and Stephen Ervin at Harvard's Graduate School of Design, he developed the concept and method for assessing ecological security on a large scale. The NESP method relies on geographic information system (GIS) analysis as well as a survey of expert opinion about both the biophysical and cultural landscapes of China.

The NESP provides a national purview but lacks detail. It is therefore best understood as a framework that can be used to develop more detailed regional and local plans. For example, Yu and his colleagues were engaged by the Beijing Land Resources Department to develop an ecological security pattern for the Beijing region. Beijing faces extreme environmental challenges in the Jing-Jin-Ji megaregion, which incorporates the adjacent city of Tianjin and the impoverished agricultural and industrial landscapes of Hebei province.

The Chinese government has largely accepted the premise of Yu's national analysis. By operating on a national scale under the aegis of the Chinese government, the NESP has the potential to marshal and coordinate the forces necessary to seriously address China's environmental challenges. In this regard the plan also raises prescient sociopolitical questions about the role and potential impact of top-down ecological planning in the 21st century.

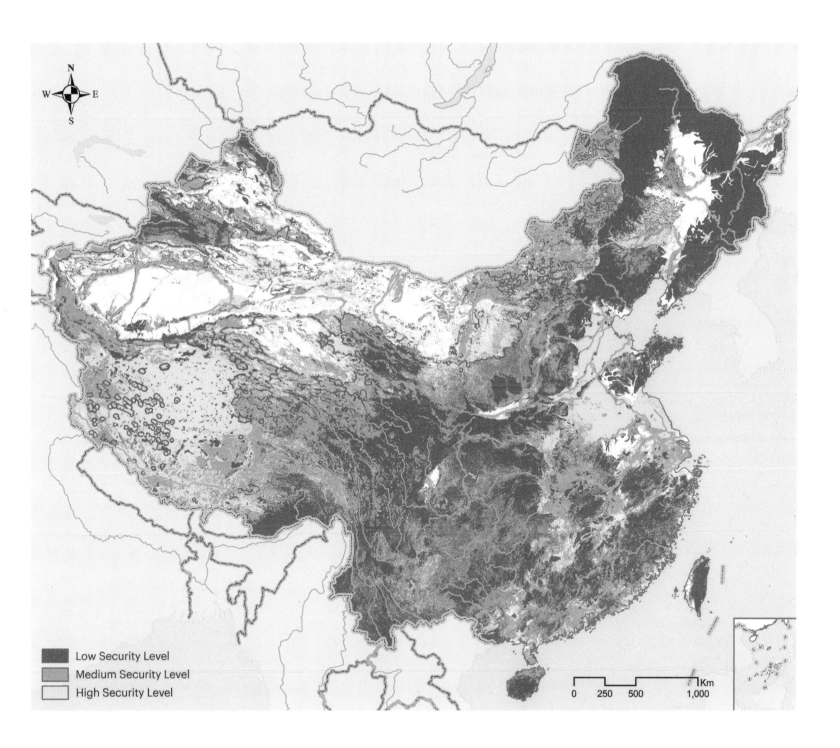

FIGURE 12.3.1 The overall National Ecological Security Pattern Plan is a composite of five primary maps, each of which comprises four to six map sublayers. © *Kongjian Yu, Peking University Graduate School of Landscape Architecture.*

Low Security Level
Medium Security Level
High Security Level

0   250   500   1,000   Km

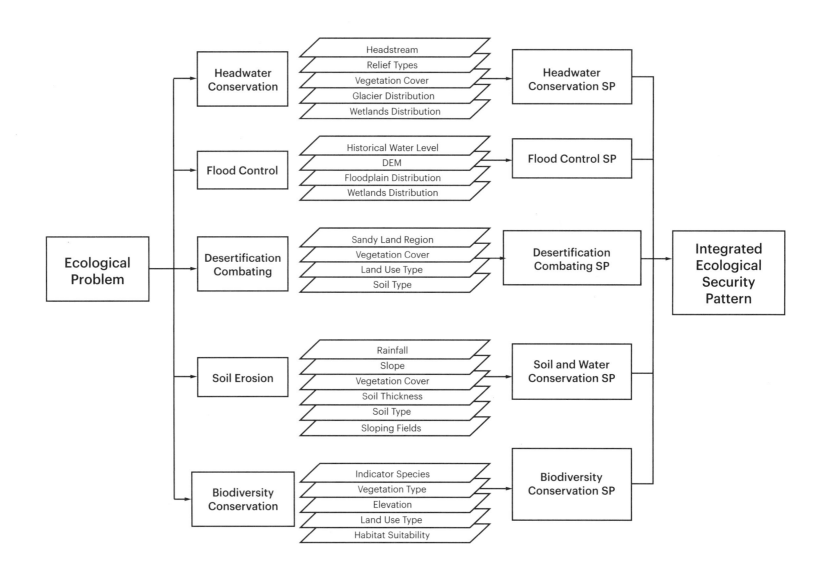

FIGURE 12.3.3 (LEFT)
Headwater Conservation Composite Map. © *Kongjian Yu, Peking University Graduate School of Landscape Architecture.*

FIGURE 12.3.4 (RIGHT)
Flood Control Composite Map. © *Kongjian Yu, Peking University Graduate School of Landscape Architecture.*

FIGURE 12.3.5 (LEFT) Combating Desertification Composite Map. © *Kongjian Yu, Peking University Graduate School of Landscape Architecture.*

FIGURE 12.3.6 (RIGHT)
Soil and Water Conservation Composite Map. © *Kongjian Yu, Peking University Graduate School of Landscape Architecture.*

Headwater Conservation

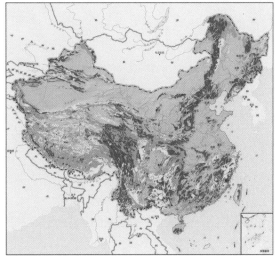

Security Level
■ Low ■ Medium ■ High

Flood Control

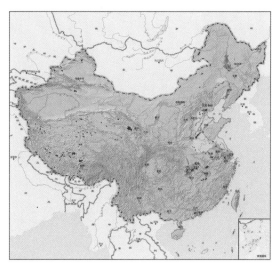

Security Level
■ Low ■ Medium ■ High

Combating Desertification

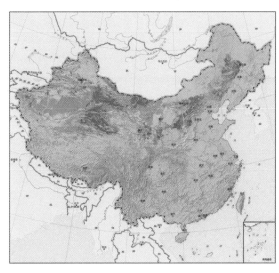

Security Level
■ Low ■ Medium ■ High

Soil and Water Conservation

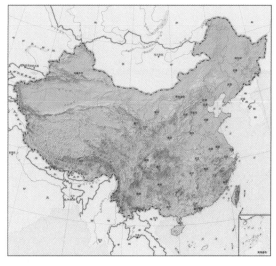

Security Level
■ Low ■ Medium ■ High

Malpai Borderlands

Arizona and New Mexico, USA

In the boot of New Mexico and the southeastern tip of Arizona along the U.S.–Mexico border, there is a 1,250-square-mile (3,238-square-kilometer) plot of land, almost entirely unbroken by highways or subdivisions. The Malpai Borderlands harbors an estimated 4,000 species of plants, 104 species of mammals, 327 species of birds, 136 species of reptiles and amphibians, and the greatest diversity of bee species in the world. In this biodiverse landscape, 53 percent of the area is privately owned and 47 percent is public—a split that has led to tensions among government agencies, cattle ranchers, and environmentalists.

What sets the Malpai Borderlands apart from other stories of conflict in conservation is how these tensions have largely been overcome in order to conserve the landscape's biological and cultural identity. Fewer than 100 families use this expansive land to graze their livestock. Despite being long loathed by environmentalists, these cattle-ranching families have led the charge to keep the land from subdivision and development.

In the early 1990s, the suppression of wildfire caused the land to revert to shrubland dominated by the invasive mesquite tree. This brushlike tree is bad for grazing and highly flammable, serving as added fuel for forest fires, which can further denude the land. Fire has historically kept the brush at bay, and when a fire broke out on July 2, 1991, ranchers pleaded with the local authorities to let it burn. They did not listen. In response, ranchers committed to stewardship of the landscape formed the Malpai Borderlands Group, which has succeeded in protecting almost 80,000 acres from development.

The success of the Malpai Borderlands Group can be credited both to their reliance on science to help manage the Malpai and to their commitment to educating others about how grazing and conservation can coexist. The first scientist on the board, Ray Turner, specialized in comparative photography, a type of ecological study that traces old photographs to their origin and takes a new picture in the same location. The floral species in the photographs are then compared in order to paint a picture of the area's ecological change. Turner and subsequent scientists have concluded, controversially, that a certain level of ranching can contribute to preserving the land's biodiversity.

FIGURE 12.4.1 An aerial view of subdivided land near Douglas, Arizona. Coronado Estates is a development built in the 1970s that has failed to prosper. © *Blake Gordon.*

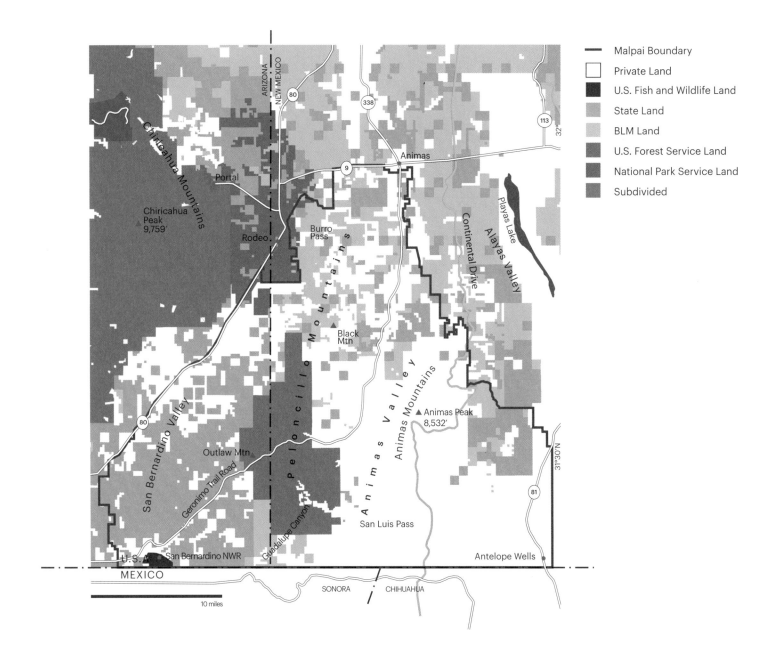

FIGURE 12.4.2 Malpai Borderlands boundary shown on a landownership map. *Map redrawn by Qi Wang based on map by Darin Jensen. With permission.*

Malpai Boundary
Private Land
U.S. Fish and Wildlife Land
State Land
BLM Land
U.S. Forest Service Land
National Park Service Land
Subdivided

FIGURE 12.4.3 Ranches with conservation easements (shown in green). *Map, Darin Jensen. With permission.*

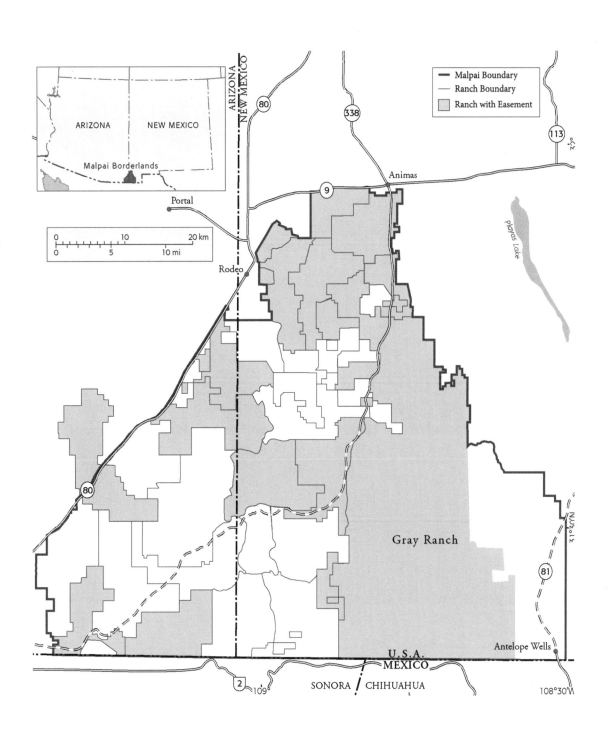

Samboja Lestari

East Kalimantan, Indonesia

Over the past half-century, East Kalimantan (Borneo) has experienced rapid deterioration of its landscape. Owing to a burgeoning population and clear-cutting of its rainforest for agricultural land, timber, and palm oil, roughly half of the Kalimantan rainforest has been razed. With the loss of habitat, the most charismatic of Indonesian animals, the orangutan, cannot find food and faces starvation or capture. Orangutans that raid agricultural lands are considered pests and are often killed.

In an effort to reconstruct a viable rainforest ecosystem and contribute to the local economy, the Samboja Lestari reforestation project began in 2001, spearheaded by the Borneo Orangutan Survival Foundation (BOS) and Dr. Willie Smits, who cofounded the organization in 1991. A ring of sugar palms was planted around the boundary of the 2,000-hectare (5,000-acre) Samboja Lestari property. Sugar palms can be planted extremely close together to create a live fence. The palms can also produce a sugar alcohol that can be tapped daily for income. Within the boundary, Smits, the BOS, and the local community cultivated the cleared land by mimicking the process of rainforest succession. First they planted fast-growing, nitrogen-fixing, pioneer tree species, typically the first species to return after a disturbance. The Smits team paid special attention to the accruing beneficial fungi and made large amounts of compost from local materials and organic waste to restore the soil. When conditions had improved, they planted the more permanent rainforest species and allowed them to become established before harvesting the pioneer species and offering the timber to local people.

The original aim was for Samboja Lestari to sustain a thousand orangutans as a breeding population large enough to survive in the event that all other orangutans were wiped out. The plan was to plant more fruiting species within Samboja Lestari than are found in a typical rainforest to feed the orangutans. In addition, the local residents would be given free land outside the greenbelt of sugar palms to farm using agroforestry techniques. These plots would help buffer the rebuilt rainforest and help the forest spread. The local population could harvest the fruit and sell it to the BOS for profit. This produce would then be used to feed the orangutans within Samboja.

Although reports vary, today over 200 orangutans are part of Samboja Lestari's program, a range of wildlife has colonized the humanmade rainforest of over 1,200 tree species, and the local population is able to harvest and sell the fruit from the sugar palms.

FIGURE 12.5.1 Access roads and terraced fields erase Sarawak's rolling lowlands. © *Mattias Klum/ National Geographic Creative.*

FIGURE 12.5.2 Restoration of forest, Samboja Lestari. *With permission, Borneo Orangutan Survival Foundation.*

FIGURE 12.5.3 Four decades of forest persistence, clearance, and logging on Borneo. Forest (dark green) and nonforest (white) in 1973, residual clouds (cyan) in map A. Areas of forest loss during the period 1973–2010 (red) in map B. Primary logging roads from 1973 to 2010 (are so extensive they are barely visible) in map C. Remaining intact forest (dark green), remaining logged forest (light green), and industrial oil palm and timber plantations (black) in 2010 in map D. *David L. A. Gaveau, et al., in "Four Decades of Forest Persistence, Clearance and Logging on Borneo," PLoS One, July 16, 2014, https://doi.org/10.1371/journal.pone.0101654.g003.*

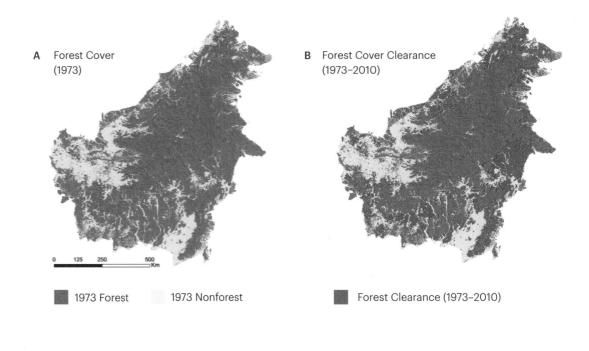

A   Forest Cover
(1973)

0   125   250   500
Km

■ 1973 Forest   ■ 1973 Nonforest

B   Forest Cover Clearance
(1973–2010)

■ Forest Clearance (1973–2010)

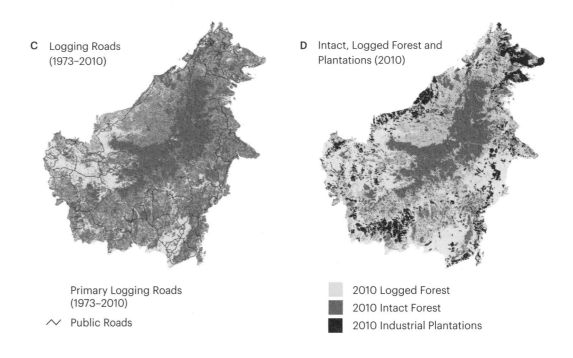

C   Logging Roads
(1973–2010)

Primary Logging Roads
(1973–2010)

⌒ Public Roads

D   Intact, Logged Forest and
Plantations (2010)

■ 2010 Logged Forest
■ 2010 Intact Forest
■ 2010 Industrial Plantations

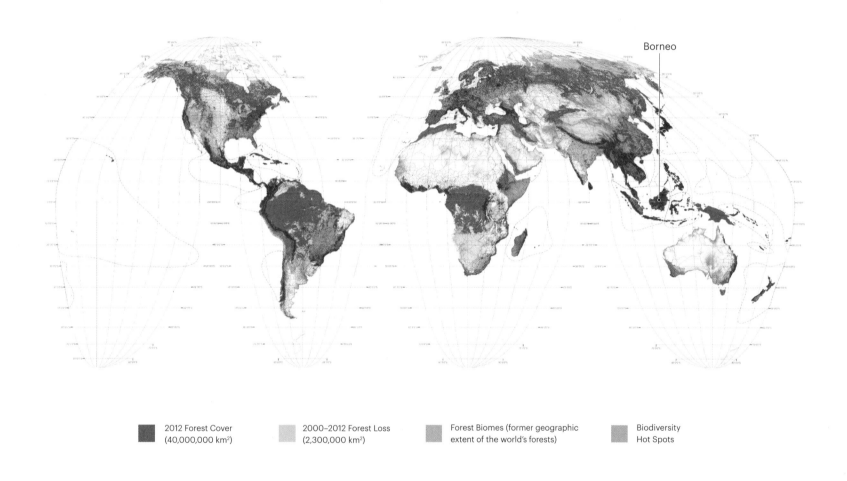

Borneo

2012 Forest Cover
(40,000,000 km²)

2000–2012 Forest Loss
(2,300,000 km²)

Forest Biomes (former geographic
extent of the world's forests)

Biodiversity
Hot Spots

FIGURE 12.5.4 Global Deforestation Map.
© 2017 Richard J. Weller, Claire Hoch, and
Chieh Huang, Atlas for the End of the World,
http://atlas-for-the-end-of-the-world.com.

Landscape Regeneration of Western Waiheke Island

New Zealand

Although New Zealand enjoys worldwide fame as "clean and green," the reality is different. New Zealand has suffered massive deforestation and huge losses of unique biodiversity over the past three or four hundred years. More than half of the country's farming landscape has been damaged by land clearance and overgrazing, and requires regenerative action.

Some New Zealanders have taken such action in the western area of Waiheke Island, on the periphery of Auckland, the nation's largest metropolitan area. The Western Waiheke project is a composite of five master plans for private landowners who initially wanted lifestyle property subdivisions. In 1987, the landscape had been almost completely denuded by monoculture farming. The landscape architect Dennis Scott persuaded the landowners and local authorities to embark on a process of landscape enhancement that is ongoing to this day.

Using McHargian land suitability analysis, the design team identified and mapped areas of land that have critical sensitivity, including steep, unstable slopes; river, stream, and coastal riparian margins; wetlands; remnant and regenerating indigenous bush areas and patches; as well as cultural features, such as archaeological sites. These areas were then used collectively to anchor an interconnected pattern of land set aside for management as a permanent framework for indigenous vegetated habitat. The result is a legally protected "landscape commons," interwoven with private property.

To date, over 430 hectares (1,060 acres) of land have been fully restored, making it the largest such project in New Zealand and a model for the nation. Over 1.3 million seedlings have been planted to mitigate soil erosion and reinstate biodiversity. Central to the project's success was the landscape

FIGURE 12.6.1 (Top) Aerial view of Western Waiheke (Church Bay and Owhanake projects) from the southeast looking northwest over Matiatia Bay, Waiheke Island, Auckland. *Photo, Whites Aviation, March 3, 1951. With permission, Alexander Turnbull Library, Wellington, New Zealand, ref. WA-26691-F.*

FIGURE 12.6.2 (Bottom) Aerial view of Western Waiheke (Church Bay and Owhanake projects) from the southeast looking northwest over Matiatia Bay, Waiheke Island, Auckland, December 5, 2016. *Photo, Sky View Photography, NZ, Ltd. With permission.*

architect's influence over local planning policy under the umbrella of the Resource Management Act of 1991, whereby additional development rights were offered to the landowners in exchange for landscape protection and restoration.

In addition to ecological restoration, the Western Waiheke project has opened up the land for recreational use by introducing nature, scenic, and sculpture trails, as well as improved access to the coast. Increased and diverse productivity results from mixed agriculture, horticulture, wineries, restaurants, tourist accommodations, and housing. The integrated environmental, social, and economic gains fulfill the purpose and promise of the New Zealand Resource Management legislation. The project shows that peri-urban expansion can be turned into a positive process if the new development takes place along with ecological planning and involves local residents in the creation of multifunctional landscapes.

FIGURE 12.6.3 Design analysis and development process, Resource Mapping Overlay Series. The combination of layers enables the designers to determine which areas should be protected and which can be developed. Waiheke Western End, Owhanake Project from *Assessment of Environmental Effects for Owhanake: Land Use and Subdivision and Related Consent Applications*, 1996. *With permission, DJScott Associates Ltd.*

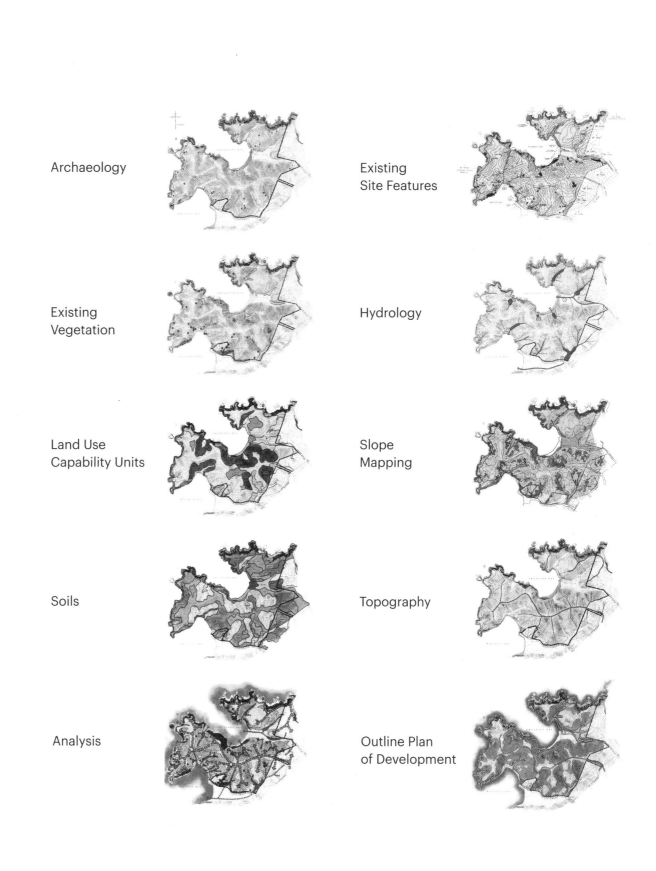

Archaeology

Existing Site Features

Existing Vegetation

Hydrology

Land Use Capability Units

Slope Mapping

Soils

Topography

Analysis

Outline Plan of Development

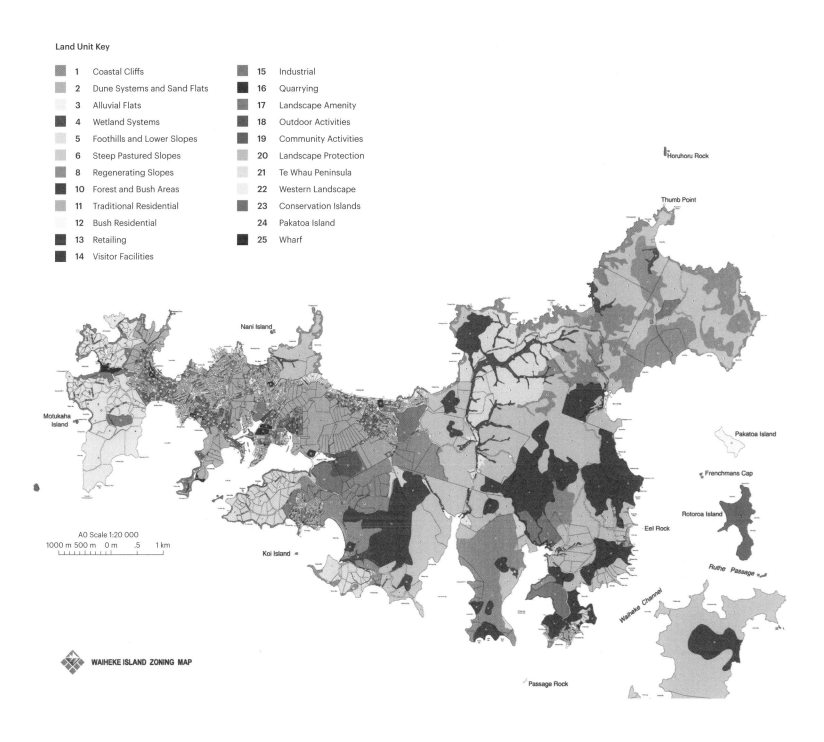

FIGURE 12.6.4 Zoning map of Waiheke Island from Auckland Council District Plan—Operative 2018 (Hauraki Gulf Island Section). © Auckland Council 2018.

Land Unit Key

	1	Coastal Cliffs		15	Industrial
	2	Dune Systems and Sand Flats		16	Quarrying
	3	Alluvial Flats		17	Landscape Amenity
	4	Wetland Systems		18	Outdoor Activities
	5	Foothills and Lower Slopes		19	Community Activities
	6	Steep Pastured Slopes		20	Landscape Protection
	8	Regenerating Slopes		21	Te Whau Peninsula
	10	Forest and Bush Areas		22	Western Landscape
	11	Traditional Residential		23	Conservation Islands
	12	Bush Residential		24	Pakatoa Island
	13	Retailing		25	Wharf
	14	Visitor Facilities			

AO Scale 1:20 000

1000 m 500 m   0 m   .5   1 km

WAIHEKE ISLAND ZONING MAP

FIGURE 12.6.5 View of Western Waiheke (Owhanake project) from southwest looking northwest over Matiatia Bay, January 10, 2008. *With permission, DJScott Associates Ltd.*

Rising Tides

THE NETHERLANDS

Zandmotor

Ter Heijde

2050—An Energetic Odyssey

North Sea

The BIG U

New York, New York, USA

The BIG U was designed as a response to Hurricane Sandy in 2012 to protect Manhattan from subsequent flood events. Sandy killed forty-three people, flooded 90,000 buildings, and caused over $19 billion in damage along the East Coast. The BIG U was one of ten finalist projects developed for the design competition Rebuild by Design, sponsored by the U.S. Department of Housing and Urban Development. It received a portion of the $1 billion in federal funding made available through the competition. The first phase of the BIG U—known as the Lower East Side Coastal Resiliency Project—is now in the construction and documentation phase, and is expected to break ground in 2020.

The BIG U proposes a ribbon of protective berms and barriers around the most physically vulnerable and economically productive parts of Manhattan. It runs from West 54th Street, down around the southern tip of the island, and up to East 40th Street, thus forming a large U shape. It comprises two primary sections: the Lower East Side Coastal Resiliency (ESCR) Project and the Lower Manhattan Coastal Resiliency (LMCR) Project designed to avoid separating communities from the waterfront. It was conceived as a chain of smaller, neighborhood-scale flood protection projects to encourage community involvement in what would ultimately become a massive barrier system around the whole of lower Manhattan.

The BIG U faces many challenges. First, it winds through heavily congested urban territory. Second, some worry that it will promote gentrification by catalyzing an influx of luxury real estate development in one of Manhattan's only remaining vestiges of affordable housing. Third, there are concerns that floodwaters will be deflected into adjacent neighborhoods not covered by the initial phase of the project. Finally, although the design augments flood protection with a mix of social and recreational spaces, the BIG U lacks substantive ecological engagement with the water's edge, suggesting that in such heavily urbanized circumstances, nature-based strategies of protection might be impractical.

FIGURE 13.1.1 The BIG U: Aerial view of Battery Park with integrated flood protection and open space planning. *With permission, The BIG U, 2014. Bjarke Ingels Group (BIG), One Architecture & Urbanism (ONE), Starr Whitehouse, JLP+D, Level Infrastructure, BuroHappold, Arcadis, Green Shield Ecology, AE Consultancy.*

FIGURE 13.1.2 Map of the greater New York region overlaid with projections for the future floodplain. *With permission, The BIG U, 2014. Bjarke Ingels Group (BIG), One Architecture & Urbanism (ONE), Starr Whitehouse, JLP+D, Level Infrastructure, BuroHappold, Arcadis, Green Shield Ecology, AE Consultancy.*

FIGURE 13.1.3 Section of the "bridging berm," a raised public park serving as resilient infrastructure. A floodwall in the berm at the site of a present-day service road would double as a bridgehead. *With permission, The BIG U, 2014. Bjarke Ingels Group (BIG), One Architecture & Urbanism (ONE), Starr Whitehouse, JLP+D, Level Infrastructure, BuroHappold, Arcadis, Green Shield Ecology, AE Consultancy.*

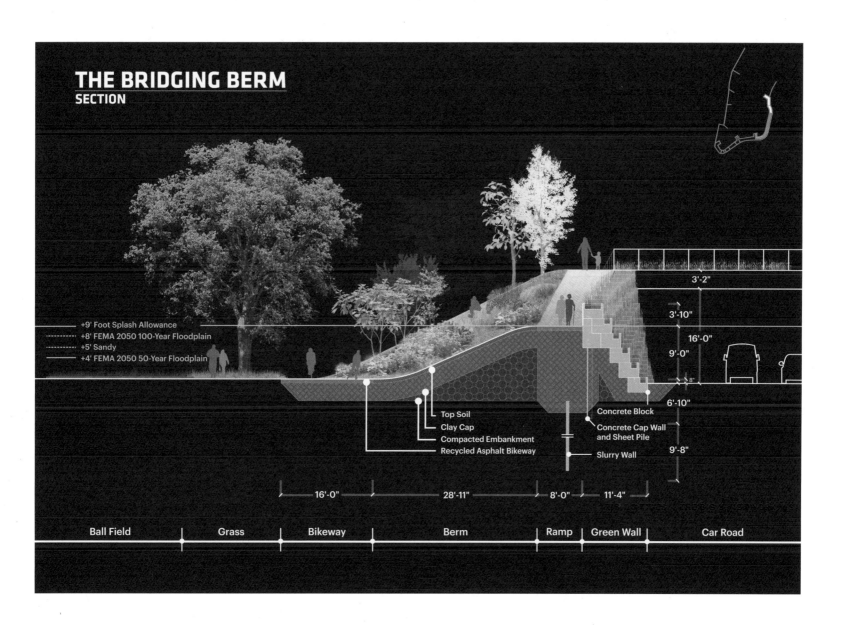

THE BRIDGING BERM
SECTION

+9' Foot Splash Allowance
+8' FEMA 2050 100-Year Floodplain
+5' Sandy
+4' FEMA 2050 50-Year Floodplain

Top Soil
Clay Cap
Compacted Embankment
Recycled Asphalt Bikeway

Concrete Block
Concrete Cap Wall and Sheet Pile
Slurry Wall

3'-2"
3'-10"
16'-0"
9'-0"
8"
6'-10"
9'-8"

16'-0"
28'-11"
8'-0"
11'-4"

Ball Field | Grass | Bikeway | Berm | Ramp | Green Wall | Car Road

FIGURE 13.1.4 Initial exploration of how a simple flood wall can double as "social infrastructure" integrated with recreational programming and public armature. *With permission, The BIG U, 2014. Bjarke Ingels Group (BIG), One Architecture & Urbanism (ONE), Starr Whitehouse, JLP+D, Level Infrastructure, BuroHappold, Arcadis, Green Shield Ecology, AE Consultancy.*

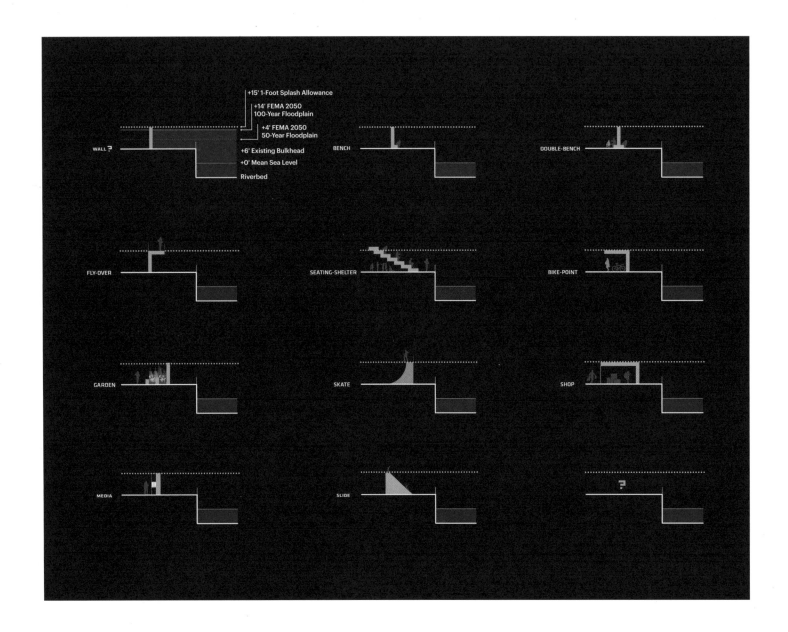

FIGURE 13.1.5 Section of flip-down deployable flood walls attached to the underside of FDR Drive, a coastal highway encircling lower Manhattan. In the "open" position (top), the flood walls would allow for pedestrian access along the waterfront esplanade. In the "storm event" position (bottom), the flood walls would defend adjacent neighborhoods from inundation and flooding caused by storm surge. *With permission, The BIG U, 2014. Bjarke Ingels Group (BIG), One Architecture & Urbanism (ONE), Starr Whitehouse, JLP+D, Level Infrastructure, Buro-Happold, Arcadis, Green Shield Ecology, AE Consultancy.*

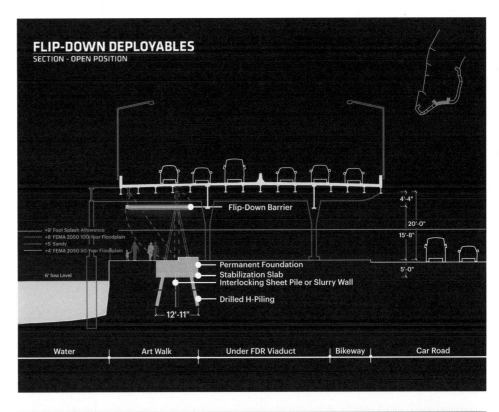

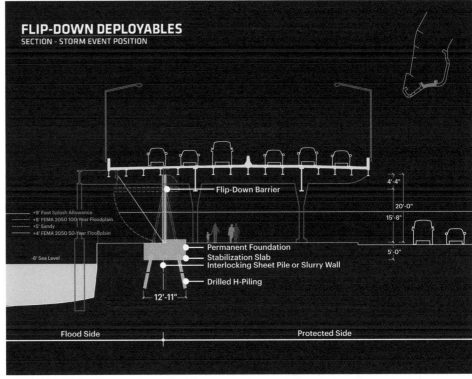

A New Urban Ground

New York, New York, USA

In 2010, the Museum of Modern Art and the P.S. 1 Contemporary Art Center commissioned five works for the exhibition *Rising Currents: Projects for New York's Waterfront*. The catalyst for this was the 2010 book *On the Water: Palisade Bay*, in which Guy Nordenson, Catherine Seavitt, and Adam Yarinsky document their research about the potential impacts of climate change on coastal areas of New York and New Jersey.

The New Urban Ground proposal by the design firms ARO (Architecture Research Office) and DLAND-studio challenges how we engineer the interface between cities and water with a variety of measures from the water's edge to the urban core. Although the proposal would raise the ground level at the water's edge, absent from the plan is an explicit seawall or levee to mitigate sea-level rise and storm surge. A New Urban Ground focuses instead on treatments known as "nature-based solutions" and "ecosystem-based adaptation" in conjunction with new forms of upland gray infrastructure. Moving communications and energy lines into waterproof vaults under sidewalks would protect critical infrastructure and make the streets available to manage upland stormwater.

In the proposal, lower Manhattan's ground surface is repaved with a mesh of cast concrete covering engineered soil, making it porous enough to absorb excess water from heavy rains and periodic storm surge. The surface will also support a community of salt-tolerant plants. In addition, the city is ringed by a series of wetlands in areas where development is all but guaranteed to be overtaken by the sea in the coming centuries. These wetlands would buffer the city from storm surge and create a filter for the stormwater runoff produced by the city. At the southernmost tip of Manhattan, surrounding Battery Park, a series of small barrier islands made from dredge and aggregate-filled geotextile sacks is proposed. The plan would add 2 miles of new shoreline to Manhattan with a new crenelated edge that alternates wetlands with development zones.

With its iconic image of wetlands in the foreground of Manhattan, this project heralds a shift in design thinking from creating a hardened line of resistance to a hybrid landscape and architectural zone of resilience.

FIGURE 13.2.1 Proposed "greening" of lower Manhattan. Parks and wetlands create new ecosystems, facilitating the ecological interconnectivity of the region, improving water quality, and enhancing opportunities for habitat growth. *With permission, DLANDstudio/ Architecture Research Office.*

FIGURE 13.2.2 This series of sections illustrates the various ways the streets, sidewalks, and utility infrastructure can be redesigned to allow more space for absorbing and holding water while improving the quality of public spaces with increased tree canopy, pedestrian areas, and light-rail transit to ease traffic flow. The east side of lower Manhattan (shown far right) is extended with landfill by one block to create an esker parallel to the shoreline, as well as a park and a saltwater marsh. *With permission, DLANDstudio/Architecture Research Office.*

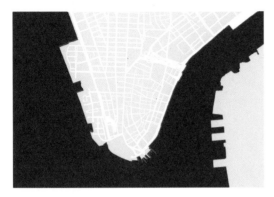

FIGURE 13.2.3 Existing seawall in 2010. *With permission, DLANDstudio/Architecture Research Office.*

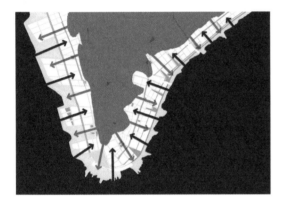

FIGURE 13.2.4 Diagram of water flow in lower Manhattan shows water entering (storm surge) and leaving (stormwater drainage). *With permission, DLANDstudio/Architecture Research Office.*

FIGURE 13.2.5 Porous street system. Up to the reach of a category 2 storm surge, the streets are rebuilt as a connected series of porous conduits that drain stormwater without impeding vehicular circulation. In anticipation of a future in which fewer automobiles are allowed in Manhattan, lighter traffic and less need for parking will allow for more urban green space. *With permission, DLANDstudio/Architecture Research Office.*

⬚ 2100 Category 2 Storm Surge Area		Water	
2100 Saltwater Marsh		2100 Sponge Streets	
2100 Freshwater Marsh		2100 Water Basins	
2100 Street Paths		◀◀◀ Combined Sewer Overflow	

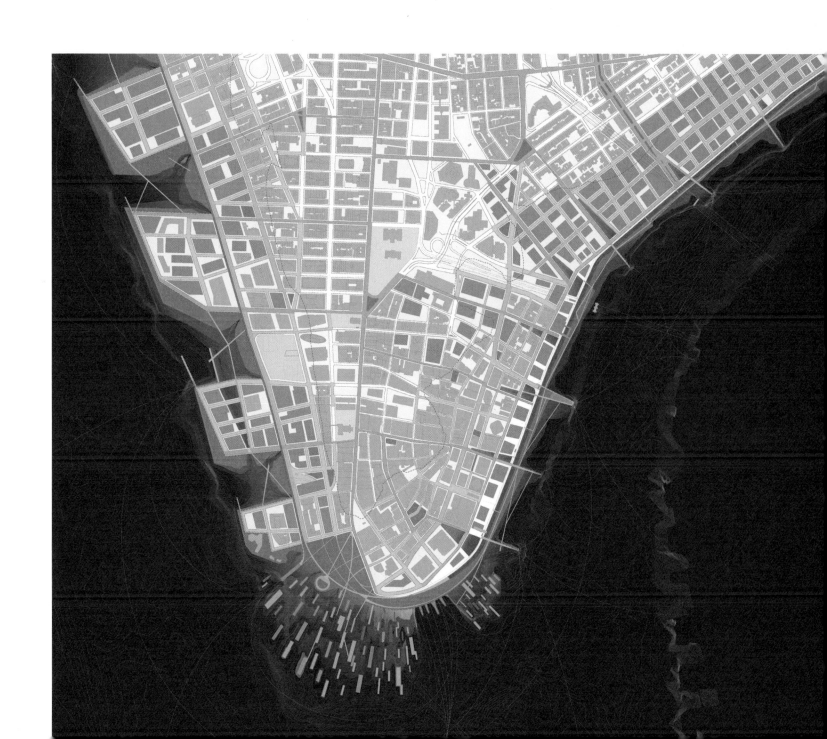

FIGURE 13.2.6 Lower Manhattan in 2100. The tip of Manhattan becomes a large natural habitat extending into the harbor. Dark green areas are upland parks, medium green areas are freshwater wetlands, and light green areas are saltwater marshes. The plan adds 2 miles (3.2 kilometers) of shoreline to Manhattan, and a new, continuous ecosystem encompasses the island's edge. *With permission, DLANDstudio/ Architecture Research Office.*

Fingers of High Ground

Norfolk, Virginia, USA

This proposal, led by Anuradha Mathur and Dilip da Cunha of the University of Pennsylvania, was one of four projects sponsored by the Rockefeller-funded Structures of Coastal Resilience initiative, which asked teams from four universities to propose coastal adaptation strategies in the North Atlantic region. The aim of the initiative was to provide recommendations that would complement the work to be undertaken by the United States Army Corps of Engineers under the Disaster Relief Appropriation Act of 2013, which was enacted in the wake of Hurricane Sandy.

Instead of establishing a division between land and sea that can be reinforced, defended, or retreated from, the Fingers of High Ground project creates a system of high and low grounds open to the rising sea where settlements and coastal ecologies are interlaced. Fingers of High Ground (FHG) are constructed landforms that accommodate rain and tides rather than confront the sea with a barrier.

FHG are inspired by a careful analysis of the morphology of the lower Chesapeake, an estuary where rivers meet sea, creeks meet rivers, and rills meet creeks in webs between protrusions of high ground. As engineered landforms, FHG likewise operate at multiple scales. They are conceived to extend into creeks, rivers, and the sea while reaching inland to connect with each other at higher elevations. Their form and orientation create slopes and gradients of salinity that can support a range of species and accommodate the migration of their habitats as sea levels rise. In the short term, the higher grounds can provide places of refuge for coastal communities, as well as create retention areas for rain, exit routes for people fleeing storms, and protective barriers from storm surges. In the long term, they can be new grounds for human settlement designed with ecologically sensitive and economically productive infrastructure.

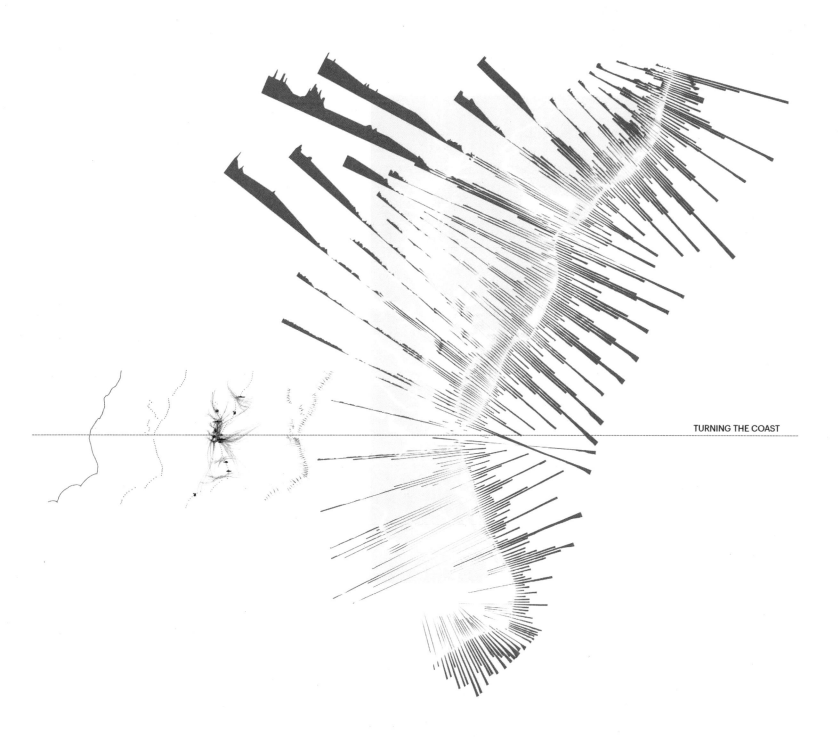

FIGURE 13.3.1 Turning the coast. In the lower Chesapeake, the sea extends deep into the continent, creating dynamic gradients in space and time—gradients activated by animals, plants, and vessels. This coast is not a line; it is a series of points that are open to accommodating the sea. *With permission, Mathur and da Cunha.*

TURNING THE COAST

FIGURE 13.3.2 Fingers of High Ground as found and designed features. The natural and built environment of the lower Chesapeake can be read with an imagination toward developing Fingers of High Ground—places where a meaningful gradient between falling rain and rising tide can be made. The top two images of each column show "found" places; the bottom row are designed features that were inspired by these found places. *With permission, Mathur and da Cunha.*

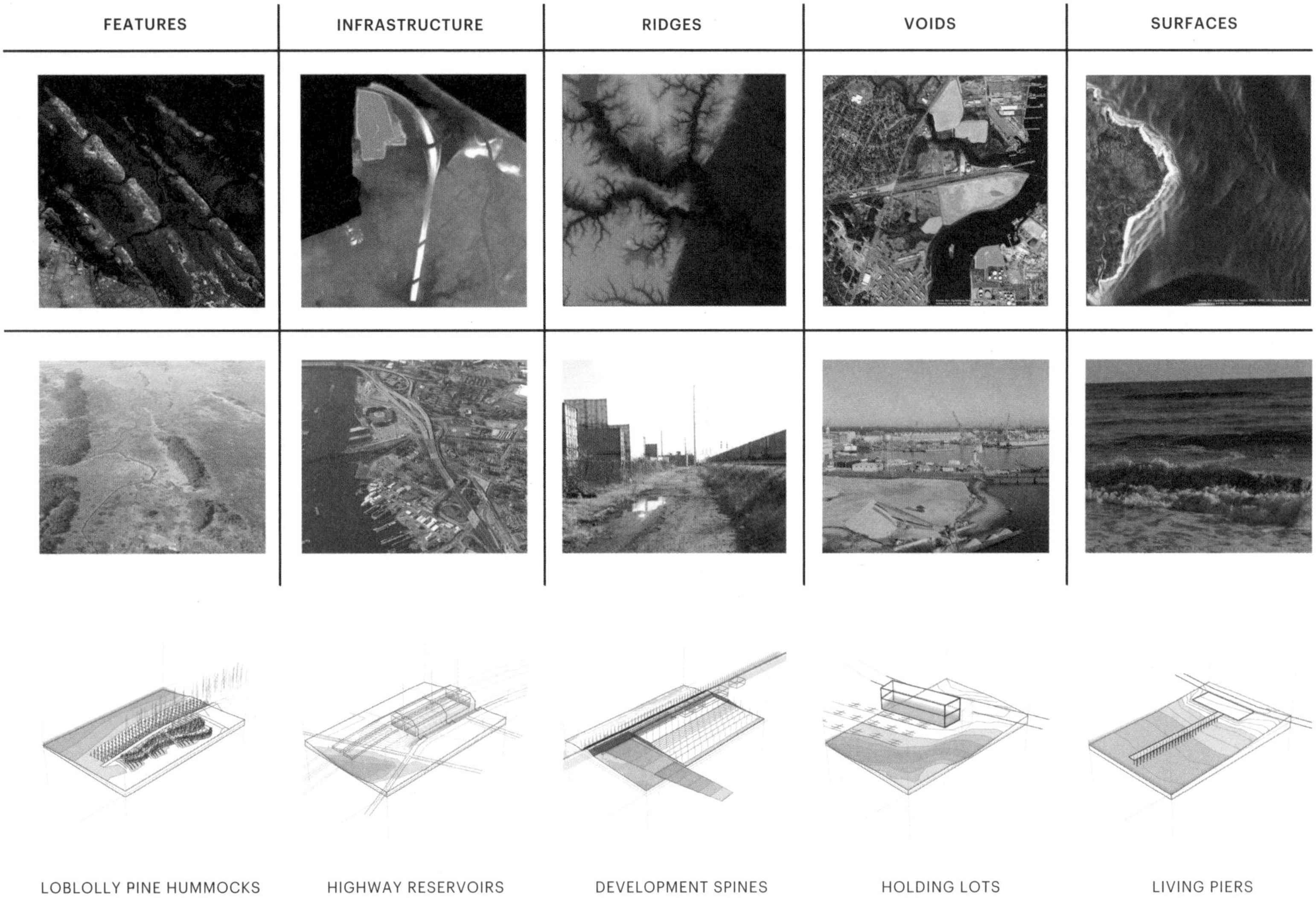

FEATURES	INFRASTRUCTURE	RIDGES	VOIDS	SURFACES
LOBLOLLY PINE HUMMOCKS	HIGHWAY RESERVOIRS	DEVELOPMENT SPINES	HOLDING LOTS	LIVING PIERS

FIGURE 13.3.3 Fingers of High Ground and Associated Low Grounds. FHG are natural features of the lower Chesapeake. They can also be a design feature and the basis of a systemic strategy for building a resilient coast. *With permission, Mathur and da Cunha.*

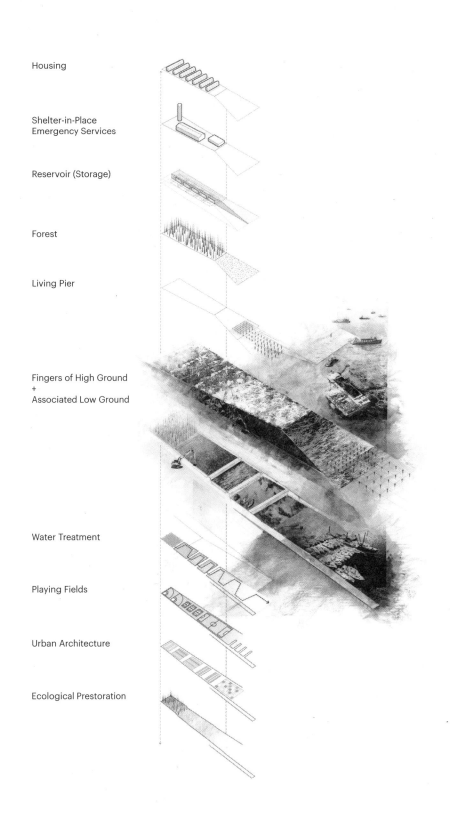

Housing

Shelter-in-Place
Emergency Services

Reservoir (Storage)

Forest

Living Pier

Fingers of High Ground
+
Associated Low Ground

Water Treatment

Playing Fields

Urban Architecture

Ecological Prestoration

FIGURE 13.3.4 Mapping high waters. In the Lambert's Point proposal, the matrices show mapped visualizations of predicted flooding from storm surge for observed climate conditions (1980–1999) and future scenarios in the periods 2020–2029, 2050–2059, and 2080–2099. For each of these time periods, probabilistic flooding is shown for the 1-year (top row), 100-year (second row from top), 500-year (third row), and 2,500-year (bottom row) storm events. Probability of exceedance refers to the percent chance that a storm of a certain size or greater will occur over a specified period of time. *Modeling, Michael Tantala and Julia Chapman for the Structures of Coastal Resilience project. With permission, Mathur and da Cunha.*

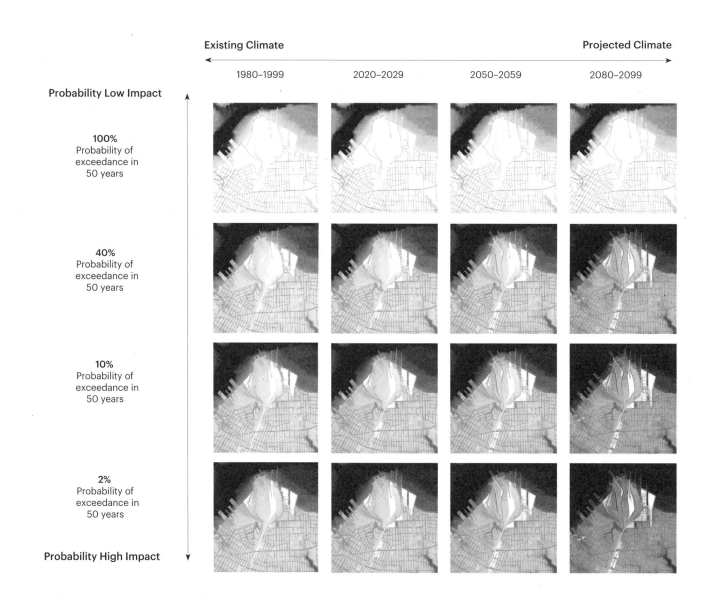

Existing Climate → Projected Climate

| | 1980–1999 | 2020–2029 | 2050–2059 | 2080–2099 |

Probability Low Impact ↑

100% Probability of exceedance in 50 years

40% Probability of exceedance in 50 years

10% Probability of exceedance in 50 years

2% Probability of exceedance in 50 years

Probability High Impact ↓

FIGURE 13.3.5 Various locations within the Chesapeake Bay were studied for their potential to be testing grounds for the Fingers of High Ground concept. These drawings focus on a proposal for Lambert's Point in Norfolk, Virginia. The bottom series shows how the Fingers of High Ground would be built up and extended inland over time. *With permission, Mathur and da Cunha.*

Norfolk Southern Coal Pier #6

Lambert's Point Golf Course (Landfill Site)
Wastewater Treatment Plant
Lambert's Point Rail Yards
Buried Historic Creek
Robertson's Park
Community Garden

Hampton Blvd Underpass / Evac Route
Warehouse District

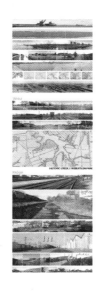

- Commercial
- Institutional
- Industrial
- Light Industry
- Open Space
- Residential

1 Norfolk Southern Coal Pier #6
2 Historic Pier
3 Living Pier
4 Wetland Terraces
5 Lambert's Point Golf Course
6 Wastewater Treatment Facility
7 Sports Platform
8 Wetland Park
9 Overflow Channel
10 Berm Walk
11 Rail Tracks/Biofilter
12 Urban Forest
13 Warehouse Redevelopment
14 Water Reservoir
15 Shelter-in-Place
16 Mixed-Use Development
17 Forest + Biofilter
18 Water Reservoirs
19 Public Amenities

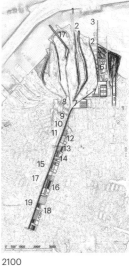

2014

2025

2050

2100

Zandmotor

Ter Heijde, The Netherlands

Zandmotor (Sand Motor in English) is a novel beach replenishment program completed in the Netherlands in 2011. The project is located between Kijkduin and Ter Heijde, just south of The Hague and downriver from the city of Rotterdam.

Much of the Dutch coastline has retreated inland over the past millennium owing to erosion from wind and ocean currents. Every five years since 1990, sand was dredged from the North Sea to rebuild beaches and dunes. In addition, the coastline faces new threats of sea-level rise and intense weather patterns due to climate change. To make the dredging process more efficient, Marcel Stive, professor of coastal engineering at Delft University of Technology, dreamed up the idea of a beach nourishment program that uses the natural power of waves, currents, and wind to redistribute sand slowly and continuously.

The idea behind Zandmotor is quite simple: dredge boats moved 21.5 million cubic meters (28.2 million cubic yards) of sand from the floor of the North Sea into a giant bent peninsula of sand that is 2 kilometers (1.2 miles) wide at its base and 1 kilometer (0.6 miles) in length. The design of this massive sandbar was based on careful calculations of wind, waves, and currents. The peninsula is expected to continue replenishing local beaches and dunes through the 2030s and will have the added benefit of eliminating the disturbance of the sea floor caused by constant dredging.

In addition to the geomorphological goals of the project, the coalition involved in Zandmotor was concerned with ensuring coastal safety, creating areas for recreation and habitat, and above all, improving knowledge about the dynamics of coastal management. The area impacted by Zandmotor is currently the best monitored and most studied section of beach in the world.

FIGURE 13.4.1 Zandmotor, April 11, 2011. *Photo, Joop van Houdt. With permission, Ministry of Infrastructure and Water Management and Province of South Holland.*

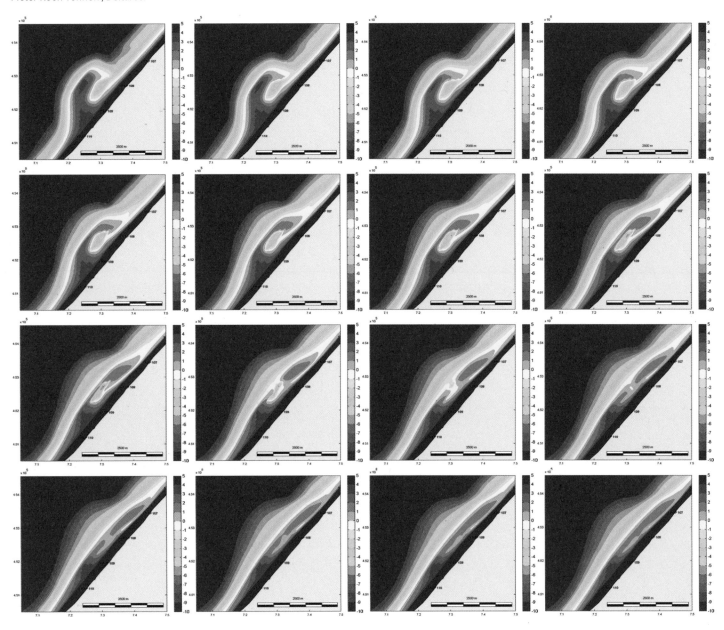

FIGURE 13.4.2 Simulation of shoreline morphology over a twenty-year period. Colors show elevation (darkest red is highest, darkest blue is lowest).*With permission, Pieter Koen Tonnon /Deltares.*

FIGURE 13.4.3 Zandmotor, October 13, 2011. *Photo, Joop van Houdt. With permission, Ministry of Infrastructure and Water Management and Province of South Holland.*

FIGURE 13.4.4 Zandmotor work begins, March 3, 2011.
© Harry Reeken. With permission, Ministry of Infrastructure
and Water Management and Province of South Holland.

FIGURE 13.4.5 Zandmotor, July 19, 2016. *Photo, Jurriaan Brobbel. With permission, Ministry of Infrastructure and Water Management and Province of South Holland.*

2050—An Energetic Odyssey

North Sea, The Netherlands

2050—An Energetic Odyssey, an immersive installation consisting primarily of a thirteen-minute video with maps, diagrams, and drawings, asks the question: What would it look like if the Netherlands and its neighbors were to switch to renewable energy production at a large enough scale to meet the Paris 2015 carbon emissions goals? 2010—An Energetic Odyssey (the Odyssey) is not a plan; it is a narrative that recasts the landscape architect as provocateur. It uses techniques of data visualization to make complicated issues understandable to a broad, policy-oriented constituency.

The Odyssey envisions 25,000 wind turbines with a net coverage of 57,000 square kilometers (22,000 square miles) that would enable 75 percent of the North Sea countries' current energy to be converted to renewable energy by 2050. Most of these turbines would be clustered on wind farms off the coastline of the North Sea countries. There is, however, one no-table exception: a proposed cluster of wind farms on Dogger Bank, an ecologically vital sandbank submerged more than 50 meters (approximately 55 yards) below the water's surface in the middle of the North Sea. To produce the necessary energy, a construction island and massive cluster of wind farms would need to be placed on Dogger Bank.

Therefore, the proposed construction method would minimize impacts on sea mammal navigation and avoid conflict with the migratory pathways of birds. The zone closest to the coast, which birds use for orientation, would be left untouched wherever possible, and wind turbines could be temporarily taken out of operation if sensors detected birds approaching. In addition, the wind farm locations could be combined with new marine reserves. Finally, the visual impact of the wind farms would be mitigated by siting the farms more than 12 miles out from the coast so that the Earth's curvature would reduce visability.

FIGURE 13.5.1 Carbon dioxide map at one point in time in the North Sea region. Red shows highest concentrations of the gas. © *International Architecture Biennale Rotterdam, 2016.*

FIGURE 13.5.2 The Princess Amalia offshore wind farm. The wind farm consists of sixty wind turbines and is located in block Q7 of the Dutch continental shelf, 23 kilometers (14 miles) from shore. © *Siebe Swart, 2013.*

FIGURE 13.5.3 Selected details (right, and opposite) from a section drawing showing the sizes of various system components. © *International Architecture Biennale Rotterdam, 2016.*

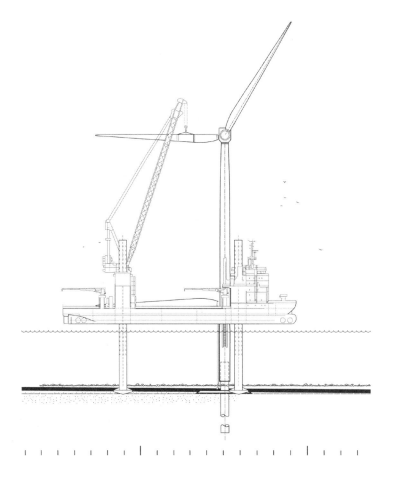

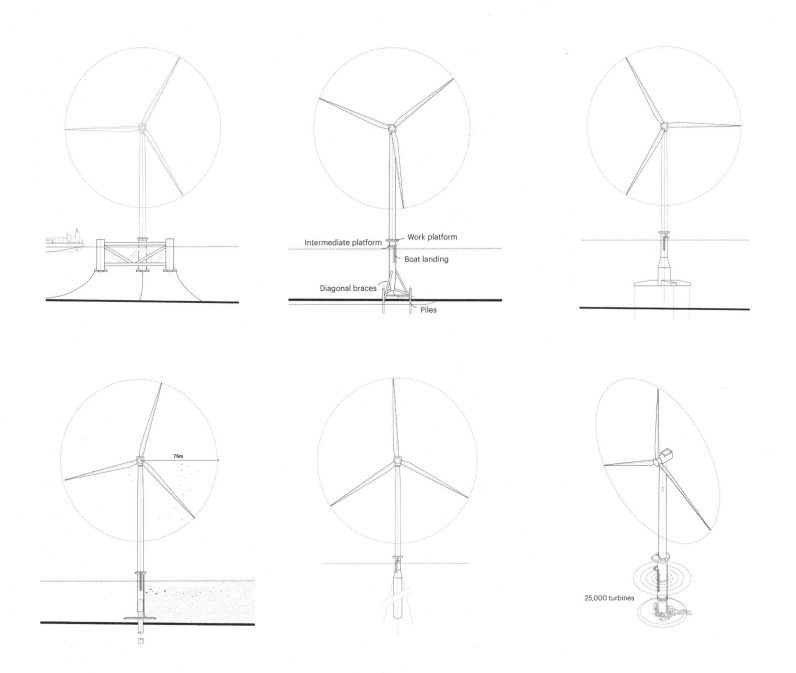

Intermediate platform
Work platform
Boat landing
Diagonal braces
Piles

76m

25,000 turbines

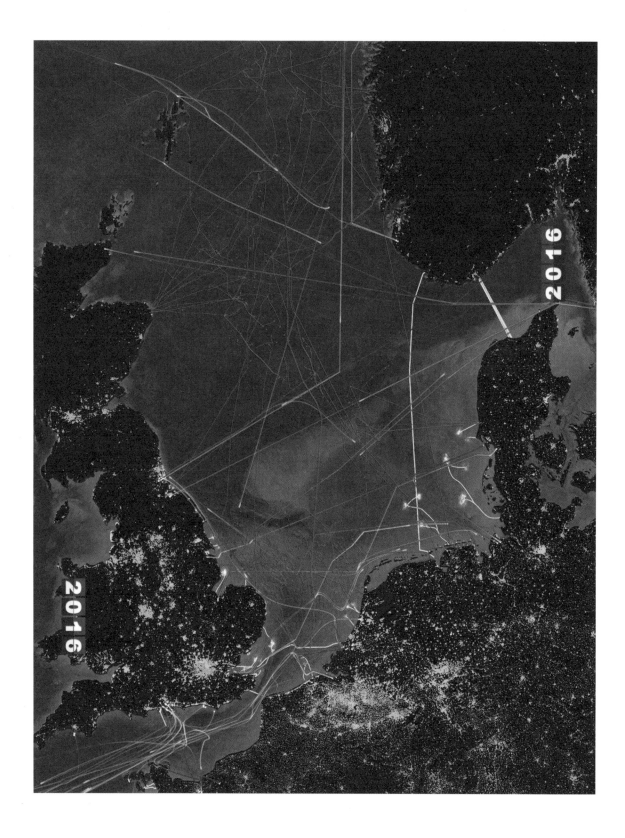

FIGURE 13.5.4 Spatial occupation of the North Sea, including shipping routes (blue lines), oil and gas rigs (red lines and dots), fishing areas, and international crossings (yellow lines).
© *International Architecture Biennale Rotterdam, 2016.*

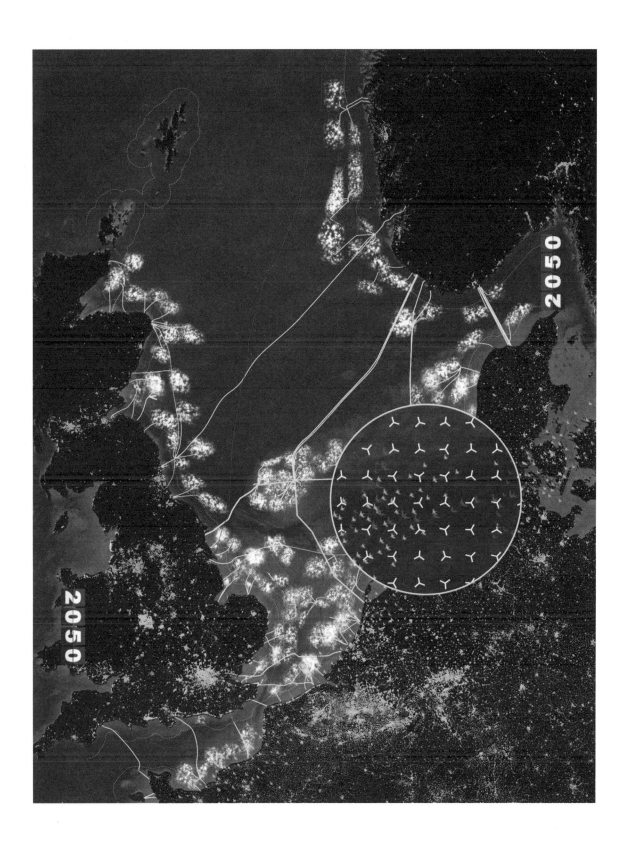

FIGURE 13.5.5 Projection of wind farm locations in 2050 (white areas). © *International Architecture Biennale Rotterdam, 2016.*

Fresh Waters

THE NETHERLANDS

Room for the River

CHINA

Weishan Wetland Park
Jining

Healthy Port Futures

Great Lakes Region, USA

The environmental quality of one of the world's largest inland water bodies—the Great Lakes of North America—is the focus of Healthy Port Futures. The project stems from a series of events held in 2015 under the rubric of DredgeFest Great Lakes by Dredge Research Collaborative. DredgeFest's symposiums, exhibitions, and speculative design workshops address the cultural and industrial ecologies associated with sediment management along the coasts of the United States. The aim is to reimagine mud and sediment as resources, rather than treating them as waste or by-products.

Similarly, Healthy Port Futures focuses on sediment management in small, working ports around the Great Lakes. Typically, the port authorities and the United States Army Corps of Engineers (USACE) dredge sediment to maintain shipping channels and dump or dispose of the material as a waste product. The Healthy Port Futures project improves on this process in two ways: it uses dredged material in an ecologically and socially constructive manner to create new landscapes, such as wetlands and recreational areas; and it reduces sediment buildup in shipping channels by using passive and adaptable sediment management systems to redirect sediment flow.

After a phase of analysis, the Healthy Port Futures project is now working at two scales. Regionally, the project is conducting outreach, surveys, and research in order to leverage sediment management for the benefit of the larger Great Lakes Basin. Locally, the project is moving toward implementing a pilot project in Ashtabula, Ohio, where the USACE and the state of Ohio are collaborating to test the potential of sediment management in generating high-quality wetland habitats suited to local environmental conditions. The idea is to contain sediment and leakage in order to restore its flow and deposition patterns within the longshore system. Construction is planned for 2019–20, and if it is successful, ideas from the process will be used in additional ports of the Great Lakes.

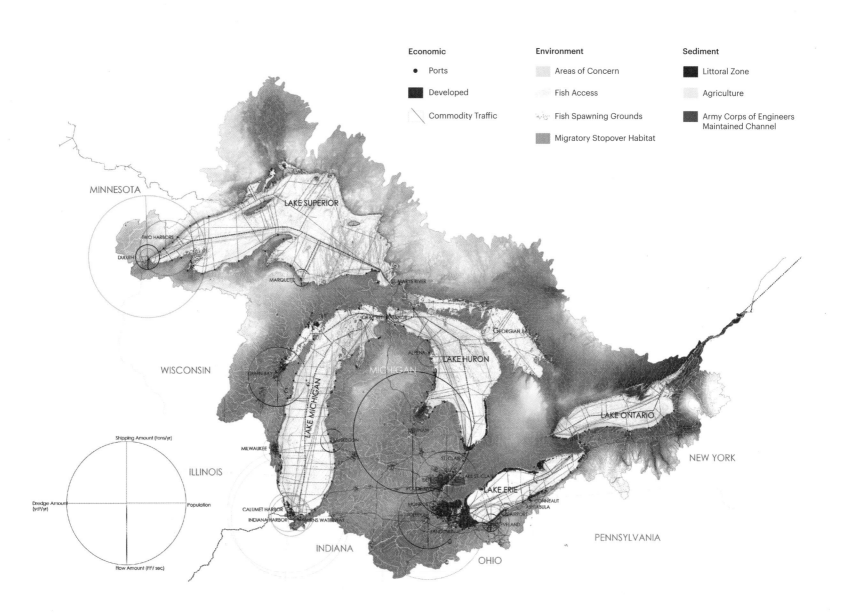

FIGURE 14.1.1 Great Lakes sediment constituencies. This map shows the vast array of actors affected by sediment within the Great Lakes Basin. Economic and environmental considerations create challenges and have led to regional partnerships in sediment management. *With permission, Healthy Port Futures: Sean Burkholder, Brian Davis, and Theresa Ruswick.*

Economic
- Ports
- Developed
- Commodity Traffic

Environment
- Areas of Concern
- Fish Access
- Fish Spawning Grounds
- Migratory Stopover Habitat

Sediment
- Littoral Zone
- Agriculture
- Army Corps of Engineers Maintained Channel

FIGURE 14.1.2 High-performance wetlands, Ashtabula, a small industrial port in northeastern Ohio. In many cases the creation of high-functioning coastal habitat is the highest and best use of dredged or suspended sediment. In Ashtabula, the design of this type of wetland is under way, created from dredged sediment that is then made more ecologically complex through management with wave energy and water currents. *With permission, Healthy Port Futures: Sean Burkholder, Brian Davis, and Theresa Ruswick.*

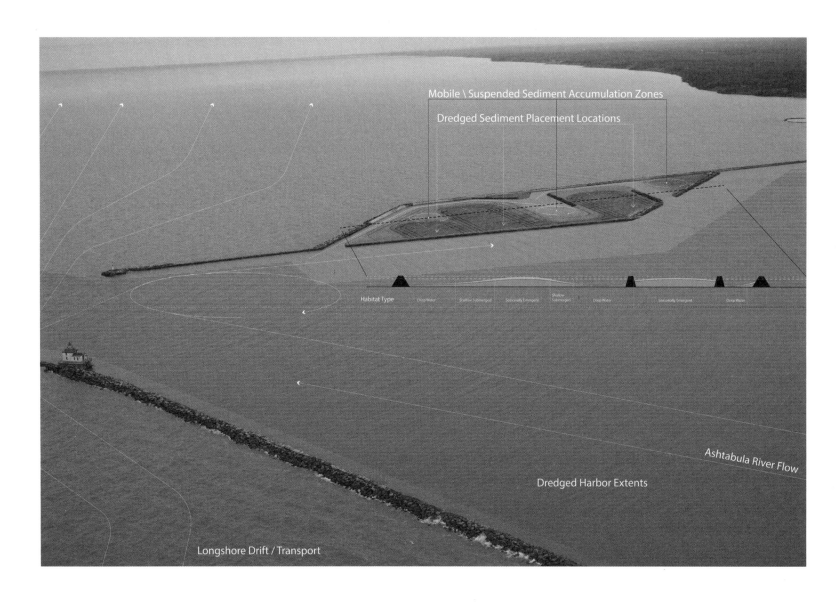

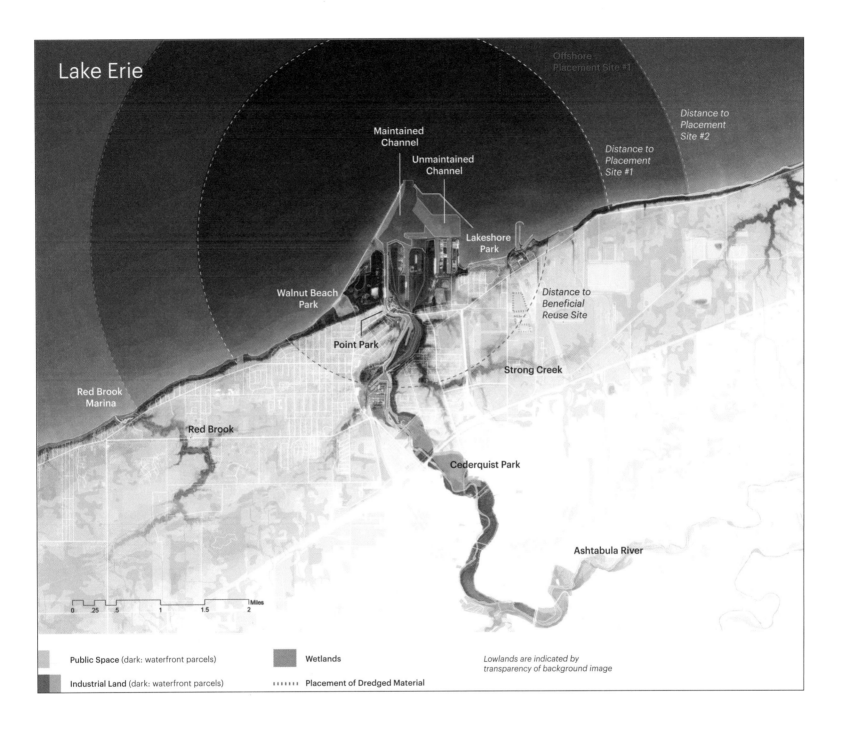

Lake Erie

Offshore Placement Site #1

Distance to Placement Site #2

Distance to Placement Site #1

Maintained Channel

Unmaintained Channel

Lakeshore Park

Distance to Beneficial Reuse Site

Walnut Beach Park

Point Park

Strong Creek

Red Brook Marina

Red Brook

Cederquist Park

Ashtabula River

Miles
0   .25   .5   1   1.5   2

Public Space (dark: waterfront parcels)

Wetlands

Lowlands are indicated by transparency of background image

Industrial Land (dark: waterfront parcels)

Placement of Dredged Material

FIGURE 14.1.3 Ashtabula sediment constituencies. This image shows the collection of actors and systems that are tied to sediment and sediment management in the Ashtabula region. Maps such as this show the long-term regional implications of sediment; its management is not a one-time issue to be addressed and forgotten. *With permission, Healthy Port Futures: Sean Burkholder, Brian Davis, and Theresa Ruswick.*

FIGURE 14.1.4 Model integration. The use of physical and digital models is linked in a system that provides rapid prototype development and testing. The effects that different structural mound configurations have on mobile sediment (shown in the physical model on the right) are vetted before being incorporated into more complex digital models. The digital simulation (left) shows the varying water velocities (blue, lower; red, higher) and bedform deformation that occur with different obstructions. *With permission, Healthy Port Futures: Sean Burkholder, Brian Davis, Matt Moffitt, and Theresa Ruswick.*

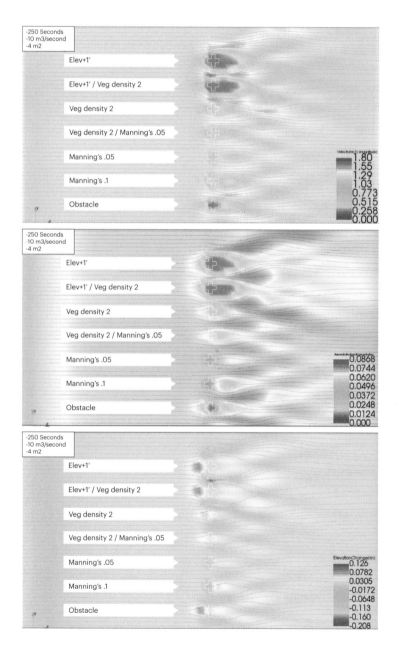

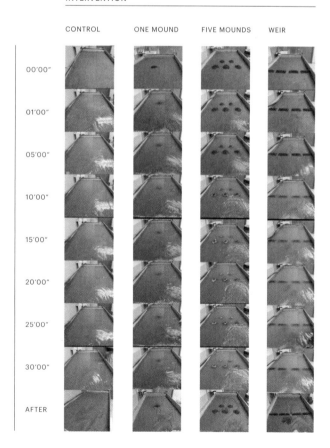

FIGURE 14.1.5 Context-calibrated proposals. Using principles derived from modeled experiments, in-place proposals can begin to illuminate the implications of particular design outcomes in a specific context. In this image, sediment-collecting devices are organized in an area with degraded habitat and a need for waterfront public space. *With permission, Healthy Port Futures: Sean Burkholder, Brian Davis, Matt Moffitt, and Theresa Ruswick.*

- **Rip Rap "Obstacles"** (approx. 5–9 cu/y per)

  Activated Pedestrian Access

  Site Extents

Future Wetland Restoration (*Inorganic suspended solids removed from site start to site end 6–9%*)

Room for the River

The Netherlands

The modern Dutch program of national water management began after the coastal flood of January 1953, when major dikes were breached in eighty-nine places and over 1,800 people were killed. The plan that arose in the wake of this tragedy promoted engineering of numerous dams and dikes in a massive nationwide project that was to take twenty-five years to complete. The environmental movement of the 1970s and 1980s, however, led to a new water management strategy that promoted "ecology and economy in balance," and that initiated the development of riverine habitats outside the dikes. After a period of relative calm, the country experienced major flood events again in 1993 and 1995, at which time the government made flood protection a top priority, paying special attention to climate change implications. At the turn of the 21st century, the idea of giving more room to the rivers first gained traction.

A 2002 study determined that the maximum carrying capacity of the Rhine to avoid overflowing the dikes was 15,000 cubic meters per second (mps); the overarching goal for the Room for the River project was to increase that capacity to 16,000 cubic mps. The Rijkwaterstaat (an executvie agency of the Ministry of Infrastructure and Water Management of the Netherlands) defined nine broad strategies that could be deployed to increase river capacity: dike improvement, dike relocation, flood channels, water storage, groyne lowering, depoldering, floodplain excavation, riverbed excavation, and removal of obstacles.

Room for the River is not a single project but a collection of thirty-four projects located along rivers throughout the Netherlands. Planned and constructed between 2007 and 2015 at a cost of 2.3 billion euros, each project has two goals. The first goal was to develop flood abatement strategies in order to safely increase the carrying capacity of the major Dutch rivers—the Waal, the Nederrijn/Lek, and the IJssel—all of which flow out of the Rhine River near the German border. The second goal, to create a more attractive river landscape, was given equal weight, but the deliverables were much harder to define.

Dirk Sijmons, the Dutch government's advisor on landscape issues, was charged with assembling a team of people to ensure that the projects all contributed to the "spatial quality" of their regions. This commitment to the improvement of local quality of life at such a large scale is what sets Room for the River apart from other forward-thinking projects in water management.

FIGURE 14.2.1 IJssel Delta in 2017. Reevediep bypass as it merges with Drontermeer Lake, one of the IJssel Delta projects affecting the IJssel River. *With permission, Rijkswaterstaat.*

FIGURE 14.2.2 The city of Nijmegen on the Waal River during high water levels before construction of the bypass. © *Thea van den Heuvel /DAPh.*

FIGURE 14.2.3 Same view showing the river park under construction. © *Johan Roerink-Aeropicture.*

FIGURE 14.2.4 *Noordwaard polder, November 13, 2015. With permission, Rijkswaterstaat.*

FIGURE 14.2.5 Map of Room for the River project locations along the major rivers, the Netherlands. *With permission, Ministry of Infrastructure and Water Management/ Rijkswaterstaat. https:// www.ruimtevoorderivier.nl /english/.*

Los Angeles River Master Plan

California, USA

The Los Angeles River was channelized after several destructive floods in the nineteenth and early- to mid-twentieth centuries. Between 1938 and 1960, this formerly meandering waterway was engineered into a 51-mile long concrete channel in an attempt to convey rainwater flow from the nearby mountains to the ocean. Though the river often runs dry, in 2010, the Environmental Protection Agency declared the river to be navigable, thereby subjecting it to the rules and regulations mandated in 1977 by the Clean Water Act. The LA River Master Plan update by the firms OLIN and Gehry Partners is the most recent, and perhaps most promising, manifestation of many years' struggle to breathe life into the river.

The master plan builds on more than twenty years of advocacy by Los Angeles landscape architect Mia Lehrer, local planning agencies, the Army Corps of Engineers, and others—all of whom have expressed a different vision for the future of the river. OLIN and Gehry began the process of updating the 1996 and 2007 master plans in 2015; conducting new research on the ecological and social conditions of the river (including demographics of adjacent neighborhoods and current uses of the river); and mapping more than 1,500 individual projects associated with the river, ranging from stormwater conveyance and water distribution to parks, green streets, and urban agriculture.

The river corridor passes through more than a dozen cities. The master plan addresses aspects of water use in various contexts: safety—protection from flooding, loss of life, and property; sustainability—catching, cleaning, and using water in reservoirs, wetlands, and aquifers; creating habitat for a range of species; and human use for the health of the region and populace. The corridor offers opportunities for recreation, exercise, and improving the health of tens of thousands of people. The master plan proposes developing habitat for resident and migratory birds, beneficial insects, terrestrial animals, and aquatic species wherever compatible with adjacent communities in created wetlands and portions of the river where functionally ecological conditions can be established or retained. Finally, this extensive territory of public land offers an opportunity to connect communities separated from each other for decades with new and much-needed cultural facilities for all of the arts.

FIGURE 14.3.1 Edward Koehn (left), chief of flood control design for the Los Angeles district, explains to colleagues the water action in plywood model demonstration of the proposed channel improvements for the Los Angeles River, 1948. *With permission, Los Angeles Herald Examiner Photo Collection/Los Angeles Public Library.*

FIGURE 14.3.2 Los Angeles River, aerial view of the 1938 flood and Victory Blvd. *United States Army Corps of Engineers, Report on Engineering Aspects, Flood of March 1938 (Los Angeles: U.S. Engineer Office, 1938).*

FIGURE 14.3.3 The Los Angeles River watershed. The Los Angeles River drains an area of 827 square miles (2,142 square kilometers) and flows 51 miles (82 kilometers) from its confluence to its mouth at Long Beach. *With permission, OLIN, for Los Angeles County Public Works, LA River Master Plan.*

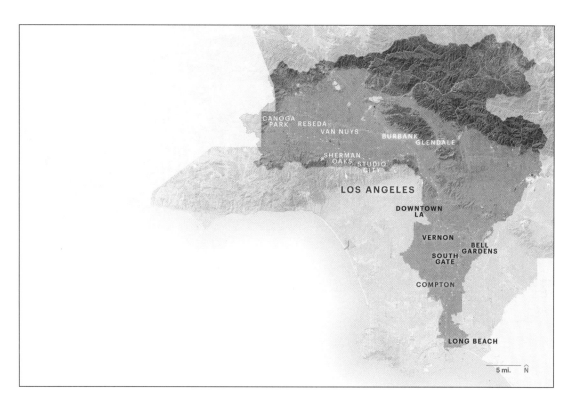

FIGURE 14.3.4 Aerial view, facing south, of the Los Angeles River at the Artesia Freeway overpass. June 12, 2003. North Long Beach. © *Lane Barden.*

FIGURE 14.3.5 Views along the Los Angeles River. Though fully channelized, existing conditions along the river include both concrete and vegetated soft bottom sections as well as a tidal estuary at the mouth. *With permission, OLIN.*

River Mile 51: Canoga Park

River Mile 43: Sepulveda Basin

River Mile 39: Studio City

River Mile 28: Atwater Village

River Mile 24: Elysian Park

River Mile 22: Downtown Los Angeles

River Mile 12: South Gate

River Mile 2: Long Beach

River Mile 0: River Mouth

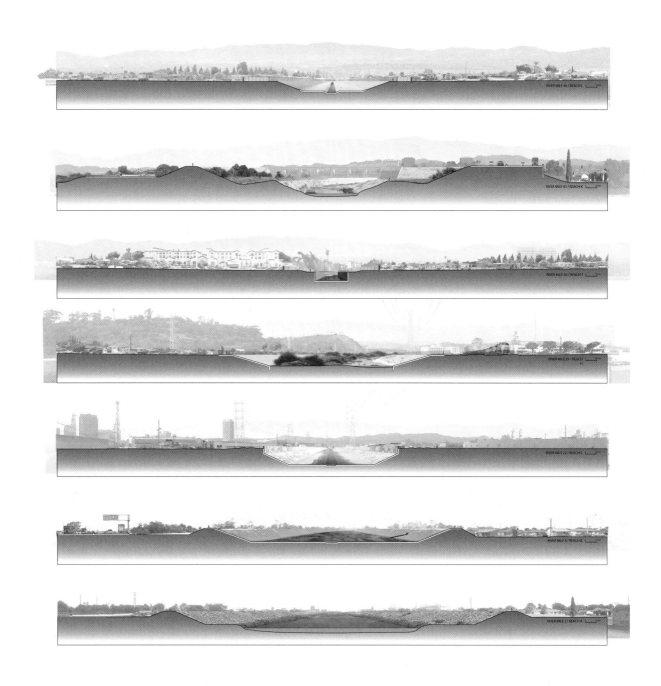

FIGURE 14.3.6 Structure of the Los Angeles River channel. The river varies in width, shape, and material, responding to the physiography and hydrology of its context. *With permission, OLIN.*

FIGURE 14.3.7 The California Floristic Province is one of five Mediterranean global hotspots. The Los Angeles River basin sits in one of the world's few Mediterranean climate zones, which host 20 percent of the world's plant species. The area is home to 3,500 plant species, over half of which are endemic. *With permission, OLIN, for Los Angeles County Public Works, LA River Master Plan.*

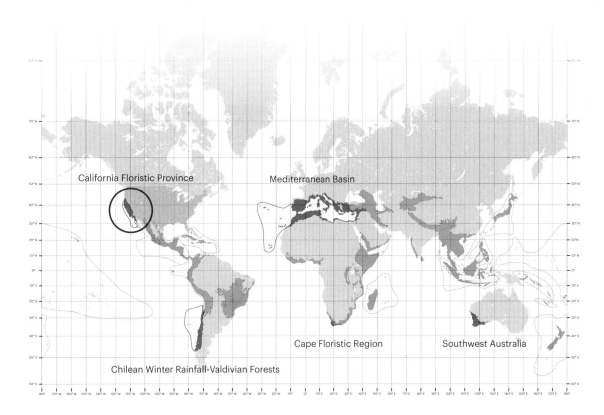

Source: Conservation International, Biodiversity Hotspots Revisited, 2004.

FIGURE 14.3.8 Species observations within 1 mile (1.6 kilometers) of the Los Angeles River. Analysis of iNaturalist community science observations is one indicator of ecosystems that are present along the length of the Los Angeles River. *With permission, OLIN, for Los Angeles County Public Works, LA River Master Plan.*

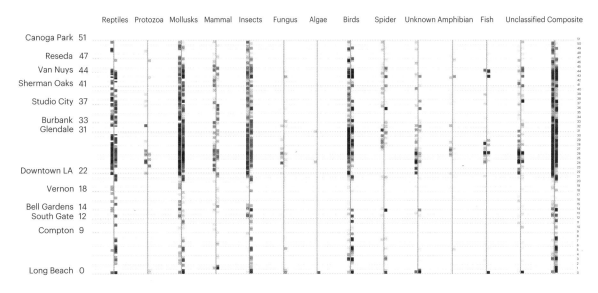

Source: iNaturalist.org, accessed 18 April 2018.

Weishan Wetland Park

Jining, China

The first phase of the Weishan Wetland Park in the town of Jining in China's Shandong Province was completed in 2013. The impetus for this 39-square-kilometer (15-square-mile) park was the adjacent development of a new urban center just south of the existing city of Weishan, near the southeastern edge of the expansive Nansi Lake (also called Weishan Lake). This new southern town will eventually have 50,000 residents in an area that was previously agricultural. The Weishan Wetland Park will filter polluted water from the future development, and it is hoped that it will be the centerpiece of a larger program of nature-based tourism in the region. The proximity to Nansi Lake, one of the country's largest and most polluted lakes, makes the park's purification function especially important, as the lake is a part of China's ambitious, though ecologically and socially disruptive, South-North Water Diversion Project, which redirects fresh water from the Yangtze River in the south to the more arid Yellow River basin in the north.

The master plan is structured around the creation of five zones: core protection, natural restoration, limited human activity, development, and a village community. Various types of wetland were restored or created from scratch, with the intention of attracting diverse species of waterfowl and enticing tourists to the park. There is some access to the park by vehicle, but much of the sightseeing can be done only on elevated pedestrian walkways built with local recycled wood and steel.

Although the water filtration and purification techniques used are not novel in the field of landscape architecture, their scale and integration into the new town mark a significant shift in thinking about water, both within the Shandong Province and in China as a whole. As of 2015, 1.3 million hectares (3.2 million acres) of new wetland park had been created and 130,000 hectares (321,000 acres) of wetland had been restored throughout the province.

China is in the process of rethinking its water infrastructure in the face of rapid urbanization and climate change. The national government's renowned "sponge cities" initiative in 2015 funded the development of ponds, filtration pools, and permeable roads and public spaces in sixteen cities to improve flood and drought resilience.

FIGURE 14.4.1 Boardwalk through the Weishan Wetland Park. *With permission, AECOM.*

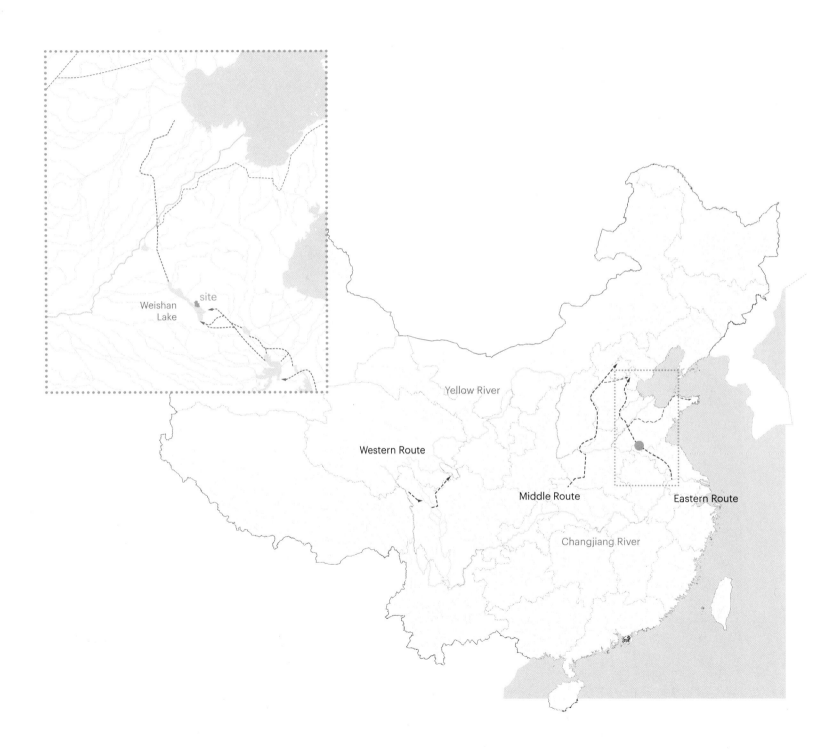

FIGURE 14.4.2 South-North Water Diversion Project (bottom); Eastern Route Project (inset). *With permission, AECOM.*

Weishan Lake

site

Yellow River

Western Route

Middle Route

Eastern Route

Changjiang River

FIGURE 14.4.3 The organic revetment is made of wicker and poplar timber piles harvested on-site. Wicker woven around the timber piles will sprout in the spring, consolidating and stabilizing the soil around them. *With permission, AECOM.*

FIGURE 14.4.4 Tiering and diverse plantings create seasonal interest and opportunities for outdoor science education. *With permission, AECOM.*

GreenPlan Philadelphia

Pennsylvania, USA

In 2012, the city of Philadelphia entered into an agreement with the Environmental Protection Agency (EPA)—the result of the enforcement of the Clean Water Act that empowers the EPA to regulate combined sewer overflows (CSOs) when they damage the health of urban streams and water sources. Philadelphia was not the first city to enter into such an agreement. CSO issues are common in communities throughout the postindustrial Northeast, where aging stormwater infrastructure and a proliferation of impervious surfaces can overwhelm municipal water utilities. But what set Philadelphia's response apart from its predecessors' was its focus on addressing the city's CSO problem by investing in a distributed network of green infrastructure. This approach was engendered by the city's strong culture of community organizing by environmental nonprofits and the precedent of Anne Whiston Spirn's work with the Mill Creek community in West Philadelphia.

In 2006, GreenPlan Philadelphia was unveiled—a comprehensive vision for open space in Philadelphia that focused on green infrastructure. The development of GreenPlan Philadelphia included WRT, LLC, as lead consultants, the firm that had been originally established as Wallace McHarg Roberts & Todd in the 1960s.

GreenPlan Philadelphia became part of a multiyear planning process that led the city to adopt a variety of green infrastructure-driven reforms to its comprehensive plan, its water utility's operations, and its municipal sustainability office. These efforts produced two additional initiatives: GreenWorks, the strategic plan to establish and grow Philadelphia's Office of Sustainability; and the Green Cities, Clean Waters Initiative, a series of pricing and planning reforms within the large, innovative Philadelphia Water Department. Led by a progressive mayor, Michael Nutter, GreenPlan Philadelphia became a vehicle for transforming the city's vast network of vacant land into one of the nation's most robust networks of urban green infrastructure.

FIGURE 14.5.1 Stormwater Management Tools Opportunities Map showing the areas of the city that use combined and separate sewer systems. *With permission, WRT, LLC.*

STORMWATER MANAGEMENT TOOLS OPPORTUNITIES

- Currently Impervious Surfaces
- Combined Sewer Service Areas
- Separate Sewer Service Areas

FIGURE 14.5.2 Combined sewer under construction in bed of Aramingo Canal, Philadelphia, Pennsylvania, June 7, 1900. *With permission, Philadelphia Water Department Historical Collection.*

FIGURE 14.5.3 The locations of Philadelphia's current green infrastructure projects. *With permission, WRT, LLC.*

○ Green Streets
○ Green Schoolyards
○ Parks and Recreation Spaces
○ Trails

FIGURE 14.5.4 Philadelphia has an abundance of vacant land that can be used as part of the city's stormwater management. *With permission, WRT, LLC.*

VACANCY

Vacant Structures

Vacant Land

FIGURE 14.5.5 Various stormwater management practices used by the Philadelphia Water Department. *Drawing, WRT, LLC. With permission, Philadelphia Water Department.*

Mid-Block Stormwater Bumpout

Stormwater Planter

Corner Stormwater Bumpout

Rain Garden

Stormwater Basin

Wetland

Stormwater Tree Trench

Green Roof

Control Structure

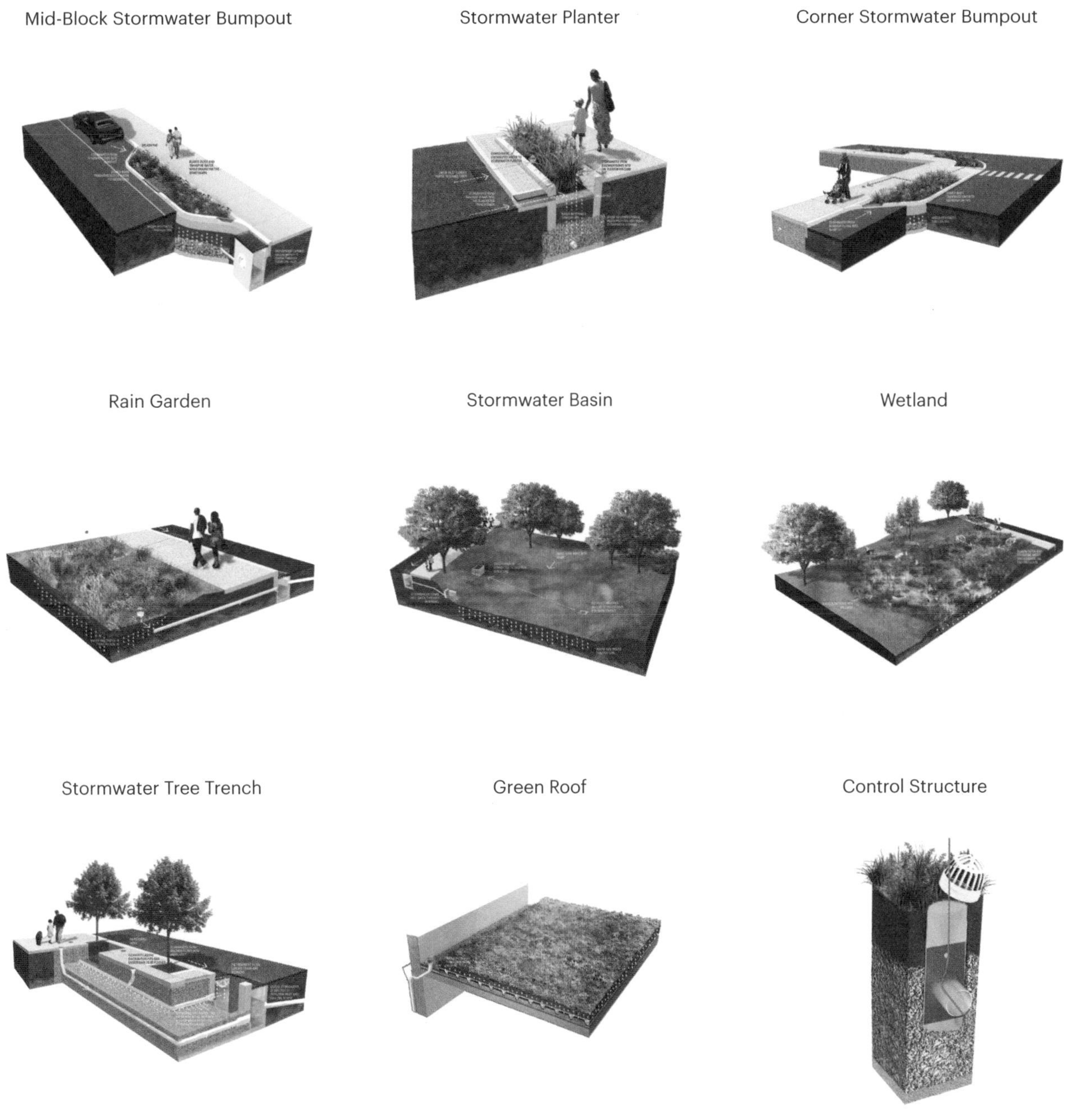

Toxic Lands

Queen Elizabeth Olympic Park
London

Emscher Landscape Park

Ruhr Valley, Germany

The International Building Exhibition Emscher Park (in German, Internationale Bauausstellung or IBA), which ran from 1989 to 1999, generated important economic and environmental ideas for renewal of the formerly industrial Ruhrgebiet (Ruhr region). Because the Ruhrgebiet had long been dominated by coal mining and steel manufacturing, by the end of the 1980s its landscape and waterways, including the Emscher River, were heavily polluted and unsuited for recreation.

At the conclusion of the IBA, a regional planning body worked with seventeen municipalities, many of which began as models of Ebenezer Howard's "Garden City" workers' towns, to adapt the IBA's concepts by developing a multipronged plan to transform the connective landscape spaces around and through the region's cities and towns. This plan envisioned an east-west green corridor along the Emscher River connecting seven north-south regional green corridors that already existed, thanks to prescient regional planning by Robert Schmidt during the 1920s. The aim of this planned area, now called the Emscher Landscape Park, was to fundamentally change the public perception, environmental quality, and ultimately the economic foundation of the region through interventions in the regional landscape. Former ore transportation routes, for example, have been turned into a network of pedestrian and cycling pathways.

A significant part of the vision for the Emscher Landscape Park, famously exemplified by the landscape architect Peter Latz's project in the Landschaftspark in Duisburg-Nord, is to repurpose and maintain the industrial ruins as iconic elements within a revegetated landscape. As of 2016, the Emscher Landscape Park includes 20 municipalities and 406 implemented projects in 457 square kilometers (177 square miles) of rehabilitated landscape.

FIGURE 15.1.1 Aerial photo of Duisburg-Nord, 1985. © *KVR, Essen.*

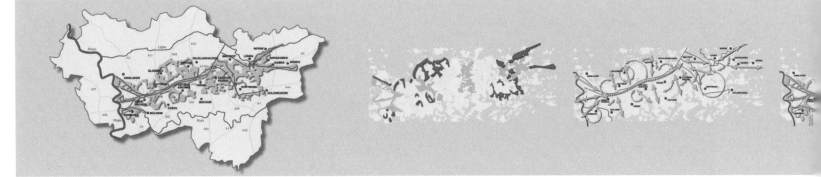

FIGURE 15.1.2 Masterplan Emscher Landscape Park, 2010. © *PRG, Essen.*

Footprint of Emscher Landscape Park

Realized Projects

Realized Localized Projects

Future Projects

Future Localized Projects

Realized Regional Park Trails

Future Regional Park Trails

Emscher Path

Landmarks

Future Landmarks

New Emscher Valley Development Zone

Realized Regional Green Links

Future Regional Green Links

Realized Local Green Links

Future Local Green Links

Urban Development Axes

Implemented Water Expansion

Planned Water Expansion

Community Borders

Highways

FIGURE 15.1.3 Landscape Park Duisburg-Nord, 2005. © *Michael Schwarze-Rodrian, Essen.*

FIGURE 15.1.4 Hoheward coal mine.
Tip piling phases in 1984, 1993, and
2005 (top to bottom), Herten.
© *KVR, Essen.*

Stapleton

Denver, Colorado, USA

Stapleton is a planned mixed-use development in the city of Denver that began in the late 1990s and is projected to be completed by 2021. The Stapleton Development Plan, commonly known as the Green Book, has guided the project. The concept was for the district to be a model for responsible urban development—an alternative to the sprawling, automobile-dependent patterns common throughout the Denver metropolitan region.

Stapleton is the outcome of transforming a heavily polluted brownfield that was previously home to the Stapleton International Airport into a healthy residential and commercial area. Approximately 3,000 acres (1,214 hectares) of concrete on the site was recycled and converted into road base aggregate. The design team conducted a deep reading of the geological and hydrological processes of the site and region to help guide planning and design. A central creek was unearthed from beneath the runway and restored as the spine of the public open space. The mixed-use urban form of the development was shaped by the ecological capacity of the sand prairie it was built on and by the goal to create access to new schools and community services needed by the residents. New governance, regulatory, and financing systems were created to make the development possible.

Stapleton has influenced developers of other urban infill projects, especially other former airfields such as the Lowry Air Force Base (also in Denver) and the Mueller Municipal Airport (in Austin, Texas). Stapleton pioneered tangible design responses to site-specific issues such as sustainability, walkability, and affordability, which are now the mainstream aims of most urban infill developments.

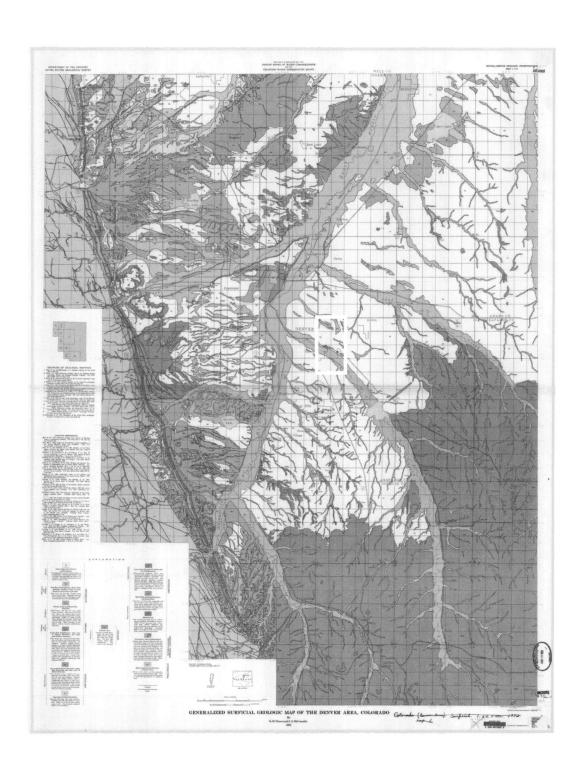

FIGURE 15.2.1 USGS Surficial Geology Map of Denver, Colorado, 1972. Light brown shows the South Platte River; other colors show a range of geological layers. The surficial geology of the site and its position in the region were a source of inspiration. The sand prairie retains moisture, supporting deep-rooting grasses, herbs, and forbs that will become a rich prairie habitat in the open space system. *U.S. Geological Survey.*

FIGURE 15.2.2 (LEFT) Regional Physiography. A first step in the master plan was to show the public that the site sits near the edge of two surficial geologies—thin soils to the west and deep sands to the east—both of which create distinct patterns of hydrology and topography. *With permission, Civitas, Inc.*

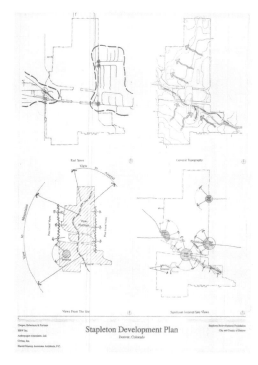

FIGURE 15.2.3 (RIGHT) Urban Analysis Diagrams. Simple diagrams were used to help the public understand the underlying structure and context of the site, as well as key assets that inform the master plan. *With permission, Cooper Robertson and Civitas, Inc.*

FIGURE 15.2.4 (LEFT) Stormwater Detention, Water Quality, and Conveyance Diagram. The backbone of the master plan is this concept for moving, cleaning, and detaining urban stormwater in a system of vegetated channels, swales, and basins that form a connected open space system. *With permission, Andropogon.*

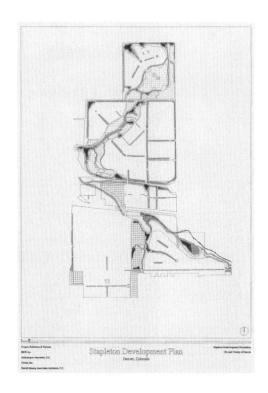

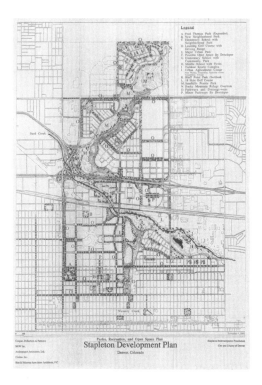

FIGURE 15.2.5 (RIGHT) Parks, Recreation, and Open Space Plan. The master plan connects the surrounding urban patterns with the core open space system, distributing open space to every neighborhood. *With permission, Civitas, Inc.*

FIGURE 15.2.6 Aerial view, including downtown Denver and the Front Range. Stapleton has become a district of mixed neighborhoods developed around a central park and connected by the restored Westerly Creek.
With permission, Forest City Stapleton.

Freshkills Park

New York, New York, USA

The general public's negative view of marshland as wasteland in the 1940s helped determine the location of landfills throughout New York City. Fresh Kills landfill is one example. It was opened in 1948 as a temporary landfill on Staten Island on the banks of the Fresh Kills estuary. Robert Moses, a key figure in the city's planning, promoted the landfill at Fresh Kills, hoping to later reclaim its marshland for real estate development and to build an expressway connecting Staten Island to New Jersey and Brooklyn.

Despite strong opposition, the Fresh Kills landfill remained, becoming permanent in 1953. At its peak in the 1980s, the landfill received 29,000 tons of refuse daily and averaged 2.8 million tons annually over its life span. Over time, its four garbage mounds grew from a few feet above sea level to 225 feet (69 meters) tall. Until its closure in 2001, Fresh Kills reigned as the largest landfill in the world.

From 2003 to 2006, the design firm James Corner Field Operations and its consultants worked to create a master plan for the site. Capping a landfill and converting it to public open space is hardly a new practice, but creating a viable ecology in such a hostile location requires innovation and experimentation. First the landfill was capped and the infrastructure for methane extraction was set in place. Then, since importing good topsoil to cover the vast landfill (which was nearly three times the size of Central Park) was not feasible, the designers developed methods of in-situ soil development through a highly curated process of plant succession. Various planting strategies have been tried, monitored, and adjusted. The creation of Freshkills Park is a work in progress and is not expected to be completed until 2036. Once built, the new park will enlarge the existing 3,000-acre (1,214-hectare) Staten Island Greenbelt and connect it to the William T. David Wildlife Refuge, offering the community a full range of recreational activities.

FIGURE 15.3.1 Layers of impermeable fabric are laid over the waste landfill to protect methane gases from escaping into the air and to prevent water from migrating downward into the waste and becoming contaminated. These fabric layers have microspikes along their surface to help prevent slippage. They are subsequently covered with soil and planted with grasses for slope stabilization. © Alex S. MacLean/Landslides.

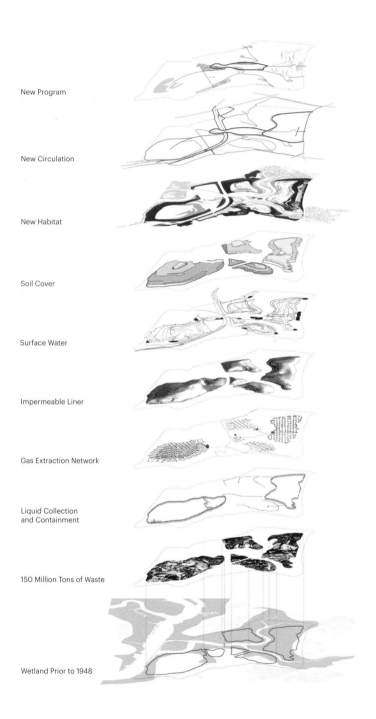

New Program

New Circulation

New Habitat

Soil Cover

Surface Water

Impermeable Liner

Gas Extraction Network

Liquid Collection and Containment

150 Million Tons of Waste

Wetland Prior to 1948

Grassland Strip Cropping

Strip cropping is an inexpensive, industrial-scale technique for increasing the organic content of poor soils, chelating metals and toxins (inhibiting their uptake by plants), increasing soil depth, controlling weeds, and increasing aeration.

A crop rotation system is proposed to improve the existing topsoil cover without importing large quantities of new soil (shown in orange and yellow).

The cultivated soils will support native prairie and meadow. In the wetter areas of the mounds, shallow-rooted successional woodland will ultimately diversify the grassland biotopes (where orange and yellow change to light green in later phases).

Woodland on the Mounds

Two to three feet of new soil will be required for cultivation of denser, stratified woodland on the mounds in early stages of the park's development. The new soils would be stabilized and planted with native grassland initially to create a weed-resistant matrix for the gradual interplanting of young tree stock.

Proposed woodland on the mounds is located in areas adjacent to proposed lowland and swamp forests to widen the habitat corridor while conserving the amount of new soil to be imported.

A total of 220 acres of woodland on the mounds is proposed—with 65 acres on the north and south mounds, and 55 acres on the east and west mounds.

Lowland Forest

When a supply of native saplings and tree plugs are available (particularly in early years of park construction when other areas are being prepared for planting), lowland and swamp forests are planted in overlapping ecotonal bands on existing soil to build the woodland rim.

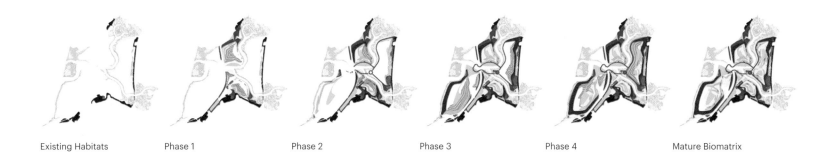

Existing Habitats Phase 1 Phase 2 Phase 3 Phase 4 Mature Biomatrix

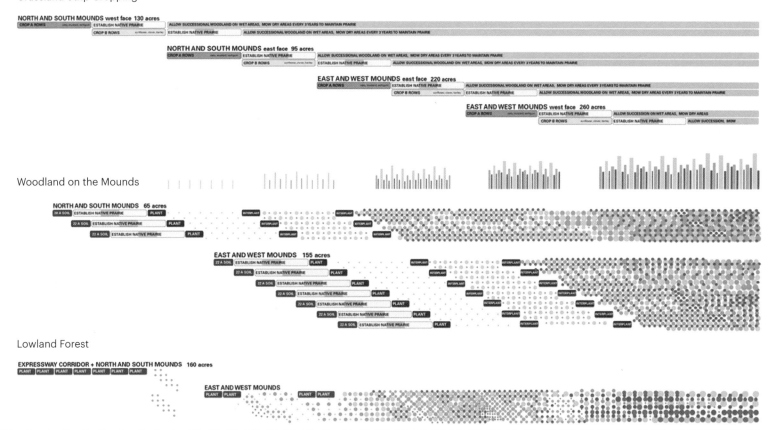

Grassland Strip Cropping

Woodland on the Mounds

Lowland Forest

YEAR 1 2 3 4 5 6 7 8 9 10 11 12 13 14 15 16 17 18 19 20 21 22 23 24 25 26 27 28 29 30 31 32 33 34 35 36 37 38 39 40

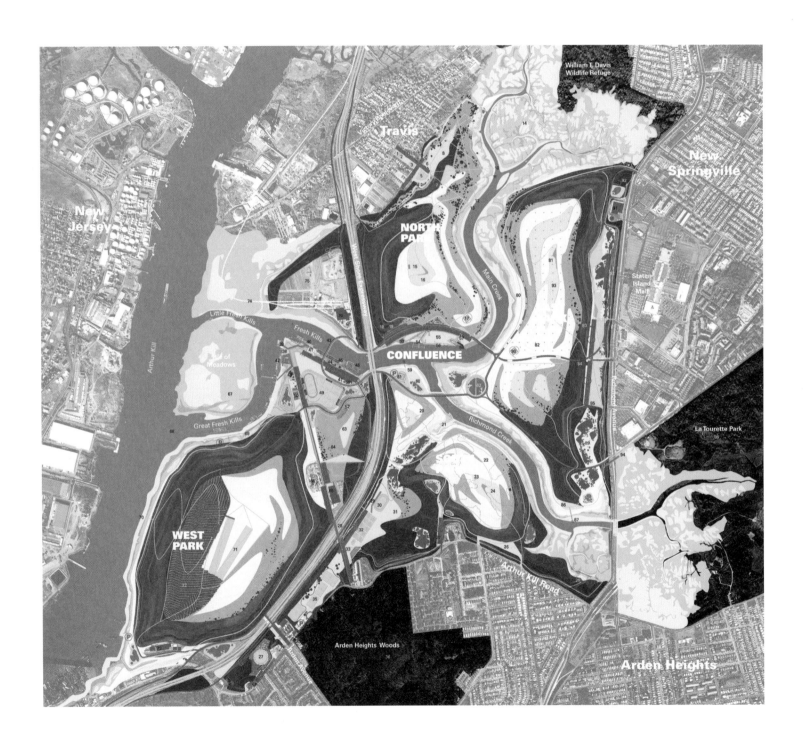

FIGURE 15.3.4 Freshkills Park illustrative plan. *With permission, James Corner Field Operations.*

FIGURE 15.3.5 Restored wetlands are visible in the foreground of a capped landfill mound. © Alex S. MacLean/Landslides.

Queen Elizabeth Olympic Park

London, England

Queen Elizabeth Olympic Park was designed and constructed to host the 2012 London Olympic Games. At 274 acres (110 hectares), it is one of the largest urban parks built in Europe in 150 years, underpinning what were touted as the "greenest games in history." The design converted the heavily polluted site into a high-performance ecological and recreational space. The heart of this transformation was the restoration of the River Lea, which runs through the park, along with the development of a biodiversity action plan to provide over 100 acres (40.5 hectares) of habitat comprising woodlands, constructed wetlands, reedbeds, and meadows. In all, 2 miles (3.2 kilometers) of waterways were restored, 1.5 million cubic yards (1.15 million cubic meters) of contaminated soil was washed and reused, 300,000 wetland plants were added, and over 4 miles (6.4 kilometers) of new trails and bike paths were laid.

Notably, the design of the public space, led by Hargreaves Associates with local support by LDA Design, was conceived to unfold in three stages: the games, transformation, and legacy. In addition to serving the logistics of the games themselves, the project was designed to be retrofitted as an urban district after the event. The designers, working in partnership with the London Organizing Committee of the Olympic and Paralympic Games (LOCOG), devised ways to deconstruct and narrow the wide bridges; repurpose the programmatic spaces; and redevelop areas of the park for housing, office, and retail space. The park, which at this writing in 2018 is still in the "transformation" phase, already serves as a hub for the five surrounding boroughs.

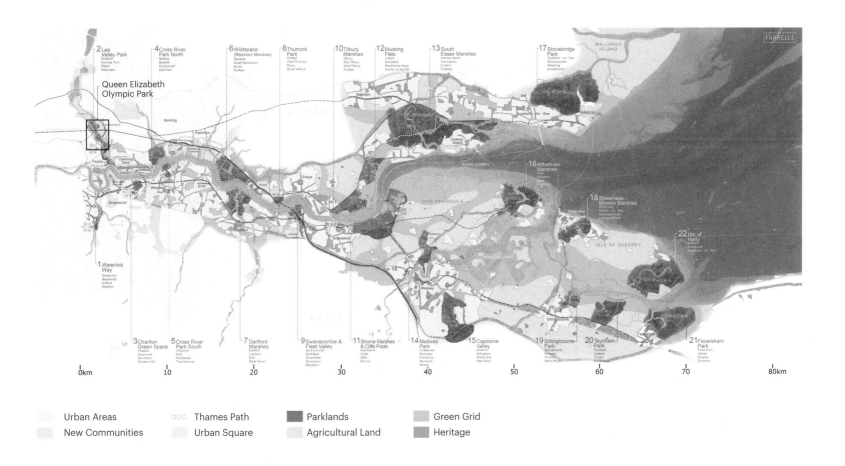

FIGURE 15.4.1 Queen Elizabeth Olympic Park (upper left in box) is shown here as part of a larger network of landscapes envisioned as the Thames Gateway Parklands. © *Farrells*.

Queen Elizabeth Olympic Park

2 Lea Valley Park
Stratford
Canning Town
Poplar
West Ham

4 Cross River Park North
Barking
Beckton
Creekmouth
East Ham

6 Wildspace (Rainham Marshes)
Rainham
South Hornchurch
Aveley
Purfleet

8 Thurrock Park
Purfleet
West Thurrock
Grays
South Stifford

10 Tilbury Marshes
Tilbury
East Tilbury
West Tilbury
Purfleet

12 Mucking Flats
Linford
Southfield
Stanford Le Hope
Horndon-on-the-Hill

13 South Essex Marshes
Canvey Island
Corringham
Corryton
Fobbing

17 Stonebridge Park
Southend-on-Sea
Shoeburyness
Wakering
Southchurch

16 Allhallows Marshes

18 Sheerness - Minster Marshes
Sheerness
Minster-on-Sea
Queenborough
Halfway Houses

22 Isle of Harty

1 Waterlink Way
Greenwich
Blackheath
Catford
Deptford

3 Charlton Green Space
Charlton
Greenwich
Silvertown
Streeters Hill

5 Cross River Park South
Plumstead
Erith
Plumstead
Thamesmead

7 Dartford Marshes
Dartford
Erith
Slade Green

9 Swanscombe & Fleet Valley
Swanscombe
Northfleet
Greenhithe
Gravesend
Ebbsfleet

11 Shorne Marshes & Cliffe Pools
Gravesend
Chalk
Cliffe
Shorne

14 Medway Park
Chatham
Rochester
Frindsbury
Wainscott
Strood

15 Capstone Valley
Chatham
Gillingham
Walderslade
Park Wood

19 Sittingbourne Park
Sittingbourne
Murston
Milton Regis

20 Teynham Park
Teynham
Lynsted
Conyer
Greenstreet

21 Faversham Park
Faversham
Uplees
Oare
Oespole
Graveney

0km   10   20   30   40   50   60   70   80km

Urban Areas   ○○○ Thames Path   Parklands   Green Grid
New Communities   Urban Square   Agricultural Land   Heritage

FIGURE 15.4.2 Site of London Olympic Park prior to construction. © *Anthony Charlton. With permission, London Legacy Development Corporation.*

FIGURE 15.4.3 The site and stadiums were already under construction (left scheme) when the new team, led by Hargreaves Associates, was hired. Based on an analysis of crowd modeling (center), the design changes led to the creation of two distinct parks environments (north and south). The river was given more primacy through a significant reduction in paving, which afforded better visual and physical access to it, provided more room for biodiverse habitats, and reduced overall costs. *With permission, Hargreaves Associates.*

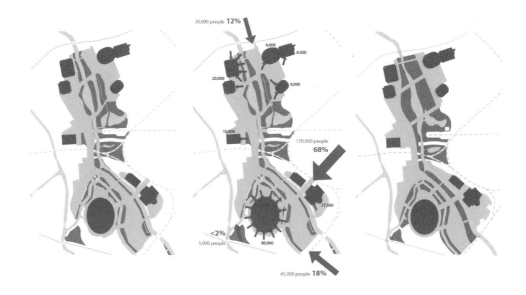

Previous scheme hardscape to greenspace comparison

Testing of crowd flows

New scheme expands greenspace and reveals park as centerpiece

FIGURE 15.4.4 Queen Elizabeth Olympic Park Site Plan—Games. The Games stage of the design showing broad avenues and bridges to accommodate large crowds. *With permission, Hargreaves Associates.*

FIGURE 15.4.5 Queen Elizabeth Olympic Park Site Plan—Legacy. The Legacy stage of the design showing reduced paving, smaller bridges, and expanded park and garden space. *With permission, Hargreaves Associates.*

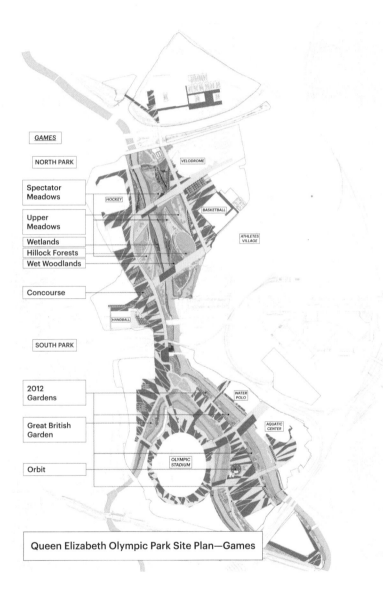

Queen Elizabeth Olympic Park Site Plan—Games

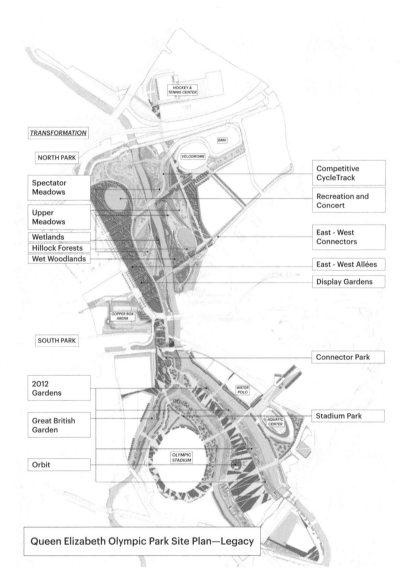

Queen Elizabeth Olympic Park Site Plan—Legacy

FIGURE 15.4.6 Aerial view of the London Olympic Park, almost complete, in 2011. © Anthony Charlton. With permission, London Legacy Development Corporation.

FIGURE 15.4.7 North Park eye-level view—opening games. *With permission, Hargreaves Associates.*

FIGURE 15.4.8 North Park during the opening of the Olympic Games in 2012. *With permission, Hargreaves Associates.*

FIGURE 15.4.9 North Park eye-level view—post-games. *With permission, Hargreaves Associates.*

211

Urban Futures

USA

Willamette River Basin
Oregon

Envision Utah
Salt Lake City Region

COLOMBIA

Medellín

SPAIN

CHINA   Barcelona Metro Region

Qianhai Water City
Shenzhen

Barcelona Metro Region

Spain

Like many metropolitan areas, the Barcelona region faces challenges of urban growth, degrading natural land, shrinking farmland, insufficient and contaminated water, traffic congestion, and climate change. In 2002, Harvard landscape ecologist Richard T. T. Forman completed the *Mosaico territorial para la región metropolitana de Barcelona* (Land Mosaic for the Metropolitan Region of Barcelona). The project's objective was to envision solutions and outline spatial arrangements to enhance natural systems and associated human land uses for the long-term future of the greater Barcelona region.

For this large area, the project highlighted five perspectives: nature, farmland, water, built areas, and built systems. Forman used large satellite images showing every building in the region and more than forty GIS maps and descriptions of diverse regional resources. To understand the place, people, culture, nature, flows, and movements, Forman spent almost a month with his team of four regional experts, crisscrossing and recording observations in every part of the region. The principles of landscape ecology provided an organizing framework.

In a series of logical steps, first the team identified a set of primary ecological principles, such as protecting riparian corridors and achieving connec-

tivity, to guide the project. Second, they compared these primary principles, represented as simple spatial models or diagrams, with the specific landscape patterns in the region. From this, they developed and evaluated two to four options for each principle by simply listing the ecological benefits and disadvantages. The third step, basically a best-judgment iterative process, was to combine the preferred options. These steps led to three comprehensive spatial solutions (most promising, solid, and minimal) for the region's conflicting land uses. These were presented to the local leaders so that they could select priorities. Each solution highlighted how pieces of the land mosaic fit together and could be implemented over time.

This process produced a set of flexible land use patterns that would sustain natural systems and people, including large connected patches of biodiverse natural land; high-quality stream valleys; large agricultural areas and smaller agriculture-nature parks; better water supply reservoirs; strategic places for growth and no-growth; an iconic floodplain park by the city; locations for industrial areas and transportation; generic solutions for features like wetlands, gullies, and highways; and flexibility and stability for the region's future.

The Land Mosaic for the Metropolitan Region of Barcelona was published in 2004. Six years later, the Catalan government completed its regional plan, *Pla territorial metropolita de Barcelona* (Metropolitan Territorial Plan of Barcelona), which incorporated many concepts from Forman's plan. His land mosaic plan also led to the book *Urban Regions*, a delineation and analysis of small-to-large urban regions (including the Barcelona model) on all continents. *Mosaico territorial para la región de Barcelona* established a model for how the valuable and often-overlooked land surrounding a city can absorb urban growth while protecting nature, local food production, water resources, and a rich array of human needs and values.

FIGURE 16.1.1 Metropolitan Territorial Plan of Barcelona. *La Generalitat de Catalunya.*

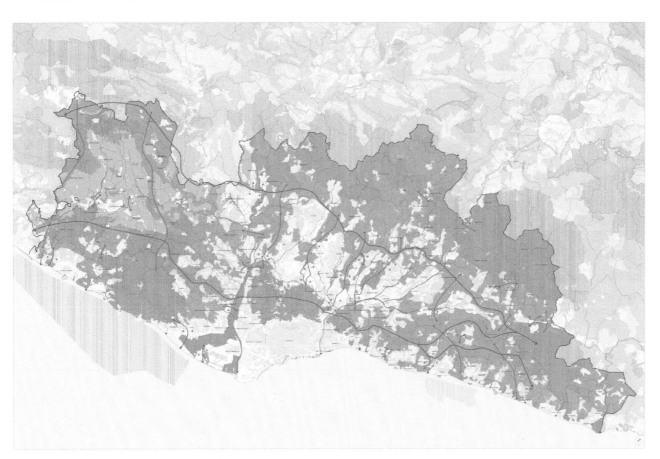

 Spaces With Supra-Municipal Legal Protection; Natura 2000 Network, PEIN Spaces, Parks of the Diputacio de Barcelona and Other Consortiums in Urban Areas

Special Protection for Natural and Agricultural Areas

 Special Protection for Vineyards

 Landscape Corridors to Connect Habitat Patches

Landscape Corridors Threatened by Urbanization

River Corridors

FIGURE 16.1.2 Diagrams from "Patches, Edges and Boundaries," in Wenche E. Dramstad, James D. Olson, and Richard T. T. Forman, *Landscape Ecology Principles in Landscape Architecture and Land-Use Planning*, 1996. © Harvard University Graduate School of Design and the President and Fellows of Harvard College, 2018. With permission.

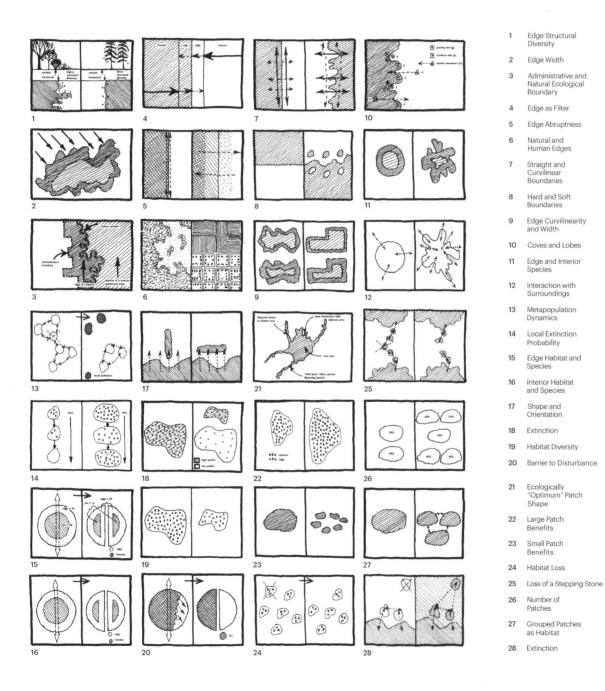

1. Edge Structural Diversity
2. Edge Width
3. Administrative and Natural Ecological Boundary
4. Edge as Filter
5. Edge Abruptness
6. Natural and Human Edges
7. Straight and Curvilinear Boundaries
8. Hard and Soft Boundaries
9. Edge Curvilinearity and Width
10. Coves and Lobes
11. Edge and Interior Species
12. Interaction with Surroundings
13. Metapopulation Dynamics
14. Local Extinction Probability
15. Edge Habitat and Species
16. Interior Habitat and Species
17. Shape and Orientation
18. Extinction
19. Habitat Diversity
20. Barrier to Disturbance
21. Ecologically "Optimum" Patch Shape
22. Large Patch Benefits
23. Small Patch Benefits
24. Habitat Loss
25. Loss of a Stepping Stone
26. Number of Patches
27. Grouped Patches as Habitat
28. Extinction

FIGURE 16.1.3 Aerial photos of metropolitan Barcelona, 2001. *Photos, Marc Montlleó. With permission, Barcelona Regional.*

FIGURE 16.1.4 Aerial photos of metropolitan Barcelona, 2001. *Photos, Marc Montlleó. With permission, Barcelona Regional.*

FIGURE 16.1.5 View of Barcelona, 2009.
© J. Oliver-Bonjoch.

Medellín

Colombia

The city of Medellín suffers from extreme inequality that is reflected in its housing types and the broader-built environment within the city's valley section. The wealthy tend to live in central, well-serviced enclaves, while the poor live on peripheral steep slopes in self-constructed settlements. Since 2003, the city has undergone an internationally recognized urban transformation, coinciding with a restoration of peace in what was once the most dangerous city in the world.

In 2004, Medellín began rapidly linking what it identified as "nodes of development" in some of the city's poorest neighborhoods—libraries, schools, and public spaces—to public transportation. It built gondolas, escalators, and bridges over steep ravines to link those neighborhoods to the city's metropolitan transit system. Public space projects have also been built to bring more life to the channelized river. The Medellín River Parks Master Plan is a linear sequence of public spaces along the river that bisects the city and is where the oldest formal elements of the city are located. The construction of the first phase of the park required a section of the highway to be buried beneath the new park, and bridges have been built across the river, connecting the two parts of what had been a divided city.

These projects are an outgrowth of a philosophical and practical shift in planning first described in the city's *Plan de Ordenamiento Territorial* of 1998, a document that built on existing United Nations efforts to provide basic services to the informal communities, or *comunas*, on the urban periphery. This document is still used and was updated in 2017, with an added focus on sustainability, walkability, accessibility, and the revitalization of the urban core. Practically and symbolically, the poorest residents were able to connect to the city and to the civility and services it promises its citizens.

Though Medellín has successfully provided services to informal settlements on its periphery, the question of how informal settlements arise in the first place and whether their growth can be planned is also relevant to the millions of people expected to migrate to rapidly urbanizing cities this century. A significant planning document that addresses this larger issue is the recently completed BIO 2030 Plan—a strategic plan to structure future growth through cooperation among the ten municipalities of the Aburrá Valley—produced by governmental bodies in collaboration with the Center for Urban and Environmental Studies (Urbam), an organization led by Alejandro Echeverri, faculty of the Finanzas e Instituto Technológico,

Universidad Medellín (EAFIT). This comprehensive plan documents the geology, hydrology, ecology, and fragmentation of the entire valley and, using these layers as a base, provides detailed designs for different developments. Similarly, professors of landscape architecture and urban design David Gouverneur and Christian Werthmann, among others, are developing projects with students related to the social, ecological, and political challenges of designing informal settlements. Gouverneur's Informal Armature approach offers a framework for self-constructed neighborhoods, prior to the occupation of the land, and Werthmann's team, building on the work of Urbam EAFIT, offers detailed construction techniques to minimize risks from earthquakes and landslides and maximize access to basic infrastructure.

FIGURE 16.2.1 View of Medellín from La Cruz, 2014. © *Joseph Claghorn, Institute of Landscape Architecture, Leibniz Universität Hannover.*

FIGURE 16.2.2 Section of Aburrá Valley. Alcaldía de Medellín, Área Metropolitana del Valle de Aburrá, Urbam EAFIT, 2011. © Bio 2030. *Plan Director Medellín, Valle de Aburrá. Un sueño que juntos podemos alcanzar. Medellín: Valle de Aburrá. Un sueño que juntos podemos alcanzar. Medellín: Urbam EAFIT.*

Upland Scrub Vegetation

Disturbed Secondary Forest

--------- Limit of Urban Zone

Key Plan

Plains Zone

Hillside Zone

Red line shows where section (right) is cut

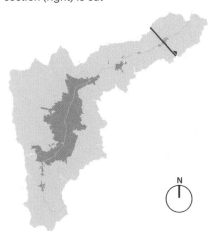

Section (distances in meters)

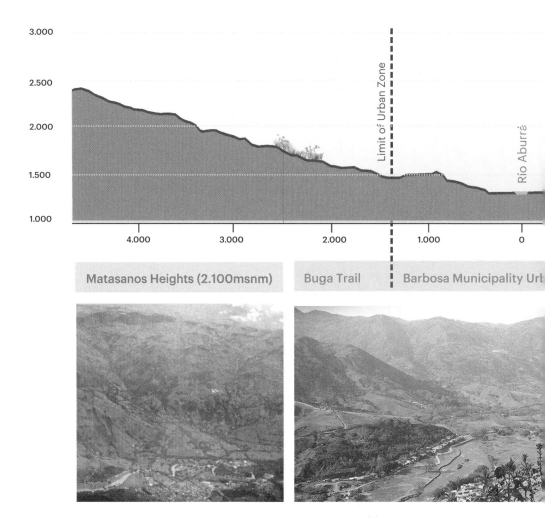

FIGURE 16.2.3 The systems of Aburrá Valley. The built and natural systems of the Aburrá Valley, including transit, recreation areas, hydrology, and ecological corridors. Alcaldía de Medellín, Área Metropolitana del Valle de Aburrá, Urbam EAFIT, 2011. © Bio 2030. *Plan Director Medellín, Valle de Aburrá. Un sueño que juntos podemos alcanzar. Medellín: Valle de Aburrá. Un sueño que juntos podemos alcanzar. Medellín: Urbam EAFIT.*

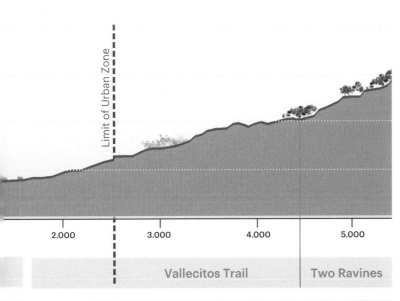

Limit of Urban Zone

2.000   3.000   4.000   5.000

Vallecitos Trail   Two Ravines

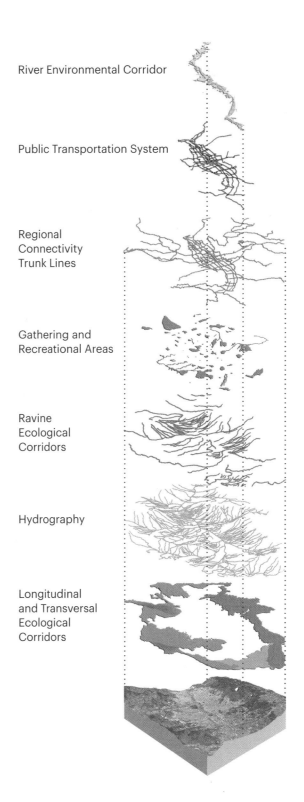

River Environmental Corridor

Public Transportation System

Regional Connectivity Trunk Lines

Gathering and Recreational Areas

Ravine Ecological Corridors

Hydrography

Longitudinal and Transversal Ecological Corridors

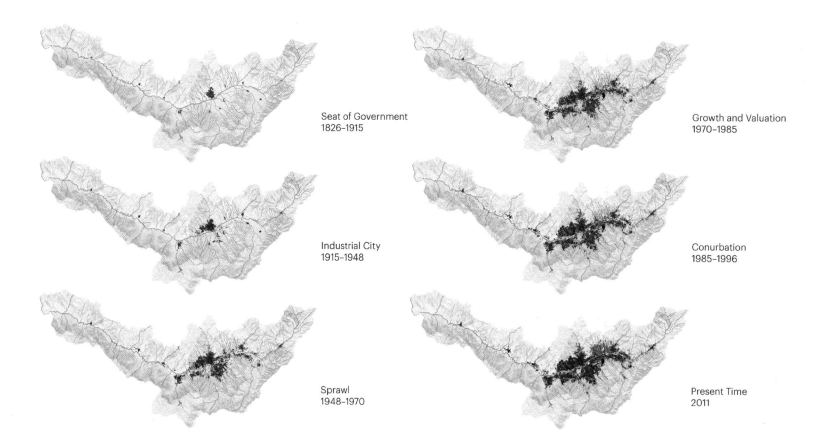

FIGURE 16.2.4 Aburrá Valley growth. Alcaldía de Medellín, Área Metropolitana del Valle de Aburrá, Urbam EAFIT, 2011. © Bio 2030. Plan Director Medellín; Valle de Aburrá. Un sueño que juntos podemos alcanzar. Medellín: Urbam EAFIT.

Seat of Government
1826–1915

Growth and Valuation
1970–1985

Industrial City
1915–1948

Conurbation
1985–1996

Sprawl
1948–1970

Present Time
2011

FIGURE 16.2.5 Components for the conceptual design of informal armatures: corridors (top), patches, and stewards (bottom). Corridors are connective landscape elements such as habitats, hydrology, public spaces, or mobility. Patches are land made available for self-constructed neighborhoods and for communal, urban, or metropolitan services that the informal city cannot provide. Stewards are nonprofit organizations, community organizations, or governmental entities supporting the transformation of corridors and patches while keeping informality from occupying sensitive sites or the public realm. *Drawings, David Gouverneur. With permission.*

FIGURE 16.2.6 Medellín's new settlers construct their houses on steep slopes. Path construction and the excavation of escarpments open up the vegetation cover and the risk of landslides increases, 2015. Slope stabilization techniques are needed to address this issue (opposite page, top right). © Marcus Hanke, Institute of Landscape Architecture, Leibniz Universität Hannover.

FIGURE 16.2.7 Shifting Grounds pilot projects in informal settlements: cooperative microfarming, slope stabilization, reforestation, and warning system. © *Institute of Landscape Architecture, Leibniz Universität Hannover (ILA, LUH) / Centro de Estudios Urbanos y Ambientales (Urbam) / Escuela de Administración, Finanzas e Instituto Tecnológico, Universidad Medellín (EAFIT).*

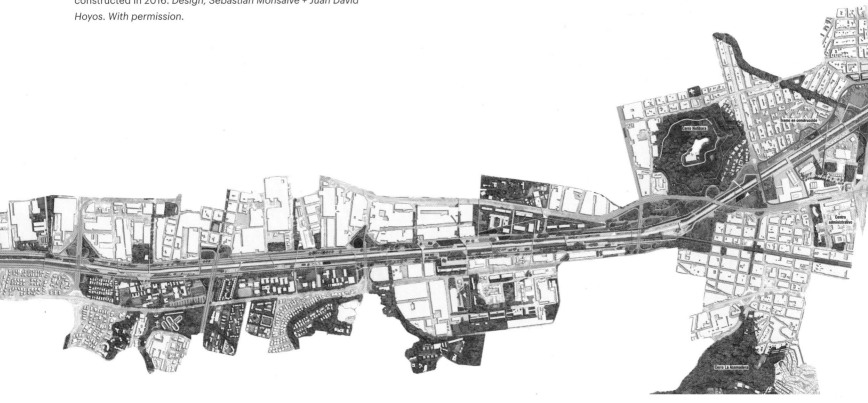

FIGURE 16.2.8 The Medellín River Parks Master Plan includes more than 10 miles (17 km) of public space that will be built in eight phases. The red outline shows the first phase, which was constructed in 2016. *Design, Sebastian Monsalve + Juan David Hoyos. With permission.*

FIGURE 16.2.9 Aerial view of the first phase of the Medellín River Parks, constructed in 2016. *Photo, Alejandro Arango Escobar. With permission.*

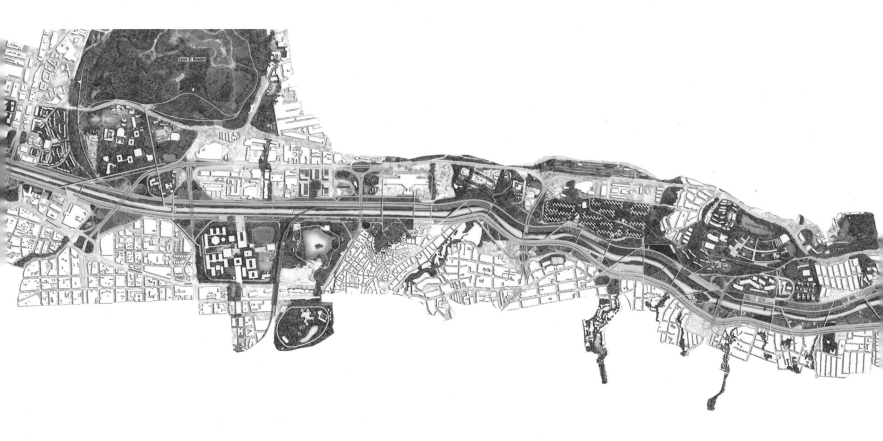

Willamette River Basin

Oregon, USA

In 1996, the U.S. Environmental Protection Agency (EPA) initiated a five-year scientific research effort to support community-based environmental planning. Because citizen groups in the Willamette River Basin (WRB) in Oregon were already attempting to address complex environmental issues, the EPA selected the WRB as one of its focal areas for the initiative. The EPA formed the Pacific Northwest Ecosystem Research Consortium, which consisted of thirty-four scientists at ten different institutions, including Oregon State University, the USDA Forest Service, the University of Oregon, and the University of Washington.

With the population of the WRB expected to grow by 1.7 million people by 2050, nearly doubling the 2002 population, the research was focused on accommodating population growth while preserving natural resources. The consortium examined the complexity of the relationships among people, land, water, and other life in the WRB, as well as the cumulative effects of land use and landownership policies over time and in different political jurisdictions. Four main questions drove the research: How has the WRB been altered by human activity in the past 150 years? What is the range of plausible human modification to the WRB in the next 150 years? What are the expected environmental consequences of these modifications?

What management strategies will have the greatest positive effect on conserving natural resources?

The consortium studied current landforms, water resources, biotic systems, human population, land use, and land cover within the WRB. Where possible, this information was compared with the relatively pristine ecosystem of pre-European colonization. Following a collaborative, citizen-led process, three alternative visions for the future of the WRB were selected to encompass the range of plausible policy options and diverse stakeholder viewpoints: (1) a plan trend scenario (policies stay as they are); (2) a development scenario (environmental protection policies are loosened); and (3) a conservation scenario (policies place greater emphasis on ecosystem protection and restoration). The likely environmental impacts of these three scenarios on the WRB were then projected, focusing on the condition of the Willamette River and its tributaries, water availability and use, and terrestrial wildlife.

Outcomes of this research resulted in land acquisition (through fee-simple purchase and conservation easements) and on-the-ground restoration of floodplain forest and channel reconnections. In 2008, the Oregon Watershed Enhancement Board allocated funding for the Willamette Special Investment Partnership to re-establish channel complexity and length and reconnect floodplains in the historic meander corridor (the natural pathways) of the Willamette mainstem and selected tributaries. These initiatives have led to a decrease in the water temperature, an increase in fish species richness and riparian forest, and a reduction in invasive plant cover.

FIGURE 16.3.1 Aerial view of Oaks Bottom Wildlife Refuge and Ross Island. Portland, Oregon, skyline in the background. *With permission, Mike Houck, Urban Greenspaces Institute.*

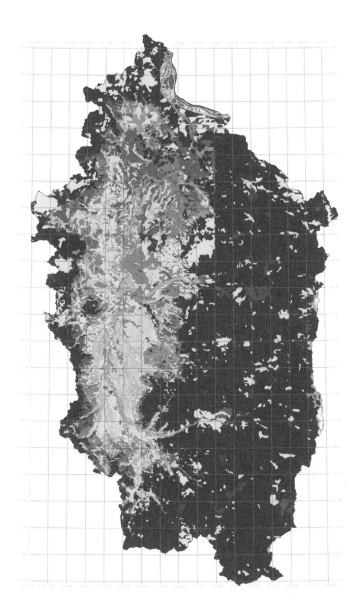

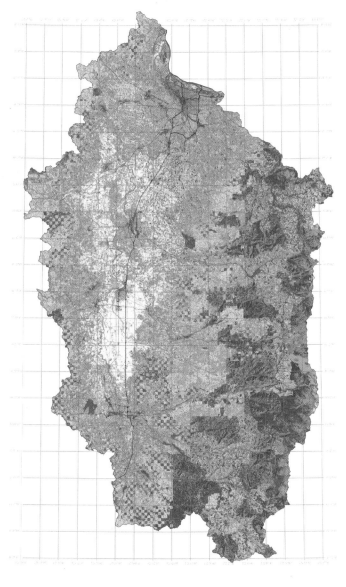

FIGURE 16.3.2 Pre-European colonization. Dark green shows conifer forests, orange shows oak savanna, and yellows are wet prairies and grasslands. *With permission, David Hulse, Lead Editor, Willamette River Basin Planning Atlas.*

FIGURE 16.3.3 Plan Trend Scenario 2050. Dark green areas show conifer forests, blueish-green shows hardwood and mixed forests, pink shows built up areas (residential, commercial, roads, etc.), and gray shows agricultural zones. This trend will lead to loss of terrestrial habitat and aquatic richness, though landscape changes and projected environmental effects remain less than 10 percent compared to the 1990 baseline. *With permission, David Hulse, Lead Editor, Willamette River Basin Planning Atlas.*

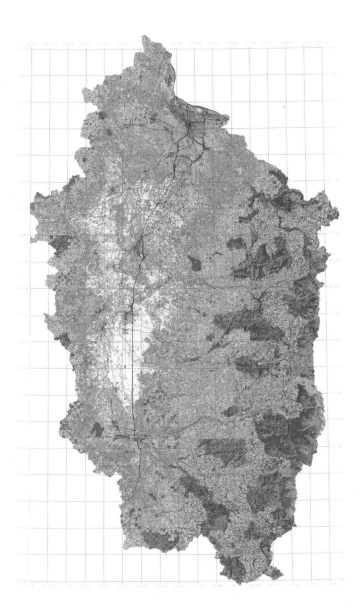

FIGURE 16.3.4 Development Scenario 2050. Dark green areas show conifer forests, blueish-green shows hardwood and mixed forests, pink shows built up areas (residential, commercial, roads, etc.), and gray shows agricultural zones. This scenario projects double the losses of terrestrial habitat compared to the Plan Trend, which is 39 percent more wildlife species lost compared to the 1990 baseline, as well as a loss of 24 percent of farmland. *With permission, David Hulse, Lead Editor, Willamette River Basin Planning Atlas.*

FIGURE 16.3.5 Conservation Scenario 2050. Dark green areas show conifer forests, blueish-green shows hardwood and mixed forests, pink shows built up areas (residential, commercial, roads, etc.), gray shows agricultural zones, and orange shows oak savannah. This scenario recovered 20–70 percent of terrestrial and aquatic habitat losses that have occurred since colonization. Though this trend also shows loss of farmland (15 percent compared to 1990), the farmland would convert to natural vegetation rather than urban and rural development as it would under the Plan Trend and Development Scenarios. None of the scenarios showed improvement in water consumption levels (all increased 40–60 percent compared to the 1990 baseline). *With permission, David Hulse, Lead Editor, Willamette River Basin Planning Atlas.*

Qianhai Water City

Shenzhen, China

Qianhai Bay is located in the Pearl River Delta, west of Shenzhen on the shore of the South China Sea. This area is a key point in the Pearl River estuary at the crossing of the east-west axis of Shenzhen and the north-south axis of Guangzhou to Hong Kong. Officially approved by China's State Council in 2010, the Qianhai Shenzhen–Hong Kong Modern Service Industry Cooperation Zone was established to serve as a pilot business zone for closer cooperation between Mainland China and Hong Kong in the financial, logistics, and information technology services sectors.

In 2009, James Corner Field Operations (JCFO) won the international competition to develop the master plan for Qianhai Water City. Over an area of 4,500 acres (1,822 hectares) of landfill, the master plan is defined by so-called water fingers. The water fingers are linear parks designed to collect, retain, filter, and cleanse stormwater in a series of terraces and ponds. Widened and extended from the existing water tributaries, these parks define the main zones of public space and delimit future urbanization.

Each of the five development districts shaped between the water fingers is defined by varying scales and typologies of the block structure of each neighborhood to promote walkability, as well as a rich mixture of building type and program (residential, commercial, or other). The five districts are linked by three ring-shaped boulevards for motor traffic. The central transit hubs in each district connect to the regional transit ring of the Pearl River Delta–Shenzhen–Hong Kong megalopolis. Metro lines, the intercity rail line, and an express rail line between Shenzhen and Hong Kong Airport all converge in the transit hubs.

Guiwan Park is the first water finger to be built and is anticipated to open in 2021. Its design naturalizes the existing tidal corridor to create various water edge habitats within continuous sculpted topography. The water finger protects against flooding while retaining and cleaning stormwater.

When all the fingers are completed, they will provide the public with large linear parks accessible by foot from the center of each district. The landscape spaces of the Qianhai Water City master plan define the structure, character, health, and logistics of an entire city.

FIGURE 16.4.1 Qianhai Water City Physical Model. Linear green areas show the water fingers. *With permission, James Corner Field Operations.*

FIGURE 16.4.2 Qianhai Shoreline Evolution. Lightest blue is oldest fill (1979); darkest blue is newest fill (2010). Intermediate fill stages are 1990 and 2000. *With permission, James Corner Field Operations.*

FIGURE 16.4.3 Guiwan Water Finger Tidal Study. Low tide (top), high tide, annual extreme high tide, and 200-year high tide (bottom). *With permission, James Corner Field Operations.*

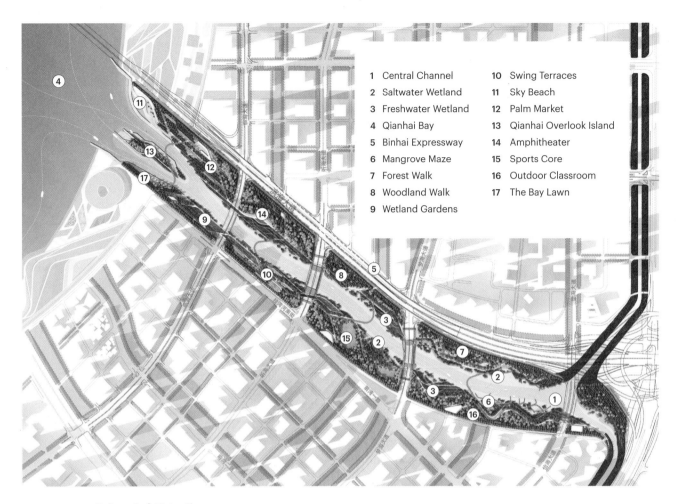

1	Central Channel	10	Swing Terraces
2	Saltwater Wetland	11	Sky Beach
3	Freshwater Wetland	12	Palm Market
4	Qianhai Bay	13	Qianhai Overlook Island
5	Binhai Expressway	14	Amphitheater
6	Mangrove Maze	15	Sports Core
7	Forest Walk	16	Outdoor Classroom
8	Woodland Walk	17	The Bay Lawn
9	Wetland Gardens		

FIGURE 16.4.4 Guiwan Park Water Finger Plan. *With permission, James Corner Field Operations.*

FIGURE 16.4.5 Pre-competition photograph of the drainage channel. *With permission, James Corner Field Operations.*

| Parkland Terrace | Water | Freshwater Terrace | Saltwater Terrace | Flood Channel |
| > +4.5 m | Tank | +3.1 - +4.5 | +0.5 - +3.1 | +0.5 - +3.1 |

FIGURE 16.4.6 Guiwan Park Water Finger
Sectional Perspective. *With permission,
James Corner Field Operations.*

FIGURE 16.4.7 Water Finger Layers include pedestrian network (top), tree canopy, wetland and channel, soft surfaces, and the combination of all layers (bottom). *With permission, James Corner Field Operations.*

Envision Utah

Salt Lake City Region, USA

The population of the Salt Lake City region in Utah is expected to reach 2.7 million by 2020—over a million more residents than in 1995, the year Envision Utah began. Five million residents are projected to live in the region by the year 2050. The region's growth and developable land are bound, in large part, by a series of natural features—the Wasatch Mountain Range, the Great Salt Lake, Utah Lake, surrounding desert, and federally owned land.

Envision Utah was organized to bring public and private entities together to coordinate activities, urban growth, and development in the region. A diverse group of community leaders from business and government came together to form Envision Utah, a nonprofit organization committed to facilitating bottom-up, nonpartisan, collaborative decision-making processes to help Utahns plan for the future. Envision Utah reached across jurisdictional boundaries and incorporated ten counties, including ninety cities and towns along the Wasatch Front and Back.

Envision Utah organized a series of workshops to broaden the community's understanding of the existing trends and challenges and enable stakeholders to develop four alternative future visions. Scenario A showed how the region could develop if the pattern of dispersed development occurring in some communities today were to continue; Scenario B showed how the region would develop if state and local governments followed their 1997 municipal plans; Scenario C showed how the region might develop if much of the new development were in walkable and transit-served communities with nearby opportunities to work, shop, and play; and Scenario D showed how the region might develop if Scenario C were taken one step further, concentrating nearly half of all new growth in existing urban areas. Following extensive public outreach—town hall meetings; radio, television, and newspaper ads; and a press conference and tour—the public's preferred strategies and outcomes from Scenarios C and D became the foundation of the Quality Growth Strategy (QGS).

The QGS has six primary goals: (1) enhance air quality; (2) increase mobility and transportation choices; (3) preserve critical lands, including agriculture, sensitive natural areas, and strategic open lands; (4) conserve and maintain availability of water resources; (5) provide housing opportunities for a range of family types and incomes; and (6) maximize efficiency in public and infrastructure investments to promote the other goals.

The QGS became the guiding tool for local, government, and private sector planners for the Greater Wasatch Area. It resulted in a 22 percent decrease in average single family home lot size, over 140 miles of added rail transportation, over 40 percent of new apartment construction occurring within walking distance of a rail station, a significant reduction in water usage, infrastructure savings on both capital and maintenance costs, and preservation of land previously slated for development.

The Greater Wasatch Area continues to grow at a rapid rate, as does the rest of the state of Utah. With a need to look further ahead, Envision Utah has facilitated another vision using the processes developed for the QGS, this time for the entire state. Your Utah, Your Future is a broadly supported vision for 2050 that establishes statewide goals and strategies critical for planning.

FIGURE 16.5.1 The Salt Lake Valley is the most densely populated region in Utah. The valley faces unique air quality challenges given its topography and climate. It experiences periods of intense inversion despite air quality that is improving each year. *With permission, Envision Utah.*

Population Density
Salt Lake City Region
(persons/acre)

- <1
- 1–2
- 2–5
- 6–10
- 10+

Water Features

- Body of Water
- Floodplain & Wetland

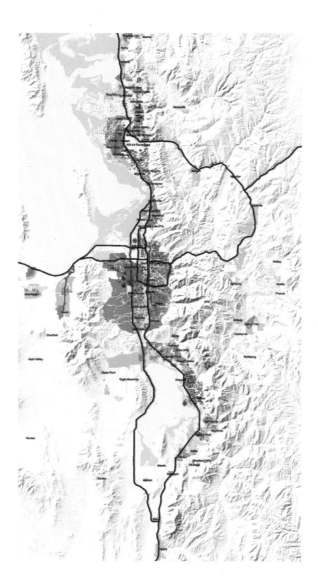

FIGURE 16.5.2 Scenario A shows how the region could develop if the pattern of dispersed development occurring in some communities were to continue. *With permission, Envision Utah.*

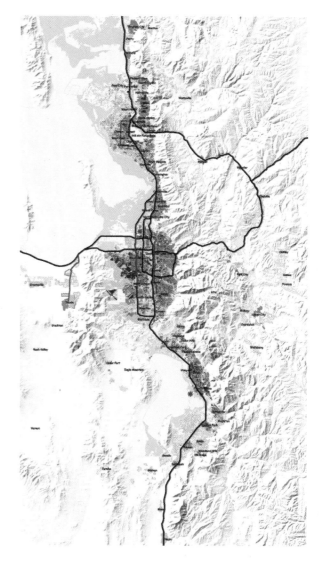

FIGURE 16.5.3 Scenario B shows how the region would develop if state and local governments followed their 1997 municipal plans. *With permission, Envision Utah.*

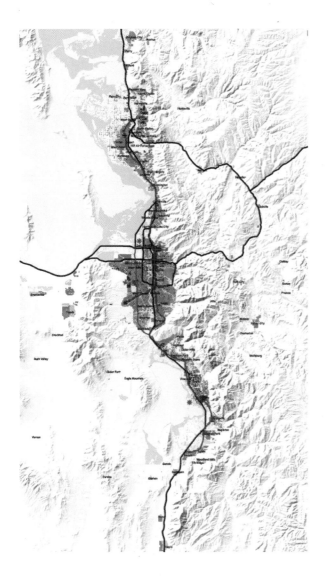

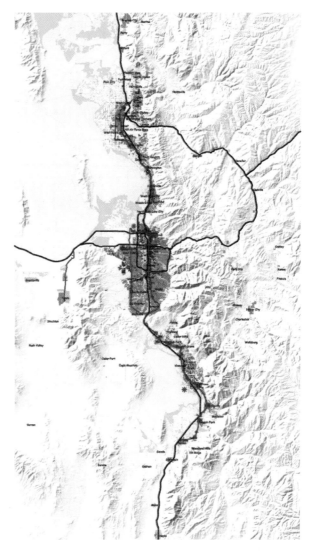

FIGURE 16.5.4 Scenario C shows how the region might develop if much of the new development were in walkable communities that contained nearby opportunities to work, shop, and play. *With permission, Envision Utah.*

FIGURE 16.5.5 Scenario D shows how the region might develop if Scenario C were taken one step further, concentrating nearly half of all new growth in existing urban areas. *With permission, Envision Utah.*

Projects:
Commentaries

CHAPTER 17

The Planetary Optic and Finding the Real Ground

Alan M. Berger and Jonah Susskind

DURING THE LATE 1960s, when Ian McHarg and his colleagues began launching their campaigns against the prevailing practices of ad hoc suburban development, their critiques underscored the birth of environmental thinking in the United States. The baby boom was tapering off, and an era of concern over planetary stewardship was emerging. Since then, the global population has more than doubled, and human-induced environmental catastrophes continue to intensify.[1] Recent decades have accelerated the environmental impact of human settlement by dramatically eclipsing the incremental pace of 20th-century development. Vast swaths of arable land have been transfigured by the rapid construction of new urban megaregions, while elsewhere basic resources such as clean air, potable water, and natural habitat have become limited by the sustained effects of climate change. In response, comprehensive multinational treaties and enforceable policies such as the Kyoto Protocol and the Paris Agreement have been established to reduce global greenhouse gases and ensure the long-term survival of earthly life.[2] Meanwhile, the metabolic processes that are required to sustain urban growth continue to rely on global networks of resource extraction and industrialized agriculture, which only exacerbate the problems McHarg foresaw. McHarg's virtuosic skill was his ability to forecast these scenarios, convince others of their impending repercussions, and tenaciously assemble the resources for changing their trajectories. It was not only his discipline as a researcher, but also the richness of his imagination and capacity for communicating complex ideas that allowed him to apprehend the impact of the oncoming ecological crisis and help bring it into the mainstream cultural agenda.

Since then, few issues have garnered more attention, debate, or concern than the immediate and future effects of climate change. The scale and scope of these issues has triggered the birth of a new "planetary optic"—a framing of the human experience through a global lens, and the inverse perception of Earth as vulnerable to the effects of human occupation. This vision of a planet that is both susceptible and modifiable has had a two-sided effect. On one hand, ambitious environmental initiatives have begun to embrace much larger scales of intervention.[3] From new cost-effective afforestation strategies taking root throughout the Amazon to weather manipulation projects for increasing annual rainfall in China, these elaborate initiatives have served as a critical testing ground for new multinational collaborations and expanded stewardship regimes.[4] On the other hand, this planetary optic has offered a viewpoint far removed from the local nuances and regional specificities that have historically underpinned the skillsets of planners and landscape architects. Satellite imagery and data-driven models have abstracted the planet and its manifold terrestrial systems through new modes of graphic reduction, allowing planners, designers, developers, policy makers, and just about anyone else with an agenda to oversimplify wicked problems in the name of consensus building.

This double-edged effect (expanded stewardship plus oversimplification) continues to force planners and designers into an age-old, self-laid trap of overpromising and underdelivering results. This trap is made extra hazardous by the perceived urgency of climate change, which has triggered an abundance of reactionary project proposals in search of shovel-ready, silver-bullet solutions that often grossly undermine the fundamental complexities of large-scale environmental and economic systems. For spatial planning and design to remain relevant in the face of projected climate-change scenarios, we must ensure that regional knowledge and local nuance do not disappear at the increasing scales of practice.

This essay highlights two megaregional initiatives: 2050—An Energetic Odyssey in the North Sea and the Great Green Wall Initiative (GGWI) in the Sahara and Sahel region of Africa. Both demonstrate the evolution of project scale from the two sides of the planetary optic, revealing tensions between new global imperatives and traditional design applications. As McHarg did half a century ago when he sounded the alarm and catalyzed a disciplinary turn toward the guiding principles of ecology, these projects signal a fundamental awakening to what is at stake given today's unprecedented flows of material, capital, waste, and destruction.

An Energetic Odyssey

In December 2015, 195 countries signed the Paris Agreement, committing to take actions designed to keep global temperatures from rising more than two degrees Celsius from preindustrial levels. The treaty constitutes a stunning shift in international policy and global industry—and perhaps most pointedly, in our cultural perception of environmental risk and responsibility—not seen since the Environmental Protection Acts of the mid-20th century. The sheer magnitude of this challenge and the degree of global coordination required to address it have led to the formation of several international coalitions charged with one central task—decreasing carbon emissions as quickly and comprehensively as possible.

The process of untangling the global economy from its associations with fossil fuels requires an almost superhuman capacity to visualize the aggressively complex, decentralized networks that prefigure human settlement patterns in the 21st century. European leaders have agreed to reduce carbon emissions by a staggering 80 to 95 percent by 2050, and the designer-led initiative 2050—An Energetic Odyssey is hoping to play a key role in demystifying the process for both policy makers and the general public.

This design research project was commissioned by the 2016 International Architecture Biennale Rotterdam

(IABR) under its curatorial theme, "The Next Economy." The immersive multimedia project, which has since been repackaged as a narrated video, is designed to reframe the conversation around European carbon targets by deemphasizing environmental risks and focusing instead on shared economic opportunities. The fourteen-minute sequence simulates an implementation strategy for energy transition on the North Sea—an area where, according to the project's narrator, Europe "will either win or lose the battle for renewable energy."[5]

The central element of this proposal hinges on the installation of some 25,000 wind turbines by 2050, or an average of fifteen turbines per week. The narrator begins by describing some of the project's challenges: "Our story is set in the most intensively used coastal waters in the world. With fishery and shipping routes cutting right across, it contains designated nature reserves and military zones, oil rigs the size of skyscrapers, countless oil and gas pipelines and there are already several wind farms. Moreover, the North Sea is used as a sink for pollutants and residual heat from our industries."[6] If this proposal is taken seriously, the basic challenges of permitting, installation, operation, and maintenance will be unprecedented. Yet, as the narrator ultimately contends, it is achievable.[7]

2050—An Energetic Odyssey is not a master plan. Instead, it is a communication schema, created by landscape architects, aimed at catalyzing a deep shift in perception among the public and policy makers alike. The project operates as a public relations tool for building consensus through a single, comprehensive vision of the future. It is an intentionally simplified abstraction of a complex idea that is made to seem feasible when visualized through a diagram. Although the narrator does identify some of the fundamental challenges, the visual scenarios remain separated from most of the real-world externalities that could

otherwise appear as logistical roadblocks or political sticking points. Hidden from view are the physical effects of global warming, sea-level rise, and natural disaster as well as the uneven distribution of resources and social burdens associated with these phenomena. The proposal also seems to disregard the fact that carbon levels continue to rise in spite of international agreements.

Projects like this foretell an evolving role for spatial designers as media producers, and the cultural appetite for this type of abstraction underscores the challenges of governance and communication in an increasingly complex and "mediatized" world. Dutch political scientist, planner, and coauthor of the project, Maarten A. Hajer, contends that today's policy makers must be able to "perform" through a dynamic range of narrative media in order to effectively persuade a multiplicity of publics.[8] Given that hitting global carbon targets will require universal buy-in from a widespread range of diverse parties, designers will likely find themselves increasingly tasked with communicating both the issues and the strategies of multinational climate governance through various forms of media production. Historically, this has meant repackaging dynamic multiscalar phenomena through extreme editorial reduction, which is useful in the short term but raises important questions about long-term effectiveness. Will the persuasive power of large-scale scenario modeling be strong enough to sustain a robust consortium of key personnel through political, technological, and generational changes? How will the perceived authority of these visualizations help support a more atomized implementation framework, scaled back down to the real-world operational constraints of territorial reconfiguration? And perhaps most important, who are the primary beneficiaries of such projects—local energy consumers (in this case) or a wider indirect audience of global citizens?

As Ian McHarg writes in *Design with Nature*, "Many of the problems that society confronts are of such inordinate complexity that it takes the greatest dedication and zeal to assemble the necessary data, analyze and prescribe."[9] In the fifty years since those words were published, access to data and the tools necessary for analyzing it has increased by an order of magnitude. Planners and designers have been able to leverage these tools in order to gain access to new professional opportunities at larger geographical scales, yet there are still very few revolutionary environmental solutions coming from the past twenty years of projective "landscape mapping."[10] In the future, the long-term success of projects like these will likely depend on how effectively they can transition from singular comprehensive visions to more granular local initiatives that will flourish because of—not in spite of—their plurality.

The Great Green Wall

The origins of the planetary optic, as we know it today, are rooted in other parallel histories of world making. To a large degree, any cultural acknowledgment that humans can (and do) radically alter the Earth has been preconditioned by the legacies of colonial terraforming. In Africa, colonial foresters from France and England were the first to propose a continental shelterbelt for combating the perceived encroachment of the Sahara Desert into agricultural lands along its southern edge.[11] In the early 1950s, the English forester Richard St. Barbe Baker lobbied for the construction of a "green front" barrier of trees to contain the spreading desert. Twenty years of droughts beginning in the 1970s gave wings to the idea, and in 2007 the African Union approved the Great Green Wall Initiative, which was drawn up as a contiguous band of

trees, more than 15 kilometers (9 miles) wide and almost 8,000 kilometers (5,000 miles) long, spanning the entire continent from Senegal to Djibouti.[12]

The central premise of the initiative has been more or less the same since the late 1920s, when French foresters coined the word "desertification," which has been used to suggest that African deserts and drylands are spreading outward from their historical extents owing to poor regional land management practices such as overgrazing and deforestation. This narrative has garnered substantial influence in sub-Saharan Africa and has been leveraged to secure public resources for monumental shelterbelt projects around the world, including in the United States, China, and the Middle East.[13] Today twenty-one African governments have agreed to participate in the project and have collectively received pledges of more than $4 billion in institutional funding.[14] The desertification narrative, which pits environmental forces against the ingenuity of human intervention, has helped to generate this type of international support, but it has also facilitated a grossly oversimplified understanding of desert ecologies. It has fundamentally ignored the role of climate change, naturally occurring cycles of drought, gradual species migration, and the history of indigenous stewardship practices that have facilitated human settlement in the region for countless generations.

If there is a single abiding characteristic of dryland environments, it is their extreme variability. These biomes, which cover about 40 percent of the terrestrial planet, undergo dramatic seasonal and annual changes predicated on natural cycles of rainfall, grazing, drought, and wildfire. In the case of the Sahel region, these perennial cycles have been extended and restructured by the effects of climate change and population growth.[15] Nevertheless, for centuries the desert has provided opportunities and livelihoods for the many communities that have learned how to both endure and exploit this regional variability. The GGWI, which has been branded as the image of a single green line meandering across the continent (reflecting the original colonial vision as described by Baker in 1954), has persisted as a clear idea but has struggled to perform meaningfully on the ground.

Since its inception, roughly 80 percent of all trees planted in the Sahel have perished, mostly owing to a lack of local support and stewardship planning, but a steady string of misguided policies has also contributed to the misappropriation of local resources.[16] Although these failures have been widely used to demonstrate flaws within the larger systems of African governance that surround this initiative, they also illuminate the shortcomings of singular landscape management strategies when deployed across huge territories and diverse cultures without direct input from the scientific community or local experts.[17]

In spite of these early failures, there are scattered instances of increased tree cover throughout the Sahel, especially in Niger.[18] This new growth is not the direct result of any top-down supranational landscape engineering project, but rather the effect of grassroots farmer-led initiatives to adopt traditional silvopastoral agroforestry practices—that is, farming that integrates trees and shrubs with crops and pastureland. Beginning in 2007, a heavily modified GGWI framework was drafted in response to these local successes. The new focus no longer emphasizes the singularity of a wall, but rather a mosaic of land use practices that may ultimately meet the performance expectations of the original wall concept.[19] These locally born practices help to ensure that long-term stewardship goals are met, and may in fact be used to sustainably precondition land for increased human settlement.

McHarg wrote that "city, suburb, and countryside become comprehensible in terms of the attitudes to nature that society has and does espouse."[20] In the case of the Sahel, the reductive logic of a fuzzy green line drawn across the map reflects the attitudes of Western colonists with little knowledge of dryland ecologies and a latent distrust of indigenous land management practices.[21] To assert that such a reductive framework could ever perform adequately as a landscape infrastructural planning tool exposes the hubris of designers and policy makers when faced with the overwhelming urgency of environmental risk. McHarg insisted on planning processes that could sustainably merge the aspirations of resource-intensive development with the dynamic sensitivities of regional landscape systems. In order to achieve this balance across larger continental scales and address the planetary imperatives of climate change, McHarg's methods must be expanded, fortified, and creatively reimagined to accommodate more nuance, detail, and complexity—not less.

A Return to Complexity

McHarg's process of collecting and superimposing spatial information to determine the most suitable land use designations began with a relatively straightforward knowledge of environmental science and his clients' needs. Generally, this allowed him to fine-tune his methods to target a predefined problem. McHarg's mappings added complexity to his clients' limited knowledge of the site, which in turn revealed a more carefully calibrated perception of wider regional systems and their relationship to planned urbanization. In the decades since *Design with Nature* was first published, the rapid proliferation of satellite vision, big data, and digital mapping software has continued to expand our perception of even larger-scale environmental systems with more accuracy. For planners

FIGURE 17.1 Aerial view of traditional agroforestry management in Niger, 2004. *Gray Tappan, EROS Center, U.S. Geological Survey.*

and designers, this has opened the door to new disciplinary arenas, but it has also fundamentally changed their professional roles and client relationships. Today policy makers, despite the complexity of planetary-scale problems, must present straightforward solutions in order to secure financial and political support. This often puts pressure on planning and design professionals to create empirical narratives that oversimplify the underlying dynamism of regional human-environmental systems.

McHarg identified a distinct directionality within both the creative process and evolution itself, which he described as "moving from simplicity to complexity, from uniformity to diversity, from instability toward dynamic equilibrium."[22] This observation became a fundamental element of his lectures and writings and underscored the value of an ecological viewpoint for planners and designers. He wrote, "The benefits of the ecological view seem patent to me,

but equally clear are the profound changes which espousal of this view will effect."[23] Indeed, this ecological view, framed by a growing environmental urgency, has drastically expanded the role of planners and landscape architects across much broader territories. Designing with nature now requires them to actively participate in the growing arena of climate governance without underrepresenting the complexities of climate science or ecological uncertainty. New tools of measurement and representation can empower a new generation of global stewardship if designers adopt a renewed commitment to applied research, scientific landscape knowledge, and local participation. Designers must find ways of building consensus for large projects without reducing them to one-liners or claiming to have a silver bullet. Otherwise, the double-edged effect of the planetary optic will continue to stand in the way of any meaningful or lasting innovation.

CHAPTER 18

Saved by a Salt Marsh

Thomas J. Campanella

THE MARINE PARK neighborhood of Brooklyn, New York, is a leafy streetcar suburb just north of Gerritsen Creek, a tidal estuary on the western rim of Jamaica Bay. The land here was inhabited by the Canarsie Indians for over a thousand years before being settled by Dutch *bouwers* in the 1630s. Incredibly, it was still under cultivation when Gotham's street grid rolled across it in the mid-1920s—Brooklyn's last agricultural landscape. The street I grew up on went from cabbages to Tudor homes in a couple of years. Marine Park itself, namesake of the neighborhood, was the subject of grand schemes and dreams before it ever became a park. It was one of the sites proposed for Gotham's first municipal airport (later built at nearby Floyd Bennett Field) and was nearly chosen for a 1932 exposition to commemorate the bicentennial of George Washington's birth—what was ultimately realized in Flushing as the 1939 New York World's Fair.

Plans for Marine Park eclipsed even these. The design by Charles Downing Lay—a cousin of the inimitable Andrew Jackson Downing and one of Frederick Law Olmsted Jr.'s first students at Harvard—called for transforming 1,800 acres (728 hectares) of pristine salt marsh into a hardscape Versailles. Larger than Central and Prospect Parks combined, Marine Park was a playground on steroids, a colossal machine for intensive urban recreation—with 200 tennis courts, 80 baseball diamonds, bocce pitches, bowling greens, three Olympic pools, a skating rink, a zoo, a golf course, a casino, and a theater grove large enough for 30,000 people. Gerritsen Creek itself was to be bulkheaded into the 2-mile (3.2-kilometer) Long Canal and a harbor for racing shells and sailing canoes. A new beach was to be created on Rockaway Inlet, anchored by great bathing pavilions. The crown jewel was to rise on the north side of Avenue U—the largest stadium in the world, with seats for 125,000 spectators, or twice the capacity of Yankee Stadium at the time.

Ironically, Charles Lay possessed a nuanced appreciation for the very sort of estuarine landscape his park would have rubbed out. "Of the beauty of tidal marshes," he wrote in a 1912 article for *Landscape Architecture*, "no one who has lived near them and watched their changing color with the advance of the seasons can speak too enthusiastically. They come to have a place in the heart which mountain scenery, with all its grandeur and fearfulness, cannot equal. Nowhere except at sea does the sky become so much a part of one's life, and nowhere is there greater beauty of line than in their curving creeks and irregular pools." He also understood their ecological complexity. "The tidal marsh," he wrote, "is a delicately balanced organism. It has a flora and fauna of its own, and it depends for its life upon the recurring tides, which bring soil and fertility and moisture for the plants at home there."[1]

None of this stopped Lay from plotting the destruction of one of New York's last great tidal wetlands. Fortunately, construction on Marine Park was delayed by the Depression and had only just gotten under way when Fiorello LaGuardia was sworn in as New York City's mayor in 1934. LaGuardia's park commissioner, Robert Moses, recognized Lay's plan for what it was: a costly ecological train wreck. He tossed the scheme in the wastebasket and ordered his design staff to restrict park improvements to a series of perimeter ball fields and the already-filled creek channel north of Avenue U (present-day Marine Park, bounded by Fillmore Avenue and East 33rd Street). "For the rest," he told his staff, "I am satisfied that Marine Park should be left largely as it is." Though extensive wetlands along Flatbush Avenue were filled in the 1960s for a golf course, the Gerritsen estuary has miraculously survived the many improvement schemes directed against it.[2]

Nonetheless, by the 1970s the creek had become a sad and forbidding place—with abandoned cars on the mud flats and discarded washing machines rusting in the marshes. Feral teens from nearby Gerritsen Beach tore up the trails with dirt bikes, and nearly every fall weekend a brushfire would be set that brought a dozen fire trucks roaring into the neighborhood. There was natural beauty at Gerritsen Creek, to be sure—rabbits and ring-necked pheasants, mummichogs, and horseshoe crabs in the shallows—but it was a marginal and troubled place, the forlorn edge of town where only kids and homeless people went.

How ironic, then, that this neglected estuary would save the very neighborhood that dismissed it. When Hurricane Sandy struck the city in 2012, tide-swelled Gerritsen Creek filled with a tremendous surge of water pushed ahead of the storm. The creek rose to more than 10 feet (3 meters) above mean sea level, the water coming up to the very edge of Avenue U. But it never spilled over. Had it breached this threshold, seawater would have raced inland unimpeded to Avenue R, filling the basements of thousands of homes—including my own. That did not happen because Gerritsen Creek was never paved and channeled into the hardscape monstrosity envisioned by "Landscaper Lay," as Moses called him. It had been left in a more or less natural state.

In fact, much of the estuary had only just been restored when the storm struck. The Gerritsen Creek Ecosystem Restoration Project was led by an agency better known for draining swamps than rebuilding them—U.S. Army Corps of Engineers—in a partnership with the New York City Parks Department. It involved stripping the estuary's vast monoculture of *Phragmites australis*—an invasive species that colonizes nutrient-poor fill to the exclusion of nearly all other flora and fauna—and augmenting White Island with dredge spoils from Rockaway Inlet. In all, more than 40 acres (16 hectares) of tidal marsh and coastal grassland were constructed and planted with a variety of native grasses. Gerritsen Creek is today a Forever Wild Nature Preserve, and the largest restored coastal wetland ecosystem in the New York metropolitan region. It was done in the nick of time. The restoration was completed in late summer 2012, marked by an opening ceremony on August 14. Hurricane Sandy arrived just eleven weeks later, the most powerful hurricane to strike the region in at least 300 years. The Gerritsen marsh was thus in fine form to carry out some of the most basic functions of tidal estuaries—buffering waves, reducing surge velocity, and acting as a reservoir to absorb a vast influx of water from the sea.

These functions lie at the heart of several innovative schemes proposed for New York City's vulnerable waterfronts in the years just before and after Hurricane Sandy. Disasters beget plans, to set things right and to make long-needed improvements to a city's layout and infrastructure. Most—like the half-dozen schemes to rebuild London after the Great Fire of 1666 or the countless plans for post-Katrina New Orleans—are doomed to oblivion, for one of the timeless truths about urban disaster is that cities get rebuilt more or less as they were before calamity struck.[3] In New York, however, real action is under way to protect the waterbound behemoth from the next big storm.

The most ambitious of the post-Sandy plans is the BIG U, a multipartner collaboration led by Bjarke Ingels Group (BIG) and the city of New York, focused on a critical 10-mile (16-kilometer) band of Manhattan waterfront from West 57th Street on the Hudson down to the Battery and back up the East River to East 42nd Street. The BIG U was one of several winning entries in the 2013 Rebuild by Design competition, an initiative of President Barack Obama's Hurricane Sandy Rebuilding Task Force. More than $300 million has since been made available by the U.S. Department of Housing and Urban Development to develop and implement the plan. The BIG U divides the waterfront into a series of autonomous flood protection zones known as "compartments," which—together—form a contiguous defensive hull to shield Manhattan's lowest, most vulnerable topography from the sea. Channeling Robert Moses and Jane Jacobs, the icons of Gotham's contested urban identity, the project considers both physical and social infrastructure. Each compartment—East River Park, Two Bridges and Chinatown, and Brooklyn Bridge to the Battery— is equipped with hard defensive measures against flooding that simultaneously provide an array of communal amenities in response to input from a series of neighborhood workshops.

The 64-acre (25-hectare) East River Park—phase one of the BIG U, now in development as the East Side Coastal Resiliency Project—features a serpentine "bridging berm" that is linked back to the street grid via ramps and "green bridges." The berm is designed to keep out storm surge and rising seas while providing new open space and recreation facilities for local residents. This is stealth infrastructure of the most benevolent sort, where the serious business of protecting 130,000 area residents is concealed by a saltwater-tolerant overlay parkscape that puts the berm to work for the people. "You won't see it as a flood wall that separates the life of the city from the water," explained Bjarke Ingels in 2014: "When you go there you'll see landscape, you'll see pavilions, but all of this will secretly be the infrastructure that protects Manhattan from flooding."[4] A similar strategy will be deployed at the southern tip of Manhattan, where additional berms will form a belt of high ground across the Battery. Just as the present Battery Oval replaced the Moses-era landscape designed by the firm Clarke and Rapuano—noteworthy for its forced-perspective mall—the Oval will be replaced by a "continuous protective upland landscape" behind which ventilation ducts and other transit infrastructure (not to mention some of the most valuable real estate on the Eastern Seaboard) will be safe from high water. The high ground will be anchored at one end by the Reverse Aquarium—an "architecturally optimistic building" that serves as a flood barrier while enabling visitors to peer into the harbor itself, to witness both its diurnal flux and its steady rise over time.[5]

The plan is not without its flaws. Compartmentalizing the shoreline is a seductive idea, but one reminiscent of the tragically flawed hull design that was meant to make the *Titanic* unsinkable. The great ocean liner was lost because no one anticipated the possibility of several hull compartments being breached simultaneously, as happened when the ship collided with a massive iceberg. According to parallel logic, the BIG U will only be able to perform as promised when every compartment on both sides of the island is in place and functioning. Given how things usually go in politically messy and fraught cities like New York, it will be a very long time before the BIG U's watertight hull is ready for a storm. Until then, each of the completed compartments will just be a lovely green playground waiting for its day in the rain. Implementation will be lengthy, especially if, as promised, the plan moves forward with a high degree of Jacobsian stakeholder engagement and community participation. Democracy is a wonderful thing, but—as Moses well understood—it tends to get in the way of getting things done.

Close in spirit to the BIG U is a joint project by Brooklyn-based DLANDstudio and Architecture Research Office, A New Urban Ground, that was commissioned for a prescient 2010 exhibit, *Rising Currents: Projects for New York's Waterfront*, at the Museum of Modern Art (MoMA). A New Urban Ground envisions an ecological infrastructure for the lower Manhattan waterfront that works in concert with the city's existing street and stormwater grids. A "quietly radical rethinking of urban design" that exemplifies Ian McHarg's idea of design with landscape, it consists of two primary components—a network of porous upland streets to keep precipitation from overloading the city's notoriously temperamental combined sewer system; and a "graduated edge" along the waterfront to receive both street runoff during major storms and influxes of high water from the sea. The edge itself will consist of a belt of upland parks with freshwater wetlands and brackish salt marshes below.[6]

Also commissioned for the 2010 MoMA *Rising Currents* show was the memorably named Oyster-tecture proposal for Brooklyn's Red Hook waterfront. Conceived by the landscape and urban design firm SCAPE, it proposes the construction of a living reef just offshore made of a woven web of "fuzzy rope" to support a variety of fish and other marine life. Seeded with oysters and mussels, the reef would gradually expand into a structure robust enough to attenuate waves and storm surge while also cleaning—through the biotic filtration processes of its mollusk colonies—millions of gallons of polluted seawater a year (a single adult oyster can pump through 50 gallons, or 190 liters, of water daily). Oyster reefs were once extensive in New York Harbor and, like coral reefs, played a vital role in protecting the shoreline from wave action and storm surges. Oysters, too, were a popular delicacy in New York City, until untreated sewage and channel dredging destroyed the vast beds in the 1920s (some of the sweetest oysters, served in the great hotels of Brighton Beach, were farmed in the brackish waters of Gerritsen Creek). SCAPE's Oyster-tecture effort led to a related project for Staten Island's Raritan Bay—Living Breakwaters—also a winning scheme in the Rebuild by Design competition. It consists of 3,200 linear feet (975 meters) of submerged breakwater along the Tottenville shore to be seeded with oysters by the Billion Oyster Project, an infrastructure that serves the dual objects of shoreline protection and restoration of Raritan Bay's once-rich oyster beds. The project has been granted $60 million in federal funding and is currently in the early stages of implementation.

Collectively, these projects represent a profound cultural shift away from the old clenched-fist way of defending cities against so-called acts of God, the man-against-nature approach championed by the Corps of Engineers for well over a century. All are variants of a "living shoreline" strategy to mitigate the effects of coastal flooding caused by rising sea levels and increasingly frequent and more potent storms. In essence, such plans look to the ecological infrastructure of the littoral zone to augment or create afresh—often in tandem with more traditional hard-structure defensive solutions—nature-based systems and structures to protect the shoreline from the ravages of extreme tides and storm surges. This approach to the problem of coastal resilience—conciliatory, synthetic, mediated—is a categorical rejection of the testosteronic hard-structure defensive tactics we have traditionally used to defend cities from the sea—dikes, seawalls, floodgates, bulkheads, revetments, jetties. Captain Ahab has set aside his harpoon, in effect, to negotiate with the troublesome whale. Of course, this is not to say that sharp harpoons are no longer necessary. No one in their right mind would suggest removing the levees that protect New Orleans or Shanghai from floodwaters. But engineered hard-structure solutions are costly to build and maintain and—because they are fixed and inflexible—are ultimately prone to catastrophic failure. They also produce unanticipated side effects. The long rock jetty at the western tip of Rockaway peninsula, built by the Corps of Engineers in the 1930s, blocked the natural westward drift of sand along the shore, triggering a rapid buildup of shoals and beach at Breezy Point.

Nature knows how to protect itself. A 2016 global study of shoreline habitats found that mangroves reduce wave heights by 31 percent, coral reefs by 70 percent, and salt marshes by 72 percent.[7] Replicating such systems—designing with landscape—is often counterintuitive: to reduce the risk of flooding, let the floodwaters in. A version of this plays out in the forests of the Mountain West. As a college student in the early 1980s, I spent summers on firefighting crews with the U.S. Forest Service and Bureau of Land Management. Wildland fire management was just beginning to change, with a new generation of foresters

and ecologists questioning time-honored suppression policy and practices. The traditional attitude toward forest fire was a macho-Manichean matter of good versus evil. "Fire is the enemy," we were told, and firefighting the "last moral equivalent of war." All blazes were to be extinguished—even those sparked by dry lightning in remote wilderness areas. Of course, this obdurate, ecologically ignorant credo produced a calamitous buildup of understory vegetation.

Fire is a natural and recurring part of forest ecosystems throughout the West. Trees like Douglas fir and ponderosa pine, which coevolved with fire, have thick bark that insulates the cambium from all but the hottest flames. Some tree species require a fast, light burn in order to reproduce—lodgepole pine, for example, whose serotinous cones pop open with intense heat. Excluding fire from forest ecosystems creates, over time, a powder-keg landscape that inevitably leads to killer conflagrations of the sort that blackened much of Yellowstone National Park in 1988—fires that burn so hot they destroy all vegetation and are very difficult, dangerous, and costly to control. Today, foresters use prescribed burns to fight fire with fire, preemptively depriving a wildfire of fuel by strategically reintroducing a natural part of the forest ecosystem.

The American landscape architecture profession has reached three major moral-ethical summits since its founding. The first, of course, was the Olmsted era, driven by a noble, if paternalistic, ideal of public service. That birthright was squandered by 1920, when most designers were content to make gardens for the rich and powerful. The profession's public service mission was revived, however, during the New Deal—the second summit—a heroic era that created a rich legacy of parks and parkways throughout the United States. After World War II, the profession was handmaiden to the highway builders, urban renewalists, and tract housing developers who destroyed our cities while leading us down the disastrous garden path of suburban sprawl. Modernism made an appearance, of course, but a minor one largely confined to gardens for a new generation of elites. Not until the 1960s and Ian McHarg did the profession reach its third summit, guided by a new vision of design with landscape.

The work reviewed here suggests that we may well be on the upper flanks of a fourth summit. Indeed, it is hard to think of a time when landscape architects were in a stronger or more vital position to ensure the future vitality and even survival of our cities. If Frederick Law Olmsted and his generation of park builders helped save the city from itself, it is the challenge of our time to save the city from the sea. Effective, sustainable countermeasures against rising sea levels, more frequent and increasingly powerful storms, and other threats induced by a warming planet constitute the moonshot of our age, and—as these projects testify—one that landscape architects are uniquely qualified to lead.

CHAPTER 19

Design with Change

Rob Holmes

DESIGN WITH NATURE opens on the Jersey Shore. "Sea and Survival," the first of the book's methodological studies, is remarkable for how it anticipates contemporary focus in landscape architecture on issues of coastal urbanization, storms, and soft infrastructure. Focusing on dunes as landforms that protect coastal communities from storm surge, Ian McHarg depicts dune growth through a time series of abstracted sections, which relate wind, sand, dune grass, and other plant species, as well as smaller diagrams that describe a sandy beach as it is affected by littoral drift, erosion, and groins. McHarg acknowledges the dynamic character of this landscape—"The New Jersey Shore . . . is continuously involved in a contest with the sea; its shape is dynamic"—and proposes to reorganize coastal development, giving the dunes space to evolve over time.[1]

Decades later, prompted by Hurricane Sandy in 2012, designers returned to the Jersey Shore. As part of the Structures of Coastal Resilience project, Paul Lewis's Princeton-based team proposed an "amphibious suburb" that would elevate roads as "berms with benefits" while allowing water in through canals to achieve "controlled permeability."[2] This idea resonates closely with McHarg's recommendation that the shore's communities not only preserve dunes, but

also look to Dutch dikes as a model.[3] Blue Dunes, proposed for the Rebuild by Design competition by WXY Architecture and West 8's multidisciplinary team, recommended lining the coast with new dune-topped barrier islands.[4] Another Rebuild project, SCAPE Landscape Architecture's The Shallows, showed "dredge wetlands" in Barnegat Bay.[5] All three projects reconfigure the relationship between coastal development and natural processes in order to adapt to the hazards of living along a now-rising ocean: Amphibious Suburb accommodates change in water levels; Blue Dunes constructs new landforms that would evolve with the dynamics of wind and waves; and The Shallows depicts a more beneficial relationship between wetlands and the industrial cycle of dredging. In proposing softer infrastructure to address the tension between settlement and sea, these projects share a clear lineage of concerns with McHarg.

Stability and Change

But this continuity conceals deeper differences. Despite McHarg's repeated invocation of "process" in *Design with Nature*, his acknowledgment of the short-term and long-term dynamism of coastal landscapes, and his interest in the dune as soft infrastructure, McHarg's conception of nature and, more important, his vision of what it means to design with nature, is too deterministic and does not account for the escalating scope of anthropogenic change. This should not be surprising. McHarg wrote as modern ecological science was still maturing and at the dawn of the Great Acceleration.[6] Developments in ecology since then have made it clear that change is a prominent feature of landscapes, and increasing awareness of the scale of human influence on Earth systems has made it clear that change is accelerating. Both these vectors of change are altering landscape practice.

In the decades since the publication of *Design with Nature*, the way ecologists conceptualize the phenomena they study has undergone a paradigm shift.[7] Where ecologists once pictured the Earth in terms of a self-regulating "balance of nature" oriented toward "equilibrium and stability," "influenc[ing] both [ecology's] theory and its practice," the newer paradigm is characterized by "nonequilibrium, heterogeneity, stochasticity, and hierarchical properties of ecological systems."[8] Landscape architects and allied professionals soon realized that this shift has significant implications for design practices, manifesting in new goals and new methods, including emphasis on the role of change.[9]

A key implication of this shift has concerned how the overall tendencies of landscapes are conceptualized and, as a result, how goals for intervention in ecological systems are framed. McHarg's method assumes a deterministic relationship between the elements of the "layer cake" that does not always exist,[10] and that cannot be assumed to be fixed over time. This descriptive determinism contributes to the perception, shared by most environmentalists of McHarg's time, of stability and balance in nature, leading to the enshrinement of those qual-

ities as goals.[11] Landscape architectural theories that incorporate the more recent insights of ecology will have subtler goals, preferring, for instance, dynamic adaptation to stability and diversity to balance.[12] Design practices that incorporate the scientific principles of adaptive management, emphasize the fluidity of ecological processes across notional site boundaries, and utilize processes as both instruments and objects of design have arisen in response.[13]

At the same time, awareness has been increasing that disequilibrium, indeterminacy, and change characterize not just ecological systems, but also the larger Earth systems processes that frame ecologies, such as global biogeochemical cycles, erosion and sediment transport, or weather and climate processes.[14] Moreover, not only have these processes always been subject to change, and not only have their oscillations long impacted humanity,[15] today their rate of change is increasingly locked in an accelerated feedback loop with processes of urbanization. Deforestation, for instance, binds processes of urbanization and global climate processes together. It is accelerated by urban populations' demand for timber, land clearance, and climate change. At the same time, deforestation produces greenhouse gas emissions and accelerates climate change, intensifying pressure on urban populations to compensate for that change by consuming more resources. An array of such impacts make humans true planetary change agents.[16]

Because he wrote before this became so clear, McHarg does not deal with the implications of this status. The construction of new island chains in Blue Dunes and the transformation of dredged material into wetlands in The Shallows propose designed nature of a scope that exceeds anything McHarg envisioned or advocated. Similarly, large ecological restoration projects under way today, in the Everglades, the Salton Sea, the Mississippi River Delta, California's Bay-Delta, and many other places, are far more ambitious in constructing novel natures (and weaving them together with human systems) than the term "restoration" suggests. Awareness of this capacity places designers in the position of being ethically responsible not just for preserving nature, but also for constructing it, even when they choose, often rightly, not to do so.[17]

But McHarg is not alone. Despite the certainty of landscape change, the fields that organize urbanization, including urban planning, logistics, infrastructure engineering, and politics, rarely account for it.[18] The typical expectation is that landscapes will remain fixed beneath buildings and infrastructure. But landscapes have never behaved this way, and they certainly do not now. This incompatibility between the dynamism of landscapes and people's desire for stability produces conflicts: between people affected unequally by changing landscapes; between stabilizing structures and the forces of moving winds, water, soil, and rock; and between economies that seek continuity and landscapes in constant migration.

Such tensions cannot be resolved by eliminating change because landscapes are not only subject to change, they are dependent on it, from beaches and barrier islands to deltas and rivers. To stabilize them is to destroy them. We need to learn to *design with change*, to organize urbanization around and as change.

This is not an entirely novel imperative.[19] Landscape architecture theorists have long recognized the centrality of change, and this focus has only grown in recent years.[20] Landscape urbanism, the most cohesive body of landscape architecture theory intended to focus on the approach of landscape architects to urbanization since McHarg, took flux, process, and indeterminacy as central concerns.[21]

What evidence can be found, though, that this theoretical agenda is impacting practice? Presuming that designing with change requires new methods, just as McHarg's project required overlays and the layer cake, what will those methods be? Three partial answers to these questions are illuminated by three projects included in this volume, all of which deal with the issues of infrastructure, urbanization, and coastal environments raised in McHarg's chapter "Sea and Survival."

Abandon Landscape Solutionism

The term "solutionism" was popularized by critic Evgeny Morozov to describe "an intellectual pathology," which he ascribes particularly to Silicon Valley, where problems are predefined on the basis of the capacity of contemporary technology to address them.[22] More generally, in a *solutionism*, the capacity for producing a solution precedes and defines problems. This results in a tendency to see the world in terms of solvable problems, ignoring aspects of the world that are not problems or not solvable.

For landscape architects, solutionism presents in the tendency to see landscapes as collections of problems that landscape architecture has the means to solve. This temptation multiplies when landscape architecture practices prove robust in responding to urgent needs. Landscape architects can offer ecologically superior and aesthetically preferable alternatives to civil engineering's systems of drainage, retention, and detention; therefore, we often reduce urban sites to mere stormwater problems, even in cases where gentrification and displacement are more significant problems. And because landscape architects have helped lead the (good and necessary) revaluation of wetlands as soft infrastructure, we often see coastal issues in terms of problems that wetlands can solve. We are susceptible to this framing because it is often powerful: if we can solve a problem, particularly if we can solve a problem better than anyone else, then we can probably convince someone to pay us to do it.

However, even where it seems to advance our agenda, landscape solutionism simultaneously undermines landscape architects. There are two major reasons why this happens. First, a solutionist framing of our work unintentionally pushes us away from the capacities that distinguish our field relative to the scientific and engineering fields that presently dominate the terrain of coasts, urbanization, and infrastructure. Where those fields are positivist, oriented toward efficiency, and relentlessly pragmatic, design, as a process, is recursive, debatable, and elusive. Solutions in design are always contingent because they are explicitly subject to reframing.[23] The task of problem-setting—the act of framing that organizes some components of a situation into givens while labeling others as variables—is both critical and, critically, not to be completed once and then considered solved, but, rather, always open to renegotiation.[24] Solutionism, in narrowing the framing of problems toward those that landscape architecture has already demonstrated the means to solve, is blind both to these strengths and to the inapplicability of landscape architectural precedent in new terrain. Emphasizing our designerly expertise in reframing is critical because landscape architects who hope to work beyond the traditional territory of the profession will have the most agency when we can demonstrate that our discipline offers capacities that other disciplines do not.

Relatedly, a solutionist framing fails to recognize the peculiar suitability of design for working in dynamic, complex situations where the effects of change are unpredictable, volatile, and politically contentious. These are precisely the contexts that demand design with change. In them, opposing interests seek incompatible ends while the climate and associated environmental processes are destabilized and accelerated by human action.[25] Put another way, contemporary culture is increasingly characterized by epistemic ambiguity at the same time that it is being swept along by accelerated environmental indeterminacy. Such a slurry of instabilities makes simplistic problem-setting hazardous and clear solutions undefinable.[26] Methods that submerge values are ineffectual when values are the primary medium of conflict. Under such conditions, design's recursion, debate, and elusion become strengths that equip designers to synthesize conditions and act intelligently in the absence of solutions.[27]

For their work in Norfolk, Virginia, as part of the "Structures of Coastal Resilience" study, the Penn team led by Anuradha Mathur and Dilip da Cunha contrasts their method with the typical way in which designers approach storms and sea-level rise. Rather than assume a problem, they first critically attend to the representational and linguistic choices that frame the situation. This critical attention began with a spatial metaphor, "turning the coast," questioning how the coast might be seen differently if it were mapped and conceptualized not as a dividing line between land and water, but as "a dynamic and porous coast of gradients in space and time" where "the sea extends deep into the continent."[28]

Their first means for constructing this alternative vision of the coast was mapping. A series of drawings traces "fingers of high ground," the fractal alternation of high and low elevations produced as rivers, streams, and creeks make their way to the Chesapeake in Virginia's Tidewater. Studies of a series of "offsites," such as the Fall Line's riverine scarps in Jamestown and Poquoson, ground the spatial metaphor of the turned coast in regional particularities. From these offsites, the team moved to a pair of test sites. Both are characterized by a tangle of infrastructure and development overlaid on a landform with the potential to be elevated into a constructed "finger" (figure 19.1). These new elevated spines draw on regional morphology to invent an alternative to levees, walls, and barriers.

Unlike such traditional flood control infrastructure, these earthworks are not intended to "solve" flooding. Rather, the designers ask how Norfolk might live differently with water. The fingers welcome water in, accepting and generating ecological and geomorphological change as components of future urbanism. They do not presume permanence; they are tied to climate scenarios with limited life spans. This rightly leaves open the need to reconsider Norfolk in future decades. They abandon one given—that the city can maintain its current form indefinitely—and inject a replacement: the water will come.

The purpose of avoiding solutionism is not just to defend the value of aspects of landscape practice that do not solve anything, but also to recognize that there are ways to act that do not rely on applying preconceived solutions to only the problems that fit those solutions well. The opposite of solutionism is not acceptance or passivity in the face of challenges; the opposite is critical, reflective, and meaningful practice.

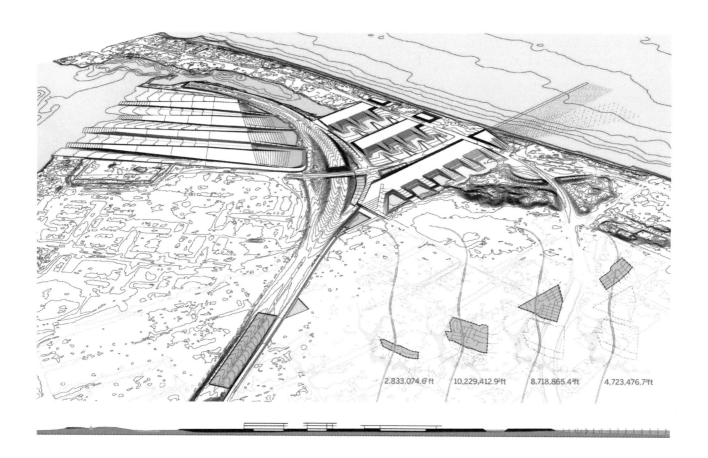

FIGURE 19.1 Fingers of High Ground channel flooding from rain and tides into alternating gradients at Willoughby Spit. *With permission, Mathur and da Cunha.*

Employ Cartography Generatively

Mathur and da Cunha's work also illustrates a key element of many design processes that avoid solutionism: they use cartography as a reframing device. Cartography has the potential to perform in a similar fashion in other nonsolutionist approaches to dynamic landscapes. James Corner, whose early work includes arguably the most influential account of cartography in landscape design processes since *Design with Nature*, argues that the generative potential of cartography is catalyzed by unconventional and eidetic representational strategies.[29] However, more conventional cartography can also undermine assumptions, reveal the contingency of givens, and interrogate values.[30]

Structures of Coastal Resilience emerged from a lineage that began a decade earlier with a multidisciplinary team led by engineer Guy Nordenson, landscape architect Catherine Seavitt, and architect Adam Yarinsky. They produced a study of the consequences of climate change for the New York–New Jersey Upper Bay, *On the Water: Palisade Bay*.[31] That book inspired the Museum of Modern Art's *Rising Currents*. In that exhibit, the design teams of *Rising Currents*, including one led by Yarinsky's firm ARO with landscape architect Susannah Drake and DLANDstudio, produced an array of speculative responses to coastal change near New York City. After Hurricane Sandy, multiple studies followed, including the city of New York's plaNYC, Structures of Coastal Resilience, and Rebuild by Design.[32]

On the Water thus prefigured a great deal of design work that has, in its best iterations, often engaged coastal climate change in a nonsolutionist fashion. How did it have this effect? *On the Water* consisted of two main components: speculative proposed interventions in the estuary's infrastructure and a rich, multidisciplinary mapping effort, which sought to lend scale, clarity, and precision to the challenges climate change poses for the Upper Bay. Data collection and reconciliation using ArcGIS produced a seamless digital topobathy model of the New York–New Jersey metropolitan area, which, together with built infrastructure and demographic data, became the base inputs for a digital flood model, enabling the quantification and spatialization of hurricane flood risk. The project team carefully studied the sectional and material character of the Upper Bay's full coastline, producing an "edge atlas" that rigorously fills a gap in existing data.

The maps produced for *On the Water* are representationally conventional, but they clearly depict possibilities, such as flooded streets, damaged homes, and endangered communities, which became realities when Hurricane Sandy arrived. Mapped threats gained urgency, the reigning assumption that conventional settlement on the coast could continue indefinitely was undermined, and post-Sandy design work was backed by government and private funders.[33]

This is not to say that mapping deterministically produces design responses. The two design proposals for lower Manhattan included in this volume, DLAND and ARO's A New Urban Ground and Bjarke Ingels Group's BIG U, both emerging from the *On the Water* lineage—though the former via the exhibition *Rising Currents* and the latter via Rebuild by Design—are radically different responses. A New Urban Ground shows lower Manhattan's edges softened and pixelated in a blur of park, wetlands, and marshes. The contrast with the BIG U, which deploys a U-shaped berm around the base of the island, is clear. Where the BIG U promises a wall to keep the water out, fortifying Wall Street and the Financial District, A New Urban Ground can be read—particularly in light of its direct relationship, via Adam Yarinsky's leading role in both teams, with the estuarywide islands, piers, slips, and wetlands of *On the Water*—as a first step toward a larger archipelago of softened edges that would be distributed democratically around the Upper Bay, so that when the water comes, it comes equally for all.

Model Differently

This contrast between the BIG U and A New Urban Ground points not only to the crucial role of framing and values, but also to the need for design methods that interrogate future change. Without such methods, politicians, publics, and planners who expect predictability will almost always prefer proposals that aim to fix nature statically in place over efforts to design with change.

Where efforts are made to model change in relationship to landscape and urbanism, this work is typically done by scientists and engineers, using numerical, physical, and computational models of varying complexities and precisions. These models are rarely dynamically incorporated into design processes. Because such models are so resource-intensive, it is typically unrealistic to model more than a few options. This excludes modeling from participation in the iterative, dense, and rapid consideration of alternatives that design requires.

If landscape architects want to improve how their proposals interact with future change, then they will need native modes of modeling. These modes should have at least two key qualities. First, they should permit more rapid iteration than typical scientific and engineering models accommodate, so that modeling does not prevent the exploration of a robust set of possibilities. Second, they should be aimed at understanding form as consequential trajectory. Form needs to be modeled not merely as static configurations of matter and space, but as dynamic matter with comprehensible trajectories, both in terms of internal configuration (the propensities of a form over time) and external relationships (how a form both has its own trajectory bent by external forces and bends the trajectories of other forms).[34]

A variety of emergent work is now hinting at how such modeling might develop.[35] Of the projects featured in this volume, Sean Burkholder and Brian Davis's work for the Dredge Research Collaborative (DRC) on the Great Lakes–focused Healthy Port Futures project stands out.[36] Burkholder and Davis are working with a team of modelers and engineers, including faculty at the University of Minnesota's Saint Anthony Falls Laboratory, which specializes in physical hydrological modeling, and experts from the U.S. Army Corps of Engineers. They have developed a three-part modeling process, which roughly progresses from broadest and fastest in the hands of the landscape architects to slowest but most precise by the Corps of Engineers.

The first of the three parts in this process, design-led physical modeling, can be distinguished from typical uses of modeling in multidisciplinary design projects because it serves a generative role.[37] That is, modeling is used in the initial iteration of design options rather than to evaluate designs that have been produced using other criteria. Such modeling accords landscape architects greater agency. If landscape architects do not participate in modeling, then their position in the design process is either downstream or upstream of modeling. Being downstream of modeling constrains the landscape architect's starting point, reducing the capacity of the landscape architect to freely evaluate relationships between form and value. Being upstream may allow the landscape architect full freedom in selecting starting points, but divorces the process of selecting those starting points from responsive feedback about consequential trajectory. In contrast, landscape architects who understand and use models of change can investigate questions about the behavior of form that permit them to integrate traditional landscape architectural concerns, such as concern for program, material, and space, with concerns that are pressing in dynamic landscapes, such as the movement of water, the accumulation of sediment, and the behavior of plant species.[38]

This capacity to open diverse options, particularly options that diverge from traditional practices, is crucial to design with change. The pace of, scale of, and, in many cases, threat posed by contemporary environmental change require rethinking settlement. Given the insoluble complexities and zero-sum nature of many of the situations produced by this accelerated change, this rethinking must avoid solutionism and embrace the propensity of design practices to challenge the framing of problems. Cartography can play a key role in nonsolutionist landscape architecture, as it is often the means by which a situation is framed and givens selected. And when novel framings are in place, designers require procedures for evaluating alternatives in new contexts where mere precedent is inadequate. New forms of modeling are one such procedure. Design with change will require the continual refinement of disciplinary tools to translate theoretical insights into convincing procedures, projects, and proposals.

CHAPTER 20

Hybrid Thoughts

Kathleen John-Alder

IAN McHARG BELIEVED that good stories, like good design, provide life with meaning, particularly when these accounts instill human action with moral purpose. He had a habit of repeating the ones he liked best and turning them into ecological axioms.

One of his favorite, oft-repeated anecdotes was one he heard from the anthropologist Loren Eiseley during a discussion on the television program *The House We Live In* in the spring of 1961. McHarg, who served as the host of the show, had invited Eiseley to discuss the environmental repercussions of human ascendance to the position of dominant species on Earth. Eiseley responded with a sweeping narrative of evolutionary history that described the emergence of life and its maturation into a living web of plants and animals adaptively united by chance, calamity, and unimaginable creative possibilities. The novel products of this interactive system included the human mind, technology, and urban civilization. But here, he cautioned, danger lurked, as evidenced by the increasingly elaborate mechanical constructs, both real and imagined, that caused people to lose contact with "the earth from which we sprang and upon which we are still dependent." Human thought, he further warned, was unconstrained by physical limits; therefore, it was imperative to balance scientific and

technological progress against the knowledge of ourselves as organisms embedded within and responsive to the world like all other living creatures. According to Eiseley, to act otherwise could be dire, as the rebound of the natural world in response to human action was "apt to be more terrific" than anticipated. He then observed that the modern city, with its veinlike anatomy of concrete highways and buildings, is a perfect example of what happens when an organism renounces limits and escapes, for a moment, from the living web of life. "If one flies over any extended area of the country I think that one can almost see this as one might look at a fungus spreading on an orange," Eiseley stated.[1]

I was reminded of the exchange between McHarg and Eiseley, and of Eiseley's likening of human behavior and spatial patterns to the spread of fungus on an orange, when I was first introduced to the project 2050—An Energetic Odyssey in June of 2016. I was sitting in Irvine Auditorium at the University of Pennsylvania listening to the notable theorists and practitioners who were invited to present at the Landscape Architecture Foundation Summit. Dirk Sijmons, one of the four speakers on the first panel, had just begun his thousand-word Declaration of Leadership entitled "Landscape Architecture: New Adventures Ahead!" when a computer animation of the North Sea at night, as it appeared from space, filled a large screen at the front of the auditorium. The image was breathtakingly beautiful, viscerally compelling, and slightly ominous.[2] The North Sea was rendered in a dark cobalt blue and laced with faint red lines that indicated the location of existing oil and gas infrastructure. The surrounding landmasses of Europe and the United Kingdom were black. Barely discernible patches of yellow indicated the location of urbanized areas. Suddenly, bright white lines of wind moved across the image. Their appearance signaled Sijmons's hope that the new adventure for landscape architecture would be the creation of a renewable energy infrastructure. As I continued to watch and listen, I learned that his excursion into the terrain of the sustainable future involved the installation of 25,000 wind turbines in the North Sea, each generating ten megawatts of power. The installation would cover 22,008 square miles (57,000 square kilometers), and its energy output would satisfy 90 percent of the region's needs in 2050. I also learned that the scheme was developed in response to the 2015 Paris Climate Accord and its tripartite mandate to adopt green energy sources, reduce greenhouse gas emissions, and limit the rise in global temperature. A digital clock on the upper-left and lower-right corners of the image chronicled the progression of the envisioned spatial changes.

As the years ticked by and the animation approached the Paris Climate Accord target date of 2050 for net-zero carbon emissions, patches of white light, which corresponded to the new wind turbine farms, appeared in the water, multiplied, and grew in intensity. Blue lights along the shore marked the location of energy distribution centers. They, too, multiplied over time. As the infrastructure system continued to develop and grow, bright blue bolts of energy burst from the distribution centers, crisscrossed the water, and created a vast sparkling web. In response, the color of the water turned from cobalt blue to shimmering gray. At the climax of the presentation, a green mesh enveloped the urban centers. It pulsed, lifelike, in unison with the diurnal rhythms of human organisms that fed on the wind-energy grid. To indicate the extent to which the project was environmentally responsive, radar detected the presence of flocks of migrating birds, and the wind turbines in their path ceased operation to allow safe passage. The power grid was monitored with such precision that this requisite shutdown produced less than a flicker of inconvenience.

As the computer animation played on the screen, Sijmons provided an accompanying narrative. During this commentary, he noted that the professional skills of spatial design, pattern recognition, and modeling enabled landscape architects to synthesize complex data into practical and imaginative solutions that addressed multiple problems. Moreover, this skill set could be used to envision future scenarios that forged consensus between conflicting political, economic, and environmental agendas, and thus endowed landscape architects with the power to shape the body politic and public will. In the case of the Energetic Odyssey, these capabilities had allowed Sijmons and his colleagues to forge a consensus among diverse parties that included the Netherlands Ministry of Economic Affairs; the Port Authorities of Amsterdam, Rotterdam, and Zeeland; the coal and nuclear power producer RWE; the electricity transmission corporation TenneT; the dredging contractor Van Oord; the petroleum conglomerate Royal Dutch Shell; and two nongovernmental organizations devoted to the environment—the European Climate Foundation and Natuur & Milieu. He proudly claimed that the visioning scenario displayed in the animation unified the disparate agendas of these groups; and further, this collective consensus had overcome the "spell of defeatism and crisis of the imagination" that had stalemated the actions outlined in the Paris Accord. Just the past week, he stated with pride, the ministers of the North Sea countries had signed a cooperative agreement to turn the untapped potential of this marine landscape into a sustainable energy infrastructure.[3]

Sijmons further claimed that the Energetic Odyssey reflected the discourse of the Anthropocene embodied by the actions of the Dutch chemical engineer and Nobel laureate Paul Crutzen. In the early 1980s, Crutzen's modeling of chlorofluorocarbon interactions revealed that the inadvertent release of these compounds into the air during industrial processes had destroyed the ozone layer and dangerously altered Earth's atmosphere. His subsequent activism against their manufacture resulted in the United Nations 1988 Montreal Protocol and the banning of their use.[4] Energized by this outcome, Sijmons emulated Crutzen and modeled his actions on the belief that human behavior could be redirected toward an alternative energy future. Accordingly, he did not seek to stop industrialization; he instead sought to alter the processes of industrial production to be less exploitive and destructive. His explanation revealed no apprehension that this strategy was in any way environmentally dangerous. The imperative was to move forward, experimenting and inventing, while also keeping ideas malleable, thoughts fluid, and actions open to change. In the new environmental reality of the Anthropocene, he argued, there was no going back to either prelapsarian innocence or the natural equilibriums that existed before the industrialization of the past two centuries.

Sijmons's language, I noted, also incorporated the technocratic jargon and ecologically coded inscriptions of landscape urbanism that are now famil-iar to most designers. These statements included the observation that the field of landscape architecture was the operative medium of urbanization; it was impossible to separate human action from natural processes; and strategic intervention was preferable to regulatory controls. The patterns of energy and materials that flickered across the screen at the front of the auditorium reinforced the close relationship of this worldview to the ecosystem models developed in the mid-20th century. This was particularly noticeable in the way the flows, events, and elements (energy subsystems) that constituted the proposed installation adjusted to each other as they, in turn, adapted to new circumstances.

From an epistemological standpoint, this logistical tour de force of human thought and scientific bravado, which Sijmons presented with technocratic precision and engineering authority, represented Donna Haraway's human-nature cyborg at its hybrid apogee (minus the irony and the plants and animals).[5] But I began to wonder if the progressive stance of this manifesto was a transformative emblem of historical progress, or, as Haraway warned and Eiseley cautioned, a chimera fantasized to represent the ambitions of energy production as a benign system of social reproduction. In other words, was the Energetic Odyssey a deceptively framed continuation of the aggressive actions that had created the anthropogenic climate problems it was purporting to fix; a solution to the threat of climate change that openly accepted past aggressions; or perhaps a little of both? The worldview displayed on the screen definitely contained the ghosts of past territorial claims, geopolitical maneuvers, and military strategies that required further investigation. Most problematic in this regard was the way the project narrative entangled objective analysis and strategic visioning with free will. As explained by Sijmons, the parties who participated in the project willingly did so because they benefited in some way. But his remarks on the distribution of economic and political power among the group members skirted the issue of equity. Entities that controlled the existing infrastructure, or that had monetary resources, clearly had the stronger negotiating position. Left unsaid was whether they controlled the dialogue.

My subsequent research on Sijmons revealed that in 2014 he had published *Landscape and Energy: Designing Transition*.[6] As a forerunner of the Energetic Odyssey, this study of urban land use explained how to institute an energy infrastructure geared toward net-zero carbon utilization through the retrofit of existing facilities. A case study on Rotterdam, for example, reconfigured the roofs of the city into a field of solar panels, building facades into green walls, residual heat from industries into home heating systems, economically worthless trees into biofuels, and wetlands into wind turbine islands.[7] The excess energy produced by the wind turbines, emulating a scheme developed in the early 1980s by the Dutch engineer Lukas Lievense, pumped water into an offshore reservoir. During calm winds, water released from the reservoir drove the wind turbines and maintained energy production.[8] In the Lievense scheme, the top of the eighty-foot reservoir wall accommodated a highway. Sijmons removed the road and designed the reservoir to be an "ecological water recreation hot spot."[9] A perspective of birds flitting among the sleek wind turbine blades and kayakers skimming around their massive foundations provided an "impression" of a prototypical wind island in the year 2020. Diagrammatic readouts of energy flow, in line with the kilowatt-hour tracking of power plants, documented the combined savings provided by this assemblage of spatial operations. Needless to say, this course of action was first and foremost concerned with energy grid redundancy, feedback monitoring, fail-safe mechanisms, and synchronized operations. Little attention was paid to qualitative values or visual aesthetics. It was assumed that these subsidiary needs would be achieved through improved urban function, comfort, and health, and through the subsequent reduction of extreme weather events.

Not surprisingly, *Landscape and Energy* based its proposed spatial reorganizations on the supposition that free will was both a moral proposition and a negotiated settlement. "Where is the world going," the text asked rhetorically, "and where do I want it to go?"[10] In response to this question, Sijmons argued that the attainment of environmentally responsible energy production required landscape architects to be adept players in the political schemes and free-market machinations of the fossil fuel economy. Entrenched political and economic groups were going to lobby for their interests, and landscape architects had to do the same. In case anyone doubted his seriousness, he quoted the master strategist Niccolò Machiavelli:

There is nothing more difficult and dangerous, or more doubtful of success, than an attempt to introduce a new order of things in any state. For the innovator has for enemies all those who derive advantages from the old order of things, whilst those who expect to be benefitted by the new institutions will be but lukewarm defenders.[11]

The full-length video created by Sijmons, Maarten Hajer, and H+N+S Landscape Architects for the 2016 International Architecture Biennale Rotterdam (IABR), Atelier 2050, in contrast to the Landscape Architecture Foundation animation, which was edited to conform to the requisite ten-minute presentations and silenced to accommodate Sijmons's Declaration of Leadership, was energized by the sound of the wind, waves, and dramatic music.[12] A woman with a prestige-enhancing Oxbridge accent provided the narration.

The IABR video began with Vladimir Putin, Angela Merkel, Barack Obama, and Xi Jinping signing the Paris Accord on Earth Day 2016. This opening sequence positioned the Energetic Odyssey as an important patrimony of this momentous political achievement and its vision of resource stewardship, world order, and cooperative power. The IABR video also contained a marine spatial map of existing shipping routes, oil rigs, underwater pipelines, military installations, and marine preserves that indicated wind farms were not a radical imposition, but instead a logical extension of previous political and economic accords.

At the conclusion of the video, it was apparent that Sijmons and his colleagues considered their energetic adventure into the future to be a stellar emblem of progress that demonstrated how to sustainably organize the environment to human advantage through the control and management of the resources at hand. In keeping with traditional notions of the economy of nature, the operative mantra of their proposal was maximum organic utility through minimum organic cost.[13] To assuage fears associated with technological hubris and resource exploitation, the work incorporated risk management scenarios calculated with comfortable margins of error. The net result was a complex process of energy production and utilization in which human action augmented natural forms and functions. This ambition, although magnitudes larger in scale, was nonetheless comparable to the outcomes envisioned for the sand engines, river reconfigurations, and storm surge barriers that have been devised over the years to defend the shoreline and people of the Netherlands from the relentless onslaught of nature. By all measures, this was Dutch terraforming at its finest—rational, methodical, and managerial, with a touch of mercantile capitalism and marketing opportunism.

The IABR video also contained paired photographs that juxtaposed the proposed infrastructure installations with images of marine organisms. For every environmental challenge that could be raised against the project, the imaginative minds of the project team conceived plausible, ecologically beneficial outcomes. These included new habitats provided by the stone footings of the wind turbines, new marine preserves to offset the thousands of square kilometers occupied by the turbines, fishing-free zones, and a piling system that minimized the impact of construction on marine organisms. This is where the project, which until then had been confident of its objectives and visioning strategies, moved into a terrain of uncertainty. The team acknowledged the project would alter water currents, temperature, nutrient composition, and sediment distribution, and thus alter where animals feed and live. Such changes are not inherently bad, but they do portend ecological winners and losers. In a similar manner, the marine spatial map indicated that the areas devoted to wind turbines, in conjunction with an increase in the size of the marine preserve, would alter fishing patterns, which possibly explained why the fishing industry was not a member of Sijmons's visioning team. But even more worrisome, this territorial map also suggested that the project's alteration of fishing patterns had the potential to negatively affect species diversity in an area vastly larger than the North Sea. This potential scenario may seem minor in relation to the overall objective of the project to advance the goals of the Paris Accord and keep Earth's temperature from rising more than 3.6°F (2°C), but it does call attention to the fact that this project would, by its very nature, engender unexpected changes and unforeseen consequences.

As I pondered the project's unresolved issues, I came to the belated realization that the Energetic Odyssey was an example of consummate environmentalism, but not in the sense that it based its objectives on a nostalgic vision of nature and the atavistic rejection of progress. I also realized that the project was indeed ironic, in the sense of Haraway, in that it did not resolve the contradictory power relations and biophysical equilibriums of the modernist project, but instead proffered a solution that maintained these imbalances in all of their progressive glory, albeit in a more figuratively sustainable and data-intensive guise. And this was where danger lurked. Sijmons, as stated in his Declaration of Leadership, was fully aware of the inherent risks, but nevertheless embraced the danger and daringly assembled conflicting ideologies and infrastructures into a hybrid organism endowed with such a high degree of complexity that it was destined to assume a life of its own as it adroitly adapted to change, successfully reproduced, and generated new social traits. In a series of actions that both flouted and embraced convention, he willingly conceded that the inventive agility of the mind would inevitably create things that moved our thoughts farther and farther away from visions of purity and dreams of innocence. By so doing, he directly faced what Haraway and Eiseley instinctively understood to be the existential anxiety underlying modernity's fantasies of power and perfection. Despite, or perhaps because of, the elegant engineering and feedback mechanisms that the Energetic Odyssey deployed to allay this apprehension, it also illustrated how difficult it has become to maintain the illusion that we are masters of the world and that technology will continue to propel us forward into noble, environmentally sustainable adventures that preserve the modern comforts and conveniences we have come to accept as our birthright. But at this stage of the game, what other alternatives exist?

Which brings this story back to the analogy of the Earth and the orange, patterns of settlement and human action. But this time, consider the image of global invasion in relationship to the starkly dramatic photographs of the Sun and the Earth that appear on the front and back covers of the first edition of *Design with Nature*.[14] In addition to signaling the vast scope of McHarg's design project, these images endow his argument with a sense of mystery, wonder, fear, and nostalgia that impel us to engage the world—the house we live in—and acknowledge the consequences of our actions. 2050—An Energetic Odyssey accepts the moral responsibility of this charge, but denies the mystery, fear, and nostalgia. This is where the project derives its power and strength, and where it makes a striking break between design with nature then and design with nature now. And yet it is also true that both projects affirm the belief that ideas and actions are relative and causal, and therefore it is best to determine the risks and benefits before formulating a plan. The need to see the connections between things and the desire to pose generative solutions to perceived challenges is the ecological axiom that indelibly links design with nature *then* to design with nature *now*.

CHAPTER 21

Design on the Edge (a Dance Between Emergence and Extinction)

Nina-Marie E. Lister

May the things of this world
be preserved to us, their beautiful secret
vocabularies. We are dreaming it over and new . . .

Jeanne Lohmann[1]

TUCKED BETWEEN THE WEATHERED FOLDS of crinkled gray bark, high on a reaching branch of an ancient red oak overlooking Lake Ontario, the golden eye winks. Pinpricks of sunshine catch its bright orange flowerlets, appearing like fireflies dancing in dappled leaf-light. The golden-eye lichen, *Teloschistes chrysophthalmus,* lives in essential synergy with its partner, microscopic algae, which are delivered by wind and water, whether in waves crashing, lapping, or simply evaporating into the trees that line the barrier beach. The lichen's relationship with the Great Lakes, as much as with its host tree, is at once timeless and ephemeral. In the Anthropocene, it is a precarious perch for this rarest of organisms, between the magic of emergence and the void of extinction.

In this suite of nested landscapes, from the lake to the trees and its branches, the golden-eye (figure 21.1)—along with other, more humble lichens—might be said to incubate as much as to represent the sublime, both in the precariousness of their being (their constituent, intertwined bodies), and in their becoming (the synergy of their living). The microscale complexity of their habitat together with the symbiosis between fungus and algae is a marvel of emergence in coevolution and (temporary) cooperation.[2] The symbiotic and physical beauty of the lichen bodies, coupled with the relatively improbable conditions for their flourishing, reveal the plurality and complexity that underscore the layered diversity of life on Earth—and with it, a powerful urgency to design with, and in, nature, now. This immediacy cannot be overstated; it brings into stark clarity the work of the human species—at once "acutely vulnerable, and the most powerful actor on an interdependent planet"[3]—the primary agent transforming the planet's future at spatial and temporal scales that are unprecedented, unplanned, and unimagined.

Embodying intricate, interdependent, emergent, and threatened relationships, the lichen is a microcosm of ecological complexity. As such, it is both metaphor and exemplar for the work ahead for landscape architecture and its allied practices. More important still are the challenges these nested relationships present for design (and designers) in contemplating and activating our collective agency to protect and steward Earth's biodiversity and the complexity of its landscape contexts. The cold caveat here is that the planet will continue with or without humans; it is ultimately human survival that is at risk—along with most of the planet's biodiversity and the complex ecosystem relationships that sustain us. The world that is transforming and emerging through the Anthropocene will be a world we *do not yet know*, almost certainly an illegible, impoverished world made less fertile, hospitable, and "manageable" by any modern measures.

Through the domination of industrial economies and urban processes, ecological relationships and landscape habitats are, at worst, fragmented, denuded, and destroyed; at best, they are altered and rendered invisible or illegible to their inhabitants, human and nonhuman. By consequence, without a diversity of landscape types and habitats, most of the globe's biodiversity—known and unknown—is at undeniable risk. Fueled by increasing urbanization and its constituent forces, millions of acres of Earth's natural and agricultural cover are lost each year through land conversion. Exacerbated by human-induced climate change, these compounding forces are leading inexorably, faster than ever, to an unprecedented and irretrievable loss of global biodiversity. The Anthropocene is the planet's sixth great extinction epoch: from almost daily extirpation to mass extinction, the wealth of the world's biodiversity is bleeding away.[4] Although there is no consensus on how much we have to lose, what is painfully certain is that most species will be lost before they are even found.[5]

So what is to be done to slow the loss, remediate, recover, and steward the species and landscapes that remain in the world as we know it? In spite of over a century of active effort to protect habitats and species, at the scale of both the community and the continent, most countries have been woefully unsuccessful at improving conservation of species, let alone reducing their loss.[6] By contrast, landscape architecture has been focused on humans, and has been arguably more effective at integrating a diversity of human uses into a rapidly urbanizing fabric. These efforts have not been without resounding benefit, as, for example, the socially and culturally progressive GreenPlan Philadelphia and Medellín's River Parks in Colombia aptly demonstrate in chapters 14 and 16 in this volume. In activating a rich mosaic of multifunctional landscape services and supports in diverse urban communities, from stormwater infiltration to pedestrian mobility, urban agriculture, and tree canopy improvement, these plans and their projects are at once timely and necessary interventions. They improve human well-being across social and economic strata and urban livability in cities of all sizes, and arguably stimulate a greater attachment to the nature of a place—a nature that is fast disappearing around these same communities. Yet on the myriad life forms that define the character and constitution of a place, these plans remain silent; they can only be read as biologically denuded in their provision of a healthy diversity of species beyond the human.

The far-reaching and compounding negative effects of human activity are well beyond the ability of any one discipline to solve. The scale and complexity of the biodiversity challenge alone demands greater human diversity, both in professional and cultural expertise and in collaboration among practitioners. Yet to date, the responsibility for biodiversity conservation has rested almost exclusively in the domain of Western scientists and environmental policy and lawmakers. Designers and artists, diverse or not, are almost never engaged in what has become a planetary endeavor. Despite Ian McHarg's clarion call to "design with nature" fifty years ago, landscape architecture scholars and practitioners remain almost entirely focused on humans and urban spaces.[7] While their work is more visible than ever over the past twenty years, in planning, designing, and making iconic and beautiful parks, reinventing performative waterfronts, activating engaging community parks and vibrant public spaces in cities (many of them celebrated in this volume), landscape architecture is virtually absent from what is arguably the most important design challenge of our time: to design for biodiversity in a world of climate change, and thus for the protection of life itself. Despite the burgeoning scholarship in the environmental humanities, the silence of landscape architects on the brink of the Anthropocene extinction is nothing less than deafening, akin to the foreshadowed silent spring of our making.

What explains their absence at this critical juncture? Design is a uniquely, perhaps defining, human endeavor. Indeed, by many measures of the Anthropocene, our political-economic industrial system has been enabled and constructed by designers. Their legacy ought to offer fertile ground for new applications and opportunities for innovation under conditions of rapid change and transformation. So, when designers are needed most to intervene and address the unintended consequences of that system, from climate change to biodiversity loss, where are they?

FIGURE 21.1 The Great Lakes population of golden-eye lichen, *Teloschistes chrysophthalmus,* is listed as endangered in Canada. Native to the shoreline of Lake Ontario, this last remaining population is harbored in a provincial park less than 200 kilometers (124 miles) from Toronto, the country's largest city and its growing metropolitan region of 5 million people. *With permission, Samuel R. Brinker.*

Another way to frame this conundrum is to suggest that the absence of the design disciplines has opened a niche that is ripe for occupation and cooperation; it has laid the groundwork for a new role for creative talents, and with these for new economic ventures, to shape a new relationship with a novel and emerging nature, one whose arrival on our doorstep is imminent.[8]

From Conservation Science to Socioecological Design

For the past century, humans have practiced various forms of resource and land conservation worldwide, including establishing protected land and water reserves for hunting and fishing, national and state parks for outdoor recreation, and more recently, large-scale conservation landscapes intended to protect vast ranges to facilitate breeding and feeding movements of large, far-moving predators, their prey, and other desirable wildlife species. The origins of this managerial approach to conservation are deeply embedded in a long-held binary and hierarchical view of nature as sacred and sublime, and humans as profane and unfit to play in its garden, yet entitled (even destined) to pillage it.[9] These and other notable large park-making efforts, in spite of advances in collaboration with local communities and indigenous peoples, are still dominated by the 20th century's resource-based conservation paradigm, with the majority of public projects found in Northern and Western industrialized countries.[10] Half of all protected areas recognized by the International Union for the Conservation of Nature (IUCN) fall into the categories of national park, monument, or species management area.[11]

While sovereign countries and their constituent states are responsible for creating and maintaining national and state parks and protected areas, the number of alternative conservation mechanisms is growing, including private conservation lands such as those owned and managed by nongovernmental organizations (e.g., the Nature Conservancy in the United States and the Nature Conservancy Canada). Others include privately owned for-profit game reserves, such as gorilla forests and safari parks now common in East and South Africa; similar models are emerging in Indonesia (e.g., orangutan reserves and bird sanctuaries) and in Australia (e.g., bush heritage and coastal reserves). The IUCN reports a global trend in the increase of privately protected areas (PPAs) and recognizes that, though difficult to evaluate and track, PPAs may hold significant advantage as a rapid response to biodiversity loss because land parcels can often be secured more quickly though private site purchase or lease than by national or state agency processes. Notwithstanding the potentially significant conservation benefits of PPAs, land acquisition has social impacts, especially in poor and vulnerable communities, which risk being dispossessed of their lands if they are converted to PPAs—a practice that the IUCN has made clear it does not support.[12]

Some of these PPAs are instrumental in providing local economic benefits from legitimate biodiversity protection initiatives by operating as ecological tourism destinations for wildlife viewing and landscape experience; others, however, are effectively mineral or timber resource extraction areas, or hunting reserves focused on prize or trophy game to be taken by tourist-hunters, sometimes at the expense of long-term sustainable benefits to both local human and wildlife communities.[13] Evidence shows that biodiversity conservation is more effective when efforts are ecosystem-focused and deployed through collaborative strategies, engaging local communities and citizens in cooperative and mutually socioeconomically beneficial relationships for the long term.[14] Collaborative conservation must also make room for and legitimize traditional knowledge and practices, which are sometimes in tension with dominant ecosystem management regimes. Typically, conservation biology remains the primary expertise used to inform the establishment and management of protected areas. It is increasingly recognized, however, that indigenous or local cultural and spiritual values, as well as contextually specific practices, may be as or more effective (and appropriate) in achieving long-term conservation outcomes. The Linea Negra sacred seashore in Santa Marta, Colombia, is one example, in which a degraded river estuary was returned to local indigenous people for restoration and comanagement using ancestral practices.[15] In a similar approach in Spain, the Santiago de Covelo "Common Hand" Community Land Project has engaged local farmers and ranchers in a woodland restoration project that permits sustainable patch rotations of livestock grazing and timber harvesting to integrate ecological, social, and agricultural benefits while restoring native biodiversity.[16] In such contexts, there are specific and important roles for landscape architecture in the emerging space of collaborative conservation, from visualizing project infrastructure to designing alternative scenarios and outcomes to spatializing ecosystem benefits. Although this is an emerging niche, government agencies responsible for parks or social services, as well as NGOs, would do well to engage landscape architects in expanding the planning and delivery of collaborative conservation ventures.

As a result of the 2010 Aichi conference and associated biodiversity targets, the global Convention on Biodiversity (CBD) now includes a wider range of opportunities for collaborative conservation.[17] These are intended to complement and enhance traditional protected area management by recognizing a plurality of management and governance structures, including those with indigenous peoples and local communities—and which implicitly support the role of design across sectors and contexts. Importantly, the CBD now also explicitly recognizes the importance of "other effective area-based conservation measures" (OECMs), which include specific areas that, though not recognized as protected, are governed and managed over the long term to result in effective biodiversity conservation with associated ecosystem services and cultural and spiritual values.[18] This expanded and complementary mechanism for conservation opens significant opportunities for landscape architects to work within human settlement areas in resource, tourism, and socioecological contexts where biodiversity conservation is either a primary outcome or an associated benefit to the community.

Yet collaborative conservation strategies need not be small-scale ventures. Africa's Great Green Wall (GGW) (La Grande Muraille Verte pour le Sahara et le Sahel) is a remarkable and unlikely example of conservation-driven collaboration among some of the world's poorest peoples in the most unforgiving of habitats. A large-scale linear conservation initiative over 8,000 kilometers (4,971 miles) long and 15 kilometers (9.3 miles) wide, stretching from Senegal to Djibouti, the Great Green Wall Initiative (GGWI) is a consortium of twenty sub-Saharan countries collectively working to slow climate change–induced desertification through aggressive and directed tree-planting in tandem with dryland agriculture and range management strategies. Rather than biodiversity protection per se, its focus is adjacent, on collective action for healthy soils and improved rural development.[19] This project is a hopeful example of conservation in the unlikeliest of places, one that defies the odds and works in different contexts at several interconnected spatial scales, with a focus on community improvement outcomes that, by extension, necessarily protect biodiversity (although that in itself is not the primary aim). As a transboundary project, the GGW demonstrates the power of collaborative strategy, grounded in local actions across and within those communities that have at once the most to gain and the most to lose. At nearly 15 percent complete, the initiative appears to have staying power, having galvanized the region over twenty years.

With some similarities to the GGWI, the Yellowstone to Yukon Conservation Initiative (Y2Y) also achieves transboundary and international conservation outcomes, although it is grounded in a landform and focused on wildlife. Y2Y's objective is to connect and protect one of the world's last intact continental mountain ecosystems with the primary mission of providing wildlife with freedom to roam—a mission impossible in most landscapes today. Centered in the North American Rocky Mountain ecosystem, the Y2Y project spans 3,218 kilometers (2,000 miles) and encompasses an area of 1.3 million square kilometers (501,933 square miles), from Yellowstone National Park in the United States to the Yukon in Canada. Engaging its mission as a "geography of hope," Y2Y uses an umbrella approach to coordinate and support many local and context-specific organizations and communities that share the common goal of conserving and connecting the large landscape habitats of the Rocky Mountains for their iconic wildlife and the ecosystems on which they depend.[20] Both the GGWI and the Y2Y projects are at work at the scale of the biome—landscapes that span continents, cultures, and countries. As such, they rely on effective partnerships and meaningful collaboration within and across their communities and watersheds. Yet, as conservation projects that emerged from research-driven ecosystem science, their effectiveness may be limited by these same practices and traditions. The

canon of reductionist science that gave rise to what some have called "the illusion of ecosystem management" is embedded in a paradigm that has set humans aside from nature, outside "the environment."[21] This paradigm has no flexibility for the messy chaos of complexity, or for its errant companion, uncertainty. Escaping its "suffocating embrace" means loosening one's grip on control, testing new tactics with imperfect data, and inviting new partners and voices to the drawing board.[22] But such a shift is not easy in practice, or under governance models that rely on clear boundaries between agency responsibilities and territories.

Perhaps it is not surprising then that few large-scale conservation projects have engaged the work of landscape architects to develop policy and design strategy, even in collaboration with scientists and planners. Nor is conservation planning and design part of the professional training curricula for landscape architects. Yet it is clear that landscape designers could play an important role in visualizing systems, developing strategy, and communicating and building the relationships (and trust) on which conservation practice relies. As facilitators, animators, and visual artists, landscape architects are trained to imagine various futures, to visualize alternative scenarios, and to realize these in novel ways, through interdisciplinary teams, transdisciplinary and perhaps irreverent approaches, or with unlikely partners. Design visualization processes help communities understand complex socioecological systems by rendering their forms and functions legible; in doing so, they can help cocreate shared values and identify benefits for long-term resilience. By revealing how ecosystems work and their benefits to communities, designers also bring ecological assets to the foreground of a project by helping to curate the sociocultural and political conditions necessary for stewardship and conservation.

In addition to best-available science and effective policy, design skills are likely to become even more important as biodiversity loss and its consequences accelerate unevenly in response to climate change. Indeed, design thinking and creative innovation may offer the only hope for biodiversity when uncertainty is high, risk is real, decisions are urgently needed— and there is no time to wait for better data.

Such urgent times are on the horizon. Although activated by grassroots communities, the GGW, Y2Y, and other large-scale national and international conservation efforts have been guided and supported by global research and science-driven leadership at the United Nations and the IUCN.[23] Since the founding of the IUCN, subsequent policies and targets for biodiversity, and thus for wilderness landscape protection, have varied widely, from the CBD goal of safeguarding ecosystems in at least 17 percent of terrestrial and inland water by 2020[24] to ecologist E.O. Wilson's ambitious Half-Earth movement to protect from development 50 percent of the world's natural landscapes.[25] Since the 1992 Earth Summit in Rio de Janeiro, at which the Biodiversity Convention was opened for signatures, 196 countries have joined and 15.4 percent of the world's land and inland waters are deemed protected.[26] Doubtless there has been progress in conserving biodiversity, but the rates of loss far outweigh the gains in habitats and recovery, and some of the most remote and wildest landscapes are furthest behind (see table 21.1). In the abstract, conservation targets (no matter the number or percentage) are blunt instruments; in practice, they need both policy direction *and* design interventions to empower action and engage the imagination, from local communities to nation-states. Regardless of the targets we set and adopt, the challenges are unevenly distributed: the largest countries by area inevitably carry a greater obligation for protection,[27] and the world's most bio-diverse places, or "hotspots" of biodiversity, lie in direct conflict with the world's most rapidly urbanizing regions, many of them among the poorest.[28] For this reason alone, the imperative to design *with* and *for* biodiversity demands new approaches, diverse voices, radical strategies, and almost certainly, uneasy alliances. From restoration sites to rewilding initiatives, from greenways to green infrastructure, from parks to protected areas, the evidence is clear that we must develop nothing less than a radical planetary strategy of biodiversity-centered landscape protection, activated through connectivity and collaboration across scales and cultures.[29]

To ignite such a radical strategy, we need new, diverse, and complementary conservation tactics, across scales and in multiple contexts. We can start with what we know has promise, particularly those interventions that favor connected, designed networks of performative or functional (living) landscape infrastructure.[30] The plants, animals, and people give these networks life. These living infrastructures are needed both for their ecological functions and to serve as physical connections, conduits for biodiversity through urban areas where only remnant and degraded habitats are likely to remain. Whether porous and soft-edged infrastructural solutions of the New Urban Ground (Museum of Modern Art) project, or engineered reinforcement structures interspersed in the BIG U (New York) and other Rebuild by Design (New Jersey, post–Hurricane Sandy) initiatives, there are many opportunities to hybridize infrastructure with living organisms (e.g., in well-established prototypes for reef structures, living walls and roofs, green bridges, and bioswales). These can and should reveal a greater range of biodiversity they can support and engage. As vital connective habitats, land and water infrastructure may become essential as "lifelines" linking local parks and other landscape refugia for a wider variety of less charismatic and unseen species, from pollinating insects to songbirds, bats, and amphibians. These are critically needed for passages, food sources, carbon sinks, and habitats alike, as our landscapes become more urbanized. Several of the more ecologically operative projects discussed in this volume (e.g., Emscher Landscape Park (Germany), Room for the River (The Netherlands), Zandmotor (The Netherlands), and Rebuild by Design) are well-known precedents for delivering performative ecologies—designed landscapes that reveal and facilitate ecosystem functions—and offering new insights and powerful potential for cultural-natural integration. For example, Emscher Park's adaptive reuse of an industrial site was among the first regional-scale projects to engage the work of nature (plants) to transform gray infrastructure into green, thereby shifting the perception of the region from rustbelt to greenbelt. In part, it linked a reconstructed landscape through social, recreational, ecological, and cultural programs, and by repurposing and redirecting the site's history, rather than erasing it. Underpinned by a similar paradigm shift at an even larger scale, the Netherlands' Room for the River project was a radical departure from flood control to flood management, accepting the inevitability of river floods as the basis for redesigning planning and management policies *with* landscape designs for three major rivers. In literally carving out landscape space for river meanders, additional channels, and naturalized floodplains, the project's premise embraced adaptation, flexibility in living, and engineered systems. Defined by hybrid infrastructures,

Table 21.1
The Largest Countries and Their Protected Lands and Waters

COUNTRY	RANKING	LAND AREA (SQ. KM)	LANDS PROTECTED (%)	WATERS PROTECTED (%)
Russia	1	16,874,836	10.42	3.23
Canada	2	9,955,033	9.69	0.87
United States	3	9,490,391	12.99	41.06
China	4	9,361,609	15.61	5.41
Brazil	5	8,529,399	29.42	26.62
Australia	6	7,722,102	19.27	40.56

Note: The overall protected-area statistics obscure several significant obstacles to improved progress: notably, the United States, one of the most influential nations in the world (and the third-largest in area) is not a party to the Convention on Biological Diversity. Similarly, while Canada was the first signatory party to the convention (and the second-largest country by area), it is the furthest behind (among the six largest countries) and is unlikely to meet its commitment to the IUCN's 2020 target of 17 percent protection. Convention on Biological Diversity (website) is www.cbd.int.
Source: UNEP-WCMC, Protected Planet (website), "Protected Area Profiles from the World Database of Protected Areas," October 2018, www.protectedplanet.net.

these projects also make space for the emergence of novel ecosystems and for the navigation of our changing relationship with and in them.

Large wilderness is becoming rare, but its vast power and promise lies in our collective imagination. On the ground, the interstitial spaces between remnant wilds are still overlooked for their ecological potential, but soon these may become the sites of everyday practice. Designing and remaking connections between remnant wild fragments will be paramount, from peri-urban edges to suburban hydrocorridors; from agricultural working lands to reserves for hunting, foraging, and harvesting; from derelict places of urban decay to postindustrial spaces made, and remade, into emerging novel and hybrid ecosystems. Together these patchwork landscapes will form a wild mosaic, from refuge to regeneration, for the next wave of conservation and restoration—and perhaps our best hope for biodiversity. The world will need design tactics informed by systemic understanding of the full spectrum of landscapes from urban to suburban to rural to wilderness.[31] The local work of the landscape architect will be humble: to stitch together the fragments, to nurture the connective tissue in between. But the cumulative design challenge is nothing less than planetary.

Accordingly, the IUCN has broadened its reach for biodiversity conservation to include strategies for a wider range of protected areas and the peoples living in them.[32] Specifically, the CBD calls for *connected and integrated spaces*:[33] this is the design challenge of our era to which landscape architecture must rise, and with it, (re)weave the tapestry of the wild back into the landscape of the future. After all, we are not so different from the lichen, embedded in its context, at once resilient in its cooperative but dynamic partnership, and precariously dependent on the structures and flows of its place. Humans, too, depend ultimately on a coevolved and still evolving relationship with biodiversity, from plankton to pollinators of flowers to fungi, from beetles to birds of all feathers. We are locked into a morphing dance with the myriad complex life forms among us, both with the ones we know and with the novel and newly emerging. To design at the edge of the Anthropocene is to learn how to see and live differently—in what Jedidiah Purdy has poignantly called "a beautiful, devastated, resilient, fragile world that threatens, inspires, and alienates us."[34] The paradox of climate change, and with it, biodiversity loss, is that it is both a human-designed problem and likely humanity's greatest design challenge. Our ability to *design differently*—for adaptation, humility, and compassion—is now paramount. We must invest with humility in the material of nature and the language of landscape,[35] in compassionate design that adapts to change, adds value, builds performance, reveals beauty, and makes meaning from experience. At the edge of the epoch, it is high time to *design with the nature we know, now*: design to (re)affirm a culture of nature, to honor the Earth, and its lifeforms and landscapes—from the humble to the majestic—that sustain us in the whole of our being, beyond any "service" we imagine it provides.

CHAPTER 22

Landscape Design and the Democratic Prospect

David W. Orr

IAN McHARG PROPOSED ecological design as a means to bridge the widening gap between humans and the natural world caused by the fragmentation of knowledge and governance.[1] The former he attributed to reductionism that divided the world into hermetically sealed disciplinary compartments; the latter, to bureaucratization that creates government agencies that often work at cross-purposes. Both are manifestations of the drive to exploit nature more efficiently in the "belief that the earth is a structure that people are licensed to plunder."[2] In McHarg's view, the accumulation of problems, dilemmas, crises, and "long emergencies" of our time grow out of the hubris that has caused us to be

> the bullies of the earth: strong, foul, coarse, greedy, careless, indifferent to others, laying waste as we proceed, leaving wounds, welts, lesions, suppurations on the earth body, increasingly engulfed by our own ordure, and, finally abysmally ignorant of the way the world works, crowing our superiority over all life.[3]

McHarg seldom minced words, and he was not a small thinker. The goal, as he put it in an essay in 1970, was not just to "reconstitute architecture" and landscape architecture, but to reconstitute "all of society."[4]

To that end, he developed a coherent and systematic method to bring the sciences, especially ecology, to bear on urban design and land use decisions at the regional scale. For McHarg, the goal of the designer was to be a "catalyst" or "enzyme" for an ecologically smarter and more resilient society. The alternative to designing with nature was "capricious, arbitrary, or idiosyncratic, and certainly irrelevant," and he wrote that such practitioners "should be handcuffed and their licenses taken away until they learn the way the world works."[5] One might similarly deal with ecological malefactors in Congress, corporations, banks, the media, and the White House who are also proudly ignorant of how the world works as a biophysical system and why that knowledge is important for what they do and for comprehending what they are undoing. But I digress.

McHarg's best years at the University of Pennsylvania coincided with the rise of the environmental movement, in which he was a powerful force. The National Environmental Policy Act became law in 1970, followed by the passage of major environmental legislation aimed to protect air and water, endangered species, rivers, and wilderness. It was a time in which large changes in the human role in the natural world seemed possible, and problems, however difficult, seemed solvable. But solutions, in McHarg's view, would require unifying academic disciplines as well as government agencies to avoid redundancy and unnecessary conflict, and the development of a capacity for genuinely ecological planning and foresight. As McHarg put it: "The greatest advance will occur when it is recognized that integration and synthesis constitute the greatest challenge and provide the greatest promise of success."[6]

McHarg said many brilliant things, but those words I consider to be among the most important. Integration and synthesis imply a system in which the individual parts fit together and interact in harmony to their mutual benefit. The work of ecological designers begins, accordingly, in the acknowledgment of that interrelatedness and our implicatedness at all levels, from landscape to ecosystem to ecosphere. Systems thinking and ecological design, however, threaten powerful interests that prefer smaller questions, partial accounting, and narrower boundaries of moral consideration. In short, ecological design and the work of integration and synthesis run counter to the oil, coal, and gas industries and their allies who still intend to build out the energy-intensive, sprawling, endlessly expanding, and technologically driven society, whatever the cost.

The political and financial power of that vandal economy goes a long way toward explaining why the years since 1980 have not been overly kind to the idea of ecological design and systems thinking more broadly. For all of our successes, and they are many, and for all of our considerable efforts, and they are admirable, we are losing the effort to save a habitable planet. The immediate causes include rapid climate destabilization, ocean acidification, and the loss of biodiversity, all driven by the expanding human footprint. With determination and effort, some damage is repairable in a timescale that matters, but much of it is irreversible. As much as one wishes that it were otherwise, it is not.[7]

Accordingly, those like McHarg with an ecological perspective are fated to "live alone in a world of wounds . . . that believes itself well and does not want to be told otherwise."[8] Since Aldo Leopold wrote those words in the 1940s, ecological designers have done many good things, but in total they do not match the scope, scale, and urgency of the challenges we presently face and that our progeny will confront through the centuries of the "long emergency."

The question, then, is what designers and planners can do seriously and soon to improve the human prospect, and not just lament our peril. The overriding fact is that we know much more about the science of ecology than we do about its implications for the design of governance, law, and policy. In other words, we do not yet know how to translate ecology and Earth systems science into laws, regulations, public institutions, and economic arrangements that support and sustain the design revolution McHarg envisioned. The upshot is that any adequate response to our predicament must begin with an understanding of political economy large enough to include ecology and Earth systems science, and the organizational capacity to make ecological design the default setting.[9]

That sea change in perception and priorities will require recognition of the fact that the use and disposition of land, air, water, forests, oceans, minerals, energy, and atmosphere are inevitably political, having to do with who gets what, when, and how. The "who" includes all who qualify as citizens, as well as the unborn and those presently excluded from our moral community. "What" includes everything derived from nature that is transformed into wealth, as well as the ecological processes that recycle the resulting waste or consign it to land, oceans, and atmosphere. The "how" of politics are the rules that govern inclusion, exclusion, political processes, and the allocation of power. For designers, there is simply no way to be apolitical. To the extent that we stand aloof from politics, we give tacit assent to the status quo and the powers that are destroying the habitability of the Earth. For ecological designers the point is that politics, policy, and political philosophy matter and should be expressed in ways that clarify, inform, provoke, encourage, inspire, and cause us to remember, imagine, and create better possibilities than those in prospect. The goal is to counter a rising tide of despairing nihilism and build a constituency of citizens who are both ecologically competent and dedicated to democracy, and who understand the relationship between the two.

Landscape designers work at scales ranging from local to regional. Their work is not overtly political, and they are seldom politicians. They work, however, in situations affected by the politics of permitting, financing, taxing, budgeting, planning, and voting with city councils, planning departments, county officials, and state agencies. In short, design of all kinds and at all scales is part of a system in which design and the political realm interact.

Most important, designers now work in a time of political decay in which democratic institutions and the "habits of heart" that undergird democracy are coming undone. Facing rapid climate destabilization, addiction, inequality, and political turmoil, what might ecological designers do to improve the human prospect? The question is not as daunting as it may first appear. Ecological designers work in public on projects that are physical and visible, and in one way or another, instructive. Design, whether of landscapes, buildings, communities, or cities, is inevitably educational. For better or worse, design informs by its sheer presence. The question, then, is not whether but how design can best instruct toward the goal of building and empowering an ecologically competent citizenry. Of many possibilities, consider the following.

First, inclusion of the public in the design process helps to stretch the boundaries of democracy that typically stop at the factory gate, outside the corporate C-suite, and well before land use decisions are made. "Planning is a political act," in the words of Frederick Steiner, and "the public should help set goals and objectives, read landscapes, determine best uses, design options, select courses for moving forward, take actions and adjust to changes."[10] By making involvement easier and more accessible, the public's participation in the decisions that shape their places makes it more likely that community values and interests will prevail. Participation is not just empowering; it also acquaints people with the sciences of ecological design and civic collaboration necessary to democracy. But a note of caution is in order. Done right, democratic planning must be inclusive, fair, and undergirded by a decent regard for the public good. Done wrong, it can reinforce biases and existing inequities.

Second, designers can create convivial places in which citizens meet face-to-face to talk, debate, argue, celebrate, and share.[11] Models for democratic spaces include the agora of classical Athens, the speakers' corner in Hyde Park, the New England village green, the Southern front porch, urban pocket parks, taverns, churches, and civic squares, including Tiananmen Square in Peking and Maiden Square in

Kiev. Democracy comes alive in public spaces where people gather, and it withers in their absence. Gathering Place in Tulsa, Oklahoma, for example, is conceived as a public space to bring people together in a city with a history of racial violence and a growing divide between classes.[12] It is the brainchild of Tulsa billionaire George Kaiser and was designed by Michael Van Valkenburgh Associates, creators of Brooklyn Bridge Park and Maggie Daley Park in Chicago. Their intention was to create a space that can help heal old wounds of racial violence and bridge the widening chasm of class and income.

Third, ecological design is a form of instruction about our interrelatedness in the web of life. From 1996 to 1997, for example, several hundred Oberlin College students and local residents participated in the design of the Adam Joseph Lewis Center and its surrounding landscape. The goal was to design so well as to cause no ugliness, human or ecological, somewhere else or at some later time.[13] The result was the first entirely solar-powered, zero-discharge building on a U.S. college campus and the first green building to monitor and display its energy and water use. Members of the design team, including William McDonough, Carol Franklin, John Todd, and John Lyle, became tutors to students and community members in creating a model of ecological design as pedagogy that inspired dozens of other projects in the region and beyond.

Fourth, ecological design can help the public to remember its past and to create a more honest and decent future. It can remind people how human decisions shaped a particular place and with what long-term results; how the history of a place affected human ecology; and how intertwined histories—ecological and human—can be made visible in design projects in ways that heal both communities and the land. The National Memorial for Peace and

Justice in Montgomery, Alabama, for example, honors the lives of more than 4,000 victims of racial terror in the South.[14] Their history is ours. Their lives mattered then and still do. The brutal racism that cut their lives short was also part of a larger pattern of exploitation that included land degraded by cotton farming and a system of sharecropping that impoverished soils and souls alike. Similarly, in Maya Lin's Vietnam Memorial made of reflective granite, one sees the names of the dead etched on a surface that reflects viewers' faces, suggesting our tacit complicity in the war.[15] At the memorial's exit, the Capitol is visible straight ahead, the place where complicity was made policy and law, and from there led to the tragedy of the Vietnam War. Perhaps the act of remembering can cause one to look forward as well. Maya Lin's designs at the Peter B. Lewis Gateway Center at Oberlin, for example, include a porte cochere with a poem written by her brother Tan inscribed in three concentric circles on the concrete; the poem describes species likely going extinct in Ohio because of climate change and those likely to thrive in a hotter future.

Fifth, ecological design is at the heart of what Thomas Berry calls our "Great Work" of healing and repair. Imagine a new public agenda to restore damaged places, ranging from local superfund sites to global waterways, lakes, seas, coastal areas, deforested regions, and deserts.[16] Imagine a global initiative to restore the Aral Sea, repair the Chesapeake Bay, reforest the Harappan forests of India, rebuild populations of threatened species in Africa. Imagine a fraction of the money spent on war diverted to restoring life of degraded ecological systems.

In various ways, the projects considered here and in the paragraphs that follow are part of this Great Work. They engage the public in design, create new public places, provide education in the art and science of ecological design, cause people to remember, and bring about healing through re-membering. To some degree, each plan includes the public in decision making. The Yellowstone to Yukon Conservation Initiative has mobilized 300 organizations, including First Nations and private landowners, around the goal of maintaining and restoring degraded lands within the corridor. The Malpai Borderlands project along the U.S.–Mexico border in Arizona and New Mexico brings ranchers and environmental advocates together to improve land management and to resolve ongoing disputes over the effects of grazing on brittle lands. This effort is notable for providing a moderate center of gravity between competing views of the science of land management. On the Willamette River in Oregon, the plan for the Willamette River Basin is exceptional for combining history, ecology, and community envisioning sessions into an atlas and reference work for future development of a rapidly growing region. Similarly, Healthy Port Futures engaged citizens in rethinking and redesigning port facilities and adjacent lands in Ashtabula, Ohio, situated on Lake Erie, which are threatened by agricultural runoff, warmer temperatures, and changing ecologies. If successful, it could lead to similar efforts in the port cities of Cleveland and Toledo.

In response to Hurricane Sandy, Rebuild by Design in New Jersey and the Museum of Modern Art's A New Urban Ground projects have engaged the public in discussions of the threat posed by rising sea levels to New York City, and by implication to all other coastal cities. The issue will grow more contentious in the coming years, driven by questions of what and whom to protect, and how, and with whose money. Likewise, these and all projects pertaining to climate change will become more urgent and more contested.

The Stapleton development, on the site of the former Stapleton airport in Denver, restored a brownfield site with the usual mix of concrete, toxic soils, and urban politics. It is now a successful "mix of neighborhoods, parks, and businesses." At a larger scale, GreenPlan Philadelphia has had the advantage of a unified focus on water management and has restored and daylighted streams and improved water infrastructure to separate storm flows from blackwater sewage. The results are encouraging, particularly for the improvement of housing and for economic development more broadly. Envision Utah has similarly engaged the public in an exercise to identify goals and development strategies in a rapidly growing but fragile ecology.

These are exemplary projects, each wrestling with the difficulties of meshing the sciences of ecological design with different ecologies, varying circumstances, and the political realities of land use decisions. In total they reflect the limits of land and time and the realization that there are far better and more practical, beautiful, and enduring ways to design and inhabit our places.

Slowly winning the effort to reverse global warming, preserve species, and heal the land and waters is the same as losing, Bill McKibben has said. If we intend to preserve a habitable planet, we will have to do much more, and do it very soon. On that, I offer two final thoughts. The first has to do with the profession of ecological design. Ian McHarg was what Jeff Schmidt calls "a radical professional."[17] He was radical in the sense of getting to the root of what ails us. He was, moreover, a dangerous radical—a danger to cant, pedantry, arrogance, pretense, obfuscation, professional protocol, and timidity. He had a historic career, but he was not a careerist curating his résumé. He had better things to do.

Second, McHarg was a systems thinker concerned to find what anthropologist Gregory Bateson called the "patterns that connect" and to create a discipline that "solved for pattern."[18] He aimed to change and enlarge the paradigm of landscape design, to create in effect what John Wood calls a "meta-discipline" that would challenge the forces of hubris and domination that are driving the world to the brink.[19] A discipline, in other words, that is dangerous to waste, greed, profligacy, and short-term thinking, but one that fosters healthy places, healthy people, beautiful landscapes, prosperity, conviviality, civility, good work, and harmony between humans and natural systems.

CHAPTER 23

Dump-Heap Naturalists

Catherine Seavitt Nordenson

THE FRESH KILLS LANDFILL on Staten Island, New York City, claims the ignoble distinction of being the largest anthropogenic earthwork on the planet, containing 150 million tons of household trash. No longer active, this former municipal waste disposal site comprises 2,200 acres (890 hectares) of refuse distributed over four capped mounds ranging in height from 90 feet (27 meters) to 225 feet (69 meters). Pinwheeling around an extensive wetland marsh system along the Arthur Kill, the "dump" mounds of Fresh Kills are identified by their compass points and municipal parcel numbers: section 1/9 (West Mound), section 3/4 (North Mound), section 6/7 (East Mound), and section 2/8 (South Mound). Meandering between the mounds are the Arthur Kill's tributary creeks—the Great Fresh Kills, Little Fresh Kills, Main Creek, and Richmond Creek—as well as the West Shore Expressway, New York State Route 440.

Robert Moses, both the commissioner of the New York City Department of Parks and Recreation from 1934 to 1960 and the city construction coordinator, established the sanitary landfill site at Fresh Kills marsh in 1948 in order to create a substrate of made land for his proposed development of new residential and commercial properties. This vast intertidal salt marsh system at Staten Island's western shore had long been considered wasteland—in 1914 the city built a garbage reduction plant at Lakes Island on the Fresh Kills tributary that would convert trash to fertilizer, glycerin, and grease for export and sale, replacing the plant at Jamaica Bay's Barren Island.[1] Though the plant would close in 1918, an ad hoc landfill continued at Fresh Kills, as it presented a convenient location for the dumping of refuse delivered by barge. In his 1951 report to the mayor, Moses characterized this territory as a "presently fallow and useless area" and declared "the Fresh Kills project is not merely a means of disposing of the city's refuse in an efficient, sanitary, and unobjectionable manner pending the building of incinerators. We believe that it represents the greatest single opportunity for community planning in this City."[2] The landfilling process was proposed as a three-year project, a deal made with the Staten Island borough president in exchange for the construction of the West Shore Expressway. However, the filling and mounding of Fresh Kills marsh with the city's refuse continued for over fifty years.[3] By 1986, upon the final closure of the other boroughs' incinerators and landfills, Fresh Kills would receive the entirety of New York City's municipal waste until its official closure in March 2001[4] (figure 23.1).

Ian McHarg examined Staten Island intensely, of course. The *Staten Island Study*, commissioned by the

FIGURE 23.1 Garbage scows bring solid waste for use as landfill to Fresh Kills on Staten Island, 1973. *Photo, Chester Higgins. U.S. National Archives, Records of the Environmental Protection Agency (548315).*

New York City Department of Parks and Recreation and executed by Wallace McHarg Roberts & Todd in the 1960s, employed McHarg's now-famous layered geospatial analytic method—an inventory of the site's geology, geomorphology, physiography, hydrology, soils, vegetation, limnology, and wildlife habitat—to determine the site's possible social value and "suitability" for various land use types.[5] Despite the fact that Moses's Fresh Kills sanitary landfill had been actively receiving municipal waste for almost two decades, McHarg makes no reference to the landfill, and it is not identified on any of his geomorphological or cultural value maps. The western edge of the island is simply categorized as a site of "tidal inundation" but also suitable for "passive recreation." Nor, in his study to identify the ideal alignment of the proposed Richmond Parkway, does McHarg acknowledge that his "rational" method for determining the preferred alignment for this highway would have set it parallel to the eastern edge of the Fresh Kills landfill, further marginalizing the community of Travis and incurring the very "social cost" he sought to avoid.[6]

But what if McHarg had taken the approach of his own straw man "Naturalist"—operating on the ground with close empirical observation and embodied perception, rather than through his high-altitude, abstract, and ecologically deterministic viewport?[7] Might he have noted a group of children from Travis selling vegetables harvested from the seeds that had taken hold in their community's backyard dump heap of Fresh Kills refuse?[8] Designing with nature now, given the social factors of environmental justice issues and the ecological components of novel ecosystems emerging from a changing climate, requires significant investment in embodied field investigation. In this new climate, McHarg's high-altitude planning must merge with—and perhaps even be subsumed by—acute on-the-ground scrutiny.

Robert Moses's foray into land building and waste management produced an ongoing conflux of two radically different New York City agencies working together at the site of Fresh Kills—the Department of Sanitation and the Department of Parks and Recreation. Since 2001, when the Department of City Planning selected the design proposal by James Corner and Stan Allen of Field Operations as the winning competition submission for the rebranded Freshkills Park,[9] and with the firm's subsequent development of a draft master plan for the Department of Parks in 2006, the challenge for these agencies has been to determine how to work collaboratively to transform the four mounds of the capped landfill into a managed, novel landscape accessible to the public. Corner studied with McHarg at the University of Pennsylvania, but Field Operations' proposal for Freshkills Park, dubbed Lifescape, presented a new model for designing with nature that significantly advanced the layered McHargian approach. The proposal was organized around three systemic strategies to be phased across the massive scale of the mounds over a thirty-year time frame. These systems—described as threads, islands, and mats—would be deployed simultaneously, but were intended to evolve and transform over time. The suggestion of an indeterminate future for the former landfill site—one that could not be represented as a fixed, pastoral condition—was a bold proposition. Corner's systemic approach allows for developmental gaps and gaskets, a design strategy responsive to contemporary ecological theories of disturbance and regime shifts, as opposed to the presumption of a design that would achieve a steady-state condition of ecological climax.[10] The designers envisioned the park as "a new form of public-ecological landscape; an alternative paradigm of human creativity and adaptive reuse . . . informed by the voice of an engaged public and shaped by time and process."[11]

As part of a discourse of designing with nature now, the Fresh Kills landfill site offers a significant opportunity for experimentation, observation, and a nonprescriptive botanical future—indeed, a "queering" of the very process of design. "Seeding" is the provocative title of Field Operations' proposed first phase, suggesting the catalytic spontaneity of floral recolonization. In the almost two decades since the closure of the landfill in 2001, spontaneous recolonization of the site has begun through the germination of seeds latent in the topsoil fill of the capped mounds, as well as those dropped by the numerous bird species both occupying and traversing Fresh Kills, given its significant location along the Atlantic flyway. Several Sanitation Department and Parks Department–sponsored plant surveys have been executed, including the Freshkills Park Natural Resources Field Survey of 2007, and more recently the BioBlitz survey of August 2015, which identified and cataloged 137 species of vascular plants, four species of mosses, and eleven species of lichens over a two-day period.[12] This return to the botanical scale of empirical observation offers a significant point of entry for the future of design at this and other disturbed sites undergoing programmatic transformation—Queen Elizabeth Olympic Park in London and Emscher Landscape Park in the Ruhr Valley, Germany, are just two of many sites encountering similar processes of botanical recolonization.

Fresh Kills inevitably conjures the description of vast scale. The very creation of the mounds by the Department of Sanitation was a sublime feat accomplished over a long period of time, entailing the logistical collection of urban refuse from a massive region to its compressed organization into the topography of Fresh Kills. Even today, the department's complex engineering and environmental control work to maintain the capped landfill continues; an extensive network of gas wells harvests and purifies the methane gas formed by decomposing trash, while the contaminated liquid leachate that flows through the landfill is drained and filtered. But what is arguably most intriguing at Fresh Kills is not the vast, but the minute. Rather than simply celebrating the panoramic views made available from the heights of the mounds, the new and novel landscape at this site is notable for the minutiae of its emergent seeded florae, which reflect the micro- and macro-processes of ecology. Waste—and waste lands—provide a germinating bed for the natural world, creating new environmental and social ecologies.

Moses's strategy of transforming the Fresh Kills wetland flats into occupiable real estate through the deposit of refuse has a long history in New York City. The colonial waterfront edges of lower Manhattan were initially marketed as underwater lots extending into the Hudson and East Rivers and were sold to such storied families and institutions as the Astors and Trinity Church. Streets were extended out to the legal bulkhead line, wooden cribbing was constructed at the bulkhead, and waste was dumped into the impounded land-side lagoon. Eventually the water would become "made land." These new shoreline extents were well documented in Egbert L. Viele's *Sanitary and Topographic Map of the City and Island of New York* (1864), the famed "water map" of Manhattan. In the 18th and 19th centuries, much of the waste material used to create this land was ships' ballast. Ballast is the heavy material required to stabilize an empty cargo ship traversing the open seas; early merchant clipper ships would sail from Great Britain and Europe with their holds loaded with stone blocks, gravel, soil, construction debris, or other materials that would be emptied in the Americas, allowing the ship to be reloaded with cargo for her return to the Old World.[13] Ballast material was welcomed at shoreline sites along the developing eastern seaboard of the United States during the mid-1800s, and was often unloaded directly at marshy lowlands destined to become new land. With the ballast came seeds, inadvertently captured in the ballast materials.

During the second half of the 19th century, plant surveys of ballast grounds were executed in earnest at commercial waterfront territories of Philadelphia and New York City. Amateur gentleman botanists, led by Aubrey H. Smith (1814–91) of the Academy of Natural Sciences of Philadelphia and Addison Brown (1830–1913) of the Torrey Botanical Club of New York, identified sites of reclaimed land formed by the deposition of ships' ballast as well as other debris.[14] Colonies of plants emerged from these so-called ballast lands or waste lands; they were dubbed "adventive flora" by the botanists—a more positive moniker than the etymologically judgmental descriptors of "invasive," "foreign," or "alien" plants. The term "adventive" describes a species that has arrived in a new locality from a different habitat, usually introduced with the help (intentional or otherwise) of humans. Hailing from Great Britain, Europe, South America, and the West Indies, the ballast plant species were identified, pressed into herbarium specimen sheets, and tracked over a series of years to determine their ability to thrive in their new environment. These botanists championed the novelty and diversity of the ballast plants, fascinated by their opportunistic adaptability to thrive in the waste land of made land. Indeed, Brown lamented New York's ongoing waterfront improvements and the inevitable loss of these rare and fragile adventive flora. "While most of them will therefore perish after a few seasons, sufficient opportunity will nevertheless be afforded to some, not hitherto reported here, to test their endurance of our climate and to compete with our native growths. The less hardy plants will be ejected by our vigorous weeds; but *Atriplex rosea*, *A. laciniata*, and *Diplotaxis tenuifolia*, and doubtless others, will maintain their ground."[15]

Field Operations' Lifescape submission notes that Staten Island is known to support a vast diversity of plant species, including many rare and endangered flora, a benefit of its location at an estuarine embayment along the Atlantic flyway. Its geographic location, glacial geomorphology, and diverse soils profile provide a variety of ecological niches for southern species reaching their northern limits as well as northern species reaching their southern limits.[16] Indeed, the rich flora of Staten Island has fascinated botanists for over a century and a half. In 1879, Charles Arthur Hollick (1857–1933) and Nathaniel Lord Britton (1859–1934) published the first edition of their ongoing work *The Flora of Richmond County, New York*, with the descriptive subtitle *A Catalogue of the phaenogamous and vascular cryptogamous plants, with occasional notes on the same, growing in Richmond County, independent of cultivation*.[17]

Like Addison Brown, both Hollick and Britton were members of the Torrey Botanical Club, and the two Staten Island natives met while students at the Columbia School of Mines (now Columbia University's School of Engineering and Applied Science). Hollick would become a respected paleobotanist as well as an active member of New York City governance, serving as the assistant sanitary engineer of the Board of Health of the city of New York.[18] Britton was a botanist and taxonomist who would cofound the New York Botanical Garden in the Bronx in 1895. He served as its first director, a position he held until 1929. As young men, both Hollick and Britton were fascinated by Staten Island's diverse plant life, and the comprehensive *Flora* was their first published work upon graduating from Columbia College (now Columbia University). It proved to be a lifelong project; the two men continued to update the volume regularly with new species lists, publishing these as addenda in the *Bulletin of the Torrey Botanical Club* through 1922, and in 1930 they produced a new comprehensive and edited *Flora*.[19] Hollick regularly pressed plants and

mounted these on herbarium specimen sheets; his collection of Staten Island plant specimens is now housed at the New York Botanical Garden's William and Lynda Steere Herbarium (figures 23.2, 23.3, and 23.4).

As *The Flora of Richmond County* developed, the newer plant lists revealed the authors' growing interests in marginal sites and less common plant species. Locations where plant species were found ("abundant on Todt Hill," "swamps, near Giffords," "near Linden Park Station") had been recorded since the first publication in 1879, and the distribution of species was generally described ("common," "not very common," "frequent in swamps," "abundant"). Yet as plant lists were added in the early 1880s, new descriptions appeared, in some ways indicating the agency of certain plants: *Tradescantia virginica*, native to the eastern United States, "escaped from gardens at Tottenville"; *Solanum rostratum*, native to the southwestern United States, "a single plant near Four Corners"; *Ranunculus aquatilis*, an aquatic plant native to Europe, "abundant in Clove Lake Swamp; has appeared spontaneously since last year"; and *Prunus mahaleb*, native to the Mediterranean region, Iran, and parts of central Asia, "escaped to roadsides near Garretson's." In addition, the identification of habitats by Hollick and Britton moved beyond mere place-name indicators to more qualified terms addressing anthropogenic influence: "introduced in ballast," "roadsides and waste-places," "waste places, one plant had grown and flourished for several successive years in the crevice of a stone wall in Stapleton," "in recently filled-in ground," "probably grew from seeds transported by birds," and "apparently established from old garden waste."[20] Hollick and Britton are the embodiment of Ian McHarg's fictitious "Naturalists": they act empirically, observe carefully, and—unlike McHarg, who claimed rational scientific objectivity—they assess, opine, characterize, and qualify the character of the new natures they observe.[21] They are both agnostic and judgmental storytellers.

Edgar Anderson (1897–1969), an American botanist and geneticist, developed the intriguing theory of dump-heap agriculture in the 1950s, positing that the origins of early plant cultivation could be traced to dump heaps and kitchen middens. Like the botanists who sought adventive pioneers in the wastelands and ballast grounds of the New York City estuary, Anderson noted that plants, being choosy about where they grew, demanded relatively open habitats in order to establish a niche. The dump heap provided this open habitat, a place where the "strange new mongrels" of agricultural practice might successfully grow. "New patches of open soil, like dump heaps, are part of our story, for these are two of the commonest scars man leaves on the landscape. When he began to spread out of his original corner and into lands previously without human inhabitants, the open habitats which he tended to create, the strange new niches where something different might get a foothold, were dump heaps and patches of open, more-or-less eroded soil."[22] Anderson notes, in conclusion, "The history of weeds is the history of man, but we do not yet have the facts that will let us sit down and write very much of it."[23]

Yet the ballast plant pioneers and other adaptive "weed" species may indeed hold clues to how humanity might face the challenges of climate change. As Ralph Waldo Emerson asserted, a weed is "a plant whose virtues have not yet been discovered."[24] The attempt by humans to control and attack weeds has produced in these plants genetic strategies of diversity and resilience, unlike the vulnerable populations of deliberately bred genetic clones produced by agricultural and horticultural techniques. Weeds are opportunists, as observed by the adventive flora champions Aubrey Smith, Addison Brown, Charles Arthur Hollick, and Nathaniel Britton. Despite all odds, they often manage to flourish in whatever habitat, disturbed or otherwise, is made available. The adventive species' plasticity and resilience makes them a fascinating model for success, given a future of certain climatic changes—and as a genetically diverse suite of colonists, this queer ecology will likely fare better than its agriculturally cultivated and domesticated descendants. These once fragile pioneers may indeed become humans' mentors for a resilient future, and critical tools for an ongoing discussion of designing with nature now.

Fresh Kills (the dump) and Freshkills (the park) provide an unmatched opportunity to consider the disturbance of ground as a productive act, and to encourage new and novel ecologies in the greatest dump heap in the history of civilization. What are the strange new mongrels that will grow here? How can closer scrutiny, at the level of the individual plant rather than a high-altitude overflight, allow us to read a new ecology at this vast new park, and develop a new, nonnormative queer plant list of adventive flora colonists for this Anthropocene landscape?[25] The "Naturalist" botanists championing the spontaneous adventive flora of the ballast grounds and waste lands voiced a note of caution toward "improvement" of the land. Indeed, these territories were already uniquely productive. Edgar Anderson's dump-heap theory posits a more complex and direct relationship among humans, waste, health, and productivity—dump-heap thinking does not seek to marginalize or hide our waste, but rather to reframe it as productive. Freshkills Park offers the opportunity to explore and seed a living, experimental, inhabited ballast ground for an indeterminate future.

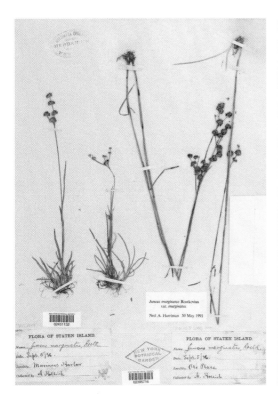

FIGURE 23.2 Charles Arthur Hollick, herbarium specimen, *Juncus marginatus* Rostk, native to North America, found at Mariners Harbor and Old Place, Staten Island, 1886. *All images this page, with permission, C. V. Starr Virtual Herbarium of The New York Botanical Garden, http://sciweb.nybg.org/science2 /VirtualHerbarium.asp.*

FIGURE 23.3 Charles Arthur Hollick, herbarium specimen, *Lepidium medium* Greene, native to the western United States and Mexico, found on ballast ground at Arlington, Staten Island, 1908.

FIGURE 23.4 Charles Arthur Hollick, herbarium specimen, *Diplotaxis tenuifolia* L., native to Europe and western Asia, found on waste grounds at Arlington, Staten Island, 1909.

CHAPTER 24

The Paradox of Security

Allan W. Shearer

SHOULD THE PLANET BE A DESIGN PROJECT? It is a question that was posed in big and bold type at the Victoria and Albert Museum's *The Future Starts Here* exhibit in the summer of 2018.[1] The show called attention to ideas and technologies of the immediate present that, if more widely distributed, could significantly affect the ways people live in the decades to come. This curatorial approach challenged museum-goers to piece together "what if?" fragments to form their own coherent mental mosaics of a world yet to be inhabited (figure 24.1).

The prompt to consider large-scale landscape change came near the end of the exhibit, as if to ground the visitor in the fact that the hundred or so objects they had seen might be used literally to shape our world, not just imaginations of it. An illuminated sign fronted a long and low open-topped box that contained fine-grained sand. Above the box was a Li-DAR (light detection and ranging) sensor that captured elevation heights across the surface of the sand. The display was meant to be touched, and the only constraint was the angle of repose. The simulated effects of topographic manipulation were displayed in real time as the data were processed and transmitted to projectors that cast colored light, which

FIGURE 24.1 From *The Future Starts Here* exhibit at the Victoria and Albert Museum, London, May 12–November 4, 2018. © *Allan W. Shearer.*

suggested natural land-cover tones, onto the sand. Piling the sand high produced snowy peaks; excavating it resulted in rivers and lakes; in between were verdant slopes.

Perhaps the changes made to the museum's tabletop model world were understood by museum visitors in the context of the emerging technologies shown in the exhibit. They might also be understood as motivated by the scale and scope of challenges that were equally on display. To be sure, relationships between means and ends are enmeshed in all aspects of life, but they are especially entangled when it comes to shaping environments. Improving lives and livelihoods by extensively and intensively transforming the land into landscape—through agriculture, industrialization, and urbanization—brought about the Anthropocene, a geologic era in which humanity has become akin to a force of nature.[2] Climate change is the most visible effect, but humanity's efforts have also led to the less noticeable but profound conditions in which new plant and animal species have evolved to live in our cities.[3] From this perspective, the planet is the product of design even though it has not been the object of design. If we accept it as a design project now, how should we align means and ends? More directly, should our designs be inspired by hope for what might be or by fear of what must not be? Both views could be advantageous, but each would enable a different relationship to our environment (figure 24.2).

The lessons offered through a close reading of Ian McHarg's *Design with Nature* allow for an informed engagement with the Victoria and Albert Museum's exhibit, its explicit question, and the implicit need to come to terms with attitudes about change.[4] As reflected by some of the built and speculative projects described in this book, and that extend its legacy, it is also true that today's practices of design, understandings of nature, and sense of the relationships between the two are not what they were fifty years ago. Some of the differences are evolutionary, others are revolutionary; all are significant for the ways problems are framed and solutions are developed.

One relatively new theme in design discourse is security, and it is engaged in several of the projects featured in this volume, including the National Ecological Security Pattern Plan for China, Africa's

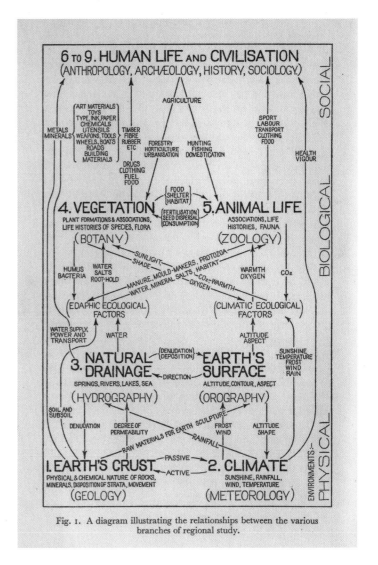

FIGURE 24.2 Diagram of relationships among physical, biological, and social environments. *Fagg and Hutchings, Regional Surveying, 1930.* © Cambridge University Press 1930. With permission.

Great Green Wall, the Netherlands' 2050—An Energetic Odyssey, and the Yellowstone to Yukon Conservation Initiative. It might be said that these pursuits of security can be accepted simply as an aspect of our global zeitgeist. But doing so is problematic. As a matter of professional practice (at least in the United States), landscape architects, architects, civil engineers, and others are licensed by government agencies for the goal of promoting health, safety, and welfare. The change in focus from safety to security does more than escalate rhetoric. Securitization both foregrounds our existential fears and seeks to offer a foundation for hope through protection. The gap between hope and fear is often great, and a question that must be asked is if the means of defense ultimately destroy our relationships to what is being protected. How should security be realized through design projects?

The economist Herbert Simon's premise that "everyone designs who devises courses of action aimed at changing existing situations into preferred ones" remains a useful starting point for thinking about intentional change.[5] But it must also be recognized that design practice is an uncertain process because design problems often lack essential information about initial conditions, the available options for action, or the desired end state.[6] Resolving these ambiguities involves abductive conjectures.[7] In science, an abductive conjecture provides a hypothesis to be tested for truth. In design, it provides a proposition to guide the development of provisional thoughts that, after refinement, will eventually be judged as satisfying or not. Once recognized as central to design, abductive conjectures can be seen as an essential aspect of creativity, but they also explicitly allow for fallibility. The abductive proposition can take many forms, but regardless of how the process starts, it ends with an argument for change.[8]

The crafting of a design argument is often further complicated by the use of "essentially contested concepts" in the formation of abductive conjectures. W. B. Gallie coined this phrase to recognize situations in which abstract ideas used to advance societal agendas are open to interpretation and, more challenging, to competing approaches.[9] Examples of essentially contested concepts include art, democracy, justice, and religion. In environmental design, the move from a concept of goodness to material form is hampered by competing models about cause and effect and by having too much or too little data—both additional aspects of "wicked problems."[10] In short, the inherent contingency of design logic cannot be underestimated: essentially contested concepts are used to frame abductive conjectures to provisionally resolve—not permanently solve—wicked problems.

Gallie's notion of essentially contested concepts focused on ideas with positive connotations, but one might wonder if doing good can go too far. The National Ecological Security Pattern Plan for China by Kongjian Yu and his colleagues explicitly raises this issue by making the argument that security should be the primary goal of environmental design.[11] On the one hand, it can seem intuitively difficult to argue against security when there seems to be so much uncertainty around us. On the other hand, security is an essentially contested concept.

Considering something as an object for security rests on how values—or in a more limited way, interests—are established, shared, and maintained.[12] It presupposes some *other* that poses a danger. So, how is the hazard manifest? From where does it come? When might it strike? Securitization reinforces ideas of aggressors and victims.[13] And because these dangers are associated with matters of survival, security trumps other political activities. It must therefore be asked who within a society has the authority to declare something a security issue, who has the responsibility to respond, and, most challenging, what (if any) are the limits of action?[14] It must also be recognized that improving security for one group or thing may lessen it for others.[15] The act of prioritization can increase the vulnerability of other entities. Prioritizing the security of the nation-state allows harm to environments and people—for example, fallout from nuclear arms testing or the poisoning of groundwater by lead and propellants. Prioritizing the security of the environment harms the nation-state by limiting military training and testing operations and harms humans by limiting economic activities.

Security also predicates present actions on images of the future. Imagine all the kinds of uncertainties people face about the future and all the kinds of actions that are taken to manage them. For simplicity, assume that these can be grouped in three categories. First, there are uncertainties that are privately inconvenient. These are addressed by personal care and habit, such as setting two alarm clocks to make sure an appointment is kept. Second, there are uncertainties that are socially important because they relate to collective health, safety, and welfare. These are typically addressed by routine government police powers and sometimes by institutional support or by markets. An example are traffic laws and signal systems to allow motorists, pedestrians, and cyclists to share roadways and street crossings. Finally, there are uncertainties that may cause existential harm. These require extraordinary powers and are addressed through practices of security.

Throughout most of the 20th century, discussions of security centered on the defense of sovereign nation-states through military means. The end of the Cold War, though, brought calls in the West to expand the definition of security to include a wider range of concerns, including the environment.[16] In broad terms, this expansion initiated a reevaluation of what constitutes a "threat" and an increasing recognition that ecological concerns play an important role in issues related to health, economics, and political stability.[17] This was also a time when it was argued that more holistic definitions of security would better allow for analysis of transboundary issues that are larger than the state and of personal or regional issues that are smaller than the state.[18]

These ideas have been woven into policy and practice. In what was possibly the first high-profile consideration of the environment as a security concern, President George H. W. Bush called attention to transboundary environmental stress as contributing to international political conflict and asserted, "We must manage the Earth's natural resources in ways that protect the potential for growth and opportunity for present and future generations," in his National Security Strategy.[19] President Bill Clinton similarly affirmed the position that environmental degradation has implications for national security.[20] Beyond policy documents, the issues of deforestation, soil erosion, and water pollution were recognized by Deputy Undersecretary of Defense for Environmental Security Sherri Wasserman Goodman as materially contributing to societal decay in Haiti, which ultimately led to intervention by U.S. forces there in 1994.[21] In the United States, interest in securitizing aspects of the environment goes beyond the obvious ties to national defense. For example, the federal Farm Bill, which provides various kinds of support for agriculture, was retitled the Food Security Act in 1985.[22] The Federal Emergency Management Agency, which was established as in independent agency in 1979, became part of the Department of Homeland Security in 2003.[23]

Not all, though, favor the idea of securitizing the environment or ecological factors. In part, it has been argued that placing ecological issues into national security discussions often confuses nonrenewable economic resources with renewable economic externalities, such as clean air and clean water.[24] Further, while aggressive actions can usually be understood as intentional, the degradation of an ecosystem is largely considered to be a by-product of some other—often beneficial—intention. Finally, it has been argued that the securitization of the environment may limit the available means to resolve the problems to the hierarchical and bureaucratic methods of statecraft that are common to nation-states.[25]

Kongjian Yu, the lead author of the National Ecological Security Pattern Plan for China (chapter 12), developed his early thinking about ecological security patterns while he was a doctoral student at Harvard in the early- and mid-1990s.[26] Trained as a landscape architect in China, he built his ideas on theories and practices of environmental planning and design, a field in which there was no apparent intersection with the literature on environmental security that was advancing in security studies. It should also be noted as a matter of academic symmetry that those in security studies did not include planning and design theories in their own literature reviews. Despite the apparent lack of overlapping bibliographies, Yu, like those in security studies, positioned the idea of security as a matter of existential threat, in this case with regard to ecological functionality, and he drew on Kozlowski's concept of ultimate thresholds at which irreversible harm occurred as a way to qualify and quantify risk.[27] A point to underscore is that Yu pursued the protection of systemwide ecological processes that supported continued ecological function and not individual elements near the brink of collapse, such as an endangered species.[28]

As might be expected, Yu cited McHarg's *Design with Nature* in his thesis and subsequent publications. One recognizable point of connection is the foundational premise from ecology that storing, movement, and use of energy within a system is of vital importance. But Yu, also understanding current theories of landscape ecology, noted that while "layer cake" techniques of analysis were necessary, they were not sufficient. Specifically, they allowed for an understanding of vertical interactions (vertical energy relationships), but not horizontal interactions.[29] The contribution of Yu's thesis was a demonstration of how to conceptualize and computationally model strategic positions and portions of the landscape to conserve, improve, and create these horizontal flows. The flow of water is one such flow that links heterogeneous ecosystems in a larger mosaic. Horizontal flows are also critical in the support of biodiversity through the transfer of genes.[30]

Yu's development of the National Ecological Security Pattern Plan was spurred by the announcement that the central government was turning its attention to the rural areas and planned to create the New Socialist Countryside.[31] Without invitation, but with concern based on the missteps the government had made in developing new urban areas, he wrote to Prime Minister Wen Jiabao suggesting security pattern analysis and ecological infrastructure as a way to protect both the still healthy ecosystems and rich cultural heritage of these areas. Within weeks, Yu was asked to assemble a team and create the plan. The roughly thirty professionals and doctoral students involved were given one year to deliver a national-scale plan that could guide more detailed regional efforts that would follow. The overall security pattern synthesized individual assessments for watershed headwater conservation, stormwater management and flood control, soil erosion, desertification, and biodiversity. The scope of the undertaking is inspiring, and its methods have been adopted for policies by the Ministry of Land Resources.

By many standards, China's National Ecological Security Pattern Plan and related ecological security studies are successful examples of designing with nature. Without hyperbole, they should be applauded as major accomplishments. But what next? Are the ecological systems to be securitized forever through this approach? The long-term implications of the rhetoric and the actions that follow from it should be considered. As noted, securitization moves decisions out of routine political processes. While doing so protects the intended object or system, it also separates it from other aspects of society.

Earlier in this essay the concept of security was discussed in relation to three levels of uncertainty, the level of potential harm, and the kinds of actions that might be taken to manage them. A point that can be emphasized by a quirk of the English language (as well as some other languages) is the distinction between safety and security, the two terms used to distinguish ideas about needs for routine safety from needs for extraordinary protection from serious harm. Other languages, including the Romance languages and Chinese, do not share this distinction and, instead, have only words for security. The lack of two words is not an insurmountable problem, but it creates a requirement for explicit qualifications to differentiate uncertainties that can be managed by formalized routines from those that demand emergency measures. Equally important is the ability to contemplate deescalation.

Climate change and environmental degradation have pushed some people beyond thresholds of resilience.[32] In the ecological security literature produced by China's scholars and practitioners, rapid urbanization over the past twenty-five years has resulted in unintentional but significant damage to the environment.[33] In this situation, it is certainly conceivable that assuming a security posture would allow various emergency measures to address the issues. At some point—perhaps of our own inadvertent making—we, as collective humanity, may have no choice but to design the planet for humanity's survival. Nevertheless, the language of security is totalizing and, without providing a path for deescalation, there is the risk of diminishing or even denying, necessary discussion and debate. But, is it expected that they—or we—will always be in crisis? From the perspective of critical security studies, can it be imagined that designing with nature no longer requires extraordinary powers, but becomes a routine safety matter? If not, our means—or worse, our imaginations—will be insufficient to confront the challenges we face.

Yes, existential threats give just reason for exceptional, security-providing action, but taking such action creates a paradox. Productively, securitization of a highly regarded object or concept focuses attention and establishes extraordinary practices in support of it. But each compromise of cultural norms and social routines marginally and cumulatively changes relationships between us and the things we are trying to protect. As Michael Dillon wrote, "For something to be secured it must be acted upon and changed, forced to undergo some transformation through the very act of securing itself. Securing something therefore violates the very thing which security claims to have preserved as it is. Securing an object is only possible on the condition that the integrity of the original thing is destroyed."[34] When ecological systems become a security referent and when security becomes the basis of our argument to design the environment, what becomes of our ideas about nature and our connections with it?

Making and remaking the landscape does more than change topography; it enables ecological relationships and affirms values based on these relationships. In *Design with Nature*, the preposition *with* provides a pivot for possibilities. For McHarg, the task of environmental design was about finding a fit between people and nature. The *with* in *Design with Nature* was, I believe, used to convey a sense of human responsibility. To offer a more explicit rephrasing: design in accord with nature. There is a good amount of humility and an inherent flexibility in this kind of approach. I believe that Yu and his colleagues also pursued the notion of fit. To test kinds of fitness, they also developed analytic techniques that are more advanced than those available to McHarg. A potential problem comes with the pursuit of their stated design logic—their chain of contingent thoughts to make an argument for change. Securitizing our planet's ecological systems without a plan for deescalation seems shortsighted and could result in one of two different ways to think about the *with* in *Design with Nature*. At one extreme, practices of design might reduce nature to a vestigial notion—that somewhere in the design is a remnant nature held as a possession. At the other extreme, *with* is used to suggest the means of action. To design with nature means to bring about change with full command of natural processes as the primary tools of our own agency.

Let us return to the Victoria and Albert Museum's exhibition and its provocative question, "Should the planet be a design project?" Since the earliest times, people have shaped the land into their own image of what the world should be.[35] As such, it was little surprise that one very satisfying aspect of the interactive spectacle was the instant gratification that came with power to make mountains and carve seas. Nearby displays, including a model for a proposed section of Africa's Great Green Wall and a golden spike encased in Lucite to mark the Anthropocene, provided ample suggestion that human agency could realize large-scale geoengineering visions. And, as if acting on cue, some visitors made sweeping transformations of long ridges and broad coastlines. Most visitors, though, modified discrete sections of territory based on wherever they happened to be standing and were careful not to cause harm to the efforts of others, as if territorial borders existed. Even when no one else was around, the majority respected well-shaped "existing" features as if they were protected natural wonders, cherished cultural landscapes, or sacred sites. Although certainly not a scientifically valid survey, the observation that most people chose to limit the extent of their changes and to leave some things untouched might suggest that we, as a species, want to find a fit with nature and not fit nature through a totalizing narrative.

CHAPTER 25

Ecology, Scarcity, and the Global South

Jillian Walliss

A NATION'S ECONOMIC GROWTH and ecological values are closely linked—a factor well demonstrated in *Design with Nature,* which Ian McHarg wrote during a period of unprecedented economic growth. Writing in the 1960s, McHarg observed that the United States, now emancipated "from oppression, slavery, peonage and serfdom," was at a place "where an unparalleled wealth has been widely distributed."[1] It was against this rare background of shared prosperity that McHarg honed his argument for setting limits to development through a greater understanding of ecological systems across the three scales of the city, suburb, and countryside.

Rotate the globe during the 1960s to the Global South and a very different economic story was unfolding. The Cultural Revolution was only beginning in China, where the population was still largely agrarian; many African and Southeast Asian countries were just emerging from the control of European colonizers. And notably, the subsequent transition of these nations into greater economic prosperity through

processes of industrialization and modernity relied largely on their own resources. The implications for ecological values were considerable.

The significant effects of this 20th-century economic disparity between the Global North and South are rarely acknowledged in the ecological discourse of landscape architecture, where instead design projects tend to be presented in an apolitical scientific or artistic manner. In adopting the lens of "scarcity," this essay explores new critiques of large-scale environmental projects in Africa and China, which acknowledge distinctive economic conditions. Scarcity is commonly defined as a shortage or a lack. However, many scholars identify its value for revealing influential social and political attitudes toward environmental resources such as water, soils, and forests. I adopt scarcity as a heuristic device for moving beyond generic ideas of sustainability to develop understandings of large-scale landscape systems that recognize the intertwining dynamics of ecology and economic growth.

The Global South

Encompassing Africa, Latin America, China, and developing countries in Southeast Asia, the term "Global South" emerged as a post–Cold War alternative to the third world, and has since expanded to include "spaces and peoples negatively impacted by contemporary capitalist globalization."[2] Whereas the Global North has achieved economic prosperity from resources (labor and physical) accessed through processes of colonization and globalization, the Global South is largely dependent on its own resources. This factor, along with the Global South's later transition into modernity, is given scant attention in Western landscape discourse. Considered against the unfolding complexities of climate change and globalization, this oversight is problematic. As David Harvey concludes, "If you think that you can solve the environmental question, of global warming and all that kind of stuff, without actually confronting the whole question of who determines the value structure. . . . then you have to be kidding yourself."[3]

Bridging economic and ecological domains, the concept of scarcity offers a valuable lens for revealing underlying values implicated in large-scale landscape systems designs. With connections to economic theory, scarcity is used extensively as a factor in formulating development and environmental policies by governments, nongovernmental organizations (NGOs), investors, and international agencies throughout the Global South.[4] Within economic and ecological contexts, scarcity is inherently about limits, and at its simplest can be considered in two ways. Absolute scarcity posits that there is an impassable limit to resources, as reflected in concepts such as carrying capacity and controlling population growth.[5] Conversely, relative scarcity claims that political

and technical factors influence the availability of resources.[6] With these framings as a starting point, this essay considers three large-scale ecological designs, beginning with Africa's Great Green Wall.

Scarcity and Colonization

At almost 8,000 kilometers (5,000 miles) long, and stretching from Senegal to Djibouti, Africa's Great Green Wall (GGW) aims to combat desertification. In 2005, the idea was ratified, with all countries of the Sahel signing the Convention Creating the Pan African Agency for the GGW.[7] Like many African environmental projects, the vision is funded by multiple national and international parties, including the European Union, the United Nations (Convention to Combat Desertification), and the African Union Commission partner countries.[8] At face value, this ambitious project is admirable. However, a closer investigation reveals a legacy of agricultural and conservation agendas grounded in colonial assessments of resource scarcity.

The GGW encompasses the semiarid region of the Sahel—a specific ecological transition zone between the Sahara and the Sudanian savanna. By 1914, all eleven countries of the Sahel had been colonized by European nations, which quickly introduced policies to address agriculture production, soil degradation, and desertification.[9] Conceived by European-trained scientists, foresters, and administrators, these policies were shaped by assessments of drylands ecology. For instance, France (with fourteen African colonies under its control) introduced policies that declared trees to be a scarce commodity. Any trees found on farmers' properties became the property of the government (farmers were threatened with fines and jail for removing or damaging trees). Simultaneously, separate forest plantations were established.[10] This separation of trees from agriculture produced clear fields, and farmers were encouraged to plough, fertilize, and plant improved species. An emphasis on increased food production also led to the adoption of animal husbandry, which contributed to a decrease in nomadic herding practices.

Within the Sahel environment, these introduced practices devastated traditional agricultural practices, such as brush firing, digging deep planting pits for water retention, and using tree shelter for crops, and led to poor yields and the loss of topsoil.[11] Commonplace throughout Africa in the 20th century, these policies constructed the environment as a problem and led to the application of "environmental solutions" that ignored established social, economic, and ecological relationships.[12] In addition, the idea of "desertification" introduced by European scientists in the 1920s claimed that the Sahara was encroaching south into the savanna—a concept now disputed by ecologists.[13] This assumption of encroachment forms the genesis for the proposal to plant a continuous barrier of trees across the Sahel to moderate winds and soil erosion temperatures, and to improve humidity levels for agricultural production.[14]

The earliest version of the GGW continued the colonial policies of compartmentalization, presenting a plantation of trees segregated from nearby villages. Its initial focus was on the technical challenge of tree planting in the desert, with a slew of foreign experts offering advice on appropriate tree species and planting techniques. Dutchman Pieter Hoff, for instance, proposed the "Waterboxx," a small round tank designed to provide environmental protection and water to a seedling, but at a high unit cost.[15]

Over time, the GGW has been significantly revised from a forest plantation into "a mosaic of in-terventions," shaped by stronger economic and ecological ambitions.[16] No longer a continuous band of trees, the GGW intersects with villages and agriculture areas to encourage more sustainable development of land resources and better living conditions for the local population. Early indications suggest that this approach is offering promising outcomes. In Senegal, for instance, communal gardens managed by women's associations provide members with fresh food, with the excess sold at market rate and profits invested in a common fund available to provide microcredit.[17]

A review of contemporary scientific and ecological reports, however, presents a confusing picture of how the GGW and other environmental projects are changing the Sahel environment. It is unclear whether the Sahel is in fact greening or browning, or whether droughts are persisting. This ambiguity reflects differing conceptual definitions of land degradation, as well as methodological and disciplinary biases.[18] For example, working at the continental scale, the Global Drylands Assessment (2015–16) uses satellite images to document tree-cover density over the drylands, identifying potential for restoration and investment.[19] Numerous researchers warn of the limitations of such coarse-resolution Earth observation data to inform policies. Hannelore Kusserow, for instance, demonstrates that the analysis of data sets covering the period from the 1970s droughts to the present gives the sense of greening, whereas including predrought data imaging would suggest browning.[20] Similarly, Kjeld Rasmussen and coauthors warn that "large-scale and long term trends do not say much about environment change processes at micro-scale and over shorter periods."[21]

For instance, initiatives in Niger include strategies for empowering small landholders to manage natural regeneration and return to indigenous land use techniques such as *zai*—a grid of planting pits that improve water retention and infiltration.[22] Establishing a balance between clearing land for agriculture and regeneration has improved soil conditions with little investment. And most important, in an era of climate change, this approach has demonstrated that in the Niger context, rainfall is not the limiting factor. Instead, the real issue is changing the farmers' perception and management of trees, attitudes and practices that can be traced back to colonization.[23]

Therefore, how disciplines, NGOs, governments, and communities define indicators of land degradation in the Sahel is fluid and reflects attitudes toward resources. Natural scientists tend to emphasize biophysical reasons (absolute), social scientists focus on human causes (relative), and villages often elevate vulnerability to attract international aid (relative).[24] Further, aerial satellite images construct representations of scarcity and abundances of land, water, and vegetation, independent of how land is owned and used.[25] Consequently, balancing local economic gains with longer-term ecological outcomes is difficult, with tensions arising over the marginalization of local people in decision making.[26] For example, large-scale planting to combat desertification may have the economic potential of substantial carbon sequestration but at the same time results in the loss of productive land, puts stress on the water system, and has negative implications for food security. The challenges of the Sahel and the GGW are therefore interdisciplinary and multiscalar and require the explicit identification of methods and values to best inform development and environmental policies.

Turning to China, we find a very different framing of scarcity. Rather than impose limits, the socialist government adopted scarcity as a powerful mobilizer of economic growth.

Scarcity and Socialism (with Chinese Characteristics)

In the period since 2010, there has been a proliferation of large-scale ecological projects in China designed by local and international landscape practices, yet rarely are they contextualized within China's unique political and cultural environment. From the outside, postreform China is particularly difficult to comprehend, presenting a mix of third-world and first-world elements, socialist and capitalist.[27] However, scarcity offers a valuable lens for understanding China's evolving relationship between ecology and economic growth.

Numerous Chinese scholars highlight the role scarcity has played in China's economic development.[28] For instance, post–Cold War embargoes and blockades imposed by the West excluded China from the world trade system, while notions of scarcity operated as a mobilizing force for the new socialist economic system in its industrialization of an agrarian society. China's progression toward an industrial modernity has been shaped by perpetual conditions of scarcity and austerity, which Lu describes as the transition from "a state of being less to a state of being lacking."[29]

Critically, Mao Zedong considered people to be China's greatest resource, with population growth vital for increasing production and building status in order to compete with Soviet Russia and the West. Although China has limited environmental resources, most notably water, a new socialist order was considered the liberating mechanism that would provide for all people.[30] In a clear demonstration of relative scarcity, China's path to modernity was not to be limited by resource availability; rather, technology (often with Soviet influences), human power, and socialist ideology, including a war against nature,[31] were considered the path to industrial growth.

Consequently, resource scarcity was a mobilizer rather than a limit, inspiring monumental technological visions such as China's South-North Water Diversion Project (SNWDP). The origins of the project are traced to Mao, who stated in 1952, "Water is abundant in the south and scarce in the north, so why not borrow a little from the south if possible?"[32] Covering over 1,200 kilometers (745 miles), this canal built between the Yangtze and Beijing is considered one of the world's most expensive infrastructures, and on completion it will transfer up to 7 percent of China's yearly water consumption.[33]

Britt Crow-Miller highlights how concepts of excess and limitations are used to validate the SNWDP, constructing water scarcity as a "natural phenomenon" related to droughts and climate change as distinct from "extreme anthropogenic pressures" on the North China Plain.[34] This framing of water scarcity is not specific to SNWDP, but common for many large-scale water projects internationally, serving to shift attention from regional issues, uneven financial distribution, and longer-term impacts.

By the late 1970s, Mao's vision for population growth (to increase the population from 540 million in 1949 to over 940 million in 1976) had become a major issue. Interventions such as the one-child policy limited population growth and, notes Jiahua Pan, provided a major impetus for the adoption of environmental protection policies and more sustainable development approaches.[35]

The declaration of an "ecological civilization" at the 18th National Congress of the Chinese Communist Party in 2012 elevated these environmental ambitions to the level of national policy. Maurizio Marinelli traces the origins of the term "eco-civilization" to agricultural economist Ye Qianji, who in the 1980s proposed a more sustainable approach to agricultural production.[36] In language reminiscent of McHarg's, Ye declared:

Humanity can both benefit from nature, and also act in the interest of nature: while humanity has a transforming effect on nature, humanity also has to protect nature, since this is the only way for man and nature to maintain a harmonious and unified relationship.[37]

This political recognition of a more ecological responsive economic development, inclusive of limits, was driven by extensive scientific research and debates over the previous decade. Kongjian Yu's influential "National Ecological Security Pattern Study" (2006–11) was an important contribution. Commissioned by the Ministry of Cultural Heritages and the Ministry of Environmental Protection, the pilot project of the Graduate School of Landscape Architecture at Peking University in association with Yu's office, Turenscape, established a nationwide strategy for balancing economic development with ecological systems.[38]

With lineage to McHargian thinking and Richard Forman's ecological language, the research method draws on Yu's Harvard Graduate School of Design doctoral thesis, "Security Patterns in Landscape Planning." Facilitated by geographic information systems, spatial patterns (SP—also known as security patterns) identified ecological conditions that influence ecological security. Mixing quantitative and qualitative parameters, classifications such as buffer zones, intersource linkages, radiating routes, and strategic points are combined with ecological habitats to establish ecological spatial patterns ranked according to three security levels. This spatial expression of absolute limits based on ecological processes presented the Chinese government with a systematic articulation of national ecological values and has subsequently been influential in reshaping Chinese development policy.[39]

Closely intertwined with the ambition for an "ecological civilization" is the "Beautiful China" vision, which introduces ecojustice concepts such as environmental rights, responsibility to future generations, and the interests of the citizens. This "new era of socialist ecological progress" has been a boon for landscape projects, particularly those involving water.[40]

Weishan Wetland Park, located in the northern Shandong Province, constructed on part of the eastern route of the SNWDP, offers one such example (figure 25.1). Championed by the designers AECOM as "a new paradigm for large parklands and the balance between water remediation, wetland conservation and tourism development," the park was completed in 2013.[41] The scheme operates at two scales. A series of treatment wetlands, bioswales, and rain gardens, along with restored agricultural fields and marshes, form an important water purification and ecological barrier between urbanized areas to the north and the extensive Weishan Lake to the south. At the urban scale, six wetland fingers extend into the new town, offering a water-driven open-space typology.

In addition to purifying water, the wetland is conceived with a strong aesthetic. The carefully designed

FIGURE 25.1 View of the boardwalk through the Weishan Wetland Park. *With permission, AECOM.*

human access, a biological habitat network that encourages animal and bird diversity, and the dramatic seasonal transformation of the wetlands facilitate many educational, tourism, and recreational opportunities.[42] A regionally significant park, the Weishan Wetland Park is an exemplar for "socialist ecological progress," offering a development model encompassing the ecological and the beautiful.

Starting from a position of relative scarcity, China's late 20th-century transition to an industrialized economy was rapid, with devastating environmental and social consequences. However, as Pan observes, China is now in a new period of slowing economic growth, almost zero population growth, an aging population, a relatively high level of social wealth acceptance, and an improving ecological environment.[43] No longer at war against nature, the environment is increasingly protected from unregulated economic development by laws and regulation, a move to renewable energies and emissions trading, and ecological conservation strategies.[44] Whether the slowing of the economy will lessen China's ecological progress is yet to be seen. However, optimistic commentators suggest that China's ecological reform could extend beyond its own borders to assume a major role in the global challenges of climate change.

Conclusion

This essay emerged from an invitation to write about a series of projects considered to exemplify what it means to design with nature now. Because I live in the Southern Hemisphere, I chose to explore projects outside North America and Europe, a decision that led to the task of identifying an appropriate lens through which to consider the work. Although a limited exploration, this engagement with characteristics of the Global South and the concept of scarcity has revealed the importance of scrutinizing values in conservation and ecological design, such as the setting of limits (absolute) and social, political, and technical dimensions that influence the availability of resources (relative).

This investigation touches on the realm of political ecology. Emerging as a discrete field in the 1980s, political ecology most broadly examines the relationship between society and land-based resources. In a major difference from Ian McHarg's 1960s context, our ecological questions are transnational, with solutions found in negotiations among international organizations, governments, NGOs, communities, and industries. With an increasingly global design practice, landscape architecture would be well served to move beyond general ideas about sustainability and ecological design to engage with core concerns of political ecology such as abundance and degradation, security and vulnerability, and prosperity and marginalization.[45] To design with nature in 2019, and into the future, is to work within global ecological and political contexts; it will require a more comprehensive engagement with the considerable populations living within the developing countries of the Global South.

CHAPTER 26

"Why Do I Have to Be the Man to Bring You the Bad News?"

William Whitaker

DURING THE WINTER OF 1954, Ian McHarg delivered a series of ten lectures on landscape architecture at The Glasgow School of Architecture. It was "the first course in landscape architecture given . . . in Scotland," he boldly claimed at the start of the first lecture.[1] In the weeks that followed, McHarg and his thirty students briskly traversed a broad history of landscape design from the "very beginning" to Modernism's advocacy of "basic principles."

The time had come to sum up the field's current state of affairs, and McHarg's attack came fast and sharp. "[The] present practice of landscape architecture derives from baseless conventions, it is superficial, undisciplined, a watered [down] and corrupt version of the English landscape tradition, its origins now unrecognizable." Landscape architects must expand their vision beyond convention and the fringes of buildings "designed by prima donna architects" if they desire to get to "the core of the problem of the environment." Choosing to do so, he pointed out, would be the foundation for a renewal of the field and

of the "opportunity and responsibility of the . . . designer to this realm."

Across the Atlantic, G. Holmes Perkins, newly positioned as dean at the University of Pennsylvania's School of Fine Arts (Penn), knew firsthand of McHarg's potential. In his previous position as chair of Harvard University's City Planning Department, Perkins had supervised McHarg's joint thesis project—a redevelopment plan for Providence, Rhode Island, done in collaboration with a number of architecture students. Perkins was working to reestablish Penn's Department of Landscape Architecture (the school's undergraduate program, established in 1924, had been shuttered in 1941). He recognized that it "would be an uphill battle for landscape architecture, to raise the profession to the level it originally had," and that "it needed somebody who would fight for it."[2] As fortune would have it, McHarg—who had returned to Scotland following his graduation—had just written to Perkins for leads on opportunities "anywhere in the United States."[3] Perkins acted quickly, as did McHarg; they

FIGURE 26.1 Ian McHarg in Portugal, July 1967.
Photo, Pauline McHarg. With permission, Ian and Carol McHarg Collection, The Architectural Archives, University of Pennsylvania.

agreed he would start as an assistant professor of city planning that fall, charged with the responsibility of developing a department of landscape architecture at Penn.

As a native of Clydebank, Scotland, Ian McHarg (1920–2001) grew up on the shadowy fringes of the Industrial Revolution. His father, John Lennox McHarg, started his professional and married life with the promise of upward mobility as a manager in a manufacturing firm. Both of his grandfathers were carters who labored transporting whiskey kegs and soft goods behind teams of Clydesdale horses. The economic depression of the 1930s took its toll on family and city alike. The time McHarg spent alongside his mother, Harriet Bain, tending the family garden—their hands working the soil together—must have awakened his curiosity about nature and the larger landscape. Young Ian's hikes from the urban grit of Glasgow to the idyllic countryside of the Kilpatrick Hills formed enduring counterpoints in his adolescent development.[4]

At the age of sixteen, McHarg resolved to be a landscape architect and dropped out of high school to formally apprentice with Donald Wintersgill, head of design and construction operations for Austin and McAlsan, Ltd., the leading nursery and seed merchants in Scotland. Service in the British Army during World War II (1938–46), including bloody fighting during the invasion of Italy, delayed the completion of his training. However, it was in these years that a parochial, "gangling . . . hobbledehoy" developed a strong sense of self-confidence and courage.[5] He had also marched through the Roman ruins in Carthage, Paestum, Herculaneum, Pompeii, Rome, and Athens, as well as the length of Greece, and returned to Scotland a worldly man.

After the war, McHarg resumed his training at Harvard University, completing a bachelor's degree before receiving master's degrees in landscape architecture and city planning. He supplemented his required courses with classes in government and economics, which had a lasting impact on his thinking. At Harvard, McHarg recalled, modern architecture was "a crusade . . . a religion. We were saved; therefore, we must save the world."[6] He had returned to Scotland in the summer of 1950 with the conviction of a reformer, but a life-threatening bout with tuberculosis diminished his professional prospects. Following four years in the Scottish Civil Service engaged in planning postwar housing and towns, McHarg packed up and sailed for America.

The Philadelphia in which McHarg arrived in early September 1954 was thinking big about the future. Postwar reformers had mounted the *Better Philadelphia Exhibition* in the fall of 1947 to introduce the virtues of urban and regional planning through a series of dazzling and engaging displays installed on two floors of the city's Gimbels department store. New ideas for revitalizing the city took a more sensitive approach to urban renewal, incorporating historic fabric and human scale. *Architectural Forum* called this approach "the Philadelphia cure," a version of clearing slums with "penicillin, not surgery" that featured works by architect Louis Kahn to illustrate recent developments.[7] Three hundred thousand citizens visited the exhibition, and the organizers' efforts came to fruition in the reform administrations of Mayors Joseph Clark and Richardson Dilworth. Both politicians supported Edmund Bacon, who served as executive director of the Philadelphia City Planning Commission (PCPC) from 1949 to 1970. Under his leadership, Philadelphia was highly regarded for its imaginative city planning, and Bacon's close ties to architects suggested that the field would have an important role to play in the city's future. As chair of the PCPC, Perkins helped to establish this atmosphere of accomplishment.[8]

Meanwhile at Penn, Perkins was working to shed the vestiges of Beaux Arts formality, but not all of its concern for the City Beautiful. The school was an energetic environment, committed to the city, with a dynamic faculty in architecture and city planning. Broadly understood, the faculty coalesced around the notion that a building, in its design, should be understood as an element integral to a larger context and that the role of the designer was, in part, to interpret how a building should relate to and grow the "patterns" around it. Denise Scott Brown, who joined the faculty in 1960 with joint appointments in landscape and city planning, championed "city physics"—the "forms, forces and functions" that shape urban settlement, particularly the social, economic, technical, and natural forces that condition and determine urban form.[9] Public and private support funded research in urban and regional studies, while universities channeled that support into curricula to deepen understanding. Research-based design studios emerged in the 1960s, as did classes and programs that focused on transforming that research into theory and action. As concern over cities shaped funding priorities in the 1950s, alarm over environmental degradation—signaled by Rachel Carson's 1962 book *Silent Spring*—sharpened priorities in the mid-1960s. President John F. Kennedy's "New Frontier" and President Lyndon B. Johnson's call for "a new conservation" catalyzed efforts at the national level.

McHarg himself began his tenure by raising the profile of Penn's fledgling landscape architecture program among architects. Advertisements built excitement by touting Penn's "experimental curriculum"; examples appeared in magazines such as the December 1955 issue of Britain's *Architectural Review*. Among the first to respond to McHarg's call were two former students, James Morris and Robert Steedman, who had attended his lectures in Scotland.[10]

FIGURE 26.2 Penn Urban Design Conference, 1958. From left to right: William I. C. Wheaton, Lewis Mumford, Ian McHarg, J. B. Jackson, David A. Crane, Louis I. Kahn, G. Holmes Perkins, Arthur C. Holden, unidentified member of Dean Perkins's staff, Catherine Bauer Wurster, Leslie Cheek Jr. Behind Cheek are Chadbourne Gilpatrick, Eleanor Larrabee, Jane Jacobs, Kevin Lynch, Gordon Stephenson, Mrs. Grady Clay, and I. M. Pei. *Photo, Grady Clay. With permission, Ian L. McHarg Collection, The Architectural Archives, University of Pennsylvania.*

He recruited Philip Johnson to lead a studio focused on the design of the plaza landscape for Mies van der Rohe's Seagram's Building, then under construction in New York. He wrote, lectured, and through his own design work, sought to improve the quality of open space in the city, often in collaboration with leading architects. In his 1957 article "The Court House Concept: Humane City Living," McHarg first praised a select group of architects before asking, rhetorically, why modern architects had yet to provide city dwellers with homes as humane as those created for the countryside.[11]

In the fall of 1959, landscape architect Karl Linn joined the department to teach the first-year studio.[12] Linn recalled his "complementary relationship" with McHarg; he would concentrate on the intimate neighborhood environment where people lived their daily lives while McHarg expanded the range of his intellectual concerns.[13] Ecology became McHarg's central focus, a lens through which a comprehensive assessment and evaluation of the environment became possible. Studio problems, as well as his professional commissions, were the primary vehicles for testing ideas and for developing the method and techniques needed to advance the ecological approach to landscape architecture. The great river basins of the Potomac and the Delaware became ideal regions for study; their boundaries were shaped by ecological forces rather than political divisions. By 1966, McHarg had successfully assembled a team of ecologists, scientists, environmental lawyers, and designers—including Nick Muhlenberg, Jack McCormick, Ann Strong, and Narendra Juneja—and was actively shaping an expansive agenda.[14]

These were exciting times for McHarg. Russell Train, then head of the Conservation Foundation in Washington, DC (and a key figure in bringing the environment onto the presidential and national agenda

FIGURE 26.3 Penn landscape students preparing for presentation of the Delaware River Basin study, "DRB II," Meyerson Hall, University of Pennsylvania, Fall 1967. *With permission, Ian L. McHarg Collection, The Architectural Archives, University of Pennsylvania.*

during the 1960s and 1970s), came to know McHarg through presidential task forces convened by the Johnson administration. Of particular interest was McHarg's service on the Potomac River Task Force. McHarg and a group of his Penn students prepared a detailed ecological study of the region during the 1965–66 academic year that became a significant milestone in the development of an ecological planning approach and central to the task force's final report. Train recognized that a book documenting McHarg's method and broad-minded thinking would engage the American public and inspire discussion about the value of land and a process for its responsible use. The promise of a $20,000 grant from the Conservation Foundation helped convince the initially hesitant author to take on the task. McHarg got down to writing in September 1966, titling his first draft "A Place for Nature in Man's World," but finalizing it as "Design with Nature" as he completed work on June 6, 1967. McHarg met with his publishers at Natural History Press the following week and then promptly departed on a much-needed six-week European holiday. He noted excitedly in his date book, "Hurray!!!!!"[15]

Although Train deserves recognition for commissioning the book, Perkins must be given credit for initiating lecture classes at Penn focused on laying out theoretical frameworks for design and giving young faculty the opportunity to teach them. In the Department of Architecture, Robert Venturi, with the assistance of Denise Scott Brown, taught "Theories of Architecture," which over a period of five years (1961–65) became the basis for his landmark book *Complexity and Contradiction in Architecture*, published by the Museum of Modern Art in 1967. For McHarg, the opportunity to teach the class "Man and Environment" enabled him to bring together leading thinkers in science, theology, and design to explore the human relationship with nature.[16] It was a groundbreaking class, drawing enrollment from beyond the School of Fine Arts. George Dessart, a producer at Philadelphia's CBS affiliate (and faculty member in Penn's Annenberg School of Communications), recognized the popular appeal of interviews with great thinkers and commissioned McHarg to bring the series to television beginning in October 1960. The program, titled *The House We Live In*, "examined the nature of the physical world, the theological positions towards it taken by the world religions and the moral implications of [people's] ability to change the world."[17] Running for two seasons and then through syndication on public television, the series established McHarg as a public intellectual and a leading voice on behalf of the environment.

McHarg worked closely with Narendra Juneja, a former student, colleague, friend, and by all accounts his right-hand man, to manage the production of *Design with Nature*. Together they designed the book's layout and created many new illustrations. Concern over the technical challenge and printing expense of these illustrations delayed the start of book production well into the fall of 1968. Ultimately, McHarg's faculty colleague Eugene Feldman, a highly regarded artist teaching in Penn's Fine Arts program, printed and bound the book at Falcon Press in Philadelphia. Feldman had collaborated with architect Richard Saul Wurman to produce *The Notebooks and Drawings of Louis I. Kahn* (1962) and, before that, with Aloisio Magalhaes on *Doorway to Brasilia* (1959).[18] Feldman presented the first bound copy to McHarg and others at a small gathering in his pressroom on April 18, 1969.

The book's cover image came from the archives of the old Hayden Planetarium at New York's Museum of Natural History.[19] The 1949 photograph depicts a "space show" on the subject of sunspots; a simplified city skyline—seen in silhouette along the bottom of the cover—provides a recognizable horizon. The back cover comprised a photograph of planet Earth—the same November 1967 NASA image used on the first edition of *The Whole Earth Catalogue*, but rotated—notably—90 degrees off-axis.

On May 16, 1969, McHarg began sending copies of the book to his closest supporters. The initial print run of 10,000 sold out before the end of the year, as did a second printing of 15,000 soon thereafter.[20] The book reached markets far beyond expectations and made clear, one *Atlanta Constitution* reviewer noted, "that it is not only the aesthetic value of the human environment which can be destroyed by irresponsible development. The point is that human technology is now capable of modifying the whole earthly environment in unpredictable and disastrous ways."[21]

McHarg brought this urgent message to the stage the following April on the first Earth Day, addressing a crowd of 30,000 assembled at Philadelphia's bucolic Belmont Plateau. He spoke "directly to the critical environmental problems," reported Penn's student newspaper, *The Daily Pennsylvanian*, beginning his remarks with the question, "Why do I have to be the man to bring you the bad news?" He then repeated the phrase "You've got no future" three times. Spellbound, the audience listened as McHarg charged that the nation's industries "are the best guarantee of your extinction" and demanded that the time had come to "toilet train American industry." "Man is an epidemic," he warned, "destroying the environment upon which [he] depends and threatening his own extinction."[22]

The student organizers involved in the Earth Week Committee of Philadelphia, many of whom had taken his "Man and Environment" class, actively engaged McHarg in planning a weeklong environmental teach-in. Events included lectures, panel discussions, large public gatherings, and even an "Ecology Action Bus Tour of Philadelphia's pollution trail." In an event billed as "Earth Day Eve" held in front of Philadelphia's historic Independence Hall, McHarg read the committee's "Declaration of *Inter*dependence," [italics in original] a statement that "repudiated the concept of man's independence [from] the other species of life on the planet. McHarg's strong, Scottish voice propelled the modern declaration's words out to the immense crowd."[23] The committee members then gathered on stage to sign the eight-foot-long document, beginning with McHarg and including Edward Furia (Earth Week Committee project director) and Austain Librach (chairman).

McHarg had come a long way from his first teaching experiences in Scotland. In less than twenty years, McHarg not only revived the program at Penn, but more important, he energized his field and established the place of design in the awakening environmental consciousness. *Design with Nature* became a bestseller and an imperative. It remains in print to this day. "My ideas were certainly not of any interest to society at all for the first 10 years I was [in the United States]," McHarg reflected. "The environment was really a matter of profound *inconsequence* [italics in original] to society at large. The only people who listened to me then were the ladies in garden clubs."[24] The pessimism (or was it realism?) in his remarks on the Earth Day stage was a call to action, an expression of outrage at the current state of affairs. People were listening and taking action; the environment had become a great unifying force.

As he approached the end of his life, McHarg was more hopeful. He spoke eloquently of a desire to "heal the earth" and imagined a great public works project to achieve this vision. In his "mind's eye," he saw himself "looking at the earth from space, viewing the shrinking deserts, the burgeoning forests, the clear atmosphere, the virgin oceans, smiling at the recovery."[25]

Acknowledgments

This book complements an ambitious program of three exhibitions and an international conference conceived to mark the 50th anniversary of Ian McHarg's classic book *Design with Nature,* and its publication coincides with the launch of the Ian L. McHarg Center for Urbanism and Ecology at the University of Pennsylvania Stuart Weitzman School of Design. As with any complex undertaking years in the making, these projects would not have been possible without the help of other colleagues, dedicated artists and designers, and generous donors. We express our sincere thanks to all those who contributed to their realization.

For their vital assistance with the exhibitions, we acknowledge the Pew Center for Arts & Heritage. Penn's Sachs Program for Arts Innovation, the Shedd Endowment for the Architectural Archives, and the LARP 100 Fund supported initial research and development. Barbara Wilks, founding principal at the Brooklyn-based firm W Architecture and Landscape Architecture, and Nanci Lanni established the Wilks Family McHarg Center Directorship through the Harry T. Wilks Family Foundation. We are grateful for the significant contributions of John Carrafiell, Ed Hollander, Larry Korman, Harvey Kroiz, and Bonnie Sellers.

The international conference was sponsored by an impressive group, including: Biohabitats; Jestena Boughton; Civitas; Carl and Roberta Dranoff; esri; Hargreaves Associates; James Corner Field Operations; Mathews Nielsen Landscape Architects; Hollander Design; Mithun; Dr. Jon Berger, Nimblesystems; OLIN; Rhodeside & Harwell Inc.; Jonathan Rose Companies; Bonnie and Gary Sellers; Temple University's Program in Planning and Community Development; W Architecture and Landscape Architecture; and WRT.

Crucial to the success of our exhibitions and this book were the enthusiastic support and participation of an inspiring group of planners, architects, ecologists, and landscape architects who gave us the opportunity to explore what it means to design with nature *now.*

Since every project like *Design with Nature Now* is necessarily a team effort, we have many individuals to thank among our colleagues at the University of Pennsylvania.

The Stuart Weitzman School of Design's indefatigable curator of the Architectural Archives, William Whitaker, orchestrated our curatorial efforts and oversaw the production of all three exhibits with the skillful staff, Heather Isbell Schumacher and Allison Olsen.

Lynn Marsden-Atlass, executive director of the Arthur Ross Gallery and curator of the University of Pennsylvania Art Collection, generously shared her experience in the creation of Laurel McSherry's installation "A Book of Days." McSherry produced the work during a Fulbright Professorship at The Glasgow School of Art, where she worked with the help and friendship of Brian Evans, Chris Platt, Anna Poston, Aoife McGarrigle, and the remarkable Ian Macfadyen. We are grateful to Marsden-Atlass and her associates at the Arthur Ross Gallery, Heather Moqtaderi, Sara Stewart, and Meg Pendoley, for their spirit of collaboration and engagement.

Michael Grant spearheaded our marketing and publicity while Jeff Snyder and Ben Ginsberg led the fund-raising effort. In addition, we thank Kait Ellis, Arden Jordan, Darcy Van Buskirk, Kristy Crocetto, Abraham Roisman, Chris Cataldo, Cathy Dibonaventura, Karl Wellman, and Sandi Mosgo for their talent, dedication, and good cheer.

We remain deeply grateful for our partnership with the Lincoln Institute of Land Policy and for the work of Maureen Clarke, Emily McKeigue, and Patricia Stillwell. Sarah Rainwater and Sarah Verity of Rainwater Studio in Providence, Rhode Island, designed the book and cover. We are grateful for their highly collaborative approach and for the production editing of Deborah Grahame-Smith and thorough copyediting of Janet Mowery of Westchester Publishing Services. Their attention to detail was exemplary.

For their sustained intellectual engagement with this project, we offer our heartfelt thanks to the contributors to this publication: Alan Berger, Ignacio Bunster-Ossa, Thomas Campanella, James Corner, Erle Ellis, Brian Evans, Ursula Heise, Rob Holmes, Kathleen John-Alder, Nina-Marie Lister, Anuradha Mathur, Laurel McSherry, Catherine Seavitt Nordenson, Laurie Olin, David Orr, Andrew Revkin, Allan Shearer, Anne Whiston Spirn, Jonah Susskind, Dana Tomlin, Jillian Walliss, and William Whitaker. Our research assistants and interns—Yaqun Cai, Christy Ka Yee Ching, Chris Feinman, Brook Krancer, Anni Lei, Robert Leventhal, Erisa Nakamura, Krista Reimer, Luke Van Tol, Erica Yudelman, Qi Wang, Yun Wang, Rosa Zedek, and Yang Zhao—offered brilliant assistance with the many details.

We offer our sincere thanks to the advisory board of the McHarg Center for their leadership, enthusiasm, and support: Jestena Boughton, Keith Bowers, Ignacio Bunster-Ossa, Carol Collier, Shannon Cunniff, Roberta Dranoff, Christian Gabriel, Jeff Goodell, Faye Harwell, Ed Hollander, Michael Kihn, Charles Neer, Steward Pickett, Joyce Anne Pressley, Elliot Rhodeside, Lucinda Sanders, Karen Seto, Barbara Wilks, and Andrew Zolli.

Finally, this project would not have been possible without the inspiration of Ian McHarg. Before his death, he entrusted his papers to the School of Design's Architectural Archives and in so doing enabled new generations of students and scholars to engage with his creative imagination and impact. His wife, Carol McHarg, added a significant group of items to those holdings; his colleague and former student Anne Whiston Spirn guided Archives staff to the remarkably intact, hidden-in-plain-sight treasure trove of records from the LARP 501 and 701 studio classes critical test beds for advancing ecological design methods. McHarg inspired a generation of designers and planners to take ecology, including the ecology of people, seriously in their work. We hope that this book will engage a new generation and empower them to employ knowledge about how we interact with each other, other organisms, and our environments in healthful, productive, and peaceful ways.

Notes

Foreword

1. Andrew C. Revkin, "A Message in Eroding Glacial Ice: Humans Are Turning Up the Heat," *New York Times*, February 19, 2001.
2. Douglas Jehl with Andrew C. Revkin, "Bush, in Reversal, Won't Seek Cut in Emissions of Carbon Dioxide," *New York Times*, March 14, 2001.
3. Andrew C. Revkin, "Ian McHarg, 80, Architect Who Valued a Site's Natural Features," *New York Times*, March 12, 2001.
4. Natalie Kofler et al., "Editing Nature: Local Roots of Global Governance," *Science* 362, no. 6414 (2018): 527, doi: 10.1126/science .aat461.
5. PBS, *Multiply and Subdue the Earth*, WGBH Media Library and Archives, http://openvault .wgbh.org/catalog/V_61A6468E2EE44DFE8 C098659C38EC075.
6. Dan Kahan, "What you 'believe' about climate change doesn't reflect what you know; it expresses 'who you are'." See Cultural Cognition Project, Yale Law School, culturalcognition.net, April 23, 2014.

Introduction

1. Specifically, we asked nominators to consider how a given work manifests, extends, and perhaps critiques:
   a. McHarg's philosophy that humanity's evolutionary teleology is to learn to live *with* rather than against the forms and flows of the ecosystem as expressed in the landscape;
   b. the role of the profession of landscape architecture as the rational and transdisciplinary stewards of this evolutionary process;
   c. the development and application of simple, universal methods for deploying digital mapping techniques based primarily on empirical, biophysical assessment;
   d. the purpose of such methods to offer unambiguous prescriptions for future land use; and
   e. an emphasis on large-scale landscape planning.

   To arrive at a shortlist, we then applied a second set of criteria. We asked:
   a. What makes a project exemplary and innovative? It could innovate in any area: design method; policy; construction and technical aspects; political reach; theory, etc.
   b. Is the project influential, and if so, why and for whom?
   c. How can the nominated project be seen to extend McHarg's theory and method into new techniques, new territories, and/or new constituencies?
   d. Does the nominated project manifest contemporary and emerging ideas of both "Design" and "Nature"?
   e. In what ways does the project point to, or open up, an expanded field for landscape architecture and environmental planning in the 21st century?
2. Will Steffen, Paul J. Crutzen, and John R. McNeill, "The Anthropocene: Are Humans Now Overwhelming the Great Forces of Nature?," *AMBIO: A Journal of the Human Environment* 38, no. 8 (2011): 614–621.

Chapter 1

1. Ian L. McHarg, *Design with Nature* (Garden City, NY: Doubleday/Natural History Press, 1969).
2. Alexander Caragonne, *The Texas Rangers: Notes from Architectural Underground* (Cambridge, MA: MIT Press, 1995), 150.
3. Ian L. McHarg, *A Quest for Life* (New York: John Wiley, 1996), 269.
4. Ibid., 363.
5. Ian L. McHarg and Frederick R. Steiner, eds., *To Heal the Earth: Selected Writings of Ian McHarg* (Washington, DC: Island Press, 1998), 71. Originally published as Ian L. McHarg, "Values, Process and Form" in *The Fitness of Man's Environment*, ed. Smithsonian Institution Staff (New York: Harper and Row, 1968), 207–227.

Chapter 2

1. Author's 1971 recollection, as a sophomore student in architecture at the University of Miami (Florida).
2. Ian L. McHarg, *Design with Nature* (Garden City, NY: Doubleday/Natural History Press, 1969).
3. See website of the Landscape Architecture Foundation at https://lafoundation.org /about/declaration-of-concern/.
4. See Landscape Architecture Foundation, "New Landscape Declaration," https://lafoundation .org/news-events/2016-summit/new-land scape-declaration/. The New Landscape Declaration was drafted by members of a Landscape Architecture Foundation committee. The committee was chaired by Richard Weller, chair of the Department of Landscape Architecture at the University of Pennsylvania.
5. McHarg left his partners in 1981, for reasons stemming from internal business disagreements. Thereafter, the firm became Wallace Roberts and Todd, LLC (WRT). The author joined the firm in 1979 and remained with it, continuously in practice, through 2015.

Chapter 3

1. Ian L. McHarg, *Design with Nature* (Garden City, NY: Doubleday/Natural History Press, 1969).

Chapter 4

1. Patrick Geddes, "The Valley Plan of Civilization," *Survey* 54 (1925): 288–290.
2. I taught the 501 studio, the foundational design studio in the Landscape Architecture Department at the University of Pennsylvania, from 1994 to 2014, with a few breaks here and there. During this time, I had the opportunity to coteach with Katherine Gleason, Mei Wu, Dennis Playdon, and from 2003 with my partner, Dilip da Cunha. I owe much to these colleagues, particularly to Dennis and Dilip, who brought structure, profound insights, and a high level of skill to 501 and taught me what it really meant to traverse.

Chapter 5

1. Ian L. McHarg, *Design with Nature* (Garden City, NY: Doubleday/Natural History Press, 1969).

Chapter 6

1. Ian L. McHarg, "An Ecological Method for Landscape Architecture," *Landscape Architecture* 57 (1967): 105.
2. Anthony Walmsley taught a course on the history of landscape architecture, but it was not oriented to ecological design and planning. He did begin to develop such a course in the late 1980s.
3. Anne Whiston Spirn, "Renewing the Great Tradition: Urban Nature and Human Design," *Journal of Planning Education and Research* 5 (1985): 39–50; Anne Whiston Spirn, "Constructing Nature: The Legacy of Frederick Law Olmsted," in *Uncommon Ground*, ed. William Cronon (New York: W. W. Norton, 1995); Anne Whiston Spirn, "Architect of Landscape: Frank Lloyd Wright," in *Frank Lloyd Wright: Designs for an American Landscape*, ed. David De Long (New York: Abrams, 1996); Anne Whiston Spirn, "The Authority of Nature: Conflict and Confusion in Landscape Architecture," in *Nature and Ideology*, ed. Joachim Wolschke-Bulmahn (Washington, DC: Dumbarton Oaks, 1997); Anne Whiston Spirn, "Ian McHarg, Landscape Architecture, and Environmentalism: Ideas and Methods in Context," in *Environmentalism and Landscape Architecture*, ed. Michel Conan (Washington, DC: Dumbarton Oaks, 2000); Anne Whiston Spirn, "Ecological Urbanism," in *Routledge Companion to Urban Design Environmentalism and Landscape Architecture*, ed. Tridib Banerjee and Anastasia Loukaitou-Sideris (New York: Routledge, 2011). An expanded version of "Ecological Urbanism" is at http://www .annewhistonspirn.com/pdf/Spirn-EcoUrbanism-2012.pdf. McHarg often claimed that he invented ecological design and failed to cite the work of many others, both historic and contemporary. Placing McHarg's contributions within the larger history of ideas and practice to which they belong permits an appreciation for ecological design and planning as an enduring, evolving tradition that encompasses both the vernacular and high design.
4. Anne Whiston Spirn, *Woodlands New Community: Guidelines for Site Planning* (Philadelphia, PA: Wallace McHarg Roberts & Todd, 1973).
5. Ian McHarg and Jonathon Sutton, "Ecological Plumbing for the Texas Coastal Plain," *Landscape Architecture* 65 (1975): 78–89. The environmental aspects of the development plan were a crucial factor in the client's successful application for a U.S. Department of Housing and Urban Development Title VII loan guarantee of $50 million.
6. Narendra Juneja and Anne Whiston Spirn, *Environmental Resources of the Toronto Central Waterfront* (Philadelphia, PA: Wallace McHarg Roberts & Todd, 1976). The project for the Toronto Central Waterfront was Narendra Juneja's. The client approached Juneja directly. He was the associate partner in charge and asked me to be project director. Since every WMRT

project had to have a partner in charge, McHarg served in that role, but only nominally.

7. Anne Whiston Spirn, *The Granite Garden: Urban Nature and Human Design* (New York: Basic Books, 1984).

8. Ian L. McHarg, *Design with Nature* (Garden City, NY: Doubleday/Natural History Press, 1969), 127.

9. Anne Whiston Spirn, *The Language of Landscape* (New Haven, CT: Yale University Press, 1998), 7. See "West Philadelphia Landscape Project" at www.wplp.net.

10. Anne Whiston Spirn, "The Nature of Mill Creek: Landscape Literacy and Design for Ecological Democracy," in *Pragmatic Sustainability*, ed. Steven Moore (New York: Routledge, 2016).

11. Spirn, *The Language of Landscape*.

12. McHarg, "An Ecological Method for Landscape Architecture," 107.

13. Ibid.

14. Ibid., 26.

Chapter 7

1. John D. Black and Ayers Brinser, *Planning One Town: Petersham—A Hill Town in Massachusetts* (Cambridge, MA: Harvard University Press, 1952).

Chapter 8

1. The Scottish Parliament was opened on May 12, 1999 (in a temporary home in the headquarters of the Church of Scotland) with the words of Dr. Winifred [Winnie] Ewing: "The Scottish Parliament, which adjourned on March 25, 1707, is hereby reconvened." See BBC website, "Democracy Live," at http://news.bbc.co.uk/democracylive/hi/historic_moments/newsid_8187000/8187312.stm.

Use of the word "discontinuity" is deliberate and echoes the geological concept of "unconformity" first observed and described by the Scottish geologist Hugh Miller to explain the discontinuity in layers of rock from different eras. See "Celebrating the Life and Times of Hugh Miller," ed. Lester Borley, at www.cromartyartstrust.org.uk/userfiles/file/Celebrating%20Hugh%20Miller%20sm.pdf.

The Scottish Parliament has created an *unconformity* in postimperial British politics and one that McHarg might have appreciated given the geological reference and his penchant for referring to the classical St. Andrew's House in Edinburgh that housed the civil service in Scotland as "the home of Scotland's puppet government." Ian McHarg, *A Quest for Life* (New York: Wiley, 1996), 94.

2. For example: Robert Louis Stevenson, Alastair Gray, Andrew Carnegie, Hugh MacDiarmid, Norman MacCaig, Robert Burns, and Charles Rennie Mackintosh. See Scottish Parliament, "Canongate Wall Quotations," at www.parliament.scot/visitandlearn/21013.aspx.

3. The quotation is from the first stanza of the poem "The Lay of the Last Minstrel," canto 6, My Native Land, Sir Walter Scott's paean to Scottish patriotism published in 1805, in which Scott makes allusion to his country and traditions.

4. McHarg, *A Quest for Life*, chap. 2. Some care is needed in drawing quotations from autobiographies, which can, on occasion, be the subject of fickle recall or wishful interpretation by the author. McHarg's own contains more than a few obvious inaccuracies, including, inter alia, consistently misrepresenting The Glasgow School of Art as the Glasgow College of Art, an institution where he studied (1936) and later taught for three years (from 1952). In this essay, however, the references to McHarg's account focus on passages where he is expressing a recollection of feeling or sentiment and his opinions on aspects of his native city and country.

5. Jane Jacobs, *The Death and Life of Great American Cities* (New York: Random House, 1961); Kevin Lynch, *The Image of the City* (Cambridge, MA: MIT Press, 1960); Edmund N. Bacon, *Design of Cities* (London: Thames & Hudson, 1967); Gordon Cullen, *Townscape* (London: The Architectural Press, 1961); Ian L. McHarg, *Design with Nature* (Garden City, NY: Doubleday/Natural History Press, 1969).

6. British children in the post–World War II era grew up reading Enid Blyton's "Famous Five" adventure stories for children published by Hodder & Stoughton. The books feature five children who go camping in nature, hiking, and on holiday together elsewhere. The settings are almost always rural and feature the simple joys of cottages, islands, the countryside, and seashores, as well as an outdoor life of picnics, lemonade, bicycle trips, and swimming. These fanciful stories instilled in the postwar generation a love of the outdoors and a compulsion in later life to take any opportunity to group things into five.

7. Photograph taken by Grady Clay in 1958 showing Lewis Mumford, Ian McHarg, J. B. Jackson, Louis Kahn, and others. Architectural Archives of the University of Pennsylvania.

8. Anne Whiston Spirn, "Ian McHarg, Landscape Architecture, and Environmentalism: Ideas and Methods in Context," in offprint from *Environmentalism in Landscape Architecture*, vol. 22, ed. Michel Conan (Washington, DC: Dumbarton Oaks Research Library and Collection, 2000), 101; see also McHarg, *A Quest for Life*, 167.

9. Spirn, "Ian McHarg," 102.

10. Shanachie is the English version of the Scots Gaelic *seanchaidh* (plural: *seanchaidhean*). In ancient Celtic culture, the history and laws of the people were not written down but memorized in long lyric poems, which were recited by bards in a tradition echoed by the *seanchaidhean*.

11. See, for example, the books of James Hunter, including *Last of the Free: A History of the Highlands and Islands of Scotland* (Edinburgh: Mainstream, 1999); *Scottish Exodus: Travels Among a Worldwide Clan* (Edinburgh: Mainstream, 2005); *Set Adrift upon the World—The Sutherland Clearances* (Edinburgh: Birlinn, 2016); Edward J. Cowan & Richard J. Findlay, eds., *Scottish History: The Power of the Past* (Edinburgh: Edinburgh University Press, 2002); Gordon Donaldson, *Scotland: The Shaping of a Nation* (Newton Abbott: David & Charles, 1974); and *A Northern Commonwealth—Scotland and Norway* (Edinburgh: Saltire Society, 1990).

12. Michael Pollan, *Second Nature: A Gardener's Education* (London: Bloomsbury, 1996), 12.

13. From the novel *Sunset Song* by Lewis Grassic Gibbon (New York: Penguin Classics, 1932). *Sunset Song* is widely regarded as one of the most important Scottish novels of the 20th century and is the first part of the trilogy *A Scots Quair*.

14. Norman MacCaig (1910–1996), "A Man in Assynt," in *The Poems of Norman MacCaig* (Edinburgh: Polygon, 2005). The quotation is inscribed in Bressay sandstone from the Shetland Islands in the Canongate Wall.

15. Hunter, *Set Adrift upon the World*.

16. Thomas Christopher Smout is the Historiographer Royal in Scotland, Professor Emeritus at St. Andrews University, and former deputy chair of Scottish Natural Heritage. See T. C. Smout, "The Highlands and the Roots of Green Consciousness, 1750–1990," Scottish National Heritage Occasional Paper no. 1 (1990), www.snh.gov.uk/publications-data-and-research/publications. This essay is the text of the Raleigh Lecture on British History, delivered by Smout at the University of Glasgow on October 24, 1990, as part of Glasgow's European City of Culture celebrations and again at the British Academy in London on November 20, 1990.

17. See for example, John Muir, *The Story of My Boyhood and Youth* (1913; Madison: University of Wisconsin Press, 1965); and McHarg, *A Quest for Life*, chap. 1. McHarg also expressed these values in conversation with those who knew and studied with him—for example, Dean Frederick Steiner, McHarg collaborator; and Robert Steedman, McHarg alumnus.

18. In the early chapters of *A Quest for Life* (pp. 13–16), McHarg makes frequent reference to the qualities of nature in the localities close to his boyhood home, learning to live "free off the land, walking many miles each day through forests of beech, mountain ash, pine and larch with water margins of flag iris with rich insect and bird life."

19. See, for example, P. D. Goist, "Patrick Geddes and the City," *Journal of the American Institute of Planners* 40, no. 1 (1974): 31–37; Mackintosh Architecture, "Patrick Geddes," www.mackintosh-architecture.gla.ac.uk/catalogue/name/?nid=GeddPat; History Scotland, "Scottish Sociologist and Town Planner Patrick Geddes," www.historyscotland.com/articles/on-this-day-in-history/scottish-sociologist-and-town-planner-patrick-geddes-was-born-on-this.

20. Patrick Geddes, *Cities in Evolution: An Introduction to the Town Planning Movement and to the Study of Civics* (London: Williams, 1915).

21. Brian M. Evans et al., "Dear Green Place: A Question of Equilibrium," in *La vita tra cose e natura: il progetto e la sfida ambientale* (Life Between Artifact and Nature: Design and the Environmental Challenge), Catalogue of the 18th International Triennale of Milan (Milan: Electa, 1992).

22. Robert Young and Pierre Clavel, eds., *Landscape and Urban Planning* 66 (October 2017), Special Issue: "Planning Living Cities: Patrick Geddes' Legacy in the New Millennium."

23. Michael Batty and Stephen Marshall, "Thinking Organic, Acting Civic: The Paradox of Planning for Cities in Evolution," and Volker M. Welter, "Commentary on 'Thinking Organic, Acting Civic,' Michael Batty and Stephen Marshall"; and "Jaqueline Tyrwhitt Translates Patrick Geddes for Post World War Two Planning," Ellen Shoshkes, in ibid.

24. Frederick Steiner and Laurel McSherry, "Observation, Reflection, Action," in "Planning Living Cities: Patrick Geddes' Legacy in the New Millennium," ed. Robert Young and Pierre Clavel, special issue, *Landscape and Urban Planning* 66 (October 2017): 55–56.

25. Spirn, "Ian McHarg," 102.

26. A note on nomenclature: In *A Quest for Life*, McHarg records his time with the Glasgow College of Art, but the institution is and always has been known as The Glasgow School of Art (GSA). He perhaps mixed the name up with that of the Edinburgh College of Art (now ESALA, Edinburgh School of Architecture and Landscape Architecture). ESALA is a school within the University of Edinburgh, whereas GSA remains an independent institution whose degrees are accredited by the senate of the University of Glasgow. Scotland's two premier art institutions are therefore underpinned by the imprimatur of the Russell Group of research universities in the United Kingdom.

27. From the lyrics of Runrig, a prominent Scottish folk-rock band who sings in both Gaelic and English.

28. Robert Burns, Walter Scott, Hugh MacDiarmid, Norman MacCaig and Lewis Grassic Gibbon are among the best known.

29. The freedom to roam, or "everyman's right," is the general public's right to access certain public or privately owned land for recreation and exercise. The right is sometimes called the right of public access to the wilderness or the "right to roam." In Scotland, the Nordic countries of Finland, Iceland, Norway, and Sweden; the Baltic countries of Estonia, Latvia, and Lithuania; and the Central European countries of Austria, Czech

Republic, and Switzerland, the freedom to roam takes the form of general public rights that are sometimes codified in law. The access is ancient in parts of Northern Europe and has been regarded as sufficiently basic that it was not formalized in law until modern times. However, the right usually does not include any substantial economic exploitation, such as hunting or logging, or disruptive activities, such as making fires and driving off-road vehicles.

30. McHarg, *A Quest for Life*, 15.

31. The most appropriate definition of "metropolitan" in the U.K. is provided by the Centre for Cities, which has defined the Primary Urban Area as a measure of the "built-up" area of a city, rather than individual local authority districts. See website of the Centre for Cities at www.centreforcities.org/puas/.

32. Doug Saunders, *Arrival City: How the Largest Migration in History Is Reshaping Our World* (New York: Vintage, 2011).

"The largest migration in human history is under way. For the first time ever, more people are living in cities than in rural areas. Between 2007 and 2050, the world's cities will have absorbed 3.1 billion people. Urbanization is the mass movement that will change our world during the twenty-first century, and the 'arrival city' is where it is taking place.

The arrival city exists on the outskirts of the metropolis, in the slums, or in the suburbs; the American version is New York's Lower East Side of a century ago or today's Herndon County, Virginia. These are the places where newcomers try to establish new lives and to integrate themselves socially and economically. Their goal is to build communities, to save and invest, and, hopefully, move out, making room for the next wave of migrants. For some, success is years away; for others, it will never come at all." (From the flyleaf)

33. McHarg, *A Quest for Life*, chap. 1.

34. New Lanark lies on the River Clyde, harnessing water power; it was founded in 1786 by David Dale, who worked with his son-in-law Robert Owen to create an industrial model village with enlightened employment conditions. Owen later became involved in the establishment of New Harmony in the U.S. state of Indiana. On the exploitation of peoples, see, for example, C. A. Oakley, *The Second City* (Glasgow: Blackie & Son, 1967). Once a source of great pride, the twin epithets "second city of empire" and "workshop of the world" have become less favored in the 21st century with the widening realization that the "wealth of empire" was founded on the exploitation of peoples and countries and on the slave trade; it also extracted a great price from Glasgow in terms of the state of its environment and the health of its people. In Glasgow, as in other cities of the United Kingdom and the United States, there is greater humility and contrition in this realization today.

35. There are numerous trusts and spiritual organizations that work with these communities. See, for example, the websites of the Iona Community at https://iona.org.uk and the Galgael Trust at www.galgael.org.

36. McHarg, *A Quest for Life*, 15.

37. One of McHarg's first students at Penn was Robert (Bob) Russell Steedman, whom McHarg recruited from the Edinburgh College of Art. He first studied at Penn and later worked for Wallace-McHarg Associates. Steedman recalls McHarg as an "archetypal blunt and charismatic Glaswegian." Author's notes from interview with Bob Steedman at the Scottish Parliament, June 6, 2018.

38. The Clyde Valley Regional Plan was published in 1946 and reprinted in 1996 to celebrate its 50th anniversary and the 20th anniversary of the Strathclyde Structure Plan.

39. McHarg, *A Quest for Life*, 15, 16.

40. Ibid., 16.

41. Ibid., 93, 112.

42. Ibid., 113.

43. After delivery of the master-plan elements, including the Seafar Forest established in response to McHarg's observations on the site, Gillespie founded his practice, William Gillespie and Partners (later Gillespies), where I also practiced for thirty-five years, from 1979 to 2015.

44. Brian M. Evans et al., "Glasgow—A City of Continuing Traditions," in *Poszukiwanie modelu inteligentnego miasta. Przykład Gdańska i Glasgow*, Monografie ekonomiczne (Warsaw: Wolters Kluwer SA, 2015).

45. McHarg, *A Quest for Life*, 110. In fact, Glasgow was awarded the title European Capital of Culture in 1990, following Athens, Florence, Amsterdam, Berlin, and Paris. Not bad for "a mean, ugly city, a testament to man's inhumanity to man" (p. 15).

46. Brian M. Evans, *Ripristino ambientale delle area abbandonate: L'esperienza scozzese* (Environmental restoration of vacant and derelict areas—the Scottish experience), in *La pianificazione nelle area ad alto rischio ambientale* (Planning in areas of high environmental risk), ed. G. Campeol (Milan: Francoangeli, 1992), 150–161.

47. Sue Evans, "Greening Central Scotland— Genesis, Vision and Delivery," in *Growing Awareness: How Green Consciousness Can Change Perceptions and Places*, ed. Brian Evans and Sue Evans (Edinburgh: RIAS, 2016).

48. McHarg, *A Quest for Life*, 112, 151.

49. Evans, "Greening Central Scotland."

50. Is this an exaggeration? In his own inimical style, McHarg claimed in 1970: "I had trained the majority of landscape architects, not only in Scotland, but in England, Wales and Ireland as well." McHarg, *A Quest for Life*, 252.

51. Ibid., 112, 151.

52. I am indebted to the archives of the University of Pennsylvania for providing access to a list of the U.K. graduates.

53. The Royal Fine Art Commission for Scotland was established in 1927 "to enquire into such questions of public amenity or of artistic importance relating to Scotland as may be referred to them by any of our Departments of State" (excerpt from the Royal Charter for the Royal Fine Art Commission for Scotland). The Countryside Commission was established in 1967 "to make better provision for the Scottish Countryside" (excerpt from the Countryside (Scotland) Act, 1968). Both commissions remained in place until the early years of the 21st century, when the devolved government of Scotland undertook an overhaul of all of Scotland's QUANGOs (Quasi-Autonomous National Government Organisations), replacing them with NDPBs (Non-Departmental Public Bodies).

54. I had the good fortune to collaborate with both Steedman and Turnbull over a period of thirty years. As a Countryside commissioner, Steedman oversaw the research that Gillespies undertook on the setting of buildings into the landscape, published in 1991 as *Tomorrow's Architectural Heritage: The Landscape Setting of Buildings in the Countryside*, ed. J. M. Fladmark, G. Y. Mulvagh, and B. M. Evans (Edinburgh: Mainstream, 1991). With a foreword by HRH The Prince of Wales, this book changed the paradigm for the manner in which Scotland's rural buildings were designed and integrated into the landscape. *Tomorrow's Architectural Heritage* informed the publication of a trilogy of Planning Advice Notes published as policy by the government in Scotland: *No. 36: Buildings in the Countryside* (1991), *No. 44: The Landscape Setting of Development in the Countryside* (1994), and *No. 52: Small Towns* (1996).

Turnbull and I established a twenty-five-year collaboration in computer-aided landscape design and regional landscape studies. The collaboration was founded on the belief that emerging computer-aided techniques in landscape design could greatly assist the delivery of the precepts of *Design with Nature*. Early work and publications in association with the University of Strathclyde (ABACUS, Architecture and Building Aids Computer Unit Strathclyde) and the University of Edinburgh (EdCAAD, Edinburgh Computer-Aided Architectural Design) led to the establishment of methods for the routing of linear developments through the landscape, notably electricity transmission lines for the South of Scotland Electricity Board, later Scottish Power (Scottish Power, 1992), now the subject of a PhD research program at MIT.

55. In 2011, the then president of the Russian Federation enacted a decree to extend the city of Moscow by some 175,000 square kilometers (67,570 square miles) to the southwest. Thereafter, a decision was taken by the president and the mayor of Moscow to stage an international design competition with three strategic outcomes: a spatial commentary on the structure of the Moscow region; a spatial plan for the new city extension area; and a master plan for a new federal administrative center in the southwest expansion area. Ten teams were selected to participate: two French, one Anglo-American, one Spanish, one Italian, one Dutch, one Russo-Japanese, and two Russian. Two prizes were awarded: one to the Anglo-American team led by Urban Design Associates (Pittsburgh, USA) and Gillespies (Glasgow, U.K.) and one to the French team led by the Wilmotte and Grumbach studios.

The competition and its outcomes have been extensively documented, most notably in a special issue of the magazine *Project Russia* entitled "Greater Moscow" (большая москва/Greater Moscow, проект Россия/Project Russia, no. 66, April 2012). I have published a number of articles in English about this competition: Brian M. Evans, "Competition for the Expansion of Moscow," in *Water Landscapes, TOPOS—The International Review of Landscape Architecture & Urban Design*, no. 81 (Munich, 2012); Brian M. Evans, "The Ecology of the Periphery," in *The Archaeology of the Periphery* (Project Meganom/Strelka Institute, Moscow Urban Forum, 2013); Brian M. Evans, "Moscow Metropolis— Edge City," *MacMag 39*, Mackintosh School of Architecture (2014): 160–161; Brian M. Evans, "Moscow River, a Living Environment," in *Resilient Cities & Landscapes, TOPOS—the International Review of Landscape Architecture & Urban Design*, no. 90 (Munich, 2015).

56. McHarg, "A Scot in America," in *A Quest for Life*, 348–349, and author's conversations with Frederick Steiner and Robert Steedman.

57. McHarg, "A Scot in America," in *A Quest for Life*, 348–349.

58. Extract from the citation by President George H. W. Bush conferring the National Medal of Arts on Ian L. McHarg in 1999. It is a statement that McHarg was rightly proud of and that he reproduced in the preface to the 25th anniversary edition of *Design with Nature* (1992) and in the conclusion to his autobiography, *A Quest for Life* (1996). Reflecting his characteristic panache, however, the quotation is different in the two books!

Chapter 10

1. E. C. Ellis, "Ecologies of the Anthropocene: Global Upscaling of Social-Ecological Infrastructures," in *New Geographies #6: Grounding Metabolism*, ed. D. Ibanez and N. Katsikis (Cambridge, MA: Harvard Graduate School of Design, 2014), 20–27.

2. B. McKibben, *The End of Nature* (New York: Random House, 1989); W. A. Steffen et al., *Global Change and the Earth System: A Planet*

Under Pressure, 1st ed. (Berlin: Springer-Verlag, 2004).

3. E. C. Ellis, "Ecology in an Anthropogenic Biosphere," *Ecological Monographs* 85 (2015): 287–331.

4. Y. M. Bar-On, R. Phillips, and R. Milo. "The Biomass Distribution on Earth," *Proceedings of the National Academy of Sciences* 115 (2018): 6506–6511.

5. E. C. Ellis, "(Anthropogenic Taxonomies) A Taxonomy of the Human Biosphere," in *Projective Ecologies*, ed. C. Reed and N.-M. Lister (New York: Actar, 2014), 168–182; Ellis, "Ecology in an Anthropogenic Biosphere."

6. Ellis, "Ecology in an Anthropogenic Biosphere."

7. Levis et al., "Persistent Effects of Pre-Columbian Plant Domestication on Amazonian Forest Composition," *Science* 355 (2017): 925–931; C. N. H. McMichael et al., "Ancient Human Disturbances May Be Skewing Our Understanding of Amazonian Forests," in *Proceedings of the National Academy of Sciences* 114 (Washington, DC, 2017), 522–527; S. Tomasz et al., "Lessons from Białowieża Forest on the History of Protection and the World's First Reintroduction of a Large Carnivore," *Conservation Biology* 32 (2018): 808–816.

8. Bar-On, Phillips, and Milo, "The Biomass Distribution on Earth."

9. L. J. Martin et al., "Evolution of the Indoor Biome," *Trends in Ecology & Evolution* 30 (2015): 223–232; L. J. Martin et al., "Biodiversity Conservation Opportunities Across the World's Anthromes," *Diversity and Distributions* 20 (2014): 745–755; M. T. J. Johnson and J. Munshi-South, "Evolution of Life in Urban Environments," *Science* 358 (2017): 607; C. D. Thomas, *Inheritors of the Earth: How Nature Is Thriving in an Age of Extinction* (New York: Penguin, 2017).

10. R. Dirzo et al., "Defaunation in the Anthropocene," *Science* 345 (2014): 401–406; G. Ceballos et al., "Accelerated Modern Human-Induced Species Losses: Entering the Sixth Mass Extinction," *Science Advances* 1 (2015): E1400253; H. S. Young, "Patterns, Causes, and Consequences of Anthropocene Defaunation," *Annual Review of Ecology, Evolution, and Systematics* 47 (2016): 333–358.

11. Dirzo et al., "Defaunation in the Anthropocene."

12. C. N. Johnson, "Ecological Consequences of Late Quaternary Extinctions of Megafauna," *Proceedings of the Royal Society B: Biological Sciences* 276 (2009): 2509–2519; L. R. Prugh et al., "The Rise of the Mesopredator," *BioScience* 59 (2009): 779–791; J. A. Estes et al., "Trophic Downgrading of Planet Earth," *Science* 333 (2011): 301–306.

13. Johnson, "Ecological Consequences of Late Quaternary Extinctions"; E. C. Ellis et al., "Anthropogenic Transformation of the Biomes, 1700 to 2000," *Global Ecology and Biogeography* 19 (2010): 589–606.

14. Ellis, "Ecology in an Anthropogenic Biosphere"; Thomas, *Inheritors of the Earth*.

15. J. E. Fa, S. M. Funk, and D. O'Connell, *Zoo Conservation Biology* (Cambridge: Cambridge University Press, 2011); E. C. Ellis, "Sustaining Biodiversity and People in the World's Anthropogenic Biomes," *Current Opinion in Environmental Sustainability* 5 (2013): 368–372; Thomas, *Inheritors of the Earth*.

16. Johnson and Munshi-South, "Evolution of Life in Urban Environments."

17. Ibid.; Thomas, *Inheritors of the Earth*; K. M. Gaynor et al., "The Influence of Human Disturbance on Wildlife Nocturnality," *Science* 360 (2018): 1232–1235; T. Merckx et al., "Body-Size Shifts in Aquatic and Terrestrial Urban Communities, *Nature* 558 (2018): 113–116.

18. Ian L. McHarg, *Design with Nature* (Garden City, NY: Doubleday/Natural History Press, 1969).

19. National Research Council, *Reducing Coastal Risk on the East and Gulf Coasts* (Washington, DC: National Academies Press, 2014); *Nature* editorial, "'Nature-Based Solutions' Is the Latest Green Jargon That Means More Than You Might Think," *Nature* 541 (2017): 133–134; C. T. Nesshöver et al., "The Science, Policy and Practice of Nature-Based Solutions: An Interdisciplinary Perspective," *Science of the Total Environment* 579 (2017): 1215–1227.

20. R. Russell, "Humans and Nature: How Knowing and Experiencing Nature Affect Well-Being," *Annual Review of Environment and Resources* 38 (2013): 473–502.

21. McHarg, *Design with Nature*, 197. S. Brand, ed., *Whole Earth Catalog* (Menlo Park, CA: Portola Institute, 1968).

22. McHarg, *Design with Nature*, 29.

23. H. L. McMillen, "Small Islands, Valuable Insights: Systems of Customary Resource Use and Resilience to Climate Change in the Pacific," *Ecology and Society* 19 (2014): 44.

24. S. A. Bhagwat et al., "Agroforestry: A Refuge for Tropical Biodiversity?" *Trends in Ecology & Evolution* 23 (2008): 261–267.

25. Tomasz et al., "Lessons from Białowieża Forest."

26. J. M. Meyer, "Gifford Pinchot, John Muir, and the Boundaries of Politics in American Thought," *Polity* 30 (1997): 267–284.

27. J. B. Callicott, "Harmony Between Men and Land—Aldo Leopold and the Foundations of Ecosystem Management," *Journal of Forestry* 98 (2000): 4–13.

28. R. M. Gunton et al., "Beyond Ecosystem Services: Valuing the Invaluable," *Trends in Ecology & Evolution* 32 (2017): 249–257.

29. U. P. Pascual et al., "Valuing Nature's Contributions to People: The IPBESA," *Current Opinion in Environmental Sustainability* 26–27 (2017): 7–16.

30. P. M. Berry et al., "Why Conserve Biodiversity? A Multi-National Exploration of Stakeholders' Views on the Arguments for Biodiversity Conservation," *Biodiversity and Conservation* 27 (2018): 1741–1762.

31. D. Haraway, "Anthropocene, Capitalocene, Plantationocene, Chthulucene: Making Kin," *Environmental Humanities* 6 (2015): 159–165; J. D. Margulies and B. Bersaglio, "Furthering Post-Human Political Ecologies," *Geoforum* 94 (2018): 103–106.

32. Ellis, "Ecology in an Anthropogenic Biosphere."

33. E. D. Dinerstein et al., "An Ecoregion-Based Approach to Protecting Half the Terrestrial Realm," *BioScience* 67 (2017): 534–545.

34. R. J. Hobbs et al., "Guiding Concepts for Park and Wilderness Stewardship in an Era of Global Environmental Change," *Frontiers in Ecology and the Environment* 8 (2009): 483–490.

35. S. T. Garnett et al., "A Spatial Overview of the Global Importance of Indigenous Lands for Conservation," *Nature Sustainability* 1 (2018): 369–374.

36. Hobbs et al., "Guiding Concepts for Park and Wilderness Stewardship," *Frontiers in Ecology and the Environment* 1 (2009): 483–490; quotation is from the abstract.

37. M. Soga and K. J. Gaston, "Shifting Baseline Syndrome: Causes, Consequences, and Implications," *Frontiers in Ecology and the Environment* 16 (2018): 222–230.

38. D. N. Cole and L. Yung, eds., *Beyond Naturalness: Rethinking Park and Wilderness Stewardship in an Era of Rapid Change* (Washington, DC: Island Press, 2010).

39. E. Fromm, *The Anatomy of Human Destructiveness* (New York: Holt, Rinehart and Winston, 1973); E. O. Wilson, *Biophilia* (Cambridge, MA: Harvard University Press, 1984); E. Marris, *Rambunctious Garden: Saving Nature in a Post-Wild World* (New York: Bloomsbury USA, 2011); E. C. Ellis, "Nature for the People: Toward a Democratic Vision for the Biosphere," *Breakthrough Journal* (Summer 2017): 15–25.

40. Ellis, "Ecology in an Anthropogenic Biosphere"; E. C. Ellis, *Anthropocene: A Very Short Introduction* (Oxford: Oxford University Press, 2018).

41. E. C. Ellis, "Too Big for Nature," in *After Preservation: Saving American Nature in the Age of Humans*, ed. B. A. Minteer and S. J. Pyne (Chicago: University of Chicago Press, 2015), 24–31.

42. H. Locke, "Nature Needs Half: A Necessary and Hopeful New Agenda for Protected Areas," *Parks* 58 (2013): 7; E. O. Wilson, *Half-Earth: Our Planet's Fight for Life* (New York: Liveright, 2016); Dinerstein et al., "An Ecoregion-Based Approach to Protecting Half the Terrestrial Realm"; Ellis, *Nature for the People*; J. E. M. Watson and O. Venter, "Ecology: A Global Plan for Nature Conservation," *Nature* 550 (2017): 48–49.

43. Wilson, *Half-Earth*.

44. Dinerstein et al., "An Ecoregion-Based Approach to Protecting Half the Terrestrial Realm"; Watson and Venter, "Ecology"; Z. Mehrabi, E. C. Ellis, and N. Ramankutty, "The Challenge of Feeding the World While Conserving Half the Planet," *Nature Sustainability* 1 (2018): 409–412.

45. B. Büscher et al., "Half-Earth or Whole Earth? Radical Ideas for Conservation, and Their Implications," *Oryx* (2016): 1–4; Mehrabi, Ellis, and Ramankutty, "The Challenge of Feeding the World."

46. Ellis, *Nature for the People*.

47. Watson and Venter, "Ecology"; J. Baillie and Y.-P. Zhang, "Space for Nature," *Science* 361 (2018): 1051.

48. Mehrabi, Ellis, and Ramankutty, "The Challenge of Feeding the World."

49. E. Ostrom et al., "Revisiting the Commons: Local Lessons, Global Challenges," *Science* 284 (1999): 278–282.

50. S. A. Pickett, "The Flux of Nature: Changing Worldviews and Inclusive Concepts," in *Linking Ecology and Ethics for a Changing World*, ed. R. Rozzi et al. (Dordrecht: Springer Netherlands, 2013), 265–279.

51. R. J. Hobbs, E. S. Higgs, and C. M. Hall, eds., *Novel Ecosystems: Intervening in the New Ecological World Order* (Oxford, U.K.: Wiley, 2013).

52. E. C. Ellis, "Distanced Authorship in the Anthropocene," *Harvard Design Magazine* (2018): 207.

53. B. Cantrell, L. J. Martin, and E. C. Ellis, "Designing Autonomy: Opportunities for New Wildness in the Anthropocene," *Trends in Ecology & Evolution* 32 (2017): 156–166; Ellis, "Distanced Authorship in the Anthropocene."

54. C. Waldheim, "Strategies of Indeterminacy in Recent Landscape Practice," *Public* (2016): 80–86.

55. D. Silver et al., "Mastering the Game of Go Without Human Knowledge," *Nature* 550 (2017): 354.

56. C. M. Laney, D. D. Pennington, and C. E. Tweedie, "Filling the Gaps: Sensor Network Use and Data-Sharing Practices in Ecological Research," *Frontiers in Ecology and the Environment* 13 (2015): 363–368; T.-H. Lin, S.-H. Fang, and Y. Tsao, "Improving Biodiversity Assessment via Unsupervised Separation of Biological Sounds from Long-Duration Recordings," *Scientific Reports* 7 (2017): 4547; M. Lacoste, S. Ruiz, and D. Or, "Listening to Earthworms Burrowing and Roots Growing—Acoustic Signatures of Soil Biological Activity," *Scientific Reports* 8 (2018): 10236.

57. D. S. Jachowski, R. Slotow, and J. J. Millspaugh, "Good Virtual Fences Make Good Neighbors: Opportunities for Conservation," *Animal Conservation* 17 (2013): 187–196; W.-P. Kang, H.-R. Moon, and Y. Lim, "Analysis on Technical Trends of Active Noise Cancellation for Reducing Road Traffic Noise," *Journal of Emerging Trends in Computing and Information Sciences* 5 (2014): 286–291; B. E. Cantrell and J. Holzman, *Responsive Landscapes: Strategies for Responsive Technologies in Landscape Architecture* (New

York: Taylor & Francis, 2015); D. S. Proppe et al., "Mitigating Road Impacts on Animals Through Learning Principles," *Animal Cognition* 20 (2017): 19–31; A. van Wynsberghe and J. Donhauser, "The Dawning of the Ethics of Environmental Robots," *Science and Engineering Ethics* (2017): 1–24.

Chapter 11

1. Karen Tei Yamashita, *Tropic of Orange* (Minneapolis, MN: Coffee House Press, 1997), 56.
2. Ibid., 57. Note that since some of the texts I discuss here use ellipses, I have enclosed my own elision marks in brackets to distinguish them from those of the authors.
3. Ibid., 80.
4. Ibid., 81–82.
5. Ibid., 33.
6. In a talk at UCLA in 2015, Yamashita indicated that she had derived this format from one of the first spreadsheet software programs to be released in the 1980s, Lotus 1-2-3.
7. As Sherryl Vint points out in her analysis of *Tropic of Orange*, "The book might also be visually represented by a geographical map, as all the action takes place in specific locations, and some of the characters separated by divergent class or racial categories come into contact only through extraordinary events that make otherwise distinct spaces contiguous." Sherryl Vint, "Orange County: Global Networks" in *Tropic of Orange*, *Science-Fiction Studies* 39 (2012): 404.
8. Yamashita, *Tropic of Orange*, 3.
9. Ibid., 217.
10. For a more detailed analysis of the universalism or global "we" that *Tropic of Orange* rejects and the type it embraces, see Sue-Im Lee, "'We Are Not the World': Global Village, Universalism, and Karen Tei Yamashita's *Tropic of Orange*," *MFS Modern Fiction Studies* 53 (2007): 501–527. See also Vint, "Orange County," for the novel's portrayal of different forms of globalization.
11. Ian L. McHarg, *Design with Nature* (Garden City, NY: Doubleday/Natural History Press, 1969), 36–39.
12. Ibid., 57.
13. Ibid.
14. Ibid., 176.
15. Ibid., 23.
16. Jon Christensen, "The Stories That Maps Tell," in *The Atlas of Global Conservation: Changes, Challenges, and Opportunities to Make a Difference*, ed. Jennifer L. Molnar (Berkeley: University of California Press, 2010), 16.
17. For a history of Los Angeles's palm trees and their cultural meanings, see Warren Techentin, "Tree Huggers," in *The Infrastructural City: Networked Ecologies in Los Angeles*, ed. Kazys Varnelis (Barcelona: Actar, 2009), 130–146.
18. Yamashita, *Tropic of Orange*, 142.

19. On actor-network-theory, see Bruno Latour, *Reassembling the Social: An Introduction to Actor-Network-Theory* (Oxford: Oxford University Press, 2007); on ecological urbanism, see Mohsen Mostafavi and Gareth Doherty, eds., *Ecological Urbanism* (Baden: Lars Müller, 2010); on landscape urbanism, see Charles Waldheim, ed., *The Landscape Urbanism Reader* (New York: Princeton Architectural Press, 2006); on urban political ecology, see Nik Heynen, Maria Kaïka, and Erik Swyngedouw, "Urban Political Ecology: Politicizing the Production of Urban Natures," in *In the Nature of Cities: Urban Political Ecology and the Politics of Urban Metabolism*, ed. Nik Heynen, Maria Kaika, and Erik Swyngedouw (Abingdon, U.K.: Routledge, 2006), 1–19; on urban environmental justice, see Julian Agyeman, *Sustainable Communities and the Challenge of Environmental Justice* (New York: NYU Press, 2005) and Ronald Sandler, Phaedra C. Pezzullo, and Robert Gottlieb, eds., *Environmental Justice and Environmentalism: The Social Justice Challenge to the Environmental Movement* (Cambridge, MA: MIT Press, 2007); on urban metabolism, see Erik Swyngedouw, "Metabolic Urbanization: The Making of Cyborg Cities," in *In the Nature of Cities*, ed. Heynen, Kaika, and Swyngedouw, 20–39; on biophilic design, see Timothy Beatley, *Biophilic Cities: Integrating Nature into Urban Design and Planning* (Washington, DC: Island Press, 2011). "Climate urbanism" was to my knowledge first used by the geographer Javier Arbona; see also Peter Calthorpe, *Urbanism in the Age of Climate Change* (Washington, DC: Island Press, 2011). The concept of "novel ecosystems" has been proposed by the ecologist Richard Hobbs and his collaborators; Hobbs used it to describe ecosystems that have been altered by humans but then left to evolve on their own. See Richard J. Hobbs, Eric S. Higgs, and Carol Hall, eds., *Novel Ecosystems: Intervening in the New Ecological World Order* (Oxford: Wiley-Blackwell, 2013). It is, however, also used for urban ecosystems—i.e., ecosystems that are still being maintained.
20. Chris Philo, "Animals, Geography, and the City: Notes on Inclusions and Exclusions," in *Animal Geographies: Place, Politics, and Identity in the Nature-Culture Borderlands*, ed. Jennifer Wolch and Jody Emel (London: Verso, 1998), 51–71; Alica Hovorka, "Transspecies Urban Theory: Chickens in an African City," *Cultural Geographies* 151 (2008): 95–11; Peter Atkins, ed., *Animal Cities: Beastly Urban Histories* (Farnham, U.K.: Ashgate, 2012).
21. Pierrette Hondagneu-Sotelo, *Paradise Transplanted: Migration and the Making of California Gardens* (Berkeley: University of California Press, 2014); Philip Howell, "Between the Muzzle and the Leash: Dog-walking, Discipline, and the Modern City," in *Animal Cities: Beastly Urban Histories*, ed.

Peter Atkins (Farnham, U.K.: Ashgate, 2012), 221–241.
22. Anastasia Loukaitou-Sideris, "Urban Form and Social Context: Cultural Differentiation in the Uses of Urban Parks," *Journal of Planning Education and Research* 14 (1995): 89–102; Paul H. Gobster, "Managing Urban Parks for a Racially and Ethnically Diverse Clientele," *Leisure Sciences* 24 (2002): 143–159.
23. Timothy Choy, *Ecologies of Comparison: An Ethnography of Endangerment in Hong Kong* (Durham, NC: Duke University Press, 2011); Catriona Sandilands, "Some 'F' Words for the Environmental Humanities: Feralities, Feminisms, Futurities," in *The Routledge Companion to the Environmental Humanities*, ed. Ursula K. Heise, Jon Christensen, and Michelle Niemann (Abingdon: Routledge, 2017), 443–451.
24. Jennifer Wolch, "Zoöpolis," in *Animal Geographies: Place, Politics, and Identity in the Nature-Culture Borderlands*, ed. Jennifer Wolch and Jody Emel (London: Verso, 1998), 135.
25. Jennifer Wolch, "Anima Urbis," *Progress in Human Geography* 26.6 (2002): 733–734.
26. Tsing is quoted in Eben Kirksey, Craig Schuetze, and Stefan Helmreich, "Introduction: Tactics of Multispecies Ethnography," in *The Multispecies Salon*, ed. Eben Kirksey, Kindle ed. (Durham, NC: Duke University Press).
27. Thom Van Dooren, *Flight Ways: Life and Death at the Edge of Extinction* (New York: Columbia University Press, 2014); Thom Van Dooren and Deborah Bird Rose, "Storied-Places in a Multispecies City," *Humanimalia* 3 (2012): 1–27.
28. Ursula K. Heise, *Imagining Extinction: The Cultural Meanings of Endangered Species* (Chicago: University of Chicago Press, 2016), chap. 5.
29. Kim Stanley Robinson, *New York 2140* (New York: Orbit, 2017), 144, 285, 279–280.
30. Ibid., 209.
31. Ibid., 120.
32. Ibid., 33.
33. Ibid., 41–42.
34. Ibid., 356.
35. Ibid., 319–320.
36. Ibid., 259.
37. Ibid., 356.
38. Ibid., 259.
39. Donna Haraway, "A Cyborg Manifesto: Science, Technology, and Socialist-Feminism in the Late Twentieth Century," in *Simians, Cyborgs, and Women: The Reinvention of Nature* (1984; New York: Routledge, 1991), 149–182.
40. Swyngedouw, "Metabolic Urbanization," 20.
41. Erik Swyngedouw and Maria Kaïka, "The Environment of the City . . . or the Urbanization of Nature," in *A Companion to the City*, ed. Gary Bridge and Sophie Watson (Malden: Blackwell, 2000): 569.
42. China Miéville, *Perdido Street Station* (New York: Del Rey, 2000), 441.

43. Ibid. The first-person narrative segments told by the character Yagharek are always italicized in *Perdido Street Station*.
44. Ibid., 38.
45. Ibid., 37.
46. Ibid.
47. Ibid., 1–2.
48. The critic Joan Gordon notes that New Crobuzon is "a bit like very far-future London, but not quite: a hyperbolic metaphor for the hybrid nature of the great cities of the contemporary world." Joan Gordon, "Hybridity, Heterotopia, and Mateship in China Miéville's *Perdido Street Station*," *Science-Fiction Studies* 30 (2003): 460.
49. Miéville, *Perdido Street Station*, 45.
50. Christopher Palmer, "Saving the City in China Miévielle's Bas-Lag Novels," *Extrapolation* 50 (2009): 228.
51. Ibid., 227–230.
52. In particular, Walter Benn Michaels's harsh critique of using biological species as a stand-in for cultural differences between humans, especially in science fiction, might be apposite here; see "Political Science Fictions," *New Literary History* 31 (2000): 649–664.
53. Jennifer R. Wolch, Kathleen West, and Thomas E. Gaines, "Transspecies Urban Theory," *Environment and Planning D: Society and Space* 13 (1995): 747.
54. McHarg, *Design with Nature*, 1, 23.
55. Yamashita, *Tropic of Orange*, 56.

Chapter 17

1. Richard Black, "Heavy Weather: Tracking the Fingerprints of Climate Change, Two Years After the Paris Summit" (London: Energy and Climate Intelligence Unit, December 2017), https://eciu.net/assets/Reports/ECIU_Climate_Attribution-report-Dec-2017.pdf.
2. United Nations Framework Convention on Climate Change (UNFCCC), "UNFCCC Process," https://unfccc.int/process#:2cf7f3b8-5c04-4d8a-95e2-f91ee4e4e85d.
3. Daniel Czechowski, Thomas Hauck, and Georg Hausladen, eds., *Revising Green Infrastructure: Concepts Between Nature and Design* (Boca Raton, FL: CRC Press, 2015).
4. See John Townsend, "The Largest Ever Tropical Reforestation Is Planting 73 Million Trees," October 31, 2017, www.fastcompany.com/40481305/the-largest-ever-tropical-reforestation-is-planting-73-million-trees; and George Dvorsky, "China's Ambitious New Rain-Making System Would Be as Big as Alaska," April 25, 2018, https://gizmodo.com/chinas-ambitious-new-rain-making-system-would-be-as-big-1825536740.
5. Dirk Sijmons, "2050—An Energetic Odyssey" (voice over text), 2016, https://iabr.nl.media/document/original/2050_an_energetic_odyssey_voice_over.pdf.
6. Ibid.
7. Maarten A. Hajer and Peter Pelzer, "2050—An Energetic Odyssey: Understanding 'Tech-

niques of Futuring' in the Transition Towards Renewable Energy," *Energy Research & Social Science* 44 (October 1, 2018): 222–231, https://doi.org/10.1016/j.erss.2018.01.013.

8. Maarten A. Hajer, *Authoritative Governance: Policy-Making in the Age of Mediatization* (Oxford: Oxford University Press, 2009).

9. Ian L. McHarg, *Design with Nature* (Garden City, NY: Doubleday/Natural History Press, 1969), 7.

10. Alan Berger, *Reclaiming the American West* (New York: Princeton Architectural Press, 2002); James Corner, "The Agency of Mapping: Speculation, Critique and Invention," in *Mappings*, ed. Denis Cosgrove (London: Reaktion Books, 1999), 231–252; Anuradha Mathur and Dilip da Cunha, *Mississippi Floods: Designing a Shifting Landscape* (New Haven, CT: Yale University Press, 2001).

11. Lars Laestadius, "Africa's Got Plans for a Great Green Wall: Why the Idea Needs a Rethink," *The Conversation*, June 18, 2017, http://theconversation.com/africas-got-plans-for-a-great-green-wall-why-the-idea-needs-a-rethink-78627.

12. Cheikh Mbow, "The Great Green Wall in the Sahel," *Oxford Research Encyclopedia of Climate Science*, August 22, 2017, https://doi.org/10.1093/acrefore/9780190228620.013.559.

13. Rosetta Elkin, "Desertification and the Rise of Defense Ecology," *Portal 9*, no. 4 (2014).

14. Kieron Monks, "The $4 Billion Great Green Wall Changes Course," CNN, September 26, 2016, www.cnn.com/2016/09/22/africa/great-green-wall-sahara/index.html.

15. A. M. Abdi et al., "The Supply and Demand of Net Primary Production in the Sahel," *Environmental Research Letters* 9, no. 9 (September 1, 2014), https://doi.org/10.1088/1748-9326/9/9/094003.

16. David O'Connor and James Ford, "Increasing the Effectiveness of the 'Great Green Wall' as an Adaptation to the Effects of Climate Change and Desertification in the Sahel," *Sustainability* 6, no. 10 (October 16, 2014): 7142–7154, https://doi.org/10.3390/su6107142.

17. Jim Morrison, "The 'Great Green Wall' Didn't Stop Desertification, but It Evolved into Something That Might," *Smithsonian*, Smithsonian.com, August 23, 2016, www.smithsonianmag.com/science-nature/great-green-wall-stop-desertification-not-so-much-180960171/.

18. Ibid.

19. Monks, "The $4 Billion Great Green Wall Changes Course."

20. McHarg, *Design with Nature*, 26.

21. Diana K. Davis, "Deserts and Drylands Before the Age of Desertification," in *The End of Desertification?: Disputing Environmental Change in the Drylands*, ed. Roy Behnke and Michael Mortimore (Berlin: Springer, 2016), 203–223, https://doi.org/10.1007/978-3-642-16014-1_8.

22. Ian L. McHarg et al., *Ian McHarg: Conversations with Students: Dwelling in Nature*, 1st ed. (New York: Princeton Architectural Press, 2007), 24.

23. McHarg, *Design with Nature*, 197.

Chapter 18

1. Charles Downing Lay, "Tidal Marshes," *Landscape Architecture* 2, no. 3 (April 1912): 101–102.

2. Robert Moses, memo to Allyn Jennings, August 27, 1936, Box 97, Robert Moses Papers, Manuscripts and Archives Division, New York Public Library.

3. See Lawrence J. Vale and Thomas J. Campanella, eds., *The Resilient City: How Modern Cities Recover from Disaster* (New York: Oxford University Press, 2005).

4. Ben Hobson, "BIG U Storm Defences 'Will Secretly Protect Manhattan from Flooding,' Says Bjarke Ingels," *DeZeen*, July 11, 2014, https://www.dezeen.com/2014/07/11/movie-bjarke-ingels-big-u-storm-defences-protect-manhattan-flooding/.

5. Rebuild by Design: The BIG "U" (New York: BIG Team, 2014), 174, 180.

6. DLANDstudio, "A New Urban Ground," https://dlandstudio.com/A-New-Urban-Ground.

7. Siddharth Narayan et al., "The Effectiveness, Costs and Coastal Protection Benefits of Natural and Nature-Based Defences," *PLoS One* 11, no. 5 (May 2016).

Chapter 19

Thanks to Justine Holzman and Brett Milligan for their comments on drafts of this essay, as well as the editors for their review and recommendations.

1. Ian L. McHarg, *Design with Nature* (Garden City, NY: Doubleday/Natural History Press, 1969), 11.

2. "Structures of Coastal Resilience" was a 2013–14 Rockefeller Foundation–supported study conducted by researchers from four universities—Princeton, Harvard, City College of New York, and the University of Pennsylvania. For the Princeton team's proposal, see https://ltlarchitects.com/structures-of-coastal-resilience/.

3. Ibid., 7–9, 15.

4. The Rebuild by Design competition was initiated by President Obama's Hurricane Sandy Rebuilding Task Force and ran in 2013 and 2014. Competition partners included the U.S. Department of Housing and Urban Development, the Municipal Art Society, the Regional Plan Association, NYU's Institute for Public Knowledge, and the Van Alen Institute. The Rockefeller Foundation was a key funding supporter. For the Blue Dunes proposal, see Jesse Keenan and Claire Weisz, eds., *Blue Dunes: Climate Change by Design* (New York: Columbia University Press, 2017).

5. For the SCAPE team's first-stage proposal, which included the Barnegat Bay work, see their 2014 report "The Shallows: Bay Landscapes as Ecological Infrastructure." See https://www.hud.gov/sites/documents/THE_SHALLOWS.PDF.

6. Mark J. McDonnell, "The History of Urban Ecology: An Ecologist's Perspective," in *Urban Ecology: Patterns, Processes and Applications*, ed. Jari Niemelä et al. (Oxford: Oxford University Press, 2011); Will Steffen et al., "The Trajectory of the Anthropocene: The Great Acceleration," *Anthropocene Review* 2, no. 1 (2015): 81–98.

7. McHarg's later writings, such as the three essays "Landscape Architecture," "Natural Factors in Planning," and "Ecology and Design," written in the late 1990s and included in *The Essential Ian McHarg*, ed. Frederick R. Steiner (Washington, DC: Island Press, 2006), show little evidence of an evolving conception of ecology. While McHarg did work after the publication of *Design with Nature* to refine his methods, he concentrated that effort on the incorporation of sociological and anthropological factors, not on assessing the potential impact of evolving ecological theory. See, for instance, his description of his method for "human ecological planning" in "Natural Factors in Planning," which is essentially unchanged from its original formulation in *Design with Nature* in its approach to natural systems. The results of McHarg's experimentation with the incorporation of human ecology are probably better seen in the work of his students, such as James Corner, Anuradha Mathur, and Chris Reed, than in McHarg's own work.

8. Jianguo Wu and Orie Loucks, "From Balance of Nature to Hierarchical Patch Dynamics: A Paradigm Shift in Ecology," *Quarterly Review of Biology* 70, no. 4 (1995): 440. Similarly, scholarship in geography, urban studies, and urban ecology has both continued to bear out the relevance of understanding change in urban systems and to emphasize the intertwinement of urban and natural systems in complex feedback relationships. Regarding the former, see, for instance, Cristina Ramalho and Richard Hobbs, "Time for a Change: Dynamic Urban Ecology," *Trends in Ecology & Evolution* 27 (2012): 3. Regarding the latter, see, for instance, Neil Brenner, ed., *Implosions/Explosions: Towards a Study of Planetary Urbanization* (Berlin: Jovis, 2014). Steward Pickett, M. L. Cadenasso, and Brian McGrath, eds., *Resilience in Ecology and Urban Design* (Dordrecht: Springer Netherlands, 2013), provides an integrated framework for conceptualizing ecological and urban processes that emphasizes change and flux.

9. Kristina Hill, "Shifting Sites," in *Site Matters: Design Concepts, Histories, and Strategies*, ed. Carol J. Burns and Andrea Kahn (New York: Routledge, 2005); Nina-Marie Lister, "Resilience Beyond Rhetoric in Urban Design," in *Nature and Cities: The Ecological Imperative in Urban Design and Planning*, ed. Frederick R. Steiner, George F. Thompson, and Armando Carbonell (Cambridge, MA: Lincoln Institute of Land Policy, 2016); S. T. A. Pickett, M. L. Cadenasso, and J. M. Grove, "Resilient Cities: Meaning, Models, and Metaphor for Integrating the Ecological, Socio-Economic, and Planning Realms," *Landscape and Urban Planning* 69, no. 4 (2004): 369–384; Robert E. Cook, "Do Landscapes Learn? Ecology's 'New Paradigm' and Design in Landscape Architecture," in *Environmentalism in Landscape Architecture*, ed. Michel Conan (Washington, DC: Dumbarton Oaks, 2000).

10. Anne Whiston Spirn, "Ian McHarg, Landscape Architecture, and Environmentalism," in Conan, *Environmentalism in Landscape Architecture*, 107–108.

11. McHarg's account of what he values in nature is subtler and more idiosyncratic than mere reference to stability and balance, though both of these qualities undergird his account. Of particular relevance are pages 46–53, 120–125, and 196–197 in *Design with Nature*, where he draws on Lawrence Henderson's *Fitness of the Environment* (New York: Macmillan, 1913). The fusion of Henderson and Darwin is the source of McHarg's conception of "fitness," which contains an explicit orientation toward increasing stability, order, and complexity in natural systems (McHarg, *Design with Nature*, 120). McHarg also emphasizes the concept of harmony, though this is as much harmony between "man and nature" as harmony within nature (McHarg, *Design with Nature*, 5).

12. Lister, "Resilience Beyond Rhetoric in Urban Design."

13. See, respectively, Nina-Marie Lister, "Sustainable Large Parks: Ecological Design or Designer Ecology?" in *Large Parks*, ed. George Hargreaves and Julia Czerniak (New York: Princeton Architectural Press, 2007); Hill, "Shifting Sites"; and Teresa Galí-Izard, *The Same Landscapes: Ideas and Interpretations* (Barcelona: Editorial GG, 2005).

14. Steven M. Manson, "Simplifying Complexity: A Review of Complexity Theory," *Geoforum* 32, no. 3 (2001): 405–414; Timothy M. Lenton and Hywel T. P. Williams, "On the Origin of Planetary-Scale Tipping Points," *Trends in Ecology & Evolution* 28, no. 7 (2013): 380–382.

15. Brian Fagan, *The Attacking Ocean: The Past, Present, and Future of Rising Sea Levels* (New York: Bloomsbury, 2014); David R. Montgomery, *Dirt: The Erosion of Civilizations* (Berkeley: University of California Press, 2012).

16. Will Steffen, Paul J. Crutzen, and John R. McNeill, "The Anthropocene: Are Humans Now Overwhelming the Great Forces of Nature?," *AMBIO: A Journal of the Human Environment* 36, no. 8 (2007): 614–621; John R. McNeill, *Something New Under the Sun* (New York: W. W. Norton, 2000).

17. Eric Higgs, *Nature by Design: People, Natural Process, and Ecological Restoration* (Cambridge, MA: MIT Press, 2003).

18. Engineering practices and paradigms, for instance, are shifting away from the static and toward the dynamic, but this movement is nascent, an uphill battle for progressive engineers, like the American Engineering with Nature program and the Dutch Building with Nature, the latter of which is represented in this volume by the Dutch Zandmotor project.

19. In answering the McHarg Center's 2017 call for short responses to the question "What does it mean to design with nature now?," four respondents focused on designing with change: Allison Lassiter, Nathan Heavers, Margaret Grose, and Anna Hersperger. See McHarg Center (website), https://mcharg.upenn.edu/conversations/what-does-it-mean-design-nature-now.

20. See, for example: Catherine Howett, "Ecological Values in Twentieth-Century Landscape Design: A History and Hermeneutics," *Landscape Journal*, special issue, 17 (1998): 80–98; Lawrence Halprin, *The RSVP Cycle: Creative Process in the Human Environment* (New York: George Braziller, 1969); Jack Flam, ed., *Robert Smithson: The Collected Writings* (Berkeley: University of California Press, 1996); Julia Czerniak, "Appearance, Performance: Landscape at Downsview," in *CASE Downsview Park*, ed. Julia Czerniak (Cambridge, MA: Harvard University Graduate School of Design, 2001); Galí-Izard, *The Same Landscapes*; Gilles Clément, *"The Planetary Garden" and Other Writings*, trans. Sandra Morris (Philadelphia: Penn Press, 2015); Margaret Grose, *Constructed Ecologies: Critical Reflections on Ecology with Design* (New York: Routledge, 2017).

21. Charles Waldheim, "Landscape as Urbanism," in *The Landscape Urbanism Reader*, ed. Charles Waldheim (New York: Princeton Architectural Press, 2006); James Corner, "Terra Fluxus," in Waldheim, *The Landscape Urbanism Reader*.

22. Evgeny Morozov, *To Save Everything, Click Here: The Folly of Technological Solutionism* (New York: PublicAffairs, 2013).

23. This contingency is also present in scientific and engineering fields, but the rhetoric of those fields submerges it, whereas the rhetoric of non-solutionist design exposes and centers contingency. On the contingency of solutions in science and engineering, see Henry Petroski's *To Engineer is Human* (1985).

24. Kyna Leski, *The Storm of Creativity* (Cambridge, MA: MIT Press, 2015).

25. Take, for instance, the case of California's Sacramento–San Joaquin River Delta, where local farmers and residents, distant cities and politicians, and environmental activists all are pursuing divergent goals for the use of water and the future of the Delta's infrastructure. At the same time, the Delta has been undergoing a rapid and irreversible ecological transition, resulting from anthropogenic impacts both local and global. In such contexts, no single solution can be equally satisfactory to all parties. See S. N. Luoma et al., "Challenges Facing the Sacramento–San Joaquin Delta: Complex, Chaotic, or Simply Cantankerous?," *San Francisco Estuary and Watershed Science* 13, no. 3 (2015); Horst Rittel and Melvin Webber, "Dilemmas in a General Theory of Planning," *Policy Sciences* 4, no. 2 (1973): 155–169; Brett Milligan and Rob Holmes, "Earthworks, Wicked Problems, and Speculative Design Scenarios" (paper presented at the conference "Landscape as Necessity," University of Southern California, September 22, 2016).

26. Dan Hill, *Dark Matter and Trojan Horses: A Strategic Design Vocabulary* (Moscow: Strelka, 2012).

27. An alternative resolution to the tension between design and planning within landscape architecture has been frequently noted, by, for example, Richard Weller and Carl Steinitz. Typically, this tension is addressed by attempting to splice design and planning together again, by pretending no schism exists, or by assigning one scale of work to designers (sites) and another, larger scale of work to planners. Instead, it would be better to see design and planning as related, complementary activities with distinct methods—and, in so doing, gain the opportunity to utilize design methods at scales that have often been reserved for planning, particularly when design methods offer distinctive capacities. See Richard Weller, "An Art of Instrumentality," in Waldheim, *The Landscape Urbanism Reader*; and Carl Steinitz, "Landscape Planning: A Brief History of Influential Ideas," *Journal of Landscape Architecture* 3, no. 1 (2008): 68–74.

28. Structures of Coastal Resilience (website), "Location: Norfolk, VA," http://structuresofcoastalresilience.org/locations/norfolk-va/.

29. James Corner, "Representation and Landscape: Drawing and Making in the Landscape Medium," *Word & Image* 8, no. 3 (1992): 243–275; James Corner, "Eidetic Operations and New Landscapes," in *Recovering Landscape: Essays in Contemporary Landscape Architecture*, ed. James Corner (New York: Princeton Architectural Press, 1999); James Corner, "The Agency of Mapping: Speculation, Critique, and Invention," in *Mappings*, ed. Denis Cosgrove (London: Reaktion Books, 1999).

30. Rob Holmes, "Synthetic Cartography as Landscape Architectural Research" (paper presented at conference of the Council of Educators in Landscape Architecture, Salt Lake City, UT, March 23–26, 2016).

31. Guy Nordenson, Catherine Seavitt, and Adam Yarinsky, *On the Water: Palisade Bay* (New York: Museum of Modern Art, 2010).

32. I detail this lineage in part to emphasize that the scale and scope of design work itself is crucial in dealing with large-scale landscape change. A single design project will never be adequate to respond to the complexities and details of a situation like a major metropolitan region located on an estuary. Moreover, the addition of multiple design teams to a project's lineage has the potential to offer key opportunities for reframing, which can push a lineage collectively away from solutionism and toward attentiveness to the perspectives of multiple actors.

33. At DredgeFest NYC, a September 2012 event organized by the Dredge Research Collaborative, Philip Orton, an oceanographer at the Stevens Institute of Technology who has partnered with SCAPE Landscape Architecture on much of their design work for the New York–New Jersey harbor, presciently noted that one of the main reasons to do speculative work—and to do design work for contexts that lack obvious funding pathways—is to be ready with ideas and images when conditions change—in this case, as a result of a hurricane that showed the urgency of reconsidering coastal infrastructure. The post-Sandy pathway for the ideas of *On the Water: Palisade Bay* clearly indicates the value of this approach to speculative design.

34. This description builds on Catherine Dee's description of form as trajectory in "Form, Utility, and the Aesthetics of Thrift in Design Education," *Landscape Journal* 29, no. 1 (2010): 21–35.

35. Notable examples include the work of Karen M'Closkey and Keith VanDerSys (PEG Office of Landscape + Architecture), Alexander Robinson (Landscape Morphologies Lab), Bradley Cantrell and Justine Holzman (formerly REAL), Alan Berger (P-REX), and Phillip Belesky (RMIT), as well as water table tests undertaken by Catherine Seavitt Nordenson's teams for *Palisade Bay* and later Structures of Coastal Resilience.

36. Like Burkholder and Davis, I am a member of the DRC.

37. These paragraphs rely on a description of Burkholder and Davis's process provided to the author in personal communication, June 2018.

38. The aim of this work is not total prediction or complete control; rather, the aim is the intelligent development and selection of options. See Alexander Robinson and Brian Davis, "From Solution Space to Interface," in *Codify: Parametric and Computational Design in Landscape Architecture*, ed. Bradley Cantrell and Adam Mekies (London: Routledge, 2018); Philip Belesky et al., "A Field in Flux" (paper presented at the conference "ACADIA 2015: Computational Ecologies: Design in the Anthropocene," Cincinnati, OH, October 19–25, 2015); Rob Holmes, "Landscape Information Modeling," 2014, http://m.ammoth.us/blog/2014/05/landscape-information-modeling/.

Chapter 20

1. *The House We Live In,* "Series 2, Program 1: Loren Eiseley (edited)," Ian L. McHarg Collection, folder 109.II.B.2.23, Architectural Archives of the University of Pennsylvania.

2. Dirk Sijmons, "Landscape Architecture: New Adventures Ahead!," Landscape Architecture Foundation Summit, www.lafoundation.org/resources/2016/07/declaration-dirk-sijmons.

3. Ibid.

4. Christian Schwägerl, "Welcome to the Anthropocene: Interview with Paul Crutzen. Environmental Society Portal," 2013, www.environmentandsociety.org/exhibitions/anthropocene/huge-variety-possibilities-interview-nobel-laureate-paul-crutzen-his-life.

5. Donna Haraway, "A Manifesto for Cyborgs: Science, Technology, and Socialist Feminism in the 1980s," *Australian Feminist Studies* 2, no. 4 (March 1987): 1–42.

6. Dirk Sijmons, *Landscape and Energy: Designing Transition* (Rotterdam: nai010 Publishers, 2014).

7. Ibid., 218–247.

8. David Scott, "Gigantic Dutch Project: Sea Storage for Wind Energy," *Popular Science* (April 1983): 85–87, https://books.google.com/books?id=qq6GBPoHQpAC&pg=PA85&lpg=PA85&dq=Lievense+Popular+Science&source=bl&ots=x3n7CPnX_X&sig=UaapM6i--ADEVA_PSP_k9wsmzpw&hl=en&sa=X&ved=2ahUKEwi_j574qePeAhXhTN8KHSk1BzMQ6AEwCHoECAYQAQ#v=onepage&q=Lievense%20Popular%20Science&f=false.

9. Sijmons, *Landscape and Energy*, 229.

10. Ibid., 310.

11. Ibid., 312.

12. IABR, 2050—An Energetic Odyssey, https://vimeo.com/199825983. The IABR Biennale, and its various ateliers, was founded as a cultural platform to generate world change through long-term research done in collaboration with the government and other stakeholders; see also IABR Mission Statement, https://iabr.nl/en/over/thema-303.

13. See Donald Worster, *Nature's Economy: A History of Ecological Ideas* (Cambridge: Cambridge University Press, 1994).

14. Ian L. McHarg, *Design with Nature* (Garden City, NY: Doubleday / Natural History Press, 1969).

Chapter 21

I thank Debra Marshall for bringing the golden-eye lichen, *Teloschistes chrysophthalmus,* to my attention; Anna Flood and Alyssa Cerbu for their thoughtful and timely research assistance; and Fritz Steiner for his leadership, feedback, and patience. This work is part of a larger project, W.I.L.D. (Wilderness Integrated Landscape Design), which has benefited from many conversations with my students in the Ecological Design Lab at Ryerson University, and with my colleagues, the "brain trust" of Ann Dale, Nik Luka, Ruth Richardson, Katrine Claassens, M. Elen Deming, Pierre Bélanger, and always, Jeremy Guth. Funding support for this work was provided in part by the Social Sciences and Humanities Research Council of Canada.

1. Jeanne Lohmann, "Invocation," in *Between Silence and Answer* (Philadelphia: Pendle Hill Publications, 1994).

2. Taxonomically classified with the fungi, lichens are "more than the sum of their parts" in that they are not individual organisms, but exist in a symbiotic relationship between two different organisms. As such, lichens are an emergent life form that have properties distinct from each constituent partner organism. Lichenologist Kevan Berg describes a lichen as "a partnership between two or more non-plant organisms, one of which is a fungus that acquires water and nutrients from rain and dust. The other [partner] is a colony of algae (or sometimes cyanobacteria) that produces food through photosynthesis. In working together, the algae and the fungus create a tiny self-sustaining ecosystem. The fungus is the dominant partner and architect in this relationship, and constitutes the external structure of the lichen within which it shades and protects the algal cells and provides them with water and nutrients. In exchange, the fungus receives [or harvests] a steady supply of sugars and other carbohydrates from its algal partner." Kevan Berg, "The Secret World of Lichen," *ON Nature Magazine* August 6, 2009, http://onnaturemagazine.com/the-secret-world-of-lichen.html.

3. Jedidiah Purdy, *After Nature: A Politics for the Anthropocene* (Cambridge, MA: Harvard University Press, 2015), 208.

4. Human activity is widely understood to be causing the acceleration of global biodiversity loss. The cumulative effects of habitat fragmentation, degradation, and destruction are caused by the human-driven processes of land conversion for agriculture, resource extraction, and urbanization. The combined effects of these anthropogenic processes characterize the current Holocene era, which many have argued is now more appropriately termed the Anthropocene era. The Anthropocene has also been coincidentally recognized as the sixth great extinction epoch. See, for example, primary research in A. D. Barnosky et al., "Has the Earth's Sixth Mass Extinction Already Arrived?," *Nature* 471, no. 7336 (2011): 51–57, doi:10.1038/nature09678; Gerardo Ceballos et al., "Accelerated Modern Human-Induced Species Losses: Entering the Sixth Mass Extinction," *Science Advances* 1, no. 5 (2015): e1400253 doi:10.1126/sciadv.1400253; and Mark Williams et al., "The Anthropocene Biosphere," *Anthropocene Review* 2, no. 3 (2015): 196–219, doi:10.1177/2053019615591020. For secondary research see also Elizabeth Kolbert, *The Sixth Extinction: An Unnatural History* (New York: Henry Holt, 2014); Edward O. Wilson, *The Future of Life* (New York: Vintage Books, 2003); and American

Museum of Natural History, "National Survey Reveals Biodiversity Crisis: Scientific Experts Believe We Are in Midst of Fastest Mass Extinction in Earth's History," press release, April 20, 1998, www.mysterium.com/amnh.html.

5. The number of identified and described species on Earth is difficult to quantify precisely because the cladistic and taxonomic data are dynamic, under constant addition, modification, and reclassification (and possible duplication) by scientists working simultaneously in different parts of the world. As such, the number of currently identified and described species ranges from 1.5 to 1.9 million. However, estimates of the total likely number of species on Earth range from conservative estimates of 8.75 to 100 million and up to as many as 1 trillion. Experts agree, however, that regardless of the total, species loss is accelerating worldwide. For a range of perspectives, see M. Julian Caley, Rebecca Fisher, and Kerrie Mengersen, "Global Species Richness Estimates Have Not Converged," *Trends in Ecology and Evolution* 29, no. 4 (2014): 187–188, doi.org/10.1016/j.tree.2014.02.002; Geoffrey Giller, "Are We Any Closer to Knowing How Many Species There Are on Earth?," *Scientific American*, April 8, 2014, www.scientificamerican.com/article/are-we-any-closer-to-knowing-how-many-species-there-are-on-earth/; Camilo Mora et al., "How Many Species Are There on Earth and in the Ocean?," *PLOS Biology* 9, no. 8 (2011), e1001127. doi:10.1371/journal.pbio.1001127; National Science Foundation, "Researchers Find That Earth May Be Home to 1 Trillion Species," May 2, 2016, www.nsf.gov/news/news_summ.jsp?cntn_id=138446; Mark Costello, Robert May, and Nigel Stork, "Can We Name Earth's Species Before They Go Extinct?," *Science* 339, no. 6118 (2013): 413–416, doi:10.1126/science.1230318; and Lee Sweetlove, "Number of Species on Earth Tagged at 8.7 Million," *Nature*, August 24, 2011, doi:10.1038/news.2011.498.

6. Currently, there are more than 91,520 species on the International Union for the Conservation of Nature's "Red List of Threatened Species," and more than 25,820 of these are critical, i.e., threatened with extinction, including 41 percent of amphibians, 34 percent of conifers, 33 percent of reef building corals, 25 percent of mammals, and 13 percent of birds. Of particular note, the number of critically endangered amphibians listed has increased by 30 times, from 18 to 547 species between 1998 and 2018, and the number of endangered bird species listed has doubled in the same period. International Union for the Conservation of Nature (IUCN), "Red List of Threatened Species. Version 2018-1," www.iucnredlist.org.

7. The origins and historical foundations of landscape architecture, as an outgrowth of landscape gardening and architecture in the

late 19th and early 20th centuries, explain the profession's early focus on human-centered design.

8. There are several notable firms whose work now engages explicitly and specifically with novel ecosystems and emerging "new natures"; see the work of Field Operations, Stoss, SCAPE, DLANDstudio, and the Dredge Research Collaborative (among others).

9. The history and origins of the North American wilderness movement and its associated paradigm of conservation are well documented in, e.g., Roderick Nash, *Wilderness and the American Mind* (New Haven, CT: Yale University Press, 1967); Donald J. Worster, *Nature's Economy: A History of Ecological Ideas* (Cambridge: Cambridge University Press, 1985); J. Baird Callicott and Michael Nelson, eds., *The Great New Wilderness Debate* (Athens: University of Georgia Press, 1988). The North American managerial approach to wilderness originated in a paradigm of hierarchical dualism in opposing domains of culture and nature, well detailed by Carolyn Merchant in *The Death of Nature: Women, Ecology and the Scientific Revolution* (New York: Harper Collins, 1980) and further in *Reinventing Eden: The Fate of Nature in Western Culture* (New York: Routledge, 2003). The prevailing notion of wilderness-without-humans was further challenged by W. Cronon, ed., in *Uncommon Ground: Rethinking the Human Place in Nature* (New York: W. W. Norton, 1995), and more recently, critically reframed by Purdy in *After Nature*. Landscape architect Richard Weller explores the effects of this dualism on and embedded in landscape in "World Park," *LA+ WILD* 1, no. 1 (2014): 10–19. The perspective of rethinking the human place in nature was not unfamiliar to McHarg himself, whose embittered observations (e.g., of humans as domineering "bullies of the earth") were captured in a 1969 PBS film, "Multiply and Subdue the Earth." See www.youtube.com/watch?v=5nBFkARCPOI.

10. The history of the wilderness movement and its binary notion of an unpeopled wild is, in fact, deeply rooted in anthropocentric ideals of pastoralism and sublime nature (e.g., those of Henry David Thoreau and John Muir). These ideals gave rise to the notion that nature is innately balanced, stable, and therefore manageable. With an emphasis on the most iconic landscapes and desirable species, the so-called charismatic megafauna, this managerial approach effectively became the focus of conservation biology. Its related scientific research was undertaken on the basis that the protection (and connection) of large rangelands and wilderness landscapes, if targeted to accommodate top predators, would necessarily capture a diversity of smaller, dependent species. For related research see the journal *Conservation Biology* for articles

by Michael Soulé, Reed Noss, Daniel Simberloff, and others. For practice, see Center for Large Landscape Conservation (website), www.largelandscapes.org; and the Yellowstone to Yukon Conservation Initiative (website), www.y2y.net (featured also in this volume). Although ecologists have since embraced a less deterministic understanding of nature (i.e., ecosystems) as more complex, diverse, and uncertain, the deeply rooted managerial paradigm both validated and facilitated an approach to conservation that remains largely entrenched in practice. See a summary in Nina-Marie Lister, "A Systems Approach to Biodiversity Conservation Planning," *Environmental Monitoring and Assessment* 49, nos. 2/3 (1998): 123–155. For a complex systems approach to landscape architecture, see Chris Reed and Nina-Marie Lister, eds., *Projective Ecologies* (New York: Actar, 2014).

11. IUCN has six categories of protected areas; see IUCN website, "Protected Areas," www.iucn.org/theme/protected-areas/about/protected-area-categories. In 2014, 50 percent of recognized protected areas worldwide fell into categories 3–5: National Park, Natural Monument or Feature, Habitat/Species Management Area; and a growing number are emerging as sustainable resource areas. See D. Juffe-Bignoli et al., *Protected Planet Report 2014* (Cambridge: United Nations Environment Program World Conservation Monitoring Centre (UNEP-WCMC), 2014).

12. S. Stolton, K. H. Redford, and N. Dudley, *The Future of Privately Protected Areas* (Gland, Switzerland: IUCN, 2014), cited in Juffe-Bignoli et al., *Protected Planet Report 2014*.

13. See, e.g., Mahesh Rangarajan, "Parks, Politics and History: Conservation Dilemmas in Africa," *Conservation and Society* 1, no. 1 (2003): 77–98.

14. There are many documented successful partnerships in conservation; notable among these are: the transboundary protection of mountain gorillas in central Africa, which relies on comanagement of habitat and ecotourism initiatives (see International Gorilla Conservation Program (website), 2018, www.igcp.org); the Great Green Wall Initiative in Africa; and the continental Yellowstone to Yukon Conservation Initiative. The latter two are profiled in this volume.

15. IUCN-WCPA Task Force on Other Effective Area-Based Conservation Measures, Case Studies 2016–2017, www.iucn.org/sites/dev/files/content/documents/collation_of_case_studies_submitted_to_task_force_on_oecms_-_september_2017.pdf.

16. Indigenous and Community Conserved Areas (ICCA) (website), ICCA Registry, www.iccaregistry.org.

17. Convention on Biological Diversity, "Strategic Plan for Biodiversity 2011–2020: Aichi

Biodiversity Targets," 2010, www.cbd.int/sp/targets/.

18. IUCN-WCPA, "(Draft) Guidelines for Recognising and Reporting Other Effective Area-based Conservation Measures," Version 1 (Gland, Switzerland: IUCN, 2018), www.iucn.org/sites/dev/files/content/documents/guidelines_for_recognising_and_reporting_oecms_-_january_2018.pdf.

19. See, e.g., United Nations Convention to Combat Desertification, "The Great Green Wall: Hope for the Sahara and the Sahel," 2016, www.unccd.int/sites/default/files/documents/26042016_GGW_ENG.pdf.

20. Charles Chester, "Yellowstone to Yukon: Transborder Conservation Across a Vast International Landscape," *Environmental Science and Policy* 49 (May 2015): 75–84; and Yellowstone to Yukon Conservation Initiative (website), https://y2y.net/.

21. Ecosystem management is a misnomer, in that while human behavior can be managed, ecosystems as adaptive complex systems are beyond the capacity of human management. For a detailed discussion, see D. Waltner-Toews, J. J. Kay, and N.-M. Lister, eds., *The Ecosystem Approach: Complexity, Uncertainty, and Managing for Sustainability* (New York: Columbia University Press, 2008). See also notes 7 and 8.

22. Aaron Ellison, "The Suffocating Embrace of Landscape and the Picturesque Conditioning of Ecology," *Landscape Journal* 32, no. 1 (2013): 79–94.

23. Established in 1948, the IUCN was the world's first global environmental union based on scientific research and cooperation for the protection of nature. In 1964, only a few years before the publication of McHarg's *Design with Nature*, the IUCN launched its hallmark "Red List," which became the world's premier mechanism and scientific resource for documenting and classifying global threatened biodiversity, and in so doing directed and reflected contemporary thinking about wild landscapes and their management. See IUCN, "A Brief History of the IUCN," www.iucn.org/about/iucn-brief-history.

24. The Global Convention on Biological Diversity (CBD) and the United Nations Environment Program (UNEP) commit signatory nations to improve the status of biodiversity in at least 17 percent of terrestrial and inland water and 10 percent of coastal and marine areas, especially areas of particular importance for biodiversity and ecosystem services. The CBD further stipulates that these lands and waters are to be conserved through "effectively and equitably managed, ecologically representative and well connected systems of protected areas and other effective area-based conservation measures, and integrated into the wider landscape and seascapes." Convention on Biological Diversity, "Strategic Plan for Bio-

diversity 2011–2020 and the Aichi Targets" (Montreal: Secretariat of the Convention on Biological Diversity, 2010).

25. Edward O. Wilson, *Half Nature: Our Planet's Fight for Life* (New York: W. W. Norton, 2016). See also Half-Earth Project (website), www.half-earthproject.org.

26. The average protected area statistic may appear encouraging but obscures several significant obstacles to making continued progress: notably, the United States, one of the most influential nations in the world (and the third-largest in area) is not a party to the Biodiversity Convention. Similarly, while Canada was the first signatory (and the second-largest country by area), it is the furthest behind (among the six largest countries) and is unlikely to meet its commitment to the IUCN's 2020 target of 17 percent protection. See Convention on Biodiversity (website), www.cbd.int.

27. Ibid.

28. Richard J. Weller, with Claire Hoch and Chieh Huang, *Atlas for the End of the World*, http://atlas-for-the-end-of-the-world.com.

29. See, e.g., *Making Europe a Wilder Place*, https://rewildingeurope.com; and a detailed account by George Monbiot, *Feral: Searching for Enchantment on the Frontiers of Rewilding* (London: Allen Lane, 2013).

30. Landscape infrastructure usually refers to human-designed vegetated infrastructures such as green roofs, living walls, bioswales, and parklands; it is also referred to as green or blue living infrastructure in contrast to the civil engineered (or gray) infrastructures such as roads, bridges, pipelines, and sewers that characterize human settlements. Landscape infrastructure can sometimes refer to forests and wetlands to emphasize the asset value of these landscape features. See, e.g., The Ecological Design Lab: https://ecologicaldesignlab.ca/projects/?research=green-blue-infrastructure.

31. Peri-urban areas in particular may have a significant role in protecting biodiversity, especially in rapidly urbanizing regions where growth outward from a dense urban core has resulted in few remaining and poorly connected greenspaces. See, e.g., discussion of the flexibility and amenity values of peri-urban areas in M. Hedblom, E. Andersson, and S. Borgström, "Flexible Land-Use and Undefined Governance: From Threats to Potentials in Peri-Urban Landscape Planning," *Land Use Policy* 63 (2017): 523–527; and Nik Luka, "Contested Peri-Urban Amenity Landscapes: Changing Waterfront 'Countryside Ideals' in Central Canada," *Landscape Research* 42, no. 3 (2017): 256–276, doi:10.1080/01426397.2016.1267335.

32. N. Dudley et al., *Natural Solutions: Protected Areas Helping People Cope with Climate Change* (Gland, Switzerland: IUCN-WCPA; and Washington, DC, and New York: Nature

Conservancy, United Nations Development Programme, Wildlife Conservation Society, World Bank, and WWF, 2010), cited in Juffe-Bignoli et al., *Protected Planet Report 2014*.

33. Convention on Biological Diversity, "Strategic Plan for Biodiversity 2011–2020 and the Aichi Targets" (Montreal: Secretariat of the Convention on Biological Diversity, 2010). See also note 26.

34. Purdy, *After Nature*, 208.

35. Inspired, naturally, by Anne Whiston Spirn, *The Language of Landscape* (New Haven, CT: Yale University Press, 1998).

Chapter 22

1. Ian L. McHarg, "Natural Factors in Planning," in *To Heal the Earth*, ed. Ian L. McHarg and Frederick R. Steiner (Washington, DC: Island Press, 1998), 74–75.

2. Ian L. McHarg, *A Quest for Life* (New York: John Wiley, 1996), 248.

3. Ibid., 3.

4. Ian L. McHarg, "Architecture in an Ecological View of the World," in McHarg and Steiner, *To Heal the Earth*, 185.

5. Ibid., 194.

6. Ibid., 77.

7. See, for example, Will Steffen et al., "Trajectories of the Earth System in the Anthropocene," in *Proceedings of the National Academy of Sciences* (Washington, DC: National Academies Press, August 2018), www.pnas.org/cgi/doi/10.1073; Somini Sengupta, "The Year Global Warming Turned Model into Menace," *New York Times*, August 10, 2018, 1. Both refer to the near onset of "cascading system failures" threatening systems that supply food, water, and energy, as well as entire economies.

8. Aldo Leopold, *Round River* (New York: Oxford University Press, 1953), 165.

9. Perhaps like the Mont Pèlerin Society formed by Friedrich Hayek, Milton Friedman, and others in advancing the cause of neoliberalism in the decades after World War II—only better thought out, grounded in ecology, much faster, and more inclusive. See Philip Mirowski and Dieter Plehwe, eds., *The Road from Mont Pèlerin* (Cambridge, MA: Harvard University Press, 2009); and Angus Burgin, *The Great Persuasion* (Cambridge, MA: Harvard University Press, 2012).

10. Frederick R. Steiner, *Making Plans* (Austin: University of Texas Press, 2018), 5.

11. John R. Parkinson, *Democracy and Public Space* (New York: Oxford University Press, 2011).

12. Patricia Leigh Brown, "Transforming Tulsa, Starting with a Park," *New York Times*, August 10, 2018.

13. David W. Orr, *Design on the Edge* (Cambridge, MA: MIT Press, 2006).

14. Campbell Robertson, "Giving Voice to the Victims of Racial Terror," *New York Times*, April 25, 2018.

15. James Reston Jr., *A Rift in the Earth* (New York: Arcade, 2017).

16. Thomas Berry, *The Great Work* (New York: Bell Tower, 1999); John Todd, *Healing Earth* (New York: Atlantic Books, 2019).

17. Jeff Schmidt, *Disciplined Minds* (Lanham, MD: Rowman and Littlefield, 2000), 265–280.

18. See Stuart Walker, *Designing Sustainability* (New York: Routledge, 2014), 39.

19. John Wood, "Meta-Designing Paradigm Change," in *The Handbook of Design for Sustainability*, ed. Stuart Walker and Jacques Giard (London: Bloomsbury, 2013), 429–445.

Chapter 23

1. Martin V. Melosi, "Fresh Kills: The Making and Unmaking of a Wastescape," in "Out of Sight, Out of Mind: The Politics and Culture of Waste," ed. Christof Mauch, special issue, *RCC Perspectives: Transformations in Environment and Society* 1 (2016): 61. For an excellent general history of the urban waste infrastructures of the United States, see also Martin V. Melosi, *The Sanitary City: Urban Infrastructure in America from Colonial Times to the Present* (Baltimore, MD: The Johns Hopkins University Press, 2000).

2. Robert Moses et al., *Fresh Kills Land-Fill: Report to Mayor Impellitteri and the Board of Estimate* (City of New York, November 1951), 13. Though viewed by Moses as "useless," Fresh Kills supported not only a vast intertidal salt marsh system, but also the traces of precontact civilizations dating back to the Paleo-Indian, Archaic, and Woodland periods. In the 17th and 18th centuries, Dutch and British settlers' farms occupied the area, and the marshes provided valuable salt hay for livestock. Early industrial manufacturing sites emerged in the 19th century, including the famed American Linoleum Company, as well as several brickworks that used the moist clay found in the marshy soils. A number of immigrant communities settled nearby, including in Travis (formerly Linoleumville) and Rossville, drawn by the plentiful factory jobs. See also Allee King Rosen & Fleming, Inc., "Phase 1A Archaeological Documentary Study: Fresh Kills Park, Richmond County, New York" (report prepared for the New York City Department of City Planning and the New York City Department of Parks and Recreation, March 2008).

3. From the 1920s through the 1950s, waste production surged, along with the city's population and postwar consumerism. Municipal waste disposal policy shifted toward favoring the sanitary landfill and the incinerator as an alternative to ocean dumping—dumping within New York Harbor and other tributary waters had been prohibited by the federal Rivers and Harbors Act of 1899, and by 1934 the United States Supreme Court ruled that the city must cease ocean dumping.

Though New York City had hoped to shift to incineration as an optimal means of waste disposal, the enactment of the Clean Air Act of 1970 resulted in the closure of the city's incinerators, which did not meet the new emissions guidelines. See Benjamin Miller, *Fat of the Land* (New York, NY: Four Walls Eight Windows Press, 2000).

4. The Fresh Kills landfill was reopened briefly after the terrorist attacks of September 11, 2001, to accommodate and sort the debris from the collapsed World Trade Center towers.

5. Ian L. McHarg, "Processes as Values," in *Design with Nature* (Garden City, NY: Doubleday/Natural History Press, 1969), 103–115.

6. McHarg, "A Step Forward," in *Design with Nature*, 31–41.

7. McHarg, "The Naturalists," in *Design with Nature*, 117–125.

8. See quotations from Molly Greene's July 2012 interview with Mark Alvorson, a Travis resident, cited in the research paper "A Mountain by the Sea: Waste-scapes, Life-scapes, and the Reinvention of Fresh Kills" (New Haven, CT: Yale School of Forestry and Environmental Studies, 2012).

9. Field Operations was founded as a collaboration with architect Stan Allen in 2001; the firm is now led by Corner as James Corner Field Operations.

10. C. S. Holling, "Engineering Resilience versus Ecological Resilience," in *Foundations of Ecological Resilience*, ed. Lance Gunderson, Craig Allen, and C. S. Holling (Washington, DC: Island Press, 2009). Note that McHarg's writings position him as a staunch proponent of the steady-state ecological climax theory.

11. Field Operations, "Lifescape," in *PRAXIS* 4 (2002): 20.

12. The Freshkills Park Natural Resources field survey of 2007 is included in the *Freshkills Park Generic Environmental Impact Statement* of March 2009; see www.nycgovparks.org/sub_your_park/fresh_kills_park/pdf/FGEIS/Vol1/10_Natural_Resources.pdf. The Macaulay Honors College of the City University of New York organized and executed the 2015 Freshkills Park BioBlitz under the direction of Kelly O'Donnell; see CUNY, Macaulay Honors College (website), https://macaulay.cuny.edu/eportfolios/bioblitz/welcome/.

13. Glenn A. Knoblock, *The American Clipper Ship, 1845–1920: A Comprehensive History, with a Listing of Builders and Their Ships* (Jefferson, NC: McFarland & Company, 2014), 52–32.

14. Aubrey H. Smith, "On Colonies of Plants Observed Near Philadelphia," in *Proceedings of the Academy of Natural Sciences of Philadelphia* 19 (1867), 15–24; and Addison Brown, "Ballast Plants in New York City and its Vicinity," in *Bulletin of the Torrey Botanical Club* 6, no. 59 (1879): 353–360.

15. Brown, "Ballast Plants," 354.

16. Field Operations, "Lifescape," 20.

17. Charles Arthur Hollick and Nathaniel Lord Britton, *The Flora of Richmond County, New York* (Staten Island, NY: Torrey Botanical Club, 1879). Note that Richmond County was incorporated into the greater New York City as the Borough of Richmond in 1898; the island was not officially called Staten Island until 1975, though this name has been used interchangeably with Richmond County since settlement by the Dutch in the 16th century.

18. As a member of the Board of Health, Hollick would work with George E. Waring on the installation of a sewage system for Staten Island from 1881 to 1891. Waring, an agricultural scientist and sanitary engineer, would be appointed in 1894 as the commissioner of the Department of Street Cleaning of the City of New York, the predecessor of the modern-day Department of Sanitation.

19. See especially Arthur Hollick, "Local Flora Notes—Staten Island" in *Torreya* 22, no. 1 (1922): 1–3. In this essay published by the Torrey Botanical Club, Hollick notes his ongoing field surveys from 1908 through 1921 at the area of Arlington on the north shore of Staten Island along the Kill van Kull, a significantly disturbed ballast ground.

20. Hollick and Britton, *The Flora of Richmond County*, addenda of 1880, 1880–1882, 1883–1884, 1885, 1886–1889, 1890, and 1891–1895.

21. McHarg, "The Naturalists," in *Design with Nature*, 117–125.

22. Edgar Anderson, *Plants, Man, and Life* (Boston, MA: Little, Brown and Company, 1952), 149.

23. Ibid., 150.

24. Ralph Waldo Emerson, "The Fortune of the Republic," in *The Complete Works of Ralph Waldo Emerson: Miscellanies*, vol. 11 (Boston, MA: Houghton, Mifflin Company, 1904), 512.

25. The ongoing collaborative work between Freshkills Park and the pioneering Greenbelt Native Plant Center in nearby Travis, led by Edward Toth of the native plant nursery for the New York City Department of Parks and Recreation, offers rich possibilities for the park's experimental planting palette. See Jeffery Sugarman, "Environmental and Community Health: A Reciprocal Relationship," in *Restorative Commons: Creating Health and Well-Being Through Urban Landscapes*, ed. Lindsay Campbell and Anne Wiesen (Newtown Square, PA: USDA Forest Service, Northern Research Station, 2009), 148.

Chapter 24

1. R. Hyde and M. Pestana, exhibit curators, *The Future Starts Here* (London: Victoria and Albert Museum, 2018).

2. P. J. Crutzen and E. F. Stoermer, "The 'Anthropocene,'" *Global Change Newsletter* 41 (2000): 17–18; S. Dalby, *Environmental Security* (Minneapolis: University of Minnesota Press, 2001); M. Morton, *Dark Ecology: For a*

Logic of Future Coexistence (New York: Columbia University Press, 2016); W. Steffen et al., "The Anthropocene: Conceptual and Historical Perspectives," *Philosophical Transactions of the Royal Society A* 369, no. 1938 (2011): 842–867.

3. C. Parmesan and G. Yohe, "A Globally Coherent Fingerprint of Climate Change Impacts Across Natural Systems," *Nature* 421 (2003): 37–42; M. Schilthuizen, *Darwin Comes to Town: How the Urban Jungle Drives Evolution* (New York: Picador, 2018).

4. Ian L. McHarg, *Design with Nature* (Garden City, NY: Doubleday/Natural History Press, 1969).

5. H. A. Simon, *Sciences of the Artificial*, 3rd ed. (Cambridge, MA: MIT Press, 1996), 111.

6. A. Newell, "Heuristic Programming: Ill-Structured Problems," in *Progress in Operations Research*, vol. 3, ed. J. Aronofsky (New York: Wiley, 1969), 360–414; W. Reitman, "Heuristic Decision Procedures, Open Constraints, and the Structure of Ill- Defined Problems," in *Human Judgments and Optimality*, ed. M. Shelly and G. Bryan (New York: Wiley, 1964), 282–315; H. W. J. Rittel, "Some Principles for the Design of an Educational System for Design," *Journal of Architectural Education* 25, nos. 1–2 (1971): 16–27.

7. N. Cross, *Designerly Ways of Knowing* (Basel, Switzerland: Birkhäuser, 2007).

8. A. W. Shearer, "Abduction to Argument: A Framework of Design Thinking," *Landscape Journal* 34, no. 2 (2015): 127–138.

9. W. B. Gallie, "Essentially Contested Concepts," *Proceedings of the Aristotelian Society* 56 (1956): 167–198.

10. H. W. J. Rittel and M. M. Webber, "Dilemmas in a General Theory of Planning," *Policy Sciences* 4, no. 2 (1973): 155–169; W.-N. Xiang, 2013, "Working with Wicked Problems in Socio-Ecological Systems: Awareness, Acceptance, and Adaptation," *Landscape and Urban Planning* 110 (2013): 1–4.

11. Kongjian Yu et al., "Primary Study of National Scale Ecological Security Pattern," *Acta Ecologic Sinica* 29, no. 10 (2009): 5163–5175; K.-J. Yu, "Reinvent the Good Earth: National Ecological Security Pattern Plan, China," in *The Ecological Design and Planning Reader*, ed. F. O. Ndubisi (Washington, DC: Island Press, 2014), 466–469.

12. K. Krause and M. C. Williams, eds., *Critical Security Studies: Concepts and Cases* (Minneapolis: University of Minnesota Press, 1997).

13. D. Baldwin, "The Concept of Security," *Review of International Studies* 23, no. 2 (1997): 5–26.

14. B. Buzan, O. Waever, and J. de Wilde, *Security: A New Framework for Analysis* (Boulder, CO: Lynne Rienner, 1998).

15. R. Costanza, "Review Essay: The Nuclear Arms Race and the Theory of Social Traps," *Journal of Peace Studies* 21, no. 1 (1984): 79–86; J. H. Herz, *Political Realism and Politi-*

cal Idealism (Chicago: University of Chicago Press, 1951).

16. S. Dalby, *Environmental Security* (Minneapolis: University of Minnesota Press, 2002); N. Matthews, "Environment and Security," *Foreign Policy* 74 (1989): 23–41; R. H. Ullman, "Redefining Security," *International Security* 8, no. 1 (1983): 129–153.

17. P. H. Gleick, "Environment and Security: The Clear Connections," *Bulletin of the Atomic Scientists* 47, no. 3 (1991): 16–21.

18. G. D. Dabelko and D. D. Dabelko, "Environmental Security: Issues of Conflict and Redefinition," *Environmental Change and Security Project Report* 1 (1995): 3–13.

19. U.S. President George H. W. Bush, *National Security Strategy* (Washington, DC: The White House, 1991), 55.

20. U.S. President William J. Clinton, *A National Security Strategy of Engagement and Enlargement* (Washington, DC: The White House, 1994).

21. S. Wasserman Goodman, "The Environment and National Security" (remarks to National Defense University, Washington, DC, August 8, 1996).

22. Food Security Act of 1985, Pub. L. No. 99-198, 99 Stat. 1504 (2002).

23. Exec. Order No. 12127, 44 Fed. Reg. 19367, 3 CFR, 1979 (March 31, 1979); Exec. Order No. 12148, 44 Fed. Reg. 43229, 3 CFR, 1979 (July 20, 1979); Homeland Security Act (HSA) of 2002, Pub. L. No. 107–296, 116 Stat. 2135 (2002).

24. D. Deudney, "Environment and Security: Muddled Thinking," *Bulletin of the Atomic Scientists* 47, no. 3 (1991): 22–28.

25. B. Buzan, O. Waevern, and J. de Wilde, *Security: A New Framework for Analysis* (Boulder, CO: Lynne Rienner, 1998).

26. Kongjian Yu, *Security Patterns in Landscape Planning with a Case in South China*, Doctor of Design thesis (Cambridge, MA: Harvard University, 1995).

27. J. Kozlowski, *Threshold Approach in Urban, Regional, and Environmental Planning: Theory and Practice* (St. Lucia, Australia: University of Queensland Press, 1986); J. Kozlowski and G. Hill, *Towards Planning for Sustainable Development: A Guide for the Ultimate Environmental Threshold (UET) Method* (Brookfield, VT: Ashgate, 1993).

28. Yu, *Security Patterns in Landscape Planning*, 31.

29. Kongjian Yu, "Security Patterns and Surface Modeling in Landscape Ecological Planning," *Landscape and Urban Planning* 36 (1996): 1–17.

30. R. T. T. Forman, *Land Mosaics: The Ecology of Landscapes and Regions* (New York: Cambridge University Press, 1995); R. T. T. Forman, *Urban Ecology: The Science of Cities* (New York: Cambridge University Press, 2014).

31. Kongjian Yu, "Think Like a King, Act Like a Peasant: The Power of a Landscape Architect and Some Personal Experience," in

Thinking the Contemporary Landscape, ed. C. Girot and D. Imhof (New York: Princeton Architectural Press, 2017), 164–184.

32. B. B. Allan, "Second Only to Nuclear War: Science and the Making of Existential Threat in Global Climate Governance," *International Studies Quarterly* 61, no. 4 (2017): 809–820; D. Wallace and D. Silander, eds., *Climate Change, Policy and Security: State and Human Impacts* (London: Routledge, 2018).

33. Examples include: Q. Lin et al., "Ecological Security Pattern Analysis Based on InVEST and Least-Cost Path Model: A Case Study of Dongguan Water Village," *Sustainability* 8, no. 2 (2016): 172, doi:10.2290/su8021172; D. Liu and Q. Chang, "Ecological Security Research Progress in China," *Acta Ecologica Sinica* 35 (2014): 111–121; S. Liu et al., "The Ecological Security Pattern and Its Constraint on Urban Expansion of a Black Soil Farming Area in Northeast China," *International Journal of Geo-Information* 6, no. 263 (2017), doi:10.3390/ijgi6090263; S. Wang et al., "The Evolution of Landscape Ecological Security in Beijing Under the Influence of Different Policies in Recent Decades," *Science of the Total Environment* 646 (2019): 49–57; Z. Wang et al., "A DPSIR Model for Ecological Security Assessment Through Indicator Screening: A Case Study at Dianchi Lake in China," *PLoS One* 10, no. 6 (2015): e0131732.

34. M. Dillon, *Politics of Security* (New York: Routledge, 1996), 122.

35. C. J. Glacken, *Traces on the Rhodian Shore: Nature and Culture in Western Thought from Ancient Times to the Eighteenth Century* (Berkeley: University of California Press, 1967).

Chapter 25

1. Ian L. McHarg, *Design with Nature* (Garden City, NY: Doubleday/Natural History Press, 1969), 24.

2. Anne Garland Mahler, "Global South," www.oxfordbibliographies.com/view/document/obo-9780190221911/obo-9780190221911-0055.xml.

3. Geographer David Harvey, cited in Jon Goodbun, Jeremy Till, and Deljana Iossifova, eds., "Themes of Scarcity," in *Scarcity: Architecture in an Age of Depleting Resources* (New York: John Wiley, 2012), 9.

4. I. Scoones et al., *Narratives of Scarcity: Understanding the "Global Resource Grab"* (Brighton, U.K.: Institute for Poverty, Land and Agrarian Studies, 2014).

5. Absolute scarcity has origins in the writings of Thomas Robert Malthus, an English scholar influential in political economy, who claimed that natural resources are limited and are subject to increasing demands from human society. Malthus's 1798 *Essay on the Principle of Population* proposed that society's increase in wealth and abundance tended to support population growth rather than maintaining a higher standard of living, a concept that became known as the "Malthusian trap."

6. Relative scarcity can be considered in two forms, as resource scarcity and as political scarcity. First, society's potential for transformation (through technological innovation) can replace or substitute for scarce resources through strategies such as recycling, extraction of lower-quality resources, or technological innovation. This concept is traced to classical economists such as David Ricardo who, writing in the early 19th century, observed that agricultural productivity was related to land quality, the level of financial capital, and the ingenuity and skills of the farmer. In contrast, political scarcity has origins in the work of Karl Marx, who argued that scarcity is perceived and manufactured to suit particular interests. Political scarcity is therefore tied to the impact of colonization, globalization, capitalism, and elite power in controlling access to and distribution of resources.

7. The partner countries of the Great Green Wall are: Algeria, Burkina Faso, Chad, Djibouti, Egypt, the Gambia, Mauritania, Niger, Nigeria, Senegal, and the Sudan.

8. David O'Connor and James Ford, "Increasing the Effectiveness of the 'Great Green Wall' as an Adaptation to the Effects of Climate Change and Desertification in the Sahel," *Sustainability* 6, no. 10 (2014): 7143–7154.

9. Wieteke Aster Holthuijzen, "Dry, Hot and Brutal: Climate Change and Desertification," *Journal of Sustainable Development in Africa* 13, no. 7 (2011): 245–268.

10. Burkhard Bilger, "The Great Oasis: Can a Wall of Trees Stop the Sahara from Spreading?," *New Yorker*, December 19 and 26, 2011.

11. Hannelore Kusserow, "Desertification, Resilience, and Re-Greening in the African Sahel—A Matter of the Observation Period?" *Earth Science Dynamics* 8 (2017): 1141–1170.

12. Piers Blaikie, *The Political Economy of Soil Erosion in Developing Countries* (London: Routledge, 2016).

13. According the United Nations Convention to Combat Desertification, desertification is defined as "land degradation in arid, semi-arid and dry sub-humid areas resulting from various factors, including climatic variations and human activities," www.csf-desertification.eu/combating-desertification/item/desertification-and-land-degradation-trend-indicators.

14. O'Connor and Ford, "Increasing the Effectiveness of the 'Great Green Wall.'

15. Bilger, "The Great Oasis."

16. Food and Agriculture Organisation of the United Nations, "Great Green Wall for the Sahara and the Sahel Initiative," www.fao.org/docrep/016/ap603e/ap603e.pdf.

17. Lea Billen and Deborah Goffner, "Gardening the Sahel," September 30, 2016, https://goodanthropocenes.net/2016/09/30/gardening-the-sahel/.

18. Kjeld Rasmussen et al., "Environmental Change in the Sahel: Reconstructing Contrasting Evidence and Interpretations," *Regulating Environmental Change* (February 2015): 1–8.

19. Food and Agriculture Organisation of the United Nations, Green Growth Knowledge Platform, "Building Africa's Great Green Wall: Restoring Degraded Drylands for Stronger and More Resilient Communities," www.greengrowthknowledge.org/resource/building-africa%E2%80%99s-great-green-wall-restoring-degraded-drylands-stronger-and-more-resilient/.

20. Kusserow, "Desertification, Resilience, and Re-Greening in the African Sahel," 1163.

21. Rasmussen et al., "Environmental Change in the Sahel," 6.

22. R. Bellefontaine et al., "The African Great Green Wall Project: What Advice Can Scientists Provide?," ed. I. Amsallem and S.Jauffret (Montpellier: French Scientific Commitee on Desertification, 2011).

23. Jim Morrison, "The 'Great Green Wall' Didn't Stop Desertification, but It Evolved into Something That Might," Smithsonian.com, August 23, 2016, www.smithsonianmag.com/science-nature/great-green-wall-stop-desertification-not-so-much-180960171/.

24. Rasmussen et al., "Environmental Change in the Sahel."

25. Scoones et al., "Narratives of Scarcity."

26. O'Connor and Ford, "Increasing the Effectiveness of the 'Great Green Wall,'" 6.

27. Duanfang Lu, *Remaking Chinese Urban Form: Modernity, Scarcity and Space, 1949–2005* (London: Routledge, 2006).

28. Ibid.; Damien Ma and William Adams, *In Line Behind a Billion People: How Scarcity Will Define China's Ascent in the Next Decade* (Upper Saddle River, NJ: FT Press, 2014).

29. Lu, *Remaking Chinese Urban Form*, 10.

30. Judith Shapiro, *China's Environmental Challenges* (New York: John Wiley, 2016).

31. It is important to note that Mao's attitudes toward the environment were not all driven by socialist ideology. Judith Shapiro argues that on some levels his views represented "an extreme form of a philosophical and behavioural tendency that has roots in traditional Confucian culture" (ibid., 8). In 2001, Shapiro published *Mao's War Against Nature: Politics and the Environment in Revolutionary China* (Cambridge: Cambridge University Press).

32. Britt Crow-Miller, "Discourses of Deflection: The Politics of Framing China's South-North Water Transfer Project," *Water Alternatives* 8, no. 2 (2015): 180.

33. *The Economist*, "China Has Built the World's Largest Water-Diversion Project," April 5, 2018, www.economist.com/china/2018/04/05/china-has-built-the-worlds-largest-water-diversion-project.

34. Crow-Miller, "Discourses of Deflection," 180.

35. Jiahua Pan, *China's Environmental Governing and Ecological Civilization* (Heidelberg: Springer-Verlag, 2016).

36. In 1982, Ye's dissertation, "Shengtai nongye—Woguo nongyede yici lüse geming" (Ecological Agriculture—A Green Revolution in My Country's Agriculture), was published as *Ecological Agriculture: The Future of Agriculture* (Chongqing: Chongqing Chubanshe).

37. Ye is quoted by Maurizio Marinelli in "How to Build a 'Beautiful China' in the Anthropocene. The Political Discourse and the Intellectual Debate on Ecological Civilization," *Journal of Chinese Political Science* (February 22, 2018): 9.

38. Kongjian Yu, "Projects Leading Policy: Water Urbanism Across Scales," in *Water Urbanism East*, ed. Kelly Shannon and Bruno De Meulder (Zurich: Park Books, 2013).

39. Kongjian Yu, Sisi Wand, and Dihua Li, "The Negative Approach to Urban Growth Planning of Beijing, China," *Journal of Environmental Planning and Management* 54, no. 9 (2012): 1209–1236.

40. Marinelli, "How to Build a 'Beautiful China' in the Anthropocene," 15.

41. America Society of Landscape Architects (ASLA), Weishan Wetland Park submission (2015), www.asla.org/2015awards/96363.html.

42. Lian Tao, "Weishan Lake National Park, Shandong," *Landscape Architecture Frontier* 4, no. 3 (2016).

43. Pan, *China's Environmental Governing and Ecological Civilization*.

44. United Nations Environment Programme, "Green Is Gold: The Strategy and Actions of China's Ecological Civilization," May 26, 2016, https://reliefweb.int/report/china/green-gold-strategy-and-actions-chinas-ecological-civilization.

45. Marcus Taylor, *The Political Ecology of Climate Change Adaptation* (New York: Routledge, 2014).

Chapter 26

The title quotation is McHarg's opening comment to the crowd at the first Earth Day, April 22, 1970. Jonathan B. Talmadge, "Thousands Gather for Earth Day Activities," *Daily Pennsylvanian*, April 23, 1970.

1. McHarg first gave these lectures at the Edinburgh College of Art and continued to do so for several years. Typescripts with annotations and a class schedule survive, documenting seven of the ten lectures; see Ian McHarg Collection, The Architectural Archives, University of Pennsylvania (call #: 109.I.B.1.18).

2. Marshall Ledger, "On Getting the Lay of the Land," *Pennsylvania Gazette* 85, no. 4 (February 1987), 35.

3. Ibid., 34.

4. For McHarg's account of his youth and education, see Ian L. McHarg, *Design with Nature* (Garden City, NY: Doubleday/Natural History Press, 1969); and Ian L. McHarg, *A Quest for Life* (New York: John Wiley, 1996). The official birth registration for McHarg lists

his given names as "John Lennox," after his father. His family must have begun using the Gaelic variation "Ian" early on. Extract of an entry from the Register of Births in Scotland, obtained by author from the General Register Office of Scotland, August 2018.

5. McHarg, *Quest for Life*, 63–64.

6. Ibid., 77.

7. "The Philadelphia Cure: Clearing Slums with Penicillin, not Surgery," *Architectural Forum* 96, no. 4 (April 1952): 112–119.

8. Thomas Hine, "[Philadelphia] Influence in Architecture on the Decline," *Philadelphia Inquirer*, September 7, 1980, M1–2.

9. Denise Scott Brown, conversation with the author, December 2, 2018. For an account of Scott Brown's experience, see Denise Scott Brown, "Urban Design at Fifty: A Personal View," in *Urban Design*, ed. A. Krieger and W. Saunders (Minneapolis: University of Minnesota Press, 2009), 61–87.

10. Morris and Steedman attended McHarg's lectures at the Edinburgh College of Art. McHarg, *Quest for Life*, 112. Also responding to McHarg's advertisement was the Englishman, Gerald M. Cope, who graduated Penn in 1957. Marshall Ledger, "On Getting the Lay of the Land," 36.

11. Kathleen John-Alder, "Toward a New Landscape: Modern Courtyard Housing and Ian McHarg's Urbanism," *Journal of Planning History* 13, no. 3 (August 2014): 187–206.

12. Karl Linn, "Karl Linn: Landscape Architect in Service of Peace, Social Justice, Commons, and Community," interview by Lisa Rubens in 2003 and 2004 (Berkeley, CA: Oral History Center, Bancroft Library, University of California, Berkeley, 2005), 79.

13. For an insightful narrative of McHarg's development in the context of environmentalism, see Anne Whiston Spirn, "Ian McHarg, Landscape Architecture, and Environmentalism: Ideas and Methods in Context," in *Environmentalism and Landscape Architecture*, ed. M. Conan (Washington, DC: Dumbarton Oaks, 2000), 97–114.

14. Ian L. McHarg, "An Ecological Method for Landscape Architecture," *Landscape Architecture* 57, no. 2 (January 1967): 105–107.

15. McHarg's datebook for 1969, Ian and Carol McHarg Collection, The Architectural Archives, University of Pennsylvania (call #: 365.II.2).

16. McHarg, in his "Preface" to the 25th anniversary edition of *Design with Nature*, notes a companion course, entitled "Ecology of the City," as a significant but secondary source for *Design with Nature*. Ian L. McHarg, *Design with Nature* (New York: John Wiley, 1992), iii–vi.

17. *Radio-Television Daily*, New York, January 17, 1961.

18. Edgar Williams, "Eugene Feldman, 54; Artist and Teacher" (obituary), *Philadelphia Inquirer*, September 27, 1975.

19. The author wishes to thank Mai Reitmeyer, senior research services librarian at the American Museum of Natural History in New York, for identifying the source and history of the image used for the cover.

20. Susan McMillan, an editor at Natural History Press, as quoted in the *New York Times*, March 28, 1970.

21. Charles Duncan, "Man Threatens Mother Nature" (book review of *Design with Nature*), *Atlanta Constitution*, August 17, 1969.

22. Beth Gillin et al., "30,000 Mark Earth Day at Fairmount Park Rally," *Philadelphia Inquirer*, April 23, 1970.

23. Maurice Obstfeld, "Earth Week Gathering Calls for Human Race to End Destruction of Environment," *Daily Pennsylvanian*, April 22, 1970.

24. Maralyn Lois Polak, "This City Planner Lives on a Farm," *Philadelphia Inquirer*, March 23, 1980.

25. McHarg, *Quest for Life*, 112.

Project Credits

12.1 Great Green Wall. Partners include: Permanent Inter-State Committee for Drought Control in the Sahel (CILSS); European Union (EU); Food and Agriculture Organization of the United Nations (FAO); Global Environment Facility (GEF); United Nations Convention to Combat Desertification (UNCCD); International Union for Conservation of Nature (IUCN-PACO); Sahara and Sahel Observatory (OSS); and World Bank Group (WBG).

12.2. Yellowstone to Yukon. Conservation Initiative is a joint Canada-United States not-for-profit organization dedicated to securing the long-term ecological health of the region. See https://y2y.net/.

12.3 Ecological Security. Kongjian Yu, Peking University Graduate School of Landscape Architecture; Dihua Li, Peking University; Zhifang Wang, Peking University; Liyan Xu, Peking University; Xili Han, Peking University; Hailong Liu, Tsinghua University; Lei Zhang, Tianjin University; Xuesong Xi, China Agricultural University; Sisi Wang, Beijing University of Civil Engineering and Architecture; Hailong Li, China Society of Urban Studies; Bo Li, Central South University; and Bo Luan, Peking University.

12.4 Malpai. The Malpai Borderlands Group is a nonprofit organization comprising landowners whose mission is to manage the ecosystem of nearly 1 million acres (404,685 hectares) of relatively unfragmented landscape. See www.malpaiborderlandsgroup.org/.

12.5 Samboja Lestari. Dr. Willie Smits and the Borneo Orangutan Survival (BOS) Foundation. The BOS Foundation is a nonprofit whose mission is to conserve the Bornean orangutan and its habitat, in cooperation with local communities, the Indonesian Ministry of Forestry, and international partner organizations. The BOS Foundation works in other areas of Indonesia as well.

12.6. Waiheke. Foundation Project—Auckland Council District Plan, Hauraki Gulf Islands Section: prepared for Auckland City Council by the Auckland Council Maritime and Rural Planning Team; Barry Kaye, Neil Rasmussen, Matthew Feary, and Jane Jennings in association with DJScott Associates Ltd., landscape architects; and A. B. Matthews & Associates, surveyors and planners.

Project 1, Church Bay and Project 2, Bush Landscape Lot, Western Waiheke Island: prepared for Nick and Annette Johnstone by DJScott Associates Ltd., landscape architects, in association with Beca, Carter, Hollings and Ferner, engineers and planners.

Project 3, Park Point and Project 4, Cable Bay: prepared for Walter and Kerry Titchener by DJScott Associates Ltd., landscape architects; and A. B. Matthews & Associates, surveyors and planners, in association with TSE Group Ltd., engineers.

Project 5, Owhanake: prepared for Waiheke Island Coastal Estates Ltd. by DJScott Associates Ltd., landscape architects and resource planners, in association with TSE Group Ltd., engineers.

The DJScott Associates Ltd. landscape architecture and planning team included Dennis Scott, Logan Anderson, Megan Moors, Glen May, Grant Kneebone, and Scott Cameron. Other prominent team members included Charles Mitchell Associates Ltd., ecology; Architage Ltd. and Rod Clough Associates, archaeology; Babbage Consultants Ltd., geotechnical engineers; and Traffic Design Group Ltd., traffic engineers. Primary project implementation contractors: Waiheke Contractors Ltd., civil contractors; Awarua Nurseries, green input and rural design, revegetation/planting.

13.1 The BIG U. Bjarke Ingels Group (BIG); One Architecture & Urbanism (ONE); Starr Whitehouse; JLP+D; Level Infrastructure; BuroHappold; Arcadis; Green Shield Ecology; and AE Consultancy.

13.2 New Urban Ground. DLANDstudio/Architecture Research Office.

13.3 Fingers of High Ground. The Structures of Coastal Resilience initiative was conceived and curated by Guy Nordenson, professor of architecture at Princeton University. The University of Pennsylvania team was led by Anuradha Mathur and Dilip da Cunha. The team included Caitlin Squier-Roper, Jamee Kominsky, Graham Laird Prentice, and Matthew J. Wiener, with assistance from Michael Tantala and Julie Chapman. See http://structuresofcoastalresilience.org.

13.4 Zandmotor. Zandmotor is overseen by the Ministry of Infrastructure and the Environment. The project was made possible with support from the European Regional Development Fund. See www.dezandmotor.nl/en/.

13.5 2050—An Energetic Odyssey. Commissioned by the International Architecture Biennale Rotterdam (IABR) in the context of IABR—2016—THE NEXT ECONOMY. Concept: Maarten Hajer and Dirk Sijmons. Realized by: Tungstenpro, H+N+S Landscape Architects, and Ecofys in partnership with the Ministry of Economic Affairs of the Kingdom of The Netherlands, Shell, Port of Rotterdam, and Van Oord.

14.1 Healthy Port Futures. The project was made possible through the generous funding of the Great Lakes Protection Fund. Supplemental support provided by Cornell University, the University of Pennsylvania, the State University of New York at Buffalo, and the Saint Anthony Falls Laboratory at the University of Minnesota.

At its inception, Healthy Port Futures was coordinated with the DredgeFest Great Lakes event in Minnesota and organized by the Dredge Research Collaborative. The Dredge Research Collaborative consists of the following members: Rob Holmes, Auburn University; Tim Maly, Rhode Island School of Design; Brett Milligan, University of California at Davis; Gena Wirth, SCAPE Landscape Architecture; Brian Davis, Cornell University; Sean Burkholder, University of Pennsylvania; Justine Holzman, University of Toronto. Project team: Sean Burkholder, University of Pennsylvania; Brian Davis and Theresa Ruswick, Cornell University; Kimberly Hill and Jeffrey Marr, University of Minnesota; Matthew J. Lewis, Michigan Aerospace; Walter Dinicola, Nathan Holiday, and Matthew

Henderson, Anchor QEA; Jeff Schaeffer, USGS Great Lakes Science Center; David Knight, Great Lakes Commission; and Matthew Moffitt, Harvard Graduate School of Design.

14.2 Room for the River. Room for the River is a cooperative effort of nineteen different entities overseen by the Ministry of Infrastructure and Water Management/ Rijkswaterstatt. See www.roomfortheriver.com/.

14.3 Los Angeles. OLIN: Laurie Olin, Richard Roark, Jessica Henson, Andrew Dobshinsky, Nate Wooten, Michael Miller, Joanna Karaman, AJ Sus, Diana Jih, David Armbruster, Danielle Toronyi. Gehry Partners: Frank Gehry, Tensho Takemori, Meaghan Lloyd. Geosyntec Consultants: Mark Hanna, Al Preston. Outreach: River LA. Client: Los Angeles County Public Works.

14.4 Weishan. Client/Owner: Wei Shan Wetland Investment Co. Ltd. Photography: AECOM. AECOM team: Qindong Liang, Lian Tao, Yan Hu, Heng Ju, Yi Lee, Jin Zhou, Enrique Mateo, Xiaodan Daisy Liu, JiRong Gu, Li Zoe Zhang, YinYan Wang, Yan Lucy Jin, Kun Wu, Qijie Huang, Jing Wang, Ming Jiang, Danhua Zhang, Junjun Xu, Shouling Chen, Gufeng Zhao, Benjamin Fisher, FanYe Wang, Shuiming Rao, Changxia Li, Donald Johnson, Agnes Soh. Contractor: Shanghai Machinery Complete Equipment (Group) Co., Ltd. Wetland consultant: Shandong Environmental Protection Science Design and Research Institute. Sculpture consultant: UAP.

14.5 GreenPlan Philadelphia. Management Group / Client Group: Fairmount Park Commission; Office of the Managing Director; Department of Commerce; Mayor's Office of Sustainability; Philadelphia City Planning Commission; Philadelphia Water Department; Department of Recreation; Zoning Code Commission. Consultants: WRT, LLC; Center for City Park Excellence, Trust for Public Land; Evergreen Capital Advisors, Inc.; SK Designworks, Inc.; Nitsch Engineering; James S. Russell, AIA; Pennsylvania Horticultural Society; Western Pennsylvania Conservancy. Funders: City of Philadelphia; Pennsylvania Department of Conservation and Natural Resources; William Penn Foundation; U.S. Forest Service; PECO, An Exelon Company.

15.1 Emscher. The International Building Exhibitions (IBA) was founded in 1901. Emscher Landscape Park was curated by IBA between 1989–1999. See www.open-iba .de/en/. Emscher Landscape Park is currently managed by Regionalverband Ruhr (RVR), a regional association of towns and counties.

15.2 Stapleton. Stapleton Redevelopment Plan: Cooper Robertson, master planning; Civitas, open space and parks planning; Wenk Associates, stormwater planning; Andropogon, ecological planning. Implementation: Calthorpe Associates, community planning; EDAW, streets and phase one parks design; Civitas, streets and phase two parks design; Dig Studio, streets and phase two parks design.

15.3 Freshkills. Project lead, landscape architecture, urban design: James Corner Field Operations. Consultant team: AKRF; Applied Ecological Services; Arup; Biohabitats, Inc.; BKSK Architects; Brandston Partnership Inc.; Jacobs (previously CH2M Hill); Daniel Frankfurt; Faithful + Gould; Geosyntec; HAKS; Hamilton, Rabinovize & Alschuler; Langan; L'Observatoire International; Philip Habit and Associates; Project Projects; Rogers Surveying; Sage & Coombe Architects; Richard Lynch (ecologist); and Sanna & Loccisano Architects (expediters).

15.4 Q. E. Olympic Park. Design lead, master planning and landscape architecture: Hargreaves Associates. Prime consultant, master planning and landscape architecture: LDA Design. Ecologist: Dr. Peter Shepherd. Meadow horticulture: Dr. Nigel Dunnet and Dr. James Hitchmough. South Park Garden plant design: Sarah Price Landscapes. North Park engineering: Atkins. South Park engineering: Arup. Sustainability assessment: National House Building Council. Landscape maintenance and management planner: ETM Associates. Lighting design: Sutton Vane Associates. Irrigation design: Waterwise Solutions. Soil scientist: Tim O'Hare Associates.

16.1 Barcelona. Mosaico territorial para la region metropolitana de Barcelona (Land Mosaic for the Metropolitan Region of Barcelona): The urban regional plan for Barcelona was produced for Mayor Joan Clos and Chief Architect Josep Acebillo by Harvard University Professor Richard T. T. Forman and his Barcelona team of Sito Alarcon, Marc Montlleo, Xavier Mayor, and Eva Serra. Preliminary meetings occurred in November 2000 and April 2001; the plan was developed and completed in fifteen months (June 2001 to September 2002). The product was translated and published as R. T. T. Forman, *Mosaico territorial para la region metropolitana de Barcelona* (Barcelona: Gustavo Gili, 2004), The 2010 plan, Pla territorial metropolita de Barcelona was produced by Generalitat de Catalunya, Departament de Politica Territorial i Obres Públiques.

16.2 Medellín (Various Projects).

BIO 2030: Plan Director Medellín, Valle de Aburrá. Un sueño que juntos podemos alcanzar. Alcaldía de Medellín, Área Metropolitana del Valle de Aburrá and Urbam EAFIT, www.eafit.edu.co/centros/urbam /articulos-publicaciones/SiteAssets/Paginas/bio-2030 -publicacion/urbam_eafit_2011_%20bio2030.pdf.

Shifting Ground / Medellín: Project team, Institute of Landscape Architecture, Leibniz Universität Hannover: Christian Werthmann, Joseph Claghorn, Nicholas Bonard, Florian Depenbrock, Mariam Farhat; Centro de Estudios Urbanos y Ambientales (Urbam) / LA Universidad EAFIT (Escuela de Administración, Finanzas e Instituto Tecnológico): Alejandro Echeverri, Francesco María Orsini, Juan Sebastian Bustamante Fernández, Ana Elvira Vélez Villa, Isabel Basombrío, Diana Marcela Rincón Buitrago, Juan Pablo Ospina, Anna Manea, Daniela Duque, Ángela Duque, Simón Abad, Lina Rojas, Maya Ward-Karet, Santiago Orbea Cevallos; Harvard Graduate School of Design: Aisling O'Carroll, Conor O'Shea.

Contracting authority: Municipal Planning Authority of the City of Medellín.

Cooperation partners: Fundacíon CIPAV, Fundación Sumapaz, Aníbal Gaviria Correa, Jorge Pérez Jaramillo, Juan Manuel Patiño M., Paola Andrea López P., Sergio Mario Jaramillo V., David Emilio Restrepo C., Mario Flores, John Cuartas, María Alejandra Rodríguez N.

Participating project specialist: Eva Hacker, soil bioengineering; Marco Gamboa, geology; Michel Hermelin, geology; Iván Rendon, sociology; Tatiana Zuluaga, urban planning.

Duration, 2011–today.

Medellín River Parks: Architectural design: Sebastián Monsalve, Juan David Hoyos. Design team: Osman Marín, Luis Alejandro Jiménez, Andrés Santiago Fajardo, Sebastián González, Juan Diego Martínez, Maria Clara Trujillo, Alejandro Vargas, Carolina Zuluaga, Daniel

Zuluaga, Sara París, Daniel Beltrán,Daniel Felipe Zuluaga, David Castañeda, Alejandro López, David Mesa, Andrés Velásquez, Juan Camilo Solís, Melissa Ortega, D. David Hernández del Valle. Landscape design: Nicolás Hermelín. Photography: Alejandro Arango Escobar, Sebastián González Bolívar. Engineering team: Consorcio EDL. Builder team: Guinovart Obras y Servicios Hispania S.A. Grupo OHL Construcción. Construction supervision team: El Consorcio integral—Interdiseños. Design audit team: Bateman Ingeniería S.A. Medellín's town hall: Aníbal Gaviria. Director of Administrative Department of Planeación de Medellín: Jorge Alberto Pérez Jaramillo. Management of Medellín River Parks: Antonio Vargas del Valle.

16.3 Willamette. Contributors to excerpts from WRB Planning Atlas: Dave Hulse, Stan Gregory, Joan Baker, Allan Branscomb, Chris Enright, David Diethelm, Dixon Landers, Linda Ashkenas, Doug Oetter, Paula Minear, Randy Wildman, Kelly Wildman, John Christy, Mieko Aoki, Warren Cohen. Funding received from U.S. Environmental Protection Agency, Oregon State University, and University of Oregon.

16.4 Qianhai. Qianhai Water City post-competition design and planning phases. Client: Authority of Qianhai Shenzhen-Hongkong Modern Service Industry Cooperation Zone of Shenzhen. Team: James Corner Field Operations; Zhubo Design Group Co. Ltd.; Buro Happold International (Hong Kong) Ltd.; Tsinghua Urban Planning and Design Institute; The Pearl River Hydraulic Research Institute.

Guiwan Water Finger Park Design. Client: Shenzhen Qianhai Development Investment Holdings Co., Ltd.

Team: James Corner Field Operations; Shanghai Landscape Design and Research Institute.

16.5 Envision Utah. Initial planning led by Calthorpe Associates Urban Designers, Planners, Architects, with participation from Fregonese Calthorpe Associates and QGET (Quality Growth Efficiency Tools) Technical Committee. Further development information can be found at www.envisionutah.org/ and https://yourutah yourfuture.org.

Index

Page numbers in italic indicate a figure or table on the corresponding page.

About the Editors and Authors

Editors

Billy Fleming is the Wilks Family Director of the Ian L. McHarg Center at the Stuart Weitzman School of Design. He is the coauthor of *The Indivisible Guide* for Indivisible, a progressive, grassroots-organizing nonprofit—and cofounder of Data Refuge, an international consortium working to preserve vital environmental data. Fleming worked on urban policy development in the White House Domestic Policy Council during the Obama administration. His work has been published in *The Guardian*, the *Houston Chronicle*, *Landscape Journal*, the *Journal of the American Planning Association*, and the *Journal of Landscape Architecture*. His next book, entitled *Sinking Cities: The Nature and Politics of Adaptation Along the American Coast*, will be published by the University of Pennsylvania Press. He earned a PhD in city and regional planning from Penn, an MS in community and regional planning from the University of Texas at Austin, and a bachelor of landscape architecture from the University of Arkansas.

Karen M'Closkey is an associate professor of landscape architecture at the University of Pennsylvania and cofounder of PEG office of landscape + architecture, an award-winning design and research practice based in Philadelphia. Most recently, M'Closkey helped lead the Stuart Weitzman School of Design's involvement in Resilient by Design: Bay Area Challenge (as part of a large team led by the San Francisco firm Bionic). M'Closkey's publications include *Unearthed: the Landscapes of Hargreaves Associates*, which received the J. B. Jackson Book Prize awarded by the Foundation for Landscape Studies; and *Dynamic Patterns: Visualizing Landscapes in a Digital Age*, coauthored with Keith VanDerSys. She is coeditor of *LA+ SIMULATION*, which explores how technologies influence the ways disciplines design with nature today. M'Closkey was the recipient of the 2012–13 American Academy in Rome Prize in landscape architecture.

Frederick Steiner is dean and Paley Professor at the University of Pennsylvania Stuart Weitzman School of Design, and coexecutive director of the Ian L. McHarg Center for Urbanism and Ecology. He served as dean of the School of Architecture and Henry M. Rockwell Chair in Architecture at the University of Texas at Austin. He taught at Arizona State University, Washington State University, the University of Colorado at Denver, and Tsinghua University. A fellow of the American Academy in Rome, the American Society of Landscape Architects, and the Council of Educators in Landscape Architecture, he has written, edited, or coedited nineteen books, including *Making Plans: How to Engage with Landscape, Design, and the Urban Environment*. Steiner earned a master of community planning and bachelor of science in design from the University of Cincinnati, and his PhD and MA in city and regional planning and MRP from Penn.

Richard Weller is the Martin and Margy Meyerson Chair of Urbanism, professor and chair of the Landscape Architecture Department, and coexecutive director of the McHarg Center for Urbanism and Ecology at the University of Pennsylvania. He is former director of the design firm Room 4.1.3 as well as the Australian Urban Design Research Center. He is an adjunct professor at the University of New South Wales in Sydney and the University of Western Australia in Perth. He has received a stream of design awards and published four books and extensive papers. In 2012 he received a national Australian teaching award and, in 2017 and 2018, was named as one of North America's most admired teachers. He is currently the creative director of the journal of landscape architecture *LA+* and is a member of the International Federation of Landscape Architects Advisory Circle. His recent research concerns global flashpoints between biodiversity and urban growth.

Authors

Alan M. Berger is the Norman B. and Muriel Leventhal Professor of Advanced Urbanism at the Massachusetts Institute of Technology. He is founding director of P-REX lab and codirector of MIT's Norman B. Leventhal Center for Advanced Urbanism. His work emphasizes the links between urbanization and the loss of natural resources and growth of waste. His books include *Drosscape: Wasting Land in Urban America*, *Reclaiming the American West*, and *Infinite Suburbia* (edited with Joel Kotkin and Celina Balderas Guzman). He is a fellow of the American Academy in Rome and Honorary Visiting Professor at the Oslo School of Architecture. Berger earned a BS in agriculture and horticulture from the University of Nebraska-Lincoln and an MLA from the University of Pennsylvania.

Ignacio F. Bunster-Ossa is a landscape architect with a forty-year practice devoted to urban environments spanning regions and building sites. He currently leads the landscape architecture practice in the Americas for AECOM, with a focus on the integration of green infrastructure in transportation and flood control. He planned the open-space system for the metropolitan areas of Panama City, Panama, and designed the SteelStacks Arts and Cultural Campus in Bethlehem, Pennsylvania, a project that merited a ULI Global Award of Excellence and the Rudy Bruner Gold Medal Award for Urban Excellence. A Harvard Loeb Fellow in Environmental Studies, he is the author of *Green Infrastructure: A Landscape Approach* (with David Rouse) and *Reconsidering Ian McHarg: The Future of Urban Ecology.*

Thomas J. Campanella is director of the Urban and Regional Studies Program at Cornell University and historian-in-residence of the New York City Parks Department. A recipient of Guggenheim, Fulbright, and Rome Prize fellowships, he has written for the *New York Times,* the *Wall Street Journal, Slate, Wired,* and *The Atlantic's CityLab.* His books include *Brooklyn: The Once and Future City; Cities from the Sky: An Aerial Portrait of America; The Concrete Dragon: China's Urban Revolution and What It Means for the World;* and *Republic of Shade: New England and the American Elm,* winner of the Spiro Kostof Award. Campanella holds an MLA from Cornell and a PhD from the Massachusetts Institute of Technology.

James Corner is the founder of James Corner Field Operations based in New York City, San Francisco, Philadelphia, London, and Shenzhen. His projects include New York's highly acclaimed High Line, Hong Kong's Tsim Sha Tsui Waterfront, and Shenzhen's new city of Qianhai. Among numerous awards, Corner received the National Design Award and the American Academy of Arts and Letters Award in Architecture. The New York Museum of Modern Art, the Cooper-Hewitt Design Museum, the Royal Academy of Art in London, and the Venice Biennale have exhibited his work. His books include *The High Line, The Landscape Imagination,* and *Taking Measures Across the American Landscape.* Named by *TIME* as one of Ten Most Influential Designers and by *Fast Company* as one of the Top 50 Innovators, Corner is emeritus professor at the University of Pennsylvania Stuart Weitzman School of Design, where he served on the faculty since 1990, and as professor and chair from 2000 to 2013.

Erle C. Ellis is professor of geography and environmental systems at the University of Maryland, Baltimore County, where he directs the Laboratory for Anthropogenic Landscape Ecology. His work investigates the ecology of human landscapes to inform sustainable stewardship of the biosphere in the Anthropocene and examines long-term changes in Earth's ecology produced by human societies. He is a member of the Anthropocene Working Group of the International Commission on Stra-

tigraphy, a fellow of the Global Land Programme, and a senior fellow of the Breakthrough Institute. He is the author of *Anthropocene: A Very Short Introduction.* Professor Ellis received a BA in biology and a PhD in plant biology from Cornell University.

Brian M. Evans is professor of urbanism and landscape at The Glasgow School of Art. As a partner with Gillespies, his teams transformed the public realm in cities, including Glasgow, Edinburgh, and Moscow, winning international competitions and awards. Dr. Evans has published over eighty articles and twenty books, including *Tomorrow's Architectural Heritage: The Landscape Setting of Buildings in the Countryside* and *Growing Awareness: How Green Consciousness Can Change Perceptions and Places;* he was the lead author of *Towards a City-Focused, People-Centred and Integrated Approach to the New Urban Agenda* for UN-Habitat. He cofounded the UK Academy of Urbanism and established a UNECE Charter Centre of Excellence at the Glasgow Urban Laboratory, which he directs at GSA. In 2019, he was appointed City Urbanist for Glasgow.

Ursula K. Heise is the Marcia H. Howard Chair in Literary Studies in the Department of English and the Institute of the Environment and Sustainability at the University of California, Los Angeles (UCLA) and a 2011 Guggenheim Fellow. Her research focuses on environmental literature, arts, and cultures in the Americas, Western Europe, and Japan; literature and science; science fiction; and narrative theory. Her books include *Chronoschisms: Time, Narrative, and Postmodernism; Sense of Place and Sense of Planet: The Environmental Imagination of the Global; Nach der Natur: Das Artensterben und die moderne Kultur;* and *Imagining Extinction: The Cultural Meanings of Endangered Species,* which won the 2017 book prize of the British Society for Literature and Science. She cofounded UCLA's Lab for Environmental Narrative Strategies (LENS).

Rob Holmes is an assistant professor of landscape architecture at Auburn University, where he teaches design studios and courses in the history and theory of landscape architecture. His research and creative work focus on infrastructure design, urbanization, and landscape change. He is cofounder of the Dredge Research Collaborative, an independent nonprofit organization that aims to improve the design and management of sediment through publications, the DredgeFest event series, and design research. Before joining Auburn, he practiced landscape architecture in Virginia and taught in Florida, Virginia, Louisiana, and Ohio. He received his MLA from Virginia Tech and a BA in philosophy from Covenant College.

Kathleen John-Alder is an associate professor in the Department of Landscape Architecture at Rutgers University. Her essays have appeared in *Landscape Journal, JoLA*, the *Journal of Planning History, Site/Lines*, and *Manifest*. A practicing landscape architect and scholar, John-Alder has received professional awards from the Van Alan Institute, the National Park Service, and the American Society of Landscape Architects for work that explores the interplay of environmental perception, representation, and design. She holds a BA from Oberlin, a BS in environmental planning and landscape architecture from Rutgers, an MS in botany from Pennsylvania State University, and a master of environmental design from Yale.

Nina-Marie E. Lister is graduate program director and associate professor of urban and regional planning at Ryerson University in Toronto, where she founded and directs the Ecological Design Lab. She was formerly visiting associate professor of landscape architecture at Harvard University's Graduate School of Design. She is the founding principal of plandform.com and focuses on the confluence of nature and culture in urbanizing regions, landscape ecology, and urban planning. She is co-editor of *Projective Ecologies* and *The Ecosystem Approach: Complexity, Uncertainty, and Managing for Sustainability*, and author of numerous other publications. In 2016, she contributed to the Venice Architectural Biennale, collaborating with Pierre Bélanger on Canada's exhibit, EXTRACTION. In recognition of her leadership in ecological design, Lister was awarded honorary membership in the American Society of Landscape Architects.

Anuradha Mathur, an architect and landscape architect, is professor in the Department of Landscape Architecture at the Stuart Weitzman School of Design, University of Pennsylvania. She is the author, with Dilip da Cunha, of *Mississippi Floods: Designing a Shifting Landscape; Deccan Traverses: The Making of Bangalore's Terrain*; and *Soak: Mumbai in an Estuary*. The two coedited *Design in the Terrain of Water*. In 2013–14, she and da Cunha led a PennDesign team for *Structures of Coastal Resilience*, a research project on Norfolk in Tidewater, Virginia, supported by the Rockefeller Foundation. In 2017, Mathur and da Cunha received a Pew Fellowship Grant for their work that imagines new possibilities for design of the built environment and challenges the lines separating land and water, urban and rural, formal and informal environments, among others. They are currently working on an exhibition titled *Ocean of Rain*.

Laurel McSherry is an associate professor and director of the Graduate Landscape Architecture Program at Virginia Tech's Washington-Alexandria Architecture Center. She is an alumna of Rutgers University and the Graduate School of Design at Harvard University. McSherry received the 1999 Rome Prize in Landscape Architecture from the American Academy in Rome. Formerly, she was section head of Landscape Architecture at The Ohio State University and faculty in the College of Architecture and Environmental Design at Arizona State University. Regarded

as a visual thought leader in landscape architecture, McSherry is the recipient of numerous awards and prizes for her design work and is widely published. In 2017–18, McSherry was honored with a Fulbright-Scotland Visiting Professorship at The Glasgow School of Art.

Catherine Seavitt Nordenson is an associate professor of landscape architecture at the City College of New York. An architect and landscape architect, she is a graduate of the Cooper Union and Princeton University, a fellow of the American Academy in Rome, and a recipient of a Fulbright Fellowship for research in Brazil. Her research explores adaptation to climate change in urban environments and the intersection of political power, environmental activism, and public health in the design of public space and policy. Her books include *Structures of Coastal Resilience; Depositions: Roberto Burle Marx and Public Landscapes Under Dictatorship; Waterproofing New York*; and *On the Water: Palisade Bay*. Her work has been published in *Artforum, Avery Review, Harvard Design Magazine, JoLA, LA+, Landscape Architecture Magazine*, and *Topos*.

Laurie Olin is one of the most renowned landscape architects practicing today. From vision to realization, he has guided many of OLIN's signature projects, including the Washington Monument grounds in Washington, DC, Bryant Park in New York City, and the Getty Center in Los Angeles. His recent work includes an award-winning design for the Barnes Foundation in Philadelphia, and Apple Park in Cupertino, California. He is emeritus professor of landscape architecture at the University of Pennsylvania and former chair of the Department of Landscape Architecture at Harvard University. Olin is a fellow of the American Academy of Arts and Letters, a fellow of the American Society of Landscape Architects, and recipient of the 2012 National Medal of Arts and the Vincent Scully Prize from the National Building Museum.

David W. Orr is Paul Sears Distinguished Professor of Environmental Studies and Politics, Emeritus, at Oberlin College. He authored eight books, including *Dangerous Years: Climate Change and the Long Emergency* and *Down to the Wire: Confronting Climate Collapse*, and over 220 articles, book chapters, and professional publications. Orr served as a board member or advisor to numerous foundations and organizations, including the Rocky Mountain Institute, Bioneers, and the Aldo Leopold Foundation. He is a trustee of the Alliance for Sustainable Colorado, the Children and Nature Network, and the WorldWatch Institute. He holds a BA from Westminster College, an MA from Michigan State University, and a PhD from the University of Pennsylvania.

Andrew Revkin is the strategic advisor for environmental and science journalism at the National Geographic Society and a member of its Executive Committee for Research and Exploration. There, after prize-winning reporting, mostly for the *New York Times*, he is working on grants and programs for innovative environment-focused journalism and communication. He received top awards in science journalism, Columbia University's John Chancellor Award for sustained journalistic achievement, and a Guggenheim Fellowship. From 2010 through 2016, Revkin taught environmental blogging and filmmaking at Pace University and was a member of the Anthropocene Working Group of the International Commission on Stratigraphy. He has written three books on climate change and *The Burning Season: The Murder of Chico Mendes and the Fight for the Amazon Rain Forest*.

Allan W. Shearer is an associate professor and the associate dean of research and technology at the University of Texas at Austin School of Architecture. With an emphasis on issues relating to the built environment, his work expands conceptual frameworks and advances methods for scenario-based studies and practice. His research focuses on critical uncertainties that may lead to national, environmental, or human security problems, and he is currently involved with NATO on military operations in future urban environments. He is a coauthor of the books *Land Use Scenarios: The Environmental Consequences of Development* and *Gaia's Revenge: Climate Change and Humanity's Loss,* as well as numerous articles. He holds a PhD, a master of arts, and an MLA from Harvard, and an AB in art history from Princeton.

Anne Whiston Spirn is the Cecil and Ida Green Professor of Landscape Architecture and Planning at MIT. The American Planning Association named her book, *The Granite Garden: Urban Nature and Human Design,* as one of the 100 most important books of the 20th century, one that launched the ecological urbanism movement. Her other books include *The Language of Landscape; Daring to Look;* and *The Eye Is a Door.* Since 1987, she has directed the West Philadelphia Landscape Project, an action research program to restore nature and rebuild community through strategic design, planning, and education programs (www.wplp.net). Spirn is the recipient of Japan's 2001 International Cosmos Prize for "contributions to the harmonious coexistence of nature and mankind," IFLA's Geoffrey Jellicoe Award, and the 2018 National Design Award for "Design Mind." In 1986 she succeeded Ian McHarg as chair of Penn's Department of Landscape Architecture and Regional Planning.

Jonah Susskind is a lecturer in the Department of Urban Studies and Planning at MIT, focusing on coastal resilience, environmental site planning, and suburban land use adaptation. He is a research associate at the Norman B. Leventhal Center for Advanced Urbanism. His work spans landscape architecture and urban design, including metropolitan climate governance, postindustrial transition, and regional wildland management. Susskind holds a degree in landscape architecture from the

Harvard Graduate School of Design, where he was awarded a Penny White Prize and an ASLA Certificate of Honor for his thesis project, "Forward from Woodward: Planning New Growth Along the American Rust Belt." He has published in the *Harvard Design Magazine,* and is a contributing author to the book *Wood Urbanism: From the Molecular to the Territorial.*

Dana Tomlin is a professor of landscape architecture and regional planning at the University of Pennsylvania Stuart Weitzman School of Design and an adjunct professor at the Yale School of Forestry and Environmental Studies. Prior, he taught at The Ohio State University School of Natural Resources and the Harvard Graduate School of Design. Tomlin holds a bachelor in landscape architecture from the University of Virginia, an MLA from Harvard, and a PhD from Yale. His work focuses on geographic information systems (GIS). He cofounded Penn's Cartographic Modeling Lab, authored *GIS and Cartographic Modeling,* originated Map Algebra, and is a member of the GIS Hall of Fame. He is among those who worked most closely with Ian McHarg in geospatial information technology.

Jillian Walliss is a senior lecturer at the University of Melbourne, where she teaches landscape theory and design studio. Her research explores the relationship between technology, culture, and contemporary design practice, and has been published extensively, including in the *Journal of Landscape Architecture, Space and Culture, Environment and History, LA +, Museum and Society, Architecture Theory Review,* and the *Journal of Australian Studies.* She is coauthor (with Heike Rahmann) of the book *Digital Technologies and Landscape Architecture: Re-conceptualising Design and Making.* Her recent work investigates a new generation of urban open spaces, which feature the explicit manipulation of climatic phenomena. In 2018, Walliss coedited a special issue of *Landscape Architecture Australia* that focused on the Asian century.

William Whitaker is curator of the Architectural Archives at the University of Pennsylvania Stuart Weitzman School of Design. Trained as an architect at Penn and the University of New Mexico, he has documented and interpreted the resources of the Architectural Archives, most notably the collections of Louis I. Kahn, Lawrence Halprin, and the partnership of Robert Venturi and Denise Scott Brown. Most recently, Whitaker co-organized "Complexity and Contradiction at 50," a celebration of Robert Venturi's seminal book, *Complexity and Contradiction in Architecture,* in collaboration with the Museum of Modern Art in New York, the Philadelphia Museum of Art, and colleagues at Penn. Whitaker is coauthor (with George Marcus) of *The Houses of Louis I. Kahn* and recipient of the 2014 Literary Award of the Athenaeum of Philadelphia.

About the Lincoln Institute of Land Policy

The Lincoln Institute of Land Policy seeks to improve quality of life through the effective use, taxation, and stewardship of land. A nonprofit private operating foundation, the Lincoln Institute researches and recommends creative approaches to land as a solution to economic, social, and environmental challenges. Through education, training, publications, and events, we integrate theory and practice to inform public policy decisions worldwide.

LINCOLN INSTITUTE
OF LAND POLICY

Cambridge, Massachusetts